TWENTY TUMULTUOUS YEARS: INSIGHTS INTO INDIAN POLITY (1973-1994)

TWENTY TUMULTUOUS YEARS

INSIGHTS
INTO
INDIAN POLITY
(1973-1994)
(In 2 Volumes)

COALITIONS, CONFLICTS AND COMMUNALISATION
(Volume II)

Ayub Syed

Edited by
Dr. Anees Syed
Dr. Shri Prakash

GYAN PUBLISHING HOUSE
NEW DELHI–110 002

TWENTY TUMULTUOUS YEARS: INSIGHTS INTO INDIAN POLITY (1973-1994)

(Political Science)

Rs. 1800 (Set)
Rs. 900 (each volume)

ISBN: 81-212-0804-1 (Set)
ISBN: 81-212-0821-1 (Vol. 1)
ISBN: 81-212-0822-X (Vol. 2)

Published in 2003 in India by
Gyan Publishing House
5-Ansari Road, Daryaganj
New Delhi-110 002
Phones: 23282060, 23261060
Fax: (011)23285914
E-mail: gyanbook@vsnl.com
Visit our website at: http//www.gyanbooks.com

Lasertypesetting by: Varsha Graphics, Delhi
Printed at: Mehra Offset Press, Delhi

Contents

9. Communalisation of Indian Polity

A. HINDUTVA—EMERGENCE AS A POLITICAL TREND

B. THE MUSLIM QUESTION AND ELECTORAL POLITICS

II

COALITIONS, CONFLICTS AND COMMUNALISATION

5

Centre-State Relations Growing Challenge to Delhi Hegemony

A. Dissidence in Congress ruled States

Confrontation

The mishandling of the Karnataka PCC crisis by the Congress high command and especially by President Brahmananda Reddy has led to the sharpening of differences between the two factions.

Y.B. Chavan, leader of the Congress in Parliament and a number of senior congressmen have expressed great concern at the rapidly deteriorating state of affairs in that strife torn state.

According to responsible Bangalore congressmen, the reappointment of K.H. Patil as PCC chief was not only a grave political error but a "mischievous move." It was obviously aimed at creating hurdles for Devraj Urs.

Urs feels he had been deliberately humiliated by Brahmananda Reddy who is in a revengeful mood because the Karnataka Chief minister opposed him in his election.

Urs has retaliated with a ferocity rarely known in the Congress. He is tough. He refuses to be intimidated or browbeaten. He has his own ways of fighting Reddy's "skullduggery", as one of his ministers pointed out. He is in no mood to compromise. In fact he had simultaneously trained his guns on Reddy too. He is after the scalp of the Congress president.

Urs derives his strength from the powerful and solid following he has built among the weaker sections, Harijans and minorities in the state. For the first time in him, Karnataka has a chief minister who has no caste, creed or religious bias. He proved his political strength and remarkable tactical skill by winning all but one seat during the last Lok Sabha elections. He is confident of winning the forthcoming Assembly

elections with an equally impressive majority.

The serious corruption charges against him and the two inquiry commissions sitting over his head have not made a big dent in his personal strength or following.

Last week's meeting which he termed as a "Congress Constructive Workers' Conference" was later hailed by his followers as a general body meeting of the PCC. This meeting "derecognised" K.H. Patil as PCC president. The action, Urs told his followers, would not lead to a split, as apprehended. "I have a majority both in the CLP and the PCC," he said. "Where is the split?" I maintain that there is no split in the party. Wait for a few days and see if there'll be one Congress or two Congresses."

His arch-rival K.H. Patil is equally a tough fighter. But he lacks the qualities of a politician who could lead his faction to victory. Patil has succeeded in gathering around him a large number of ex-ministers and some influential congressmen who derive their strength from caste base.

Last week when I met Urs he was in a fighting mood and he spoke like a general about to launch an offensive. He did not mince words.

Patil was subdued and on the defensive. He had his plus points which he explained during our interview. But he lacks a majority and democracy is a game of numbers.

What are the basic differences between you and K.H. Patil?

First, it's basically a power struggle, Patil and his friends think that I should not be in this position any more. At least not now. After the elections they had a suspicion in that I might still come to power.

Individually?

Yes, individually not the Congress. Even if the Congress were to break they would not mind as they would not mind as long as I was eliminated.

Why do they want to throw you out?

Take the history of the Congress in Karnataka. A man without a caste battle and without one man in the Assembly of his caste, has come to this position. That in itself is not the point. After the 1969 split, the ideology for which the Congress stood went before the people and was accepted. Even after the 1972 elections and the 1971 parliamentary elections, Congress has given a programme which is basically meant for the uplifting.

Uplifting of the masses?

Yes. Uplifting the poorer sections of our society. *Garibi Hatao* is oriented towards that. Starting with the basic work of land reforms we have done

our best to implement all these things. A thing like land reforms basically helps the poorer sections. There is another revolutionary idea which we have taken up: Land Tribunals. In every *taluka* we have one, two depending . . . .

To settle local disputes....

Yes. Between a tenant and a landlord. Disputes between the two are taken to these tribunals, thus saving them the tedious process of going to a court of law. We have made suitable provisions in the Act. The Land Tribunal was constituted with one official at its head and a sub-division officer and about two or three non-officials as members. These Tribunals have nearly seven lakh cases on hands. Judgement on two and a half lakh cases are expected very soon.

Two and a half lakh cases?

Yes, may be more. This could not have happened if the disputes were taken only to the courts. The Land Tribunal is a revolutionary idea. Andhra Pradesh is also trying this out. But it is only official. Here it is non-official. The members of the tribunal are able to go to the people and make on the spot inquiries as to whether they are the tenants or not. Whether what he says is true or not. When you speak to the people, you know the truth.

Besides this revolutionary step, other measures like the abolition of bonded labour has been taken up.

This then is a class war?

Definitely. These moneylenders are everywhere. They are in the city as well as the villages. The loans of those earning Rs. 2,000 a month and below have been liquidated. That means so many thousands of people have antagonised the richer class.

The K.H. Patil group represents the richer class?

Definitely.

Where will this struggle between the PCC and the government end?

In a democracy, numerical strength also counts. We have won the election because the minorities, the backward class and Harijans have stood by us. Otherwise how could I win 26 seats? I lost one seat by a thousand and odd votes during the election disputes.

You hope to repeat the same performance in the Assembly elections?

Certainly. It won't be anything less than what we have now.

They say that you are a very tough chief, because you are fighting all these forces. The centre is against you. There are two commissions of

inquiry. The PCC is against you. A lot of ministers have resigned. Yet you are hitting back.

The real secret is my complete faith in my ideology for which the organisation stands. I believe in this programme and I am convinced that it is for the poor people and my mission in life is to fight for them.

Will you form a new party?

It is not a question of forming a new regional party. Now suppose the Congress at the AICC and the high command level realise what I am fighting for and despite this they push me into a corner and the party breaks. I cannot say what shape it will take.

But why has the AICC taken up this hostile attitude?

I do not know why Brahmananda Reddy talks of prestige. I do not know what type of prestige is involved in this. Even without asking me they have imposed a leader on the party.

They say your friendship with MGR is . . .

Other Congress people were also friendly with him. Only recently the Congress and the AIADMK were friendly. How can you object if I am friendly with him?

There is a question of your and MGR coming together?

I must be friendly with my neighbour. But, politically the entire AICC was with him. Why?

You think the Congress will be able to win the Assembly elections?

Provided the people know who is going to head them.

What type of co-ordination have you established with Mrs. Gandhi?

Congressmen should understand that Mrs. Gandhi was the undisputed leader not only of the party but of the country and she was there for 11 long years. At least instead of degrading her everyday, they should keep quiet.

Some people say that she had made mistakes and she must repent.

More than once she has publicly admitted the mistakes and said that she repents for them. She has not accused others.

But they also say that she has not been telling the truth? That she does not support Brahmanand Reddy. But it was known that she supported him.

She never mentioned that Reddy should be supported, whatever she told me, I know I am not interested in what others say, not in their experiences. She said that she did not want to involve herself in this conflict.

Are you inviting her to Karnataka?
I may. I have not fixed the date.

But during your elections should she come and canvass for you?
Since she is a member of the Congress, what is wrong in inviting her? I do not feel apologetic in any way.

You have decided to fight back?
Definitely. I will fight back.

Current, 17.09.1977.
pp. (12 + 13 + 14)

Traitor they or me? Sharad Pawar

Sharad Pawar, the youngest Chief minister of Maharashtra will be watched intently by the whole country because he has taken an unusual step. His joining hands with Janata has temporarily shaken Indira Gandhi and accelerated the process of the disintegration of Congress.

The country is now ready for a much awaited polarisation. Very soon our political system will be divided into two warring camps. The field is now clear for Indira Gandhi to mobilise her forces and attack the Janata—right, left and the centre.

The Janata, too, will have its allies among the vanquished congressmen. And if it does not break then India would achieve a real two-party system at the national level.

The credit goes to Sharad for setting the pace.

Do you still consider yourself a congressman despite the Working Committee's decision to expel you? A senior CWC member, V.P. Naik has branded you a 'master defector' and your government, 'based on treachery'. Will you remain in the Congress or join the Janata?
There are some people who are physically in the Congress but mentally with Indira Gandhi. V.P. Naik is one of them. He has been constantly pleading her cause, in fact he has been operating for her within the Congress.

What do you call this kind of men?
There is only one word for them—Trojan horses. Naik is more interested in his and his family's politics. In Pusad he put up his nephew, Sudhakar and then entered into a deal with Indira Gandhi that she would not visit

this constituency. She visited the whole of Vidarbha but at the last moment cancelled her visit to Pusad.

As a result, even though the Congress was defeated all over Vidarbha, Naik's nephew was the only Congress candidate elected in that region. This in a nut-shell, is V.P. Naik's politics.

We are against this kind of adjustment with persons who are staying in the Congress but simultaneously making adjustments with other parties because of personal gains. Naik helped Indira Gandhi to win seats in Vidarbha.

Now tell me who is treacherous—he or me?

Though I am not in a position to suggest, this kind of people better join her and relieve us of their burden.

Will that strengthen the Congress?

The Congress will be much stronger.

Naik also called you a master defector?

I do not know in what way he is thinking. But his approach has always been to keep the government under his thumb. I will not entertain this kind of thinking. Naik cannot keep my government under his thumb.

Now he is conspiring to topple my government and using choicest invectives against me.

You have set a new political trend in the country by heading the first Janata government under Congress leadership. Though I would not call it a beginning of a re-alignment of forces I do feel that the Congress is on the cross-roads. Is it the beginning of the end of the Congress?

I must clarify. This is not the Janata government. We have formed Progressive Democratic Legislative Party which includes Janata, PWP, Republican – both Gavai and Kamble groups – and ex-congressmen who had joined the Janata. This front reflects the progressive and leftist stance. All its members have abiding faith in democracy. Therefore, it will not be fair to call it a one-party government. It is a coalition of all these parties who have come together on the basis of definite programmes and ideals.

I am sure the Maharashtra experience will set a new trend in our national politics. I have been advocating this view for quite some time and I am sure there is a sizeable section of congressmen who share my views.

The greatest problem is the re-emergence of Indira Gandhi with her authoritarianism. This is the main challenge we are facing. Her followers in Maharashtra have already started justifying Emergency and recently Nasikrao Tirpude publicly defended the dark era.

We are determined to fight this tendency as congressmen. We have to strengthen democracy and its fundamental principles and ideology. My appeal is that all those congressmen and other parties who have faith in democracy and who are determined to fight her authoritarianism should come together.

Janata is also committed to fight her. We must, therefore, set aside all other differences and concentrate on this vital issue.

What will be the fate of the Congress in the process? Will it disintegrate?

I do not know about that but if the Congress is left with a will to fight her and if the central leadership reconsiders its overall approach to this problem then I think Congress has a future. There are people who believe that the Congress is a democratic party.

Unfortunately in Maharashtra I am observing that some congressmen are behaving like *sardars* (knights). Like *sardars* they have lost everything yet they believe they have a domain to rule. Like *sardars* they have their big bungalows and *wadas* (palaces). But they are not mentally prepared to accept the new situation. The times have changed, the dynamics of our national life are changing. These congressmen are left with no vision to observe those changes. They are in two minds and are not in a mood to fight the Janata. They have fixed their eyes at Indira Gandhi.

They seem to be suffering from political schizophrenia.

Yes. That was the main cause of our debacle in Karnal and Azamgarh. The people can no more be taken for granted. They have made up their minds. Those who believe in democratic principles are supporting the Janata and its allies but those who are unhappy with Janata and its policies are crossing over to Indira Gandhi.

Do you mean that the country is polarised into two distinct thinking groups?

Yes. There is a clear division in the country. The people are either with the Janata and against Indira or with Indira and against the Janata.

Did you take this step because you felt that the Congress leadership has failed to understand the national trend?

Because senior congressman like Chandrajit Yadav has lost deposit. In Karnal, too, the Congress candidate lost his deposit. Both Karnal and Azamgarh were like a weathercock. They showed which way was the wind blowing. The common man has led us to think on these lines.

You took the lead in Maharashtra because of these factors?

I thought if Congress goes it alone it will neither be able to fight Janata nor Indira Gandhi. It will be disintegrated and decimated.

You are motivated by this major consideration. You thought this was the only way to prevent the re-emergence of Indira and that is why you were welcomed in the Janata fold. But do you think yours is the only way?
If we have to fight this battle in a democratic way, I do not think there is any other alternative. We must be realistic. Nothing is stagnant in politics.

Do you consider the CPI and the CPM as part of the democratic forces?
The CPM has accepted this principle but I do not know why the CPI has not yet realised this vital issue.

As you very well know, the Janata in Delhi as well as in Bombay is a combination of various warring groups. Struggling for a decisive role in giving an ideological shape to this worthless struggle for power.
In my state two things are very clear. We will not compromise our democratic principles. Secondly, ours will be a programme-oriented government.

Are you drawing some comprehensive economic and social programme?
It is practically finalised. The draft is ready prepared by a committee headed by me. It includes Uttamrao Patil, S.M. Joshi, Prabhakar Kurane and R.A. Patil.

What are the main points?
We have to implement our Employment Guarantee Scheme and schemes for agricultural and landless labour. Our first step will be to increase their wages by 20 to 25 per cent. We will revise the wage scales of the agricultural labour. We will reconsider the agricultural prices. We will also remove disparity in power tariffs between the rural and urban sectors. Power rates will be the same for industry and agriculture. This will give a tremendous benefit to the farming community. We will also implement the Monopoly Cotton Scheme. There is a sizeable vested interest opposing it. But we are determined to go ahead.

We are also launching a crash housing programme for landless labourers. We will provide them with *pucca* houses. Besides provisions will be made for drinking water in villages and interest-free loans for farmers belonging to weaker sections.

What steps would you be taking in the urban areas?
Our first programme will be slum clearance. The workers have to be given their legitimate right of 8.33 per cent bonus.

But the centre has not accepted this suggestion on bonus.
Whatever New Delhi does we have decided to implement it. Our government is for the workers, peasants, minorities, middle classes, tribals and Harijans. There should not be any doubt about this.

Are you confident that you will ultimately consolidate the progressive and democratic forces in Maharashtra?
There is no choice. There is no alternative. We will have to do this.

Are you of the view that the progressive elements should join their counterparts in Janata to continue the battle against reaction?
I do not think we should start this type of infighting at this juncture because our main target is to avoid Indira's authoritarian rule. We should forget all our differences and concentrate on this particular point.

Don't you think that a more effective way to fight Indira Gandhi is to economically improve the lot of the people?
That is true. But we have to take both the things simultaneously to preserve our democratic heritage and launch a massive programme for the upliftment of the weaker sections of society.

The Harijans and minorities have to be given a sense of security. They are a very important pillar of our democratic structure.

Your political mentor Y.B. Chavan is understood to be greatly pained at your decision to violate the CWC decision. But there is a feeling that you continue to enjoy his blessings.
I must be frank with you. Immediately after the CWC meeting I met him and said: 'Baba' I am not in a mood to accept this decision. The CWC is not realising the changing situation in the country. It's leaders are thinking on the pattern of 1975 and 74. It is 1978. The dynamics of 1978 are different.

He tried to convince me, to persuade me, and when I returned to Bombay, he rang me twice asking me not to violate the CWC decision. But my friends, and especially the young MLAs were of the view that if we do not stick to our decision the process of new thinking will not start. We respect our elders. Yeshwantraoji is our leader. But if they are not prepared to accept our position we must defy them.

Would you be able to bring around the CWC to your viewpoint?
Well, if our judgement proves correct they will one day accept us.

And Yeshwantraoji?
Yes, I am confident. It will take some time. Only yesterday Dr. Karan Singh publicly advocated our cause in Bombay.

Your joining hands with the ruling Party has proved Indira Gandhi's allegation that you and Y.B. Chavan were in league with Janata.
I do not understand the attitude of our Congress leaders Y.B. Chavan met Morarji Desai and the next day he issued a clarification that he had not

seen Desai for at least six months. He said he had never met him. Why are they so scared of meeting Desai or any other Janata leader? Indira too met Desai twice. Is it a sin to meet him or anybody else.

Not only this. She has been sending messages to Jagjivan Ram to become her Prime minister.
Yes, she does all kinds of funny things. But our people are always on the defensive. Why should we be scared of her. I am prepared to enter in alliance with anybody opposed to her.

So far Maharashtra has enjoyed stability. But the people are now not sure of it. The Janata image is synonymous with chaos and instability.
Our last government had 153 MLAs which was a wafer-thin majority. Now we have 180 MLAs. There is no danger to my government. So long as we remain committed to the people the question of instability does not arise. We will preserve our reputation of stability and progress.

What will be your attitude towards the RSS which in a way controls the Janata?
Though the RSS was born in Maharashtra, it has no base here. It is voluntary organisation and is functioning outside the Janata. There are some ex-RSS men in Janata but then they were in Congress too.

Do you think the RSS is a dominant group in Maharashtra Janata?
I do not think so. I have not so far faced any pressure from them.

What is your experience with your Janata colleagues?
Good. I am happy with them. Earlier I was under the impression that there might be fights on certain economic and political issues but they have been agreeing with me on almost every issue. They are eager to have an action oriented programme.

You mean this coalition will be an improvement on the last one.
Definitely better. My colleagues have a feeling that the new experiment in Maharashtra has to be made successful.

Do you remain wedded to the ideals of socialism and secularism.
Totally. There is no going back on these issues.

Current, 05.08.1978.
pp. (1 + 2 + 19)

Urs's war cry: I will fix her

You have lost weight I told Devraj Urs as we sat down for a two-hour long chat. He looked straight at my face and said: But I have gained confidence—in my self. I feel liberated. A new chapter in my life has begun.

The spacious lawn of Balaboorie were overflowing with people. The ground floor was packed and the first floor was humming with activity. Hundreds of party workers, ministers, MLAs and MPs were shuffling in and out. Devraj Urs was immensely aware of his historic role in giving a new shape to the country's politics. Though modest and self-effacing, he doesn't under-estimate himself.

The signs of the deadly herpes were still all over his face and he couldn't speak clearly. Yet he spoke at great length. It was almost a monologue. He wouldn't let me ask him questions and would cut me short and put his heavy hands on my shoulders to drive home his point.

I tried to provoke him. She says you have been hobnobbing with the Janata. You are afraid to fight against the Janata.

Urs instantly forgot his pain, jumped on his seat and raised his voice: I say nobody can challenge my manhood, I am not a coward. What is it? Is it a street fight? Is it a bout or a wrestling match? What is the meaning of fight? I may be meeting some of my Janata friends. But should I tell you how many messages have gone from her and to how many people in power? It does not require much of a study to criticise the others, to criticise other parties. Even a market boy who carries load from one place to another has the capacity to criticise.

Why did she suddenly turn against you? Is it because you attacked her son? Was this Sanjay phenomenon?

Yes. It was Sanjay. The whole thing rotates around him. The Sanjay phenomenon is simply this: that his mother says that little boy is trying to fight his political battle. I agree that he has a right to fight his own battles but my objection was that she should not permit him to use the Congress for his advantage and carry on his fight.

So now you are convinced that he has been using his mother to promote his designs.

I am convinced beyond doubt. I was not sure of it earlier. And I have argued about this with friends, including you. But now I am convinced that it is he who counts. I am telling you it is he who created the gulf between me and her.

I am glad you realise it now. Do you regret it?
No question of regretting. But now I have a different experience.

Do you now agree that she sabotaged your efforts to unite the two congressmen?
I do. She did.

This convention of congressmen, which you are now initiating, is a good beginning. I hope it will be minus Indira Gandhi.
Well, why should I say it should be minus Indira Gandhi? I do want all congressmen to unite and rejuvenate the Indian National Congress. There is no use floating a new party. A new party does not appeal to me. The Congress is there. It has played a historic role and I am sure that it will again rise to the occasion. It got weakened in spirit.

My idea in reviving the Congress is not merely to collect a number of people and proclaim that, here I have got them. My idea is to re-inject socialist programmes and find out the instrument to implement them. The Congress has the best socialist democratic programmes and no other party can compare with them.

You want to make this Congress an alternative to the Janata?
Yes. Things must be thrashed out at this convention.

Are you expecting all the congressmen from all the parties to respond to your call.
Let anybody who has faith in the policies of the Congress come.

Will you invite Indira Gandhi also to the convention?
I do not believe in minus this and minus that. But she will not be invited to this convention. Not now.

But if she wants to come?
Let her come. Then in that case let us call the pre-split AICC. That AICC will take care of her.

You said that she sabotaged your efforts for unity. And if she comes she will again sabotage your efforts to unite all the congressmen.
I agree. But even she may change.

Can a leopard change its spots?
But aren't there many changes taking place.

Your letter to her is a powerful indictment of her style of functioning. You have accused her of authoritarianism. But people remember you declaring umpteen times that you will shed the last drop of your blood for her. Why is she after your blood now?

My dear Ayub, I will tell you in detail if you have the patience. Once she asked me a question which is the answer to your question. She asked me two months back: Devrajji they say there is a difference of opinion between you and me. For the first time she asked me this question. It was before the AICC meeting. I replied: It is simply this. People who surround you whisper in your ears that Devraj is growing out of size. That he is dreaming of becoming the Prime minister, pushing you aside. And since these people tell you this thing almost every day, you are bound to be influenced by them. This is the only difference.

How did she react?

She kept silent. I told her: It is not so. I am not interested in the Prime ministership. It is you who has been denigrating me. Why did not you consult me before calling off the unity talks? You called Chenna Reddy to find out his opinion, but not me. Perhaps people came and told you that the Congress unity will give me a boost. I will become a bigger man. I may overshadow you. That is what you have been thinking.

But what is wrong in aspiring to be the Prime minister?

This is exactly what she asked me. I said No. There is nothing wrong in it. There is nothing wrong in my aspiring, but there is everything wrong in your thinking. If you say there is nothing wrong in my thinking it is perfectly alright, but there is everything wrong in your thinking that I am thinking like that.

Did she react?

No. She sat like a sphinx and I continued talking of the Prime ministership. I told her: You will agree with me that today I am in a position to take an over-all assessment of what is going on in the country and I am also aware of the immensity of the various problems.

And you feel confident that you will be able to solve them?

Kindly wait, do not jump. I told her: I have had 13 years of administrative experience—six plus seven. This is the 14th year. I have had legislative experience all my life. I fully understand the intricacies and complication of the administration. In the modern age and in the developing situations, day-to-day administration is getting more and more complicated. People made of ordinary stuff cannot govern this country. It is always easy for anybody to come to the position of the Prime minister. But he cannot hold it for long. Today the situation in the country is such that nobody can think of continuing as Prime minister for 11 years or 15 years. Those days are gone. If a man has got to survive for more than five years he

must keep the situation in mind. I am one of those who is fully aware of all these. That is the reason why . . . .

You told her all this and she went on listening?

Yes, yes. Please wait, listen to me. I told her that is the reason why I am not aspiring to be the Prime minister of India. I am not a fool—madam. I have enough work as the Chief minister of a state. I have so much to do in Karnataka that I am not interested in the Prime ministership. That may come sometime, but I do not know. I am not thinking of it now.

But I want to ask one question, not you, but to Madam. I asked her: By chance if you happen to come back to power, I must tell you that you too may not be able to hold this country as you did the last time. I will tell you why. Will you name half a dozen men who are efficient, who have administrative experience and who have the capability and on whom you can rely to run the administration of this country? Can you please name the people? She kept silent. I continued: So, Madam, you understand I am not a child or a stupid politician like others who hanker for things bigger and bigger as though it is going to give them *moksha*. I am not that type. Even now please think seriously about the Prime ministership. Whom have you built around you? All you have done is to put up a set of people who dance attendance on you, feed you with gossip and keep you happy. Is this the way you want to function?

What was her reply?

Reply? She sat motionless and listened to me for one and a half hours. I did not expect her to reply.

My question remains partly unanswered. Why did you want to shed your blood for her?

I did say it because they were vindictive to her, wanted to disenfranchise her. I did not want that. Though I am not with her now I hold that vindictiveness is no way to fight political battles. Let's come openly in the arena and fight.

But why did she wants to shed your blood now?

I told you that. This Sanjay Gandhi. It is he.

Why was she so ruthless. You were down with herpes, couldn't she have waited?

It's that little fellow. He wants everything, the Congress, the PCC, the Youth Congress. He tried in Karnataka too, but I stopped.

He has his boys in your state. They are riding rough.

Yes. This Bangarappa. He is his friend.

You have failed to liberate her from his influence.
Yes, I admit.

There is a popular belief that it was your base and her charisma that brought you back to power in the last elections. In her yesterday's speech in Srinagar she has challenged your base also. She gave the impression that she can even rule Karnataka by her charisma.
I claim to know my people much better than her. But I have never said that her charisma did not work. But it is not merely the charisma. It was the programmes and policies which I vigorously implemented and which were for the benefit of the people. But I do not underestimate her.

You and your colleagues implemented the Congress programmes in her name. You went around saying this is from Indira amma. That is what built her image.
That is what some of us did, rightly or wrongly. She was our leader though the programmes were initiated by the Congress.

Having built her image and promoted her charisma all these years, so diligently, would you be able to demolish it?
Yes. I am confident of it.

What methods will you adopt?
Apart from other things her removing me so unceremoniously from the KPCC and dissolving the KPCC is enough to tell my people that she has been unfair. I know my people. They will take it as an insult, not to Devraj Urs, but to Karnataka. This very act has demolished her image.

She has told her people that the main reason of your somersault is your fear of the Grover report and that you have been trying to ingratiate the Janata leaders to save your skin.
I give one month. During this one month if any Janata leader can prove that I approached him directly or indirectly to curry his favour to save myself from the Grover Commission I will resign. I take this allegation very seriously. It hurts my manliness. I am not a man to bow down my head to save my skin. I am prepared to face the consequences. Why should I go and beg anybody? Had I done this earlier, the Grover report itself must not have been come out. The fact that the Grover report has come heavily on me proves that I am not bent.

You have been meeting Chandra Shekhar and other Janata leaders. That may have aroused her suspicions.
All these leaders—Chandra Shekhar, Charan Singh, Bahuguna, Babu Jagjivan Ram—all are your good friends. They know you well. Take

them into confidence and find out whether I ever spoke to them about the Grover report. If any one of them says, 'yes', I will resign, I will quit. I beg of you, for my sake, to find out on your own. You have every right to expose me. I have no right to speak falsehood and if I have done so, you must expose me. I beg of you.

Yes I will verify. But do not feel upset. You know it is a vilification.
But you please verify. And if I am wrong, expose me.

Bangalore has suddenly become the centre of a major political development. It is not a localised event. And it will have a tremendous bearing on our national politics.
Yes, I agree with you. It's not a localised event. It will have a national impact.

Your action is bound to lead to the re-alignment of forces of which you have been talking. You have set the ball rolling.
Yes, the ball is in their court. But the re-alignment should be preferably around the Congress, the Indian National Congress. I'm wedded to programmes and policies. I believe in them as much as I believe in myself and God.

It's the people who count, their living conditions, housing, wages, employment, education, health, every Indian has a right to have them. But can we give them? And how should we do it?

What will be your first preference? Your major step?
Land reforms. It's the fore-runner of all other reforms. No revolution can be complete without the land going to the tiller. We cannot build a modern socialist society with the yoke of feudalism around our neck. We cannot bring in socialism without eradicating feudalism, Indira Gandhi took it up but she failed to implement it. It's easy to declare war, but it's not simple to select the Generals. She thought any Tom, Dick and Harry can do it. It needs a basic commitment. In Andhra Pradesh Narasimha Rao tried to do it. But he was kicked out. The feudals were after his scalp.

But you seem to have survived in Karnataka.
Yes, I have, though here too they tried to bamboozle me. But they couldn't do much. I was backed by my party. Otherwise on this very question I could have gone. I'm determined to change the structure of the society to usher in socialist programmes and I am sure I will succeed.

What is your second preference?
To give revolutionary teeth to the backward classes, minorities and the weaker sections.

You and Charan Singh seem to have similar ideas. You are coming close to him.

Whether Charan Singh comes close to me or I go close to him. I do not quarrel on that. But whether Charan Singh did it or not I have done it. I had told him that on many things he will come closer to me.

What are these things?

I told him he must go further down to the people.

Did he agree with you?

Yes he did.

That may bring you two together.

Why not? I have told him that the weaker sections and the backwards are the real socialist forces in the country.

But you are convinced that only the Congress can carry forward this gigantic task.

Yes. I believe in that. It is the only party with a definite programme. No other party has programmes which are superior to that of the Congress, including the Communist Party.

The Indian National Congress is now known as the Swaran Singh Congress.

Whether it is Swaran Singh or some other Singh. It has to be revitalised. We must all join and give it a new shape, let new leadership be thrown up.

Are you extending invitations to some of the Janata congressmen also?

Yes. If they believe in our programmes they must come.

This morning I met Bangarappa and he said the only way to test who's right—you or Indira Gandhi—is to go to the people. That means a mid-term poll. Are you ready to face a mid-term poll?

Why should I bother about it? I'm not asking for it. But if it is forced on me I am ready for it.

Current, 30.06.1979.
pp. (1 + 6 + 7)

The Congress-I is finished: we will sweep the polls in Maharashtra

Sharad Pawar is President of the Congress-S and an opposition leader in the Maharashtra Assembly. But he plays his politics through his minions in the ruling Congress. His strength and weakness lie in the 'other' party.

As his influence grows and his popularity eclipses the other Congress stalwarts, he grows stronger in the ruling party.

Sangli and Patan have undoubtedly shaken congressmen, but they are not nervous. Most of them have kept their equations with Sharad and the moment they feel the ground sliding under their feet they will jump onto his bandwagon.

Sharad is absolutely confident of sweeping the state if and when elections are held. He seems to be least concerned about national politics. The nation will dump him if he does not hold Maharashtra in his hands. And if he has his people behind him, he can take care of the nation too. "I am too young to worry about Delhi," he says with a wave of the hand. In this candid interview he reveals his strategy.

What are the implications of the Sangli-Patan by-elections results. Do you think they portend the beginning of the end of the Congress in Maharashtra.

I entirely agree with you (except that I prefer to call that party Congress-I). These two constituencies are the party's strongest pockets in the entire state. The party has never lost these two seats in the past 35 years, not even during the Samyukta Maharashtra wave when it lost heavily in the rest of the state. Yes, in 1978 Balasaheb Desai won the Patan Assembly seat as a Janata candidate. But it was essentially Balasaheb's victory, and he rejoined the Congress-I soon thereafter.

So this is the first time that Congress has lost Patan and its majority has been reduced considerably in Sangli.

That is right. You see, Sangli has been Dada's pocket borough. He has enormous control over the entire district. His sugar-factory has the highest cane yield in the country. He wields power over the entire irrigation system in the area. Every co-operative institution, from the village level credit societies to the district banks, and the administrative apparatus from the panchayat samitis to Zilla Parishad are controlled by him. So also the various educational institutions. He has done a lot of work there for a long time. Naturally, even in the 1980 Lok Sabha election when the Congress-I was in the opposition, and the state Janata Party president Rajaram Bapu Patil, who is a powerful leader of that district, was in my cabinet, Dada won the seat by a margin of over 1,67,000 votes. You can imagine his hold over the area.

Could it not be that Shalinitai's personal image caused the slump in the margin.

I must say people are not happy with her, and her candidature did prove useful to us. But do not forget, in the 1980 Assembly election she had won with a margin of 38,000 from Sangli, and only four months ago Dada won that seat by a near 40,000 margin. Practically all the seats in the district have gone to the Congress-I. I may tell you that during the last election parties other than the Congress-I were virtually unwelcome in as many as 40 per cent of the villages in the area.

In such a place now the Congress-I margin has slumped to a mere 36,000 votes. In the Sangli Assembly segment Shalinitai could muster a margin of barely 1,800 votes. In the Miraj segment, where the margin in the last election was around 38,000, she has in fact lost, with a deficit of 2,800 votes. This is a clear indication that the Congress-I has lost ground considerably.

It was perhaps because the entire opposition was combined . . . .

The opposition was combined in 1980 too. Ours being a common candidate did have its effect. But basically the Congress-I is losing its influence. Many of the older generations, those in the above-40 age group, have respect for Dada and Chavan Saheb, that was a plus point for the Congress I. But the younger generations are with us. Cutting across family, caste, religious, regional ties, the younger people have taken upon themselves the responsibility of building up opposition to the Congress-I. They acted very effectively.

So you say three factors were combined, Shalinitiai's unpopularity, decline of the influence of the Congress-I, and the younger generation's support to you. May we add a fourth factor, erosion in the influence of Yeshwantrao Chavan and Dada.

Yes, both of them are losing. In fact Shalinitai won her seat only because Dada appealed to local sentiment. He visited practically every village and pleaded with the voters that a vote for Shalinitai would be a vote for him, for their Chief minister. If they preferred the Janata candidate, he would quit Mantralaya, retire from public life, and settle down in his village. He also talked about the activities of his rivals in the party, Antulay, Babasaheb Bhosale, etc. with whom he had to fight simultaneously. This helped to rouse local patriotism. That's how Shalinitai managed to win in Sangli. But that did not work in Patan, not even Chavansaheb's influence, though Patan is in his district, very near his home town Karad. So the Congress-I has lost in its Sangli-Satara stronghold.

What about the rest of Maharashtra.

It is losing fast in the rest of western Maharashtra as well. In Marathwada

its position is worse, and in Vidarbha the opposition is gaining ground day by day.

You think the Congress will lose in the next parliamentary election.

Yes, certainly. Out of the 48 seats, the combined opposition will capture 30 to 35 seats. And in the Assembly we are sure of getting an absolute, comfortable majority.

There is a strong suspicion among people, and Congress-I leaders like Antulay, Bhosale and many others are saying it openly, that eventually Yeshwantrao, Dada and you will join hands. In the Patan election some of their key local lieutenants openly supported your candidate.

Their support was a plus point for us, and the Congress-I has expelled them. Some of them were in my party earlier, and had gone over along with Chavansaheb. They have come back. But about Chavansaheb and Dada I can positively say they will not display the courage to leave the Congress-I. I wish they would. I would be very happy, but they just won't. It is not in them.

There is an impression that you three had a secret understanding.

Not at all. In fact, their entire campaign was mainly directed against me, that was the burden of all their election speeches.

You mean to say they consider you as the main threat.

I do not want to say that I am a threat. Nor am I speaking about Chavansaheb and Dada in person. It is the Congress-I that is losing to our benefit, whether it is led by Chavansaheb, Dada, Antulay, Bhosale or Adik.

It is a decline for the Congress or for Indira Gandhi.

Both. I will put it this way : Number one, Indira Gandhi's influence in Maharashtra is waning. Number two, the Congress as a whole is losing. And number three, its local leadership is crumbling.

Are you, like N.T. Rama Rao, putting across the theme that the central leadership of the Congress-I is insulting the state, devaluing its leaders, treating the Chief minister as a peon. Are you, in other words, playing the centre versus state tune, the tune of state chauvinism.

In my public meetings I do tell the people that the Congress-I leadership is reducing the states into class III municipalities, that it has been Indira Gandhi's design since long to finish the state leadership and that she has succeeded, that Maharashtra too has been a victim of this policy. This is not chauvinism. I am only pointing out how Indira Gandhi is systematically weakening the states, concentrating all powers in the centre, in fact in her

hands. Weak state governments, always at the mercy of the centre, means a lot of the problems. The interest of the states are often at a discount.

But Indira Gandhi insists that she is for strong states and a strong centre. In any case, why should you think that a strong centre will ignore the interests of the states.

Let me give a concrete instance—utilisation of Bombay High gas. I do not say Bombay High is Maharashtra's property, never. It is the nation's property and its benefits must be divided proportionately. But what has happened in fact? When Morarjibhai was the Prime minister, it was decided that Maharashtra and Gujarat will each get a fertiliser unit based on Bombay High gas. So came about the Thal Vaishet and Hazara projects. It was also the understanding then that, with the tapping of new gas wells further units will be set up both in Maharashtra, particularly in the backward and drought-prone areas, and in other states. In the proportion of 45 per cent for Maharashtra and 55 per cent for others. But the present government has allotted four units to UP, one each to Madhya Pradesh and Rajasthan, one more to Gujarat, and none to Maharashtra. The southern states are entirely ignored.

Now about the pipeline. According to the expert committee recommendation, the pipeline would cover Ahmednagar district, Marathwada and Nagpur in Maharashtra and traverse Madhya Pradesh and then Rajasthan via Gujarat and further onto UP. But the latest decision is a straight pipeline from Iran to Gujarat by sea.

You think this has been done to humiliate Maharashtra.

It is not a question of humiliation. Not only Maharashtra's but the national interest is harmed by this decision. The point I want to make is that Maharashtra was acquiesced in this decision precisely because of its weak leadership. Indira Gandhi wants this type of leadership so that she can impose any decision she likes on the states.

So it is more a political than an economic decision.

Hundred per cent political decision. Let me cite another example. There is thus no industry district concept which the government of India has announced. Not a single district in Maharashtra is entitled to the additional incentives and preferences given under this concept.

This may be because the priority has to be to undo the national level imbalances in development. Comparatively Maharashtra has a high concentration of industries.

Over 80 per cent of the industries in the state are concentrated in the Bombay-Pune belt and in Nasik. What about the rest of the Maharashtra?

Vidarbha, Marathwada and Konkan are backward, even the hilly tracks and drought-prone areas of western Maharashtra are backward. What about these?

Let us change the subject. The NDA and UF are not coming together largely because of the BJP. How will you reconcile your national stand with the BJP? Or, are you going to allow friendly contests between the UF and the BJP.

There are basic policy differences between the NDA and the UF and the two may not be able to support each other on many issues. But there is a thinking that we should at least try to avoid triangular contests. We do not want to encourage even 'friendly contests'—everybody is blaming me for coining that phrase. There is an urge for seat adjustments and I think we can do this so that the Congress-I does not get the advantage of division of votes among opposition parties.

What is the hitch, Sharad, in forming one single party instead of the United Front you have put together.

My party has no objection, I see like-minded people in Chandra Shekhar. Bahuguna, Ratubhai Adani, Chandrajit Yadav, Mir Qasim, etc. We can certainly come together in one party. But it cannot be by one party merging with another. All the parties must dissolve themselves to join hands to form a new party. The leaders of some of these parties are in fact pondering the subject, and there could be some progress in the near future. For the time being, you see, we have joined in a single parliamentary party. That is a good beginning.

Are you facing some difficulties from the Janata side.

I do not want to name any party.

There is a great desire among the people at large that all the opposition democratic parties should unite. They would like to know what is standing in the way.

The leaders share this desire. We in the United Front have no leadership dispute, no dispute over programmes, policies, or constitution. There is a serious attempt to forge closer links. But it takes time.

Sharad Joshi has announced that his Shetkari Sangathana is going to contest the elections. Will you be trying to bring him into the UF? What are the prospects? If he goes it alone, will it be Sharad vs Sharad?

Despite the latest reports to that effect, I do not think the Shetkari Sangathana is going to enter the election fray. My personal contacts with the Sangathana gave me this impression. They will back the candidates who make a declaration supporting their demands.

Do you support Sharad Joshi's demands.

You see, my party and the UF have accepted some programmes for agriculturists which are identical to Sharad Joshi's demands.

Do you foresee a loyalists vs defectors fight within the Congress (S) once Congress-I men join you in large numbers.

Basically we do not indict anybody from the Congress-I at the state or national levels. We have given all these powers to district and block units. They have to take the decision and recommend. This is so even in the case of important people, be they MLAs, Zilla Parishad presidents or anybody. This obviates friction later.

If your old friends such as Govindrao Adik want to come back, will you follow the same procedure.

I do not think my party's district unit will accept him. That means my state and national units too will not accept him.

Will you be giving tickets to the new members, younger people.

New people and essentially professionals. At least 20 per cent professionals, lawyers, doctors, chartered accountants, teachers, professors, agriculturists. We are aiming at good administration, not just winning elections. These people can ensure that.

There is an impression that eventually you will yourself return to the Congress-I, and that all your current efforts are meant only to keep the iron hot. Probably once Dada steps down, you may aspire to be the Congress-I Chief minister in Maharashtra.

I have been replying to this question since long. It is all Congress-I propaganda, that perhaps suits them. I can tell you, I will not accept any post in a party which has leaders like Indira Gandhi and a set up which is not at all conducive to any person who has self respect, some ideology.

After Indira Gandhi, perhaps. There have been reports that you are not against Rajiv Gandhi.

It's not a question of Rajiv Gandhi, who is Rajiv Gandhi? How can he represent the real Congress just because he has been projected in the last two or three years? I do not understand why the Congress-I is accepting him as a leader. Suppose tomorrow all Congresses were to combine under the Congress spirit, Congress culture, Congress programmes, one cannot say what will happen. But not Indira Congress. The Congress-I doors are not at all open to me.

If after Indira Gandhi, all congressmen come together in that party, probably that could be the real Congress and you may think of joining it.

I do not think so, I am not prepared to accept that those in the Congress-I are representing the Congress culture. There are 50 per cent who have nothing to do with the Congress culture or Congress programmes. So, with these type of people there, with or without Indira Gandhi it is impossible to think in terms of joining that party.

But there are some good people in it too.

There are some good people like Mir Qasim, who left the party only recently. There may be a few others.

Like Shivraj Patil, for example.

Shivraj Patil is one such, but I do not know how far he will be useful.

So you have burned your boats with the Congress-I.

It's not a question of burning boats, but I am fully aware of what is going on.

Related to this, your people think you have two ambitions—to get back the Chief ministership of Maharasthra, and then, aspire for the gaddi in Delhi.

Basically my desire is to replace the Congress-I and try to associate myself with youngsters, professionals and other people and try to bring about a change in society. To be frank, I do not want to be a Chief minister just for the sake of that office. I want to show that we can join together and work at the state and national levels and solve basic problems like poverty, unemployment, and things like communal tensions. You can do this whether you are here or in Delhi.

Every party says this, Dada also says he wants to solve these problems. You mean to say the advent of Dada has not helped much.

Not at all. Initially we were expecting that Dada would be able to improve the administration, do good to the people and to strengthen his party's position. But the party is still a divided house. The way Dada and his close associates are behaving has created a bad impression. People have lost hope in Dada.

Sharad, how many sugar factories do you control, directly or indirectly? How many factories are backing your party? Maharashtra politics is sugar politics.

That is a wrong impression. Those who control sugar factories are very strong people in certain areas. They are the people with tremendous resources. They can oblige by way of vehicles and other such facilities during elections. But financially, only a bit. They have never helped us financially.

Do you control sugar factories.
No. In my district there are two or three sugar mills which are controlled by people belonging to our party.
You are constantly touring, your expenses must be heavy. Who is helping you financially?
My condition to all my district committees is that for every meeting they should contribute Rs. 40,000 and there must be about seven or eight meetings every day. This is how we collect money from the people. I travel about 20 to 25 days in a month, and the funds collected take care of my party's expenses.

Current, 03.12.1983
pp. (24 + 22)

B. CPM Politics in Bengal

Red star over Bengal
Jyoti Basu: The revolution will spread

The road to communism lies through Calcutta. The sprawling city of 10 million people packed in the bastis, slums and tenements has finally fallen under the shadow of the Red Flag.

It is not only a city of dire poverty but also stinks of riches. With the concentration of 13 out of 22 monopoly houses and the headquarters of numerous and powerful multinationals, Calcutta becomes economically and politically the most important metropolis of the country.

But the city has taken the Rise of the Red Star rather stoically. The toiling people's expectations have gone up but they remain sober and disciplined. The rich and the super-rich are not nervous, though they are not very hopeful of their future.

The star attraction, Jyoti Basu, appears a changed man. He is no more burning with the ideological zeal. He deliberately avoids mentioning the words "communism" and "revolution." He is enormously aware of the unexpected and great responsibility that has fallen on his Marxist shoulders.

He knows it will not be the success or failure of an individual but, if he succeeds, communism will triumph in the country. His failure will seal the fate of not only his party but also of communism.

Jyoti Basu occupies his swivel chair in the Writers Building with the firm determination to rule Bengal in a new fashion, new style. Gone are the crowds of favour-seekers, sycophants and contact men who used to throng Writers.

The party cadre attaches more importance to the dilapidated PHQ in the lower middle class Alimuddin street than to the imposing Secretariat in the heart of Calcutta.

The ground floor of the PHQ houses the Ganashakti daily and press. The first floor hums with activity. Young and newly-elected party legislators flock into a room occupied by party boss Promod Das Gupta, a hardliner and a disciplinarian he keeps a strict eye on the goings-on in the party and other constituents of the Left Front.

Both Basu and Gupta maintain extremely amicable relations. Basu accepts the superiority of the party over the government. But at Writers he is the boss and none of his ministers except, perhaps, Dr. Ashok Mitra (Finance) has made himself accessible to journalists.

"This government will not run the state from the Writers Building." Basu told me before I could settle down for the interview.

"We are a people's party and for the solution of each problem, we've to go to the people. We've to take them into confidence: we have to create an atmosphere of total involvement. Only then can we succeed. Our success depends on the involvement of our party and the people."

Jyoti Basu spoke in brief, crisp sentences with his Middle Temple accent. He did not smile even once throughout our sitting.

I thought I should begin by drawing his attention to the new national situations: "The political map of the country is rather intriguing." He looked straight towards me, impatient to start his reply but I continued: "We have the CPM in Bengal, Sheikh Abdullah in Kashmir, AIADMK in Tamil Nadu, the Congress in four states and the Janata controlling the rest."

Basu did not even blink. His face remained creaseless and he began his reply as though he had been briefed earlier.

"It's nothing new," he said. "The most important thing is that the centre is not in the hands of the Congress. The Janata is in Delhi and states are led by various parties. The Janata will inevitably make radical changes

regarding the treatment the non-Janata governments will receive from the centre. But they should not behave like Indira Gandhi. There should be full co-operation between the centre and the states, otherwise there can be no harmony, there can be no development and there are bound to be conflicts that will harm everybody. We think since we have fought for democracy, the Janata will not pursue the path of the previous government. On our part we'll give full co-operation to the centre."

The slogan of 'strong centre" has faded with the Congress defeat. You'll naturally favour a federal system and more powers to the states.

Yes. This is municipal powers. There is no power in us. We have a unitary system, not a federal one. All power is vested with the centre. We cannot bring about the basic changes which the centre can. When we get to the centre, we'll bring about changes and socialism slowly.

There are elements in the Janata who would like a strong centre.

What do you mean by 'strong" centre? All powers concentrated in the centre means a weak centre. In that case you do not get strong support from the people. If India is to be made strong then powers should be delegated to the people. The Congress government weakened the country by concentrating too much power in the centre. I'm sure the Janata will not behave like the Congress. It's only by giving more responsibilities to the states that it can receive genuine co-operation. And there lies its strength.

In that case who will formulate national policies?

The centre in co-operation with the states.

Differences may arise on vital questions like labour, land reforms, urban ceiling, monopoly houses and multinationals.

The people have voted us to power. We'll go back to them and tell them about these differences. We are against monopoly and multinationals. We are against conflict. But the Janata Party has not said that it is for the multinationals and monopolies. They have got a programme which has several good points.

Is there a possibility of working out a minimum common programme?

Yes. It can be worked out.

Jyoti Basu is treading warily. He first wants to improve his image as an able administrator and a man with balanced views. The economic situation in his state is so different that he can be dogmatic only at the peril of his party. He knows that he'll have to evolve a high degree of

pragmatism to meet the situation. He'll have to enter into a dialogue with industry because without rapid industrial expansion, without reopening the sick units and without increasing production, he will not be able to meet the challenge of poverty and unemployment.

He knows that there is not much of a difference between the private and the public sectors. The private sector today depends largely on official financial institutions. That's why he no more talks of nationalisation. He also knows that a lack of understanding between his government and industry will jeopardise growth and industrial peace. A meaningful dialogue between the two will in no way tarnish his image of a Leftist. To him socialism means drinking water, two meals a day and shelter. It can come about only through great industrial and agrarian activity. In the present context of Bengal socialism also means no slogans, go-slows, no strikes and no *gheraos*.

Socialism means no corruption, no nepotism and an efficient administration. Socialism will have a greater respectability and acceptability if the common citizen feels safe, if peace prevails and if law and order is not challenged.

Jyoti Basu knows all this and after my meeting with him he gave me the impression that he meant business.

"Writers" too has taken his advent with typical bureaucratic equanimity. S.M. Murshid, a seasoned IAS bureaucrat who worked with him when he was Deputy CM, described Basu as an "extremely polite and polished person, a delight for bureaucrats because he doesn't believe in unnecessary interference. His decisions are clear-cut. He doesn't mince words and is quick to take on-the-spot decisions. Politically, he puts down all orders on paper and doesn't believe in verbal comments. He trusts those bureaucrats who are trustworthy."

How would he handle the bureaucracy?
I have already stated that the government will not be run from the Writers Building, Basu said. We cannot change the bureaucracy overnight. We cannot get rid of those we do not like. Such officials can only be changed, but we cannot change them. We do not have real power. If we had power in Delhi, we would have done so many other things.

Are you in favour of a committed bureaucracy?
Yes. Committed to our policies, party, cause and programme.

Basu too is keen not to alienate any section of society and to improve the image of his administration. He still remembers Ajoy Mukherjee's

gimmicks and hatred towards him. The Bangla Congress leader had branded the CPM as "a party of dacoits."

Ajoy and his ilk no more dominate Bengal policies. The Left Front has 230 of the 294 seats. Basu's party alone controls 170, a sweeping majority. It has come into power through fire and brimstone. It lost more than a thousand members of its finest cadre during Emergency. Another thousand are still in jail. Over 20,000 had gone underground to avoid the repression and torture.

Basu shows no sign of bitterness towards the Congress. "But," he says We'll make sure it does not come back. The Congress has not changed its policies. The same leaders dominate it. They are not repentant. The danger is still there.

Are you thinking of appointing commissions?

Yes. A lot of them. Against corruption, nepotism, repression and police excesses. But ours will be from 1972 onwards. To us Emergency began five years ago. But we won't be vindictive.

You have been talking of changing the Constitution. Do you think the present Constitution will serve your purpose of bringing about socialism?

We want changes. We have been demanding this for the last four years. But nobody listened to us.

Are you in favour of proportional representation?

We are. But we have to talk to our friends in the Janata Party. Our socialist friends say that it cannot be worked out. We'll talk to them and see what can be done.

Is your party planning to make Bengal a nucleus for communist activity, a springboard for the whole country?

The nucleus is there. We want the revolution to spread. We have to get the people interested in our activities. We also want the people from the other states to learn from us.

Do you envisage any ideological clash with the Janata?

Why should there be any clash? I want to do good. The Janata would also like to do the same. The communists want competition among all parties so that the people can decide what they want from their performance.

Current, 16.07.1977.
pp. (1 + 2 + 24)

We are not scared of Indira: Promod Das Gupta

What are the major achievements of the Left Front government in the past five years?

Why don't you read our Manifesto? Our main achievement is that we have given total freedom to the people. Freedom to think and to act. We have restored civil liberties. The sword of NSA or ESMA does not hang over anybody's head in this state.

Here the government does not interfere with the democratic rights of the people. They can protest, criticise the government and organise strikes. These are their fundamental rights. They can be anti-establishment or pro-establishment. This is our great achievement.

I call this an achievement only because under the present constitutional framework, we cannot give more to the people. People have the freedom to organise. They have no fear as they have in other parts of the country, mostly in Congress-ruled states.

Secondly, in Congress ruled states whenever government employees go on strike, that period is considered a break in their service, and thus promotions are stopped. Here in Bengal there is no such victimisation and the police do not interfere with the right of the workers to go on strike.

Another important thing is that the salaries of government employees, professors and teachers have been increased, especially those of primary school teachers. Nobody gets less than Rs. 500. These benefits are irrespective of ideological affiliations.

All primary school teachers are not Leftists. None of the teachers has a temporary job. All have been made permanent. No teacher can be sacked or removed. The teachers, be they in government or private schools, get their salaries regularly.

From 1972 to 1976, the government was not able to hold examinations. If it did, that was with great difficulty. The students never knew when the examinations would be held, and even if they did, they were uncertain when the results would be announced. Even when they were announced, there was no knowing whether or not they would get their certificates and degrees.

It was an era of total uncertainty on the campus. This affected the morale of the students, and after spending money on the education of their children, the parents were uncertain about the outcome.

Things have changed now. Schools and colleges run smoothly. There are no strikes in any educational institution at any level. The life of teachers

is not threatened. Examinations are held regularly and degrees and certificates are given on time. Education is completely free up to the 12th Standard and the pupils get their books, dress, tiffin free.

At the high school and college level promotions are regular. No student is thrown out of school if he is not able to pay his fee. Poverty does not come in the way of education. This is not a small relief if you see from the context of Bengal. I do not think this has ever happened in Bengal under Congress government since Independence.

You said about the police not interfering with the worker's right to strike. Isn't it the same in Congress ruled states as well? Also the workers have the right to go on strike and the police do not interfere. In Bombay Datta Samant has paralysed the textile industry. The workers are on strike for over 100 days now, and neither the police nor the government has interfered.

That is a different thing. Datta Samant was arrested under NSA. Here we have never used NSA and have opposed it. We are against all draconian laws which curb civil liberties. There is terror in Congress ruled states.

Here you are wrong. There is no terror in Congress ruled states. There may have been police excesses, but no terror as a matter of policy. There is no terror in Bengal either.

The greatest achievement of our government is that no person has been arrested under NSA or ESMA. Sixty per cent of the working class here is non-Bengali. They are from Bihar, Orissa, UP and other states. We do not encourage the 'sons of the soil' slogan. There is total national integration here. We often hear that slogan in Orissa, Maharashtra, Bihar, MP and some other states. But in Bengal there is no trace of it. The Bengalis know that so much money is going out of their state, but they are conscious that we are a part of India.

Our other great achievement is land reforms. We in Bengal has the worst kind of *zamindari* system, created and maintained by the British who came here first and founded the East India Company. We have changed it. The share cropping system continues, but crop sharing has been legalised. They have a legal right on three-fourths of the produce and the landlord gets only one-fourth.

That means the landlords are still there.

Yes, landlords are there. They are everywhere. But the legalisation of crop sharing has tremendously helped the share-cropper and his economic condition today is much better. The share croppers are recorded in a register and nobody can play hanky-panky with them. That means they

have a right to cultivate their land. They cannot be simply thrown out of their land.

Does the share cropper have a right over the land?

No. He has right over the cultivation of the land. Previously they used to get loans from moneylenders, who were ruthlessly exploiting them. Now we have eliminated the moneylender. The share cropper gets loans from the banks at a very low rate of interest. The government stands guarantee. This is important. They are helped to purchase seeds, fertilizers, bullocks and ploughs.

Is it easy for them to get these loans? Who guides them?

It was not so earlier, but now it is really easy, because the government stands guarantee and the party workers give the guidance. If a farmer does not pay back the loan, the government is responsible and so the banks are willing to help. The total amount of loans comes to about Rs. 50 crore.

We have also fixed the minimum wage for farm labourers. It is Rs. 9 per day.

Has it been effective?

In the beginning there was some trouble. But now the government is firm and nobody dare evade the law. This has stopped the flow of people from the village to the town. In the lean season peasants used to flock to the towns. To stop this influx, we introduced the Food for Work Scheme. The food is supplied by the Central government and the state government pays for it. The scheme offers two kgs of wheat and Rs. 2 per day, and the coverage is complete. Distribution is done by the Panchayat. This is a very big achievement of our party, which has endeared us to the people.

There is a growing anti-rich feeling.

May be, what can I do? But I am not unhappy about that.

Your government, your Leftist critics say, has taken no positive steps against big business houses and multinationals. In fact, Jyoti Basu has been saying that the multinationals are a part of Bengal's economy.

How can we take any steps against them? They are controlled by the centre. But you go to the business areas and ask the businessmen in Bada Bazaar—not the Birlas or Goenkas, but the middle class businessmen—ask them how much more business they have done in these five years. They have done lots of business and good business.

There is no anti-Marwari movement here. These Marwaris are a part of Bengal. They are our people. They enjoy a feeling of security and

safety, unlike in Orissa. And if they want safety, it is in their interest to vote for us and support us.

In a way you are right. The business community in Calcutta seems to have greater trust in your party than it had in the Congress.

Yes. We do not bother them and they come to settlement with the workers. Even our trade unions do not bother them. But we do not allow them to harm the interests of the workers.

You have given a sense of security to the business community even while fulfilling the demands of the workers?

Of course, this is a fact.

The law and order situation seems to have deteriorated. The Congress party has, in a brochure, listed over 300 murders in the last two years. It has given the names, ages and addresses of the victims.

This is all false. It is a canard. What do they mean by 300 murders? All of them are not political murders. Why doesn't the Congress party talk of the hundreds of murders in UP and Bihar? They are mostly political murders. What about Phoolan Devi's butchery of Harijans, and many more such ghastly episodes?

I am not talking of Phoolan Devi and the dacoits. I am talking of political murders, CPM workers killing Congress workers.

Congress workers are killing Congress workers. The CPM does not believe in killing. We are a civilised democratic party with faith in a certain ideology.

But there have been instances of clashes between CPM and Congress workers.

There may have been confrontations. But what can I do about them? From 1972 to 1976 Congress men killed hundreds of CPM workers. Their policy was one of revenge. But after we came to power, we did not retaliate. We specifically made clear to our party workers that we should not take the law into our hands.

Indira Gandhi says there is no law and order in Bengal and that your government has let loose a reign of terror.

Is there any law and order in her family? (laughs and takes a long puff of his half-burnt cigar).

That is a family dispute. Many families have disputes.

Well, that is all right. But if she cannot manage her own family disputes, how can she manage the country (laughs loudly)? I am not going to reply

to her allegations. People of Bengal have seen her through and through, and they do not believe her cock and bull stories any more.

They make false promises. Now Ghani Khan Chowdhary has claimed that he can make Bengal surplus in power if his party gets the majority. This is a childish claim. How can he do it? And why did not his party do it when it was in power? He simply cannot. He cannot take the people of Bengal for a ride by making this kind of tall claim.

I have heard that Ghani Khan and Jyoti Basu are great chums and that they are helping each other in this election. Ghani Khan's main target is Pranab Mukherjee and not Jyoti Basu.

I will not reply to this question. It is an insinuation. But I know one thing, that Ghani Khan cannot produce electricity in six months. He is talking like a child.

Do you think the DVC cut the electric supply at the behest of the centre? Or is Luther (DVC Chairman) acting on his own?

I don't know what the real position is, but Luther cannot possibly act like this without instructions from Delhi.

Do you think the massacre of the 17 Anand Margis was a conspiracy and a provocation to postpone the elections? I understand the Margis will launch a state-wide agitation.

Let them agitate, I do not care. I have instructed my party people not to get provoked. I do not want to go into details.

How can you avoid the details? It is such a big tragedy, 17 people butchered in broad daylight by a mob of 5,000. You cannot brush aside such a ghastly tragedy.

I do not attach any political significance to the Margi murders. I think it was the result of a scare in the Kasba locality. There was a scare about the influx of child-lifters, and some of the Margis killed were carrying little children with them.

Don't you think it was an organised conspiracy aimed at creating a law and order problem?

I don't think so. I do not see in it the hand of the CBI or IB. These agencies cannot organise a mob of 5,000.

How do you finance your party? Where does the money come from?

It comes from the people, from the workers. They contribute out of their salaries.

Do you take money from industrialists?

No, we do not. We are against ill-gotten wealth. We ask for money from friends like you and we get it.

I asked Jyoti Basu if he was scared of Indira Gandhi. The impression I got is that the CPM is scared of her charisma.
She is quite capable of creating trouble. But neither I nor Jyoti Basu, nor our party is scared of her. We were not scared of the British and their bayonets, who is Indira Gandhi? After all what can she do? We do not believe in confrontation though she has been challenging us off and on. Our party is prepared for any eventuality.

What is the CPM membership?
Now about 96,000. It was 38,000 in 1977.
What is the number of your sympathisers?
It runs into a legion. I think they must be about four and a half million. The membership of our trade unions is about 7.6 million. Then there are teacher unions with a membership of about 72,000.

What is the party's attitude towards the police? I do not mean the police officers, but the ordinary constable?
Well, the police have their own role to play. Policemen get corrupt very easily.

I do not think your government has an anti-police attitude. They have served you well.
Well, they have been serving themselves too. We have increased their salaries as we have increased the salaries of teachers. We have declared their union a legal organisation. We think the policemen have every right to form their own union.
Have you been able to win their sympathy too?
Frankly, I do not care.

Have you any CPM members in the police?
I will not answer that question.

My impression is that a majority of policemen are in sympathy with you.
May be. But I will not talk about it.

Do you think there is any chance of unity between the CPI and CPM
No. We consider the CPI only one of the Left parties.

Do you see any possibility of a broad Left unity at the national level?
I do not think so.

You have a big brother attitude towards the CPI?
Well, we are big.

You can be equal, too?

No, on this issue we cannot be equal. We are big and they are small.

You are two brother parties.

May be, but how can all brothers be equal?

What is wrong with being equal?

Everything.

After all the CPI is a Marxist party. It believes in all the Leninist principles as you do.

You see, there are 294 members in the Left Front, of which CPI is a small constituent. We have our shares, and they have theirs. This cannot be called big brother attitude.

I was talking about CPM-CPI unity at the all-India level.

What does CPI have at the all-India level? They are nowhere except for a few pockets in Bihar and another few in Kerala.

Do not you think unity between the two will strengthen the leftist movement in the country?

It is a hypothetical question. Do not you think unity between the USSR and China would strengthen the socialist movement in the world?

You talk of authoritarianism, and you want to fight single-handed?

That risk is there. But unity to fight against authoritarianism is there. Otherwise why should we have brought CPI into the United Front? The CPI is divided on the issue of Indira Gandhi. The Dange faction is now fully supporting her and has completely broken away. That the founder member and holder of the Order of Lenin should behave in this way is unfortunate.

Dange's daughter Rosa, and son-in-law Bani Deshpande are as good as members of the Congress.

Why do you ask me these questions? I'm least bothered about them. These people have nothing to do with Communism. They are misguided individuals.

This is a very negative attitude. They cannot be discarded like this, Dange has been a big name in the international Communist movement.

It makes no difference. There have been many big names in the international Communist movement.

Current, 15.05.1982.
pp. (3 + 5)

Cracking the Gorkha nut

The shadow-boxing between Rajiv Gandhi and Jyoti Basu over Gorkha enfant terrible Subhas Ghising has resulted in a whimper.

Rajiv has been saying that the demand for Gorkhaland is not anti-national. Now Basu agrees with him after Ghising expressed 'regrets' on his approach to foreign powers. And Ghising came down to Delhi to discuss 'only the citizenship' issue.

The fight between Basu and Ghising will, however, continue because the Gorkha leader has not given up the demand for a separate Gorkhaland. It will be between him and the CPM, with the Congress obviously making maximum capital out of the bout.

Rajiv and Basu will be in Darjeeling, and Ghising is most likely to meet them. The scenario in pre-poll Bengal will now take a new turn in which the Marxists stand to gain considerable footage.

You called the Gorkha National Liberation Front anti-national, and now you are going with Rajiv Gandhi to Darjeeling.
There is a misunderstanding. We characterised Subhas Ghising as anti-national because he wrote letters to outsiders—to the king of Nepal, to the U.N., to others. We thought that was dangerous.

Do you feel he is no more anti-national?
If he has expressed regret, how I call him anti-national. I have seen his letter, I have a copy. Simply because he talks of Gorkhaland I do not give in and we fight on it—that is not anti-national. It was anti-national to establish links abroad.

So they invited him with your consent.
Yes, I told Buta Singh that the PM should not meet him unless he agrees to all our conditions. He assured me Ghising wanted to meet him to discuss the citizenship issue. I added that if the PM were to meet him, then the Congress, our party everybody concerned should be invited to discuss things.

Do you still feel they are anti-national?
I'll tell you what I did. I got the Congress party here with us. The Congress and we never meet outside. But on the GNLF question, we said this is not an election issue at all. This is a national issue. It is dangerous for our country. So we got together and passed a resolution on these lines.

Then, day after day, Rajiv Gandhi went on giving certificates to

Ghising, saying "he is not anti-national, I've found nothing anti-national in his movement;" and so on. He was asked in Parliament, "is it not anti-national to seek outside help?" He did not reply. In the state Assembly, the Congress party had moved a resolution calling Ghising movement anti-national. But when the resolution came up they got cold feet. They withdrew it.

Later, however, Ghising wrote a letter to Home minister Buta Singh regretting he had written to outsiders. The word regret is there, mark you. When I mentioned this to Rajiv at the airport, he said: "Yes, I have read that letter. Can I go to Darjeeling and say that GNLF is not anti-national?" I said "go ahead".

When I met Rajiv a second time, I told him, "Look, this is the second meeting I am having with you. And the message must be carried to Ghising that we do not differ with you and you do not differ with me. And let a communication go from your office on this basis, telling Ghising that since he has expressed regrets, we won't raise the issue." Some people do not perceive things the right way.

As he was seeking outside help, I said let him withdraw these letters to the UN, somebody might raise it there some day, there are so many enemies.

They invited Ghising to Delhi.

After the meeting with Rajiv, we gave three conditions: The anti-Bengal stand should be given up, the violent movement must be called off, and Ghising must not seek the division of Bengal. Apart from this, on other issues like citizenship and economic growth, we can sit down and discuss. That was all written in the communique which Buta Singh refused to give to the press.

Buta Singh rang me up. And a messenger was sent to him conveying my conditions. He came back and reported that the Home minister concurred with the view that this latest phase of the movement, the anti-Bengal phase, was poisoning the minds of the people, and should be withdrawn. Buta Singh also conveyed to us that only the citizenship issue would be discussed when Ghising came to Delhi. I told him to explain this to Ghising.

So, you agree to sit with Ghising.

If he agrees to our conditions I sit with him. Otherwise, I don't he must say, must give a statement that he will stop his violent movement. Then he should say he agrees with us that Bengal should not be divided. No Gorkhaland apart from that, there may be so many other things. Those can be discussed.

Do you think he will agree to withdraw the Gorkhaland demand.
If he doesn't, we do not talk at all.

You are going with Rajiv Gandhi to Darjeeling on February 7. You no longer call the GNLF anti-national, nor does Rajiv. So on this point you and Rajiv agree, is it not. What would be your attitude at Darjeeling on the 7th..
The same. You see, supposing he had not written this letter to outsiders, would I have called him anti-national? Rajiv Gandhi came into the picture much later. He did not understand the point, nor did his law minister Asoke Sen. Now Ghising has understood his mistake and regretted.

What will be your programme in Darjeeling.
On February 7th we are going for some other purpose—a function of the Himalayan Mountaineering Institute with which the President and the Vice-President are associated. There was to be a meeting with Rajiv. So I told him to hold it in Darjeeling, not in Delhi, since we are in any way going there.

You selected Darjeeling.
Yes, I did. I had suggested September, but Rajiv had no time. Then, suddenly, he went to Darjeeling in December on his own, for his party meeting. I was unable to go with him.

He could not hold a public meeting there because of the boycott. Now, are you planning to hold a public meeting.
We are holding the Institute meeting.

Your detractors say the Marxist Front in Bengal is a one-man show. Jyoti Basu show.
I have been hearing and reading about it. But it's not correct. We do have an organisation unlike the Congress. For the past 15 years or so there have been no organisational elections in the Congress. Our party is not like that.

You see, there are the smaller parties—Janata and others. We are the biggest, of course. We have an organisational set up in every village, every town, everywhere. We have mass organisations. Not the party alone, other wings. They have their members. So we are not a one-man show.

But what happens is that an individual has his own role to play, and if he plays it long, he comes to the forefront. The masses look up to the leader. But this is quite unlike what is happening in the Congress, which is just a one-man show. Ours is not.

You have been in power for the past ten years. Have you ever thought of retiring and giving the Chief ministership to somebody else.

No. We politicians never retire, until we die.

But you are an out of turn politician. You can experiment with somebody else in your party.

No. It is not like that. Whatever my party wants me to do, I do. That is why for the party posts, there is constant renewal, we bring in younger leaders.

Are you preparing a second line.

Yes. We have been doing it for the past five or six years. In the past five or six years in the party conferences we bring them up, encourage them to involve themselves in the discussions on major resolutions.

Do you think there are some people in your party who can replace you.

History marches on. Did not we talk about after Nehru who, after Indira, what.

I am not saying after Jyoti Basu what.

You see because I am in the forefront here. I became the opposition leader, so I am projected like that, and have some role to play. But that doesn't mean I am running a one-man show. We have an organisation, we discuss things. I do not take decisions on my own.

Let us look outside Bengal. The party system has almost collapsed, especially the Congress party has collapsed. We began with a multi-party system, then we came to a two-party system, then one-man system. It is Rajiv Gandhi who is running the system. There is no Congress party. Other parties are mere name-sakes. Even the CPM is quite weak. In this situation the masses are left with very little choice.

We should have expanded much more. We are trying that. We have built up some mass organisations. But the party has not advanced the way it should have. And there are other opposition parties. They are still there.

They have also collapsed. I do not think Telugu Desam or the AIADMK are political parties.

Janata is very much a party. Then there is Lok Dal which has influence in north India and some other states. They are all splinter groups, having influence here and there, in various pockets. These parties, which we call bourgeoisie opposition parties, have also a role to play. Because by overselves we cannot deliver the goods. We cannot confront the Congress party by ourselves. There must be some sort of co-ordination, not electoral but on principles. We have failed in that.

Why did you fail.

The conclave and all that came earlier. That is no longer there. We had brought them together in 1980.

Is there any hope of revival.

At the moment no. But anyway, we go on trying.

The successful implementation of your rural policies is not known outside Bengal.

Not much.

I think, if people in the rest of India are made aware of achievements of the Marxists in Bengal, that will have a psychological impact.

They should know more about our achievements when I go out, I find they are aware there exists a Left Front government led by the Marxists whose performance is distinct from what is happening in other parts of the country where the Congress is ruling. But they do not know enough that is true.

I tour the country quite often and find that Jyoti Basu as an individual is liked by the people. But they do not think much about the party.

That may be so. The newspapers also play up, things that way.

Not the newspapers, I am speaking of what is in the minds of the people.

I say the papers because that impression is created by what they write.

Have you noticed that in the Indian newspapers, even in the bourgeoisie press, there is no attack on you, no criticism of your government.

They sort of separate me from my party. There are people here also among the bourgeoisie section who would say, "Oh you, you are all right. But your party . . ." I say you cannot separate me from my party. I am here because of my party. I have made my contribution in building that party. But they do not take it in that light.

Your party has certain pockets of influence as in Punjab, Bihar and Kerala. But there is no expansion, as you have yourself said.

In different places for different reasons. Now, in Kerala, we have done it in a big way. But in Bihar, the CPI let us down badly. They were the major left party there. But in the last elections their strategy was to defeat us in the Congress areas. So they did not have any understanding with us, with the result they lost half their seats. Youth front, women's front, Kissan front. But their cells are not evenly distributed.

You have not gone to the grassroots.

We have in some places. We have the student front.

Any chances of unity between the CPM and the CPI.
Yes. Yes. Not a united party, but there must be united movements, united programmes. Together we are trying to join hands with Karpoori Thakur and others for a very big front in Bihar. I tell you, if this comes off, we may go to other states with a similar strategy—with the Lok Dal and others.

What are your expectations in the Assembly elections. What will be your electoral plank.
We have already issued our manifesto in which we have said we would complete various projects on hand, and initiate a few new ones. Democracy, communal harmony and so on are other issues.

Will you be in a position to improve your position in urban Bengal where you are weak.
Yes. There has been an improvement in the last two years.

You lost heavily in Calcutta in the Lok Sabha elections.
Yes. But we made up for that in the Calcutta Corporation elections. Now we are equal with the Congress.

Why has the Congress party got support in Calcutta. Is the city anti-CPM.
It is a negative vote, no doubt, but not exactly. As I told you, things were not looking up in the urban areas. Middle class attitude and all that. But soon they realised our worth and voted for us.

How many Assembly seats have you won from Calcutta.
We have 11 seats, the Congress 10.

Will you be able to improve the position.
I think so.

You had some rebel candidates from the CPM.
Rebels do not make any difference. When we expel some people they call themselves rebels.

What is the impact of the Pranab factor in Bengal.
Not much. In some districts he seems to have made a dent into the Congress influence. We see this in the size of his meetings. But he is not a major factor.

All this time he has not spoken against you or the CPM.
No, he has not. But we will have no seat adjustments with him, nor will we withdraw any of our candidates in his party's favour.

What will happen in the constituencies where there are triangular contests between you, the Congress and Pranab's party.

In some places it may help us, he may cut into the Congress vote. But in others it could go against us.

How do you view Hope '86? Some of your ministers have criticised it. How much money was collected there.

I suppose we got Rs. 50 lakh. This gentleman, Mithun Chakraborty came to me and said. "There is a strike in Bombay and we want to raise funds for you also." I said, "Very good. You have been helping me in the past. During the 1978 floods. I went to Bombay and you raised funds for me, thank you." I attended the show and stayed till 11 p.m.

Now the Congress party is launching a show Hope '87, with Amitabh Bachchan.

Amitabh was also here.

How much did they collect, and is your share coming to you.

Yes. They collected a crore-and-a-half, of which our share of Rs. 50 lakh will come to us.

Are Rajiv Gandhi's frequent visits to Bengal affecting your chances?

They mean nothing. In fact, it is good that he comes. Our people were becoming rather complacent. If he goes to a hospital and sees a rat there, it means nothing. He asks them whether they get water. I say there is no water in Delhi, why don't you get water there. Circular Road where I stay in Delhi is a posh area, no water there. I get it there by tankers.

But he has been drawing large crowds.

Yes, he does. In a TV interview I was asked about it. I said, the Prince of Wales came, the crowds were there, Rajiv is our PM, so people come to see him.

Is it a curious crowd.

Of course, most of them are that.

But they feel he may make a dent into your citadel.

It is good for congressmen to feel that way.

What is your personal assessment of Rajiv Gandhi.

I have said it so many times, I did not know him at all before he became the PM, just met him once. He is a gentleman and all that, but Indiraji was better.

Your man-to-man relations . . . .

Has not been good. And the fault is his, not mine. We were bound to differ, but he should not go on talking like he does. You see, that needs experience. He is not a Congress leader, he is the Prime minister of India.

How can be talk like that in meetings, giving figures and all that, which does not mean anything. He only gets a bad name for himself. His people are briefing him all wrong.

You must have seen during the last week, he was dismissing secretaries right and left. And the way he removed the Finance minister. What do you think of that.

There is no government in Delhi. It is only one man. Even during Indira Gandhi's time it was not like that. Who are his advisers. Nine times he has changed his ministers, officers. He is changing things overnight.

Will it have an effect in the bureaucracy.

How can anybody, minister or officer, feel safe? And in this mood, it is just not possible for anyone even to look into the files, alone take proper decisions. This is not the way a government is run.

Do you think Rajiv will complete his term.

There is no opposition. Otherwise, he would not have.

The sudden removal of the Finance minister....

That part, it is their business. When Arun Nehru was removed….

But it affects you also.

It does. I have been telling so in public meetings. I go and talk to them, convince them of something. Then, suddenly, the man is changed and a new one has taken his place. Again, I have to start at the beginning and re-establish new rapport.

Do you feel lost in Delhi.

I know whom to contact. But some of them are new. I do not know them at all. This is my personal difficulty.

Are you able to meet Rajiv Gandhi whenever you want to.

Of course, he meets me. But I do not disturb people for nothing. That is why when he came over here, I told him. "You are moving all over India and all over the world. Why don't you talk about Gorkhaland? You are going to Darjeeling, go over there too, but we have to talk. So he said, "You come over, I'll be there".

You have been in power for almost 10 years. What are your major achievements and failures.

The major achievement is that we have been there and we still enjoy the support of the majority of the people. I think we have been successful in implementing our programme, the minimum of it. I cannot claim too much. In the countryside we have done quite a bit for the peasants, agriculturists.

You mean your rural achievement is greater.

Yes, very much. I think the people in the rural area are very happy with us. You could see this in the results of panchayat elections. But in the cities, except during the last two years, we have not been able to do much. Industries are not coming up—that's weakness. The private sector is not investing in the state.

Did you approach the centre.

Many times. We have been talking to them, even during Indira Gandhi's days. But unfortunately we get no modern industries—petrochemicals or electronics.

You say not a single major industry has come up in Bengal in the last 10 years.

Not one. And I've been talking to all of them. Asking for Centrally-sponsored industries as in other states. Then only the private sector will come in.

Did you make any specific proposals.

Yes, like petrochemicals. We got a letter of intent during the Janata regime. Since then we have been trying out, but found that we cannot undertake such a big project on our own. Where are the funds? So we suggested a joint sector effort with the centre and the state to contribute 40 per cent each and the rest the public. I waited for a long time. Finally, they said they cannot spare the funds. I am now seeking out the private sector.

Has he agreed.

Yes. Of course, we are not very happy with the joint sector units set up during the Congress regime. The private partners try to take undue advantage. But in the present case, I have done plain speaking. And at long last the centre has given us the licence.

Who is in the management? Goenkas.

No, we have a board with government majority. The government should not interfere in the working of this type of project, but it must control the management.

Similarly, electronics, I wanted Bharat Electronics, or Hindustan Electronics to set up a Rs. 50–60 crore unit here. But officials advised us that since we are a border state we should not have such a unit unless the Defence Ministry clears it. I do not know what they meant.

There is industrial peace in Bengal.

Total peace.

I have been talking to local industrialists here and they seem to be far happier with you than they were with the previous Congress government.
They know one thing. We are in the government, and we are a major force in the trade unions enjoying the backing of the working class. Differences crop up, fights go on, strikes go on, we intervene. They know once an agreement is reached we have got the power, the authority and the willingness to implement it.

But their reasoning is different. They feel Jyoti Basu in power is safer. Out of it he could be troublesome. You agree with that.
I do. And we have done good work in the field of small-scale industry. We are the first in the country to start co-operatives of small-scale and cottage industries.

What are your achievements in the social and educational fields.
The Congress was in power in the state for 29 years. What did they do? But we are here for 10 years now. We have made education free up to class 12. We have opened new schools. There is no village without a school with a roof and blackboard.

Have you been able to eliminate the influence of the landlords, the jotedars.
Yes, very much. That is why the landed classes are with the Congress. They want to get back their lost influence.

You say the backbone of the Congress are the jotedars and the landlords.
Yes, the masses are not with them.

Have you been to solve the power problem.
The power situation is much better here than in many other states. We have added about 1,200 mw during the last ten years. The Congress government had installed 90 mw during the previous eight years. But the demand has gone up.

Calcutta has no power problem.
At the moment no.

You have called the Rs. 684 crore aid package announced for Bengal by Rajiv Gandhi a hoax. Why?
Because it is a hoax.

In what way.
At the end of a six-hour long meeting—his Press Information Officer was there—he told the centre was giving Rs. 684 crore. I said very good. Then he repeated the offer at public meetings. When he went back to Delhi, I wrote to him and sought clarification, the actual breakdown and

the specifics. He informed me that the concerned department was still looking into it. I was surprised and expressed it. Then his secretariat sent the breakdown figures.

There you find, for example, Rs. 210 crore allotted for the Calcutta Electric Corporation's southern generating station. A private company is running this new station. The centre took a year and a half to give it MTRP permission.

Now, it was our money, the financial institutions money and the CEC's money that was tied up for a year and a half.

Current, 07.02.1987.
pp. (1 + 6 + 7)

C. Challenges from Southern States

The writing on the Wall: southern CMs challenge centre

New Delhi should see the writing on the wall. The conclave of the four Chief ministers from the South in the Salubrious climate of Bangalore was the logical outcome of the changing mood in the country. It happens that all the four CMs are anti-centre though not anti-Indira to the same extent.

The centre these days is totally identified with Indira Gandhi, and any anti-centre feeling takes the shape of an anti-Indira stance. The South, which stood by her like granite all these years, has come out of her tight grip, and its aspirations were indeed reflected in these Chief ministers postures and pronouncements. It is just the beginning, and the fiscal demands raised by them in such subtlety are a straw in the wind.

The defeat of Indira Gandhi in the South is being considered by the people in that region as the beginning of the end of 'Central' rule and the assertion of the 'personality' of the South over the North which she has suddenly come to symbolise.

The Chief ministers—Hegde, NTR, MGR, Ramchandran—who have joined in a Council have asked for an overall review of centre-state relations in view of the changed political atmosphere. Only Kerala with its Congress government has preferred to be left out, but Karunakaran's government is a fragile conglomeration and might fall any day. Keralites were, in fact, the first to raise these demands under communist rule and would do so again if the CPM comes back to power.

The feeling in the south is that the National Development Council which is made up of the Chief ministers and most of the Central ministers with the Prime minister as its permanent chairman, has failed to reflect the aspirations of the people and is totally dominated by Indira's august personality.

Since Congress CMs who dare not even whisper in front of their leader form the majority in the NDC, that body has lost its weight as an effective instrument for safeguarding the interests of the states. Hegde made this plain when he pointed out that the Chief ministers were 'dwarfed' in the NDC, which is dominated by the Union government and the planning Commission, and lamented: "We do not get sufficient opportunity even to express our views in the NDC."

The brain behind the southern meet and the one who acted as its spokesman, Hegde demanded the setting up of a new fiscal commission with sufficient representation from the states and with powers to recommend changes in the Constitution, if necessary, to ensure equitable distribution of resources. He thought the present scale of devolution of resources was not "commensurate with the responsibility to be discharged by the states under the Constitution. The total divisible pool to be shared by the centre with the states should be increased."

Hegde is opposed to the centre's discretionary powers on the allocation of funds and has suggested that the bulk of the resources should be transferred "on a statutory basis," and this should be decided by the proposed Council of Chief ministers and not by the centre. He has thus thrown the ball into the Congrèss Chief ministers' court, knowing that Indira Gandhi would never allow such a dilution in her power and authority.

With the fiscal demands, the Chief ministers have also made two equally important suggestions which challenge Central authority. They have objected to the appointment of judges to high courts from outside the state. They think the only way to 'safeguard the independence and competence of the judiciary is to ensure that high court judges are familiar with the language of the state concerned."

The third significant demand is for, a review of the administrative relations under Article 250 and 257. Specifically they demand power for state legislatures to legislate and enact laws in the state list, as also in the concurrent list on subjects on which the states are to legislate first without having to get the President's assent. They want Chief ministers to act independent of the centre in most of the matters in which the centre's

guidance is not constitutionally enjoined. "Why should we run to the centre for every little thing, asserted Hegde.

Indira Gandhi's concept of a 'strong centre' has never before been challenged so effectively and in such an organised manner. Her argument that the centre has to be strong, and that if the centre is strong, the states too would feel reassured was stood on its head by NTR and MGR by insisting that the stronger the states, the stronger would be the centre.

The Constitution has been so framed that if a strong personality such as that of Indira Gandhi is in saddle, she can make it an instrument for concentrating power at the centre, and in case there is a 'weak' Prime minister, its provisions can be moulded in favour of the states and to promote federalism.

The Southern conclave was not of the opposition leaders; it was of the elected representatives for three very important states besides a Union Territory. Their united stand cannot be wished away or ignored.

As the Prime minister, Indira Gandhi will have to take note of this very significant development if a headlong centre-state confrontation is to be avoided. For the time being the non-Congress states including Bengal are not in a position to confront her, but the Bangalore spirit may snowball with Kashmir, Punjab and Assam imbibing similar feelings.

Communist Bengal has been fighting a lone battle for such 'federal' status and the Bangalore meet must have come as a shot in Comrade Jyoti Basu's arm. Basu has already announced that he and his party's ultimate aim is to capture power at the centre with the help of 'like-minded' Chief ministers and that the day is not far off with the 'waning image' of Indira Gandhi and the 'disintegration' of the Congress in the south, the north and the east.

His more articulate 'spokesman', Ashok Mitra, has been demanding 'more powers' for the states in a more forthright manner than the soft-spoken and subtle Ramakrishna Hegde. In a recent article in a journal published by Tatas, he explodes Indira Gandhi's strong centre plank:

"Consider the realities as they are. The very first Article of our Constitution describes India as a Union of states. This seemingly posits the states ahead of the Union, since without the states, there could be no Union; it is because the states decided to come together that there is the Union of India." And the Union government for a vast majority in the country, he argues, is an 'abstraction, a distant rumble, at most a conglomeration of ministerial names."

What Hegde, as the spokesman of the four Chief ministers, did not say was explicitly stated by Mitra who wants the whole gamut of centre-state

relations reviewed in the changed circumstances and before the situation takes a turn for the worse.

"People," he says, "usually look for redress to the government in situ, that is, the state government which exists right next to them, very much a part of their own existence, and whose ministers are, all the while, visible. If, in this kind of situation, the state government is without the financial means or administrative or legislative capability to provide relief or not set right the grievance, the system would be in danger of exploding.

"There are increasing signs that such a denouement has almost been reached . . . Forget the gloss of the Asiad, this is the underlying reality of India of 1983."

Ashok Mitra is not merely Jyoti Basu's ex-finance minister. His views reflect the thinking of many a politician in and out of power in the Congress too. It goes without saying that a popularly elected Chief minister would like to have full control over the finances of his government and also a major say in the financial resources of his state.

Ramakrishna Hegde has belled the cat.

Current, 26.03.1983
pp. (1 + 2)

Federalism must prevail

The rare unanimity with which the appointment of the Sarkaria Commission has been welcomed all over the country is in sharp contrast to the acid comments of AICC general secretary C.M. Stephen on the Bangalore conclave of the southern Chief ministers.

Unthinking Stephen was patently being more loyal than the queen when he condemned the demand made by Ramakrishna Hegde and company for a thorough review of centre-state relations. Nobody is bothered if he now looks a fool in the eyes of the public.

What is more relevant is that, characteristically, Indira Gandhi has taken a major decision which has come like a bolt from the blue to her own party's central secretariat. More characteristically, she has taken pains to say that her decision had been taken "long ago", and had nothing to do with the Bangalore meeting, nor with the specific Akali demand on the subject.

A graceful and politically mature way would have been for her to say, even if the decision had been taken "long ago" that she was responding

to the demand of the opposition parties. Such a posture would have implied strength, not weakness. In fact, her contrary stance has cast doubts over the motivation behind the appointment of the Sarkaria Commission.

Though Indira Gandhi has said that terms of reference of the Commission will be decided after consultations with Justice Sarkaria, which by itself is a healthy procedure, the stipulation that the Commission will "recommend such changes as may be appropriate within the Constitutional framework" appears to circumscribe the Commission's initiatives from the very start.

This may not be intended, for the Prime minister has also indicated the possibility of the Commission proposing changes in the Constitution, provided they are consistent with the unity and integrity of the country. But this reference is not very happy, if only because it casts aspersions on those who have been demanding greater autonomy for states.

Almost for the first time, she has said that she is in favour of "a strong centre and strong states." The advocates of autonomy have been asking for nothing more and nothing less. The difference lies in their belief that a strong centre presupposes strong states, while her attitude has been to posit the issue the other way round.

What is worse, the practice of this contrary view has in effect reduced the states to no more than municipalities depending for everything on an overbearing centre.

This is an ominous shadow of the past that will haunt the deliberations of the Sarkaria Commission. His undoubted integrity, acumen and experience should enable Justice Sarkaria to fight the shadow and break new grounds. The federal principle enshrined in the Constitution has been badgered for long. It is time to restore it to its original status.

Current, 02.04.1983.
pp. (1 + 2)

The Hegde factor
I am not ambitious, says the man to watch

Had Ramakrishna Hegde been the Prime minister in 1977 the Janata would not have broken and Indira Gandhi may perhaps not have returned to power three years later. Such is the resilience of the man that even now, if he is made head of a united opposition comprising the intransigent, recalcitrant, incorrigible, obstinate, factionalist elements

he would keep them saddled and pose a formidable challenge to Rajiv Gandhi in 1990.

He may be the Chief minister of Karnataka, but he knows the country like the lines of his palm. He is secular. He is a socialist with enough flexibility to come to terms with hard-core communists. It will not be surprising if in course of time he reveals ambitions for playing a role at the national level. And why not?

He is experimenting with what he calls 'value-based' politics, and if he can succeed in Karnataka, why not elsewhere? In Bangalore most of the younger sons and daughters of Congress leaders have voted for him, with the knowledge of their shocked parents. His popularity has broken political, religious, caste barriers. His smile is infectious, and the tinkle in his eyes melts hearts made of stone.

We have been friends for over twenty years and as friends we talked last week. Excerpts;

The general impression in the country is that the defeat of the Congress in Karnataka is your personal victory, not that of the Janata. Even Nijalingappa, who has been a Janata leader, has said so. Do you agree?

This is the general impression. But I do not think it is true. Without the party, who am I? In Karnataka the party has become strong, developed its base in the last few years. Besides the Janata Party and its predecessor, the Congress (O), had the image of a party consisting of honest people.

In the last two years you have enhanced the party's image.

What we have been able to do in the last two years is a tribute to the party. The party is headed by an individual, no doubt. In the present context in national politics the individual becomes important. Thanks to Indira Gandhi's style of functioning, it has become a sort of habit to identify a party by the leader who heads it. But honesty. I cannot really take the whole credit for our victory. It is the honesty of our purpose, the sincerity with which we work that made the people trust us.

You said the Janata Party is a continuation of the Congress (O). But I think most of today's Janata men are former Socialists. Like Deve Gowda, Bommai, Nazir Saab. You seem to be one of the very few Congress-O men left in the party.

Deve Gowda was never in the Socialist Party, nor Bommai. Bommai actually belonged to M.N. Roy's Radical Humanist Party. Both were Congress-O men ever since they joined a political party as such.

There is a group which belonged to the Socialist Party.
Of course they are there, people like Gurupadaswamy, Nazir Saab, Chandre Gowda. J.H. Patel.

Coming back to my main question, you are perhaps right that the Janata developed a base in Karnataka. Now, it did have a base in certain northern states like Bihar, Orissa, Haryana. But the party has been decimated in these states particularly because of the reputation of its leaders, like Karpoori Thakur for example, who have been party breakers. What I mean to say is that individuals who head the party do count a lot in shaping its fortunes.
Well, I do not know exactly the situation and the conditions in those states. But here in Karnataka, the only main party, apart from the Congress, is the Janata. In Bihar for instance, I do not think the Janata has been a main party in that sense particularly after it was split. In Orissa, Janata has been the main alternative party in recent years. I do not know what happened there. In fact we were expecting to win. Still we are the second party there.

Still don't you think that the individual does play an important role in sustaining the image of the party, in formulating its policies, giving it a direction—the way you have done in Karnataka. Perhaps things would have been different if there was some other leader in your place, some one whose style, motivations etc. were different. Take the case of the Congress itself. Immediately after Indira Gandhi's death, had Rajiv Gandhi not been there and somebody else had become the Prime minister, the Congress Party might have split and even disintegrated. What I am trying to say is that the personality of the leader plays an important role in keeping the party intact and winning over the confidence of the people.
I agree. After all an institution is known by the character, integrity and capability of the individual who heads it. We have seen the fortunes of the Congress fluctuating depending upon who happened to be its leader at the moment.

But you have been rather apologetic about it. When someone raised a slogan 'vote for Hegde', you resented it. You asked them to say vote for Janata. If you do concede the importance of the individual, why this reservation, hesitation. Specially, when the people did identify themselves with Ramakrishna Hegde. Had the party been headed by somebody else, I think the outcome would have been different.
Possibly yes. To that extent I agree.

And there is nothing wrong in it. Such an identification does not necessarily

have to lead to a personality cult, it did not in the case of Jayaprakash Narayan. He became the symbol of the opposition, but not as a cult leader.

Personality cult occurs when it is assiduously built up, cultivated, or developed with the help of mass media.

That is right. I am referring to the identification that we see in West Bengal, Andhra, Tamil Nadu and here in Karnataka. Jyoti Basu, NTR, even MGR with his illness – all of you symbolise something which makes people rally round you. In Maharashtra, Sharad Pawar is emerging as such a symbol. What I am saying is that the opposition also should throw up one or two individuals with whom the people can identify themselves and look up to for the fulfillment of their aspirations. Why should you fight shy of this idea.

As a matter of principle I am against it. You know the personality cult . . .

I am not talking of personality cult. I am referring to the impact an individual can make in moulding a party, in projecting it . . .

That I agree. But you know what happens. During the election campaign when we were thinking of issuing advertisement, some colleagues insisted that my photograph should be featured in them. I said no. You will have noticed that my photograph was published in none of the Karnataka government advertisements issued from time to time. I had specially prohibited it. Once we start this kind of projection, the person so projected gets an illusion that he is becoming more and more popular . . . you know, it could happen to me also.

What is wrong in becoming popular, why are you scared of yourself?

I am not scared of myself. I believe in collective leadership. You know, leadership of a single individual will sooner or later lead to dictatorship. Do you remember what Pandit Nehru said long ago? He went to the extent of writing an article under a pseudonym warning the people, as it were, about the dictatorial tendencies that he saw in himself. Of course he was not in power then. But he was the idol of the masses. Perhaps he thought that he was falling prey to their adulation. He wanted to guard himself against it at the same time warning the people about it. He rightly thought that it is not proper that a single individual . . .

The fact remains that the people's faith in an individual has an important role to play. That is what we have seen in your case, in the case of NTR, MGR, Farooq Abdullah, Jyoti Basu, and at the national level, Rajiv Gandhi. In our system the people seem to have greater confidence in an individual than in a party.

I quite agree . . .

In this context, was the Janata victory in Karnataka the victory of a person or a principle.

I think it is the victory of principles as symbolised through a person.

That is well said. Right principles as symbolised through right men will evoke people's confidence. But if the person who symbolises even the most salutary principles happens to be the wrong one, that doesn't work. Take the case of Charan Singh. Finally I have all admiration for his economic formulation. A large number of people like his views, but they do not like him. They have no faith in him because of his opportunism. They say he is not a good man. This makes a big difference. So the person who represents the principles counts a lot. And you cannot keep on avoiding it.

I agree with you. I was not apologetic just out of false modesty, but I tell you . . .

And in the case of Karnataka, was there not also the expression of some kind of regional feeling?

Look, in Karnataka regional feelings cannot be aroused very easily. Karnataka has been described as a bridge between the south and the north. It has a history and culture of open mindedness and tolerance. We have always treated those who are normally called outsiders with respect and love. In Bangalore you will find such a great cosmopolitan atmosphere, which you will not find even in Bombay now. But self-respect is something different.

But Karnataka's self-respect was not hurt. In fact under Gundu Rao's regime Karnataka's self-respect was asserted.

You may be right in a way. But the general feeling is that under the Congress dispensation the Chief minister of a state is but a pawn, just a servant . . .

A doormat, as they say.

Yes, a doormat. He doesn't have his own personality, individuality, his own say. I can understand being a part of an all-India set-up and may have to make certain compromises. But that doesn't mean that a local unit has to the central leadership for everything.

Incidentally, would you like a person to be suddenly shunted out as a Governor just one day after he is unanimously elected Chief minister? Do you like this manner of treating a Chief minister?

No, not at all. It is an insult to the institution of Chief minister, to the people who have elected the Chief minister.

Anyway, you are a Chief minister who cannot be treated in that manner. In fact, the whole country is watching you. In what way do you plan to be different from a Congress Chief minister, project your government as different from a Congress government? Have you any plan to make Karnataka a model state? For the first time you are in power with an absolute majority, a massive one. In what way would you project your government as strong, purposeful, beneficial.

I do not know if you have read our manifesto. It is different from manifestos of other parties, particularly the Congress. During the last two years I have been able to do two or three things. First, I have brought the administration very close to the people. And I have revived the confidence of the bureaucrats in the administrative machinery. You know the bureaucrats had not been treated properly. Sometimes they were given full authority and the ministers just did not bother about anything. At other times there was too much of ministerial interference. There has to be a balance. Then only the policies laid down by the government will be smoothly implemented. I think my government has taken the right steps in this direction.

But there is something much more important. I do not know how far you can call it a model government, but in three or four aspects it will be different, to begin with, our priorities will be different. We are not going for huge capital and power intensive projects. Our emphasis will be on decentralisation, both in economic and political fields. Power to the people will not be just a slogan. In fact, Panditji had given this slogan, but unfortunately both *panchayat raj* and community development programmes were destroyed under Indira Gandhi's regime.

You mean they degenerated.

Yes, degenerated. I would like to re-establish vibrant, responsive popular institutions at various levels. Secondly, the priority will be to provide every village with basic amenities such as drinking water, schools, roads, electricity and hospitals. During the last two years we started 500 primary schools in places where there were none. This is after 39 years of freedom. If we are not able to provide drinking water and a mere school to the villagers, what is the worth of freedom? In fact it is thanks to the nature of our people that there has been no revolution.

That takes me back to the personality cult we talked about, its other danger. Indira Gandhi became the symbol of everything, symbol of

people's dreams and aspirations. So elections were won just because of the magic of her name, the wave or the spell. The electorate did not even know who was the candidate they were voting for. For all they knew, he might have been absolutely third rate, corrupt, anything.

Assemblies in the northern states are packed with criminal . . . .
Yes. You know that is what it is. Leave aside this diversion. The third priority is raising the per capita income. This can be done in two ways. One is to provide employment. One important item in our programme is to provide a job to at least one person in every family. The next is to raise the level of the minimum wage. Now, we have adopted the 'rice for Rs. 2 per kilo' programme.

Many people are accusing me of adopting a populist measure. But I have studied the economic implications of the measures. I do not consider it as populist. I consider it as the primary duty of a popular government. The purchasing power of ordinary people has been eroded because of the failure of the Central government to control prices. In Karnataka, this has resulted in nearly 10 per cent of the people living on a diet whose calory content is less than half the minimum requirement. Injecting a little more purchasing power into the hands of these people by providing certain essential goods at a cheaper price cannot be dubbed populism. It can only be a measure to soften their misery.

And you expect the centre to stand by you in this effort.
Precisely.

But your budget speech gives the impression that you are getting ready for a financial confrontation with the centre. You have made a strong criticism of the Central government.
Actually I have not criticised anybody. I have just placed the facts before the public. You know in the course of the last 10 years or more, the Central government has not been able to control its non-plan and unproductive expenditure. At the same time it has been giving homilies, advices and directives to the state governments about frugality. What I have done is to tell the centre to mend its own ways before it takes objections to the state governments ways of spending.

During my first meeting with Prime minister Rajiv Gandhi, just before these elections, I suggested to him that until we are sure about dependable resources, we should not plunge into the Seventh Plan. Let us have a transitional plan for a year, so that we can have a hard look at the resources. So, you see, it is a question of the entire country's resources. And we

should not be guided or influenced in terms of state versus the centre in the matter of resources. We must have an overall view.

You are talking like a Congress minister.

Just because I am a non-Congress Chief minister it does not mean that I should be different in this matter. I belong to Punjab, UP or any other state as much as I belong to Karnataka. So when I say that the centre must put an end to its unnecessary expenditure, I am saying it as an Indian, not as a spokesman of Karnataka. And there is a lot of scope for slashing Central expenditure.

You mean thereby larger resources will be available to the states.

To the states as well as to the centre itself. And these resources will be allocated with a certain sense of priorities. When the Eighth Finance Commission came here, I told them that I was prepared to share my resources with some of the states which were just capable of raising their own resources, such as the north-eastern states, even Orissa for that matter. Or certain percentage of the national resources may be set apart for the development of those states. As a citizen of this great country, I cannot tolerate the idea of any part of the country being neglected, I should not. What I mean is that we should take a national view.

But I must say that there are states like UP, Bihar, and others who have, over the decades, continuously committed financial indiscipline, and got away with it. Why should it happen and why does the centre not restrain them. Why should only we be penalised for being prudent and frugal in our fiscal management.

Pardon me a diversion. You have said repeatedly that you will not remain a Chief minister for long. What do you propose to do, taking sanyas.

I said that not because I have something else in view. In the first place I was reluctant to come back to state politics having gone to work at the national level. You know I was the General Secretary of a national party for over six years. That gave a certain perspective which would be a handicap at the state level. Secondly, before I left for national politics I was virtually at the top level here, and returning to the state again would amount to sidelining several people who had filled the gap in my absence. That is why is was reluctant to come back, I thought I would hinder the growth of leadership in the state. Anyway, the reason why I talked about not continuing as Chief minister for long is my feeling that before this term ends there must be a smooth change—over in the state's leadership. This is my wish.

You want to go to centre.

I do not have that kind of ambition.

Running the party from the centre is part of a politician's role.

I would like to function at the national level. I would feel more at home there.

What will happen to Karnataka then.

As I said, I am sure there will be a smooth change over.

Do you think the victory of Rajiv Gandhi shows that the electorate has a particular liking for the Nehru family. Or is it just a passing phase.

I think if it were not for the assassination of Indira Gandhi people would not have taken to Rajiv Gandhi as easily as they did. The succession happened in very peculiar circumstances, and it looked as though there was no other alternative. And there was no time. Well, I do not say that there is no such thing as the charisma of the Nehru family, that the people have no feeling for the Nehru *khandan*. But it is not so strong that Rajiv Gandhi's success in the elections can be attributed solely to it. There are four things which are responsible. One is the obvious sympathy factor. Secondly, Rajiv Gandhi represented a new generation as compared to his own mother, forget about Charan Singh.

Compared to Charan Singh he is of the third generation.

Yes. And Rajiv talked about the 21st century. Whatever its implications, this made a good impression on the youth, the middle class, etc. And thirdly, which is perhaps the most important, there was a total absence of an alternative either in terms of a party or a leader. There was nobody. In Bangalore, which has been a Janata stronghold, people who normally voted for us came and told me during the Lok Sabha elections: look here, we are going to vote for Rajiv Gandhi, there is no other alternative to him. And lastly, the issues were unmistakable, unity and national integrity. You see the electorate has never voted for a weak centre. In fact, we must give credit to the people on this count.

It is said that we have a competition between two Mr. Cleans, one in Delhi and one here in Bangalore. Who do you think will win in this race.

I tell you, it is a good competition, healthy competition. Whoever wins, will have no grouse but the competition should continue.

Do you propose to wage a relentless battle against corruption in Karnataka.

Yes. I have got some plans. The Lok Ayukta and UP-Lokayukta Bill has been sent up for the President's assent. Now I have to select competent

and the best people for appointments. Then I would invite the co-operation of not only the political parties but of voluntary agencies to join hands with me in our fight. Without people's co-operation it is just not possible to eradicate corruption.

They say charity begins at home. Will you first see that your Cabinet colleagues do not indulge in corrupt practices. What machinery do you propose to have for this purpose.

The official machinery is the Lok Ayukta which has jurisdiction not only over the ministers but even over the Chief ministers. But apart from it if anybody tells me that such a minister has taken bribes and if I am convinced that there is some veracity in the complaint, I shall immediately ask the minister to resign.

How do you propose to raise funds for your party.

This is a very very important question. You see, as long as the problem of funding of elections is not solved, corruption cannot be totally eliminated. Actually that is the biggest source of corruption. I would suggest that there is need for three or four basic changes in the electoral law, and it is good that the Prime minister too is thinking on these lines.

One is compulsory voting with identity cards given to the voters. That will eliminate the chances of candidate or his party trying to bribe a voter. The second is state funding of election expenses. And thirdly every political party must compulsorily render its accounts, in fact properly audited accounts should be published in the newspapers. This is very important. The electoral reforms should include a rule to this effect.

At the national level you must have people like Sharad Pawar, Farooq Abdullah, Chandra Shekhar and you. Should you not all sit together as individuals, especially since there are no ideological inhibitions between you and these men, and promote the idea of a national party.

Efforts to bring about unity among the opposition parties did not fail because of ideological incompatibilities. They failed every time because of the incompatibility of individuals, their whims, prejudices, fancies and ambitions. I really do not know how anybody working at the national level becomes so small.

Everyone was a candidate for the Prime ministership. Now that question is out, so is there a possibility of the younger leaders coming together at the national level to provide an alternative to the Congress. How about a sort of a convention or a conclave for the purpose.

I would suggest to Chandra Shekhar to convene it. Or initiate talks with Farooq, Sharad and others.

And NTR

NTR has different ideas, you know, his Bharat Desam. I really do not know what he means.

But he is a genuine opposition man.

Yes, he feels very strongly that there must be opposition unity, and that, if not merger, there should be a federation of opposition parties.

During the election campaign, Rajiv Gandhi said that there was only one wrestler and nobody to challenge him. And the people ridiculed the opposition. You must now have a wrestler who can grow in the next five years to equal him.

This was a factor in the minds of the electorate.

You have said that the opposition should play a constructive role, that the days of confrontation are over since Rajiv Gandhi, unlike his mother, has a positive approach. What sort of constructive role have you in mind.

By constructive approach I do not mean that the opposition parties should function like the Servants of India Society or the Sarvodaya Sangh. They must not lose their political character. But you see, particularly in the past 10 or 15 years, every opposition party was obsessed with Indira Gandhi, she was their only target.

That was indeed her strength and our weakness. We fell for that approach because Indira Gandhi not only symbolised but in fact was the Congress, the government, the programme of the party, the policy of the government. There was hardly any other target, and there was plenty that could be said against her.

Now, suddenly, there is a change of scenario. Here is a man who doesn't have a political past. He was not even associated with the Emergency. You cannot attack him. He has a clean slate, and that is why we have to wait and see where and when he commits mistakes. Until then you cannot attack him, you will only lose your credibility.

I couldn't have attacked him in my election speeches till he provided me an opportunity. When he said that the Janata government's performance was a zero, then I said the people would decide. And they decided, for they know that every village has got a drinking water well, a road, school, or something in the last two years.

So we must have a constructive approach. In regard to certain national issues, whether it is Punjab or Assam, you know we have to, especially in an emergency, co-operate with the government. There is no point in opposition for the sake of opposition.

Rajiv Gandhi has displayed the kind of tolerance that a democrat should in respect for the opposition. Similarly, we too must change our attitude towards the ruling party. Only then we will get public credibility. That is the way to build ourselves as an alternative, by offering constructive alternative policies and programmes.

The Janata has no reason to feel demoralised. Chandra Shekhar should not feel demoralised because he has been defeated.

Actually he has recovered very fast.

Current, 30.03.1985.
pp. (1 + 21 + 22)

My eyes are not on Delhi *gaddi*—NTR

Nandamuri Taraka Rama Rao looks like a statue carved out of granite. Sitting on the Chief minister's chair, his head shaven, and a large vibutitilakam on his broad forehead, he laughs like a devata and talks as though he is addressing a public meeting.

The Andhrites are an emotional lot. NTR rules supreme over their hearts and minds. He is immensely aware of the greatness bestowed upon him of the people's expectations and of his own role in shaping their lives.

He is a man with charisma. His victory at the hustings has brought sunshine into the life of millions. But unlike his flock, NTR is conscious of his new role as a down-to-earth politician. He has left the celluloid world behind. He has descended from the throne to the chair. Earlier he had popularity, but no authority. Now he enjoys both. And he does speak with authority.

He was taken aback by my first question:

Are you thinking of becoming the next Prime minister?

Only God determines. I believe in destiny. But I have never thought of more than the Chief ministership.

With the whole of the south setting the pace, the temptation cannot be far too great.

No. I am not thinking about it. I must first set things right in my state.

Some of your adherents believe one day you will land up in Delhi.

Oh no. My eyes are not on the Delhi *gaddi*. Andhra is too big for me. I must serve it.

Your success in Andhra may open new vistas. The non-Congress Chief ministers may think of forming an anti-Indira front. Politics is after all a game of the impossible.

It is difficult for us to predict. Who knows what happens in future? We will cross the bridge when we come to it.

Have you ever met Indira Gandhi?

No, never. I will meet her for the first time in the first week of February when I go to Delhi.

What are your sentiments about her?

She is a great leader. I must admit it.

Then why did you fight against her?

Not against her. My fight was against her government in Andhra. I have all the regard for her.

Do you envisage any difficulty in your relations with the centre?

We will always co-operate with it.

If the centre lets you down.

The people are always there. I do not envisage any confrontation. It is a matter of adjustment. I feel I am flexible enough. My only idea is to make any state economically strong and I do not think the centre will object to this.

Why did you support Maneka Gandhi?

I sympathised with her.

She has no party, no programme. What was the basis of initiating her to your state's politics.

I did not support her for any programme or policy. There was no political alignment. It was pure sympathy.

Do you think injustice has been done to her?

I cannot go into the details. But it appeared to me that she was wronged and I said so at my public meetings.

If the clash between Indira and Maneka snowballs at the national level, whom would you support?

That will be considered later. If it happens, we shall see.

People in the North feel Telugu Desam is a temporary phenomenon, a one-man show.

We will prove it permanent. Telugu Desam started long before so many of us were born. It will outlive me, but not because of my popularity or charisma. Telugu Desam has a history of its own. Who can forget the

sacrifice of our great heroes? If I have been instrumental in building the party, it is my privilege. I have done it with the blessings of millions of Andhrites.

Teluguism is being compared with regional chauvinism.
Teluguism is in our blood. We belong to the Telugu nation. My *dhoti,* my shirt, my *tilakam*—everything reflects the Telugu man. You can see in me an authentic representative of Telugu Nadu.

That is what is described as the NTR charisma. Do you agree that it was a clash of charisma between you and Indira Gandhi, in which your charisma proved ubiquitous and you won?
That was the verdict of my people, I honour it.

Your people claim you have completely shattered her charisma.
I do not know. The Telugu Nadu supported the Congress for so long, now they have switched their support to my party. It is their democratic right.

The change in the people's thinking was brought about by you or were they themselves fed up.
They decided it themselves, they were totally dissatisfied.

You have said that yours is a victory against corruption.
Charity begins at home. I must first be pure. Only then I can think of others. Corruption will automatically disappear if I and my ministers remain honest.

What deterrents have you thought of?
Punishment, harshest punishment. No compromise.

How will you identify the corrupt?
Vigilance.

Who will keep the vigil?
The people. Nobody can escape the people.

What about the Vigilance Commission and Anti-Corruption Bureau?
All these come later. First, my party men will have to set examples of incorruptibility. We are answerable to the people. Our assets must be declared and, if we had anything more, we should be treated as criminals.

If anyone fails . . . .
He will be punished. He will be immediately handed over to the court. We will see what best can be done. We cannot take law into our own hands.

Indira Gandhi recently remarked that you have men in your Cabinet who were dismissed for corruption by the previous Congress governments.
Valmiki was a hunter before becoming a *Rishi*. Like that, a man maybe corrupt, but by associating himself with good people, he can become a saint.

So you have saints in your Cabinet.
Saheb, I hope they will behave like saints.

You are hoping for too much.
I will prove you wrong.

You talk like a philosopher.
I am a philosopher, a political one.

Are you planning to appoint some sort of a commission to investigate the charges of corruption against the members of the previous governments.
I am not planning it. I am not prejudiced. I am not vindictive. But I will not forgive the corrupt. I will fulfill the people's demand. The people have brought me to power on the issue of dishonesty and corruption. I am not empowered to forgive the corrupt.

Since Independence, hardly a politician worth his name has been caught and punished for corruption. You know the fiasco of the various commissions appointed by the Janata.
I will set an example. Otherwise why should I be here? You will soon hear from me on this matter.

Telugu Desam may be a potential force, but where is the party. You want to run the state through fan clubs.
No. We are already in the process of organising the party from the villages upwards. Soon we will have a meeting of the party members to discuss organisational questions.

Do you plan to organise Telugu Desam on the traditional pattern of the other parties?
No, not at all. It will be organised on an entirely different pattern. The Village Parishad will organise a samiti, the samiti will elect the zilla parishad and the zilla parishads will elect the kendriya parishad. And on the top of the organisation, there will be a central committee with five members—the nirnayaka parishad.

Will that be the supreme policy-making body?
Yes. The Chief minister will be one of the members of the central committee. The other four will be men known for their intelligence and integrity.

Will any of them be ministers?

No. They will fight no elections. They will have no position in the government. They will formulate the programmes and policies of the party each year.

Will the Chief minister be just a member or the chairman of the committee?

Just a member.

Who will be the chairman?

Any one of us will be selected to preside over the meetings.

Your Central Committee appears to be similar to the Soviet one.

Whatever it is, I do not know. We want to be different. We want to avoid the defect in the other parties.

Will this committee also supervise the functioning of the government?

Completely.

It means the central committee will be a super government.

Yes, because if we entrust power to any person or group, the party will go to the dogs.

Who will train your workers politically?

They will be trained in a college.

A college!

Yes, the Telugu Desam College of politics. We will soon start it. We will have students from all the 294 constituencies—graduates and post graduates only.

What will they be taught?

There will be a course, a proper syllabus. It will be a four-and-a-half year course. For three years they will study politics, undergo training and then for one-and-a-half years they will work in constituencies and submit thesis to the party on that particular constituency. The thesis will be scrutinised and if the student succeeds, he will be a candidate during the elections.

You want to raise a cadre-based party.

Yes, very much so. The party will meet all his economic needs.

What kind of ideological training will the candidate get?

Ideal behaviour, honesty, dedication to the Desam, service to the common man.

What 'ism'?

Teluguism. No other 'ism'. We are more interested in our state, in its people, than in anything else.

Is Andhra not a part of the country?
Sure, it is. We will teach the cadre about the country also, India is as much our country as it is anybody else's.

How well will this cadre fit into the national politics.
We are an integral part of India and they will play their role in Parliament.

How close do you feel to Mahatma Gandhi?
Very, very close. Like him I too wear loincloth. I could have worn a suit. But I want to identify myself with the poorest in the Telugu land. He was hailed as the Father of the nation because he totally identified himself with the poorest of the poor, the *daridranarayana.*

You feel the same affinity towards Jawaharlal Nehru.
Sure. Never will the country forget his sacrifices. I bow my head to him.

Are you planning a major shake-up in the administration.
Not a major shake-up, but I will see that the government servants are kept away from the evils of the society.

One of your ministers has suggested abolition of the Legislative Council.
We have not yet decided. We want to economise as much as possible.

In your election speeches you have promised to give equal status to women, equal share to them in the family property.
My announcement reflects the will of the women. They form nearly 50 per cent of the population. Of boy and a girl born to the same mother, why should the girl be deprived of her rights? Social and economic equality is as much her birthright as it is of the boy. I will bring legislation in this regard, if necessary.

What would be your attitude towards the minorities, especially Muslims.
They are our brothers. Their customs, traditions and language will be honoured. They will be given complete protection and opportunities to pursue their own faith.

Will you give them greater opportunities in the services.
As the situation demands, the basis should be merit. Ours is a fully secular party. We will not permit any discrimination on the basis of religion.

Current, 22.01.1983.
pp. (1 + 3)

No wave in south

This time too the south is likely to repeat 1977 irrespective of what happens in the north. A week-long visit to the urban centres of the three states—Tamil Nadu, Andhra and Karnataka—gave me the feeling that the Congress is very much taken as a symbol of stability, national unity and an even handed treatment to all the states from the centre. Voters in the south are more well-informed and concerned about stability than corruption at high levels. Bofors has not boomed here. The Janambhoomi-Masjid dispute has not given the people sleepless nights.

While I found a large number of voters in the twin cities of Hyderabad and Secunderabad inclined towards the Congress, their attitude in Madras and Bangalore was not very much dissimilar. Local factors do count. In the twin cities the TDP and its supremo NTR have hardly made any dent in the Congress fortress. In other urban centres of coastal Andhra and Telengana the middle class and the youth have much greater faith in the policies and programmes of the Congress than any regional party. The newly enfranchised 18-21 segments does not distrust Rajiv Gandhi though a fairly large number would prefer a more dynamic and mature leader.

Surprisingly the situation is still more encouraging for the Congress in Madras and Tamil Nadu appears to be in the grip of a Jayalalitha wave. She reins supreme and, if nothing goes wrong, will sweep the polls. The Congress and Rajiv Gandhi will ride to success on piggy back. Without an alliance with her the Congress would have once again been wiped out.

Cho Ramaswamy, the maverick editor of fortnightly *Tughlak* is jubilant at the turn of events. As a Jayalalitha promoter he brings a lot of solace when he says, 'Tamil Nadu is being blessed with an anti-DMK wave". He may be exaggerating but the predominant feeling in this land of the Dravidians is that the DMK and its unquestioned leader Karunanidhi are fighting a grim electoral battle with their backs to the wall.

The voluptuous, moonfaced Jayalalitha is merciless in her attacks on her arch foe. She knows power is within her reach and that the Tamilians like a touch of disdain, a whiff of arrogance. While she was negotiating with Rajiv Gandhi, through his emissary Dinesh Singh, she never did go to Delhi or hang around the Prime minister. It was Dinesh Singh who was found shuttling between Delhi and Madras and she never went to receive him at the airport or saw him off.

That's what her followers admired in her. What could be more delightful to a Dravidian than seeing the Prime minister and his blue-

blooded emissaries submitting themselves in sack cloth and ashes and seek her help in retaining power in Delhi. "You enjoy power in Delhi. I do not grudge it. But why did you deny it to me? Never behave like this in future", she told Dinesh Singh who swallowed the reprimand without batting an eyelid.

She is a phenomenon. She has hardly done anything for the Tamilians which have given them any economic or social relief. She has never enjoyed power. A pretty looking actress in her early days, she was the "other" woman in MGR's life. The AIADMK bosses despised her and most of their time was spent in clipping her wings even when MGR was alive.

Janaki amma, MGR's legally wedded wife, made every effort to keep her away from her ailing husband and, in the last election, the two tried to finish each other. Janaki amma finally lost and folded up the rival AIADMK thereby allowing Jaya to monopolise MGR's legacy.

Tamilians adore her as MGR's legatee. Huge posters have come up proclaiming her as the next Chief minister. Last week, for the first time, she addressed a public rally at the Marina Beach with Rajiv Gandhi. The turn-out was unexpectedly low but she told her delirious followers that she had entered into an alliance with the Prime minister, that he would dismiss the DMK government if the alliance won the Lok Sabha seats.

"This government will not and should not exist a day more after the November 27 results" she shouted through the powerful public address system, looking straight in the face of an embarrassed Prime minister. Rajiv Gandhi could only tell her that "we will cross the bridge when we come to it".

Jayalalitha has given 26 out of 39 Lok Sabha seats to the Congress, keeping the rest for herself and her allies. Out of its share the Congress has given one to Abdul Samad of Muslim League and one to the United Communist Party of India. In her quota, she has dropped those sitting MPs who were found shaky in their loyalty in her fight with Janaki Amma. She also refused to accommodate Deputy Speaker Thambi Dorai and Chairman of the Public Accounts Committee P. Kolandaivelu. Both had been closer to the Congress because of favours received. Her selection was strictly on the basis of personal loyalty to her. The Congress accommodated Dorai from its quota but Kolandaivelu was left in the lurch.

During the last assembly campaign, Rajiv Gandhi had directed harsh criticism at her and described MGR's regime as a "Dark Age". She made him eat humble pie when she forced him to award Bharat Ratna to MGR

posthumously and also got herself eulogised at the Marina beach meeting. Rajiv Gandhi, for the average Tamilian, is a small man compared to his mother. He is tolerated because Tamilians would generally like to have the Congress at the centre. He was heard at the Marina beach because Jayalalitha was sitting next to him. The crowd would have been far less had he made it his own show.

Rajiv Gandhi hangs on the apron strings of a lady who is riding a wave of popularity. It is the AIADMK which is fighting his battle. Before the alliance was forged she had complained about the lack of resources but now no more. The AIADMK is flush with funds while the Congress nominees bitterly complain that their leaders are starving them of required funds.

Despite being allies, at the grass root level the AIADMK and the Congress workers do not see eye to eye. The cocky AIADMK cadres treat the Congress workers with contempt and will not lift their little fingers unless their demand for enough money is met. They do not allow the Congress workers to canvass in their pockets of influence or put up the Congress posters and banners unless they are given enough money. The Congress candidates have no choice.

Jayalalitha is unsparing in her criticism of the DMK and certain recent lapses by the administration. Rice is the main factor. It is not easily available in the ration shops and if it is, then the quality is bad. The price has also gone up slightly. The public distribution system has gone out of gear, but corruption is far less than it was during MGR's period. Corruption at the top level is almost absent though Cho cynically says it is "suspended" for the time being. The DMK argues that the centre drastically reduced its quota of rice just to put Karunanidhi in an embarrassing position. But people want good rice at reasonable price. Bring it from Andhra or take a loan from Assam, the DMK followers say.

Her other complaint, which touches a sympathetic chord is the increase in bus fares and changing of some routes. The Bus system in Tamil Nadu is the main means of transport in the countryside and the fares were reduced following an outcry and she takes the credit. The other major problem was the sudden increase in cinema tickets, which also hit the common man. This too was reduced under popular pressure. She again took the credit. Karunanidhi followers were surprised how a seasoned administrator can make these mistakes on the election eve.

Karunanidhi's administration is clean. It is efficient. His government works. It is an open government and the Chief minister is accessible to the people. He is a changed man after 13 years in exile. He is held in high

esteem by the intelligentsia and local industrialists. MGR was a freak in the Tamil politics, Karunanidhi is a dyed in the wool politician with considerable academic attainments. He is erudite, a remarkable orator and a refined, cultured man. Though the DMK movement had its origins in anti-Brahminism, his top officials are Brahmins including Guhan, who functions as adviser to the Chief minister. A mature and experienced bureaucrat, he is perhaps the finest spokesman of the DMK government.

Soon after he took over as Chief minister, Karunanidhi introduced far-reaching social welfare schemes and solved the ticklish Vanniyar problem. He also introduced a few populist schemes such as free supply of *dhoti*s, *saree*s and rice for all those whose income was below Rs. 300 a month. His government also gives doles for widow marriage, for marriage of poor girls and to pregnant women in that income category. These benefits reach maximum number of people and there are few complaints of maldistribution or corruption.

Yet he is fighting the electoral battle with his back to the wall. He is on an intensive tour of the state and draws appreciable crowds but not the massive ones Jaya does. "Do not go by permutations and combinations. We are set to win 30 seats", he tells his worried party men. He is proud of his well-oiled party machine and an alert and dedicated cadre.

It is more well-organised than that of the CPM, asserts Alladi Aruna, who is facing Congress candidate Vijayantimala from South Madras. He recently changed horses midstream from Jayalalitha to Karunanidhi. His other rivals are former Foreign Secretary P. Venkateshwaran, retired DGP K. Radhakrishnan and a scientist, C.V. Seshadri.

The fight is between the DMK and the Congress but the three others seem equally determined to make their way to the Lok Sabha. "My Karma will be with me", remarks Venky who had just come back to Madras after paying a quick visit to the Shankaracharya of Kanchipuram. "The question of my losing does not arise", asserts Radhakrishnan with a policeman's authority and Seshadri is not to be found anywhere in the city because "I cannot stand the crowds". He is the grandson of Sir C.P. Ramaswamy Iyer, former Divan of Travancore.

In the last Lok Sabha election, the Congress AIADMK alliance had bagged 37 seats leaving only two to the DMK but this time "the situation has changed", emphasises Karunanidhi, there has been a 13 per cent increase in the electorate since 1984 and another 9 per cent had been added with the enrolment of the 18-20 age group. He refers to Rajiv Gandhi's remark that the DMK came to power in the Assembly election on a small 32 per cent votes. This he takes as the Prime minister's hint at

dismissing his government if the Congress-AIADMK combine swept the polls. "But we are not afraid. The Congress would never come back to power. It is the National Front which will form the government" he says with confidence.

Like Maharashtra, Karnataka in the deep south too is involved in multicornered fights for the 28 Lok Sabha and 233 assembly seats.

Tall, dark, bald and soft-spoken Deve Gowda, who heads the fledgling Janata Party, is the fly in the ointment. His opponents say he is a Congress plant. His main rival and the head of the Janata Dal Ramakrishna Hegde believes he is an outright Congress agent fully equipped and financed by Rajiv Gandhi whose only aim in Karnataka is to eliminate him. The result is a stiff triangular fight and it is simply impossible to predict who will get a workable majority.

A much harassed KPCC chief Virendra Patil, who is seeking an assembly seat, having surrendered his Gulbarga Lok Sabha seat to his son-in-law, is sure of getting a comfortable majority and forming the government with himself as the Chief minister. He has been the main target of his rivals in the party since the announcement of the elections. They have adopted all kinds of dirty tricks to break him, and have even asked party workers to *gherao* him, to shout abuses at him and to physically assault him.

More than once the police had to rescue him. The chirpy Patil had unsuccessfully opposed Indira Gandhi from Chikmagalur as the Janata Party nominee. Before that he was the Congress Chief minister of Karnataka. Once Indira Gandhi was in power she brought him to Parliament and made him a minister. Her son has made him the PCC President and if the party comes to power he is the most likely man to be Chief minister once again.

Gundu Rao will be his most formidable rival though he is contesting for the Lok Sabha from South Bangalore. He comes back on the centre stage after five years in wilderness, and what a comeback it is. When he was thrown out of the party and its parliamentary board, he had described Rajiv Gandhi as a disaster for the Congress. In turn, the Prime minister identified him as one of the power brokers along with Antulay and Pranab Mukerjee. All of them are back and cooing, 'Rajiv is the only hope.'

Gundu Rao's rebirth is ascribed to his mentor R.K. Dhawan and he is bound to play an important role if he comes back to Delhi as an MP. He is most likely to come back, and in a big way. He has taken Bangalore by storm. Thousands of party workers, mostly youth, throng his house in the

heart of the town from early morning offering their services in various capacities.

He has no dearth of resources. In the last one week he has been on the road doing expensive *Padyatra* followed by hundreds of enthusiastic slogan-shouting followers. He is opposed by former Janata Dal minister Raghupati who is no match to Gundu Rao's resourcefulness.

Interestingly some powerful Janata Dal leaders are seeking election for the assembly from this, most prestigious parliamentary constituency including Ramakrishna Hegde and his former ministerial colleague Jivaraj Alva. Gundu Rao has taken to the election once again as duck takes to water and I saw him welcoming Rajiv Gandhi on the stage at a city public meeting with a broad smile Rajiv did not betray his embarrassment but he was not at ease. The meeting was jointly organised by Gundu Rao and Union minister Jafar Sharief who is seeking the Lok Sabha seat from adjoining North Bangalore.

It has perhaps the thinnest public rally the Prime minister has addressed during his campaigning. He was pacing on the stage looked jittery and spoke in a lacklustre way. Jafer Sharief apologised for the poor attendance and assured him that the Congress will not lose despite the indifferent attitude of Bangalorians. It is becoming clear that the people not only in Bangalore but everywhere in the south have lost interest in him and if they vote for the Congress it will be for some other more positive reasons.

In fact most congressmen are highly critical of his style of functioning, his total inaccessibility and his contempt for the common man. And even if they support the Congress it is despite him, not because of him. It is loyalty to the party. The Congress will surely improve its position at least in the assembly though it might lose half a dozen Lok Sabha seats. It might emerge as the largest single party but it may not get an absolute majority.

The tie will be between the Janata Dal and the Janata Party. In case no party gets a majority—Hegde is expecting absolute majority and at least in Lok Sabha seats—he has gained more confidence in the last one week after touring large parts of the state in his Vijayanta, a luxuriously furnished bus with a hydraulic system which hoists him to the roof of the vehicle fitted with a public address system.

The crowds in south Canara were unprecedented and the response in the old Mysore areas was equally enthusiastic—the Congress has never known defeat in this region but "this time it is an upsurge against the Congress" he says with a glint in his eyes. He is sure to get anywhere between 100 to 120 seats and form the government without of course,

Deve Gowda. The Janata Dal too is not short of resources. All its assembly and parliament nominees are financially comfortable with a fleet of cars and jeeps.

The undivided Janata Party has won 139 seats in the last assembly election while the Congress bagged 66 seats. In the last Lok Sabha election, the Congress had lost only four seats out of 28. Union minister Shankaranand is perhaps the weakest candidate and both the Janata Parties are bent on defeating him while the Congress is averse to any idea of a coalition government.

The leaders of the two Janata are slowly moving to a common point. At least Deve Gowda has no reservations. "My mind is open. It will have to be a coalition between us. I surely will not fall on the Congress for help. I have seen the fate of Bhaskar Rao and others. And I have no basic differences with the Janata Dal. It was a clash of personalities. I have taken a vow to humble Hegde. The Janata will form a government but minus Hegde" he said bluntly.

The sturdy Vokkaliga leader is expecting not less than 90 seats. "I will fall short of a few seats and I am sure my friends in the other Janata will oblige me. After all we have been struggling together to keep the Congress out of power for over two decades. I will, under no circumstances allow the Congress to form the government. That is sure".

Despite these brave assertions Deve Gowda remains a suspect in the eyes of his other Janata opponents.

He is not speaking says Hegde it is Rajiv's money power that is prompting him. The post-election picture is quite clear. In case the Janata Dal wins, Hegde is already acknowledged as the Chief minister. In case of a coalition between the two Janata it will be a marriage of convenience between Hegde and Gowda. They are bound to fight it out.

The situation will be entirely different if a non-Congress government takes over at the centre. It will then be Hegde all the way.

Current, 18.11.1989.
pp. (1 + 2 + 3)

6

Emergence of Regional Leadership

A. Punjab, Peace with Dignity

We cannot afford Khalistan

This time the demand for a Sikh Homeland is as ominous as it was for a Muslim Homeland in the early 1940s. The country paid the price letting Mohammed Ali Jinnah ride the crest of a Muslim resurgence. The country will again pay an equally heavy price soaked in blood if the lunatics of the Dal Khalsa are allowed to pursue their Khalistan 'dream'.

The demand for Khalistan should no more be taken as a law and order problem. The Sikhs are as much and as good Indians as the Hindus of Punjab. Dal Khalsa will have to be dealt with on an entirely different footing.

Lack of evidence does not allow us to see a 'foreign hand', but such a big and dangerous movement for the dismemberment of India has to have foreign collaborators.

The officially controlled media in Pakistan—newspapers, radio and TV—have been highlighting the Khalistan demand as if it is the main national cause of the military regime. The Union Home Ministry has no evidence, but it does suspect Pakistan's 'role'.

Sardar Ganga Singh Dhillon, an American-based Khalistan leader, was Zia's personal guest some time back.

The CIA has definitely not written off India, and Punjab can be an excellent beginning with Pakistan as the only 'foreign' neighour of the state.

It is illegal to quote from the banned Five More Arrows, a booklet declaring Khalistan as the birthright of the Sikh nation, but it reflects the determination of this 'lunatic' group of Sikhs to attain their ideal. The

contents of the book have been discussed widely in numerous seminars held by the 'Sikh Sophisticated Forum' and attended exclusively by Sikhs.

The first thing our intelligence should do, and do it immediately, is to find out whether 'Khalistan' is a purely domestic problem or its epicentre is somewhere else.

The movement is spreading like cancer. It has its own passport, currency, coins, stamps and rules and regulations. Its leaders along with Jarnail Singh Bhindranwale run a parallel government. Sikhs in Chandigarh, Amritsar and all over Punjab danced with joy when the news of the Boeing hijack by the Dal Khalsa activists broke out.

With Assam still in a cauldron, Punjab can be ignored at the cost of an integrated India. On her return from abroad, Indira Gandhi will have to apply her mind to the solution of this problem before she gets bogged down in other issues.

The Union Home minister's announcement at Hyderabad that the centre has no proposal at present to impose President's rule on Punjab may be reassuring to all those interested in the speedy restoration of law and order in that border state. But there is every likelihood of the Home minister's assessment being reversed after the Prime Minister's return from her foreign tour.

Indeed the Punjab situation is being given the topmost priority in the intelligence wings of the centre, and everyone concerned with law and order both at the centre and in the state have been put on the alert to gather material for a situation report to be presented to the Prime Minister so that she can decide on the next move.

Even without the hijack incident, the centre has reacted sharply to the events culminating in and arising from the arrest of Sant Jarnail Singh Bhindranwale. The hijacking episode in which five supporters of the Khalistan movement could force the pilot of a Srinagar-bound aircraft to fly to Lahore merely on the display of Kirpans has heightened the centre's anxiety.

The events in Punjab during the past month have established a few points which need to engage the serious attention not only of the centre but of all sections of Indian opinion irrespective of party affiliations.

The problem that has risen before the country in the shape of the demand for Khalistan is not one which should be treated lightly. After all people of the generation of the 1930s and 1940s had never believed that the slogan for Pakistan would one day be translated into reality, but it was and that too within a very short time.

The centre, and particularly the Prime Minister, can no more be complacent and believe that supporters for the movement exist only in the United states and Canada.

First, the Punjab armed police need to be given a reorientation course in mob psychology to enable them to tackle crisis situations in future with greater tact than they displayed after the surrender of Bhindranwale.

Secondly, the Punjab government needs to wake up to the fact that the state has any number of extremists—both religious and political— and that their activities are gaining ground. It is the primary duty of the state to identify these extremists and keep the centre posted about their activities.

The state also must immediately undertake a census or survey of the licensed arms in the state. It is said that for a population of 170 million there are only two lakh licensed arms which works out to less than two per cent. But more than the licensed, there is no accounting for the unlicensed arms which can flow into the state across the border from Pakistan. Unfortunately the fact that the Sikhs are enjoined by religion to carry arms makes it all the more difficult to get a fair assessment of the unlicensed arms in circulation.

Fourthly, the state and central governments must now proceed on the assumption that the demand and the movement for Khalistan is a serious one, and to achieve it extremist Sikhs are willing to make sacrifices. The issue can no longer be brushed aside as of no consequence.

The centre must intervene immediately and effectively to tackle what is clearly developing as a rising tide of Sikh communalism. The tragedy of the Indian situation is that one kind of communalism inevitably provokes a chain reaction and begets another type of communalism.

To prevent an ugly communal situation developing in a state where the Hindus and Sikhs have lived in amity all these years is a task to which the Prime Minister herself will have to give the closest attention. The entire issue assumes critical significance in the light of the fact that Punjab is a border state and that belligerent noises are even now being heard from across the border.

The demand for Khalistan may sound new because a precise name has been given to the movement, but it is only a repetition in a new form and with new conditions of the old demand for a separate state for the Sikhs. It was once known as Punjabi Suba and occasionally also as Sikhistan, but now the protagonists have fixed the nomenclature of the new state as Khalistan based on the holy concept of Khalsa.

And the movement has begun to tell, though it was launched in a concerted manner just over three years ago when 15 young men set up

what is called the Dal Khalsa, and followed it up the next year with the publication of a book titled *Five More Arrows*, which was promptly banned.

The reference obviously was to the five arrows which Guru Gobind Singh was supposed to have left for his successor to continue to fight the Moghuls then ruling from Delhi and discriminating against the Sikhs. The name Dal Khalsa itself is a pick-up from Sikh tradition—the 'party of the pure' that the Gurus set up to fight the Moghuls.

Dal Khalsa is admittedly involved in the hijack episode, and five of its original 15 members have been apprehended in connection with the hijack.

It was with the assistance of the hijack leader Gajendra Singh that a sacked employee of the Punjabi University (Patiala) had set up the Dal Khalsa in 1978. That man is Harsimrat Singh who is now the president of the Dal. It was no coincidence that when Gajendra Singh was announcing his demands in Lahore, Harsimrat was making similar demands at a press conference in Chandigarh.

The hijackers' strategy of enhancing their appeal by listing the release of Bhindranwale as one of the condition for giving up the Boeing was matched by their effort to associate the memory of the gurus with their movement.

It was similarly a calculated move when they picked up the Khalistan slogan, first raised by Kapur Singh, a retired ICS officer who entered politics with a vengeance and became an Akali MP way back in 1962. Both Kapur Singh, now convalescing at the Chandigarh Medical Institute, and Dr. Jagjit Singh who is recruiting adherents for the Khalistan movement from America where he stays, are treated as heroes by the Dal Khalsa activists.

Basically the demand has no justification because the Sikhs already form a majority in Punjab. Politically the Sikhs have enjoyed a predominant position, and not so curiously the demand for Khalistan was never raised when the Akali Dal was in power in the state. Mostly Sikhs alone have been Punjab's Chief ministers barring perhaps Ram Krishan who had been inducted into the office for a short while.

The Sikh demand for Chandigarh as the exclusive capital has also been virtually conceded. Till now the Sikh community has had no grievance at all about their representation in the armed forces.

But if the demand has arisen in sharper focus all of a sudden, it is because the Sikhs seem to be afraid suddenly that their majority is in danger. The last census has shown that the rate of growth of the Hindu community has been impressive.

Secondly, as alleged by the Dal Khalsa, the extreme youth group owing allegiance to Dr. Jagjit Singh, 'Hindu imperialism' was posing a threat to the Sikh religion. By Hindu imperialism what the Dal Khalsa means is that attempts are being made to project the Sikh gurus as worshippers of Hindu gods and to give similar other interpretations to the Sikh scriptures "to dilute the Panthic entity".

Chief minister Darbara Singh is reported to have appealed to Sikh Gurdwara Prabandhak Committee President Gurcharan Singh Tohra to do something to prevent the use of places of worship by those suspected of complicity in any crime. Surely some via media can be found which can maintain the respect for the place of worship and at the same time enlist the co-operation of the Gurdwara authorities.

Recently the Akali Dal submitted a memorandum to the centre listing what it termed the genuine and long-felt grievances of the Sikh community. Among the demands made in the memorandum are:

Transfer of Chandigarh and nearby, Punjabi-speaking areas of Haryana, Himachal Pradesh and Rajasthan to Punjab…

Direct transmission by radio of religious hymns from the Golden Temple at Amritsar. Permission to Sikhs to carry Kirpans during travel by Indian Airlines and Air India.

Transfer of the Bhakra Nangal head works to Punjab.

Revocation of the elections to the Delhi Gurudwara Prabandhak Committee.

Enactment of all-India legislation for the management of the Gurdwaras in the country on the Punjab Prabandhak Committee pattern.

The centre must also examine the depth of the grievance that the Sikhs are being reduced to a minority in Punjab. There has been a great deal of migration of the Sikhs to foreign lands.

Simultaneously there has been some influx of labourers mostly agricultural who are being brought by the wealthy Sikh farmers. These labourers, it is said, tend to settle down in the state. Hundreds and thousands of them have already voted in the last elections, and by the time the next Assembly elections come around their number may swell. It is feared that this can wipe out the 2 per cent majority the Sikhs enjoy today over the Hindus.

Whatever the merits of the Sikh grievances, it is obvious that the stage is past when the Khalistan demand can be swept under the carpet or dismissed as a dream of the lunatic fringe among the Sikhs. The more responsible among the Sikh community has not yet joined hand to run down the Khalistan demand. They have also been complacent. But one

hopes that they have been shaken as much as others in the country by the hijacking episode.

It is clear that the extremists are whipping up religious sentiment to gather support for the Khalistan movement. They are telling their co-religions that the ancient gurus have already laid down that *'Raj karega Khalsa, age rahe na koyi'* (the Khalsa shall rule, their enemies will be crushed).

Reports from Chandigarh, Amritsar, Ludhiana and Jullunder suggest that when the hijack news broke, there was jubilation among the Sikhs and slogans were raised. This shows that the Khalistan demand is not entirely without sympathy.

The secessionists have printed Khalistan maps. They are issuing postage stamps, passports and Khalistan 'currency'. Letters are being posted to various addresses in Punjab and are being defaced with the Khalistan mark.

There is another aspect to the political situation in Punjab which deserves the Prime Minister's attention. It is no more a secret that Union Home minister's Zail Singh and state Chief minister Darbara Singh are political rivals. Because of this the state government and the Union Home Ministry have been working at cross purposes.

It is also said in Chandigarh that Congress-I elements opposed to Darbara Singh and supporting Zail Singh calculatedly built up an atmosphere of support to Sant Jarnail Singh Bhindranwale. Report also say that there is a strong campaign against the Darbara Singh government with a view to toppling it and imposing President's rule.

Darbara Singh has also complained to the Prime Minister that his own party men were conspiring against him at the behest of certain central leaders.

Current, 10.10.1981.
pp. (1 + 3).

If she wants a settlement, let her talk to me here—Bhindranwale

Sant Jarnail Singh Bhindranwale runs a parallel government in strife-torn Punjab. He is a rule unto himself and his word is law to the Sikh masses who flock to him in hundreds everyday in the precincts of the sacred Golden Temple.

Outside the temple there is an eerie calm and the city is perched on the tip of a volcano. In the daytime he moves to the spacious terrace of

Langer Building, a red-bricked structure, holds the mike in his hand and pours unadulterated venom against the centre, the "Hindu Brahmin Indira Gandhi".

The congregation listens to him in awe and reverence. Two gun-toting young Sikhs stand by his side. There is no check or restriction on the people wanting to join the crowd.

He is frail, but words come out from his mouth like bullets. He spotted in the crowd young Hindustan Times correspondent K.L. Tomar who was accompanying. Holding the mike at me, he invited us to enter into public dialogue with him. Don't be afraid, ask any question you want.

But he does not allow the question to be completed. And his reply is a speech for the benefit of his overawed audience. "Do you want to ask what will happen if the police enter the Golden Temple," he asks, and replies himself: "First of all they dare not, and if they do they will have to walk over hundreds of dead bodies." His voice is heard all over the Golden Temple.

There is not a single Hindu among the people who flock to the temple from early morning till late in the evening. The temple is as much revered by the Hindus as by the Sikhs. But the situation has changed now. Punjab is like a shattered glass. The Hindus and Sikhs who lived like an integrated family find themselves torn into narrow social and religious fragments, and Bhindranwale couldn't care less. In fact, his daily utterances add fuel to the fire.

Don't you care for national unity, I asked. "Why should I? There can't be unity between a slave and a master. Sikhs have been treated like slaves, and until I liberate them from this serfdom I will not take rest".

I insist on having an interview without the audience and he meets me in the evening in a dingy room on the third floor of the Akal takht. On the first floor the Granthis are reciting from the huge Guru Granth Saheb. Young, heavily armed Sikhs swarm the place.

The sant speaks in pure Punjabi interpreted by equally extremist Harminder Singh Sandhu, leader of the All-India Sikh Students Federation. He is a proclaimed offender, and has been evading a number of warrants.

Bhindranwale has just finished his dinner served to him from the Langar. He lies down on the floor with a huge sword tied to his waist and covers himself with a quilt. His long-flowing beard rests on his chest. The small, low-ceiling room is filled with his followers. He is never alone. He is a narcissist. A crude reprint of Guru Gobind Singh stares at him from the wall.

He is interrupted every now and then by excited messengers who keep him posted with the latest news of violence: A sub-inspector killed near

Taran Taran along with an amritdhari. He listens to the news with his small eyes closed, and then suddenly resumes talking.

Sandhu cannot interpret properly and a pro-Bhindranwale Sikh correspondent of a local daily takes his place. Wouldn't you speak in Hindi, I plead, "No, why should I speak in Hindi? It's not my language. I speak in the language of the Gurubani, that's all the fight is about. We do not want Hindi. It is not our language."

There is a clear unmistakable rift between him and the soft-spoken Akali Dal chief Harchand Singh Longowal. He does not mention him by name and holds moderate leaders like Prakash Singh Badal in contempt. The Golden Temple is like a fief ruled by two chieftains. Longowal lives on the first floor of the Teja Singh Samudri Hall.

Bhindranwale totally disapproves of the tripartite talks held in Delhi. He would not be a party to any settlement reached over his head and one not in the spirit of the Anandpur Saheb declaration. Why should the talks be held in Delhi at all? Why should the Akalis go to Delhi? The talks have to be held in Amritsar and directly with Indira Gandhi.

Would he like to initiate talks with the centre? "No. Why should I? What is the centre? Indira Gandhi should take the initiative. She must come to Amritsar and talk to me directly. If she could go to Kashmir and talk to Sheikh Abdullah and hand over the state to him, why can't she come to Amritsar and talk to me?"

"It is I who represent the Panth. The settlement will have to be through me." He places his hand on the sword and asserts with a raised voice. "She is the cause of all the troubles, and it is she who will have to bear the brunt". He wants to talk to her about the liberation of the Sikhs.

Why do you feel the Sikhs are slaves.
I talk only of the Sikhs. Why should I talk about the others? We have fought for the freedom of others, we made a major contribution in gaining the freedom of the country, and yet we remain slaves. Now, in our struggle, others do not fight for us. The people of Haryana and Himachal were given their states without batting an eyelid. But Punjab was not given to us. Chandigarh was taken away from us, and the river waters are not ours and our power goes to the whole country. Grave injustice has been done to us and now we have to undo this injustice. We are not free in this country, we are treated like second class citizens.

The Hindus got their Hindi states without making any sacrifices. Has any Hindu made any sacrifices for getting their rights? They got trains

named after their religious places. They got the water they wanted. They got the government they wanted. But if the Sikhs want Punjabi Suba they have to go to jails. Over 50,000 Sikhs had to go to jail for the creation of Punjabi Suba. Yet the Suba is incomplete.

The Sikhs have to wage a bitter struggle to have their separate identity acknowledged. They can't even have a separate transmitter for relaying Gurbani, and the Hindu government in Delhi has not declared Amritsar a holy city. Over two lakh Sikhs have been jailed and hundreds have laid their lives. Yet their rights are not recognised. On the contrary they are branded as communal.

Do you think the Sikh are a separate nation.

Yes. Hundred per cent. You should know that everybody is a born Sikh. He becomes a Hindu or a Muslim only after he grows and his hair is shorn or he is circumcised. The real image of god is a Sikh. It is the scissors which make a man non-Sikh.

In Sikhism everybody has a place. In Quran non-Muslims have no place and in Gita non-Hindus have no place. It is only in Sikhism that everybody has a place. That's why Sikhs are a separate nation.

And Sikhs are brave and one Sikh is equal to one and quarter lakh non-Sikhs, and this is why the Sikhs are a separate nation. The Sikhs are neither Hindu nor Muslim and that is why they are a separate nation. It is as plain as that.

Even Mahatma Gandhi admitted that India has three nations—Hindus, Muslims and Sikhs. The Sikhs do not recognise the constitution of India, and the Sikh representatives in the Constituent Assembly had refused to sign the constitution . Even today this document is not recognised by us. Its Article 25, which clubs us with the Hindus, the Buddhists and the Jains, is not recognised by us. We want to burn it.

This constitution will have to be changed to give the Sikhs a separate status as has been given to the Muslims. They have their separate personal law. We are not Hindus and we must have our own personal law, and it has to be recognised by the constitution . Only then will we accept it.

What exactly do you want.

We want to abolish the slavery of the Sikhs, we want to help the oppressed. We want the total implementation of the Anandpur Saheb resolution.

Whose slaves do you think the Sikhs are.

The government has virtually made us slaves. And the greedy leaders who agreed to the partition of India have also treated us like slaves.

Do you want the liberation movement to be peaceful or violent.

The Sikhs do not believe in violence. They always believe in fighting for their rights. We are agitating peacefully, but if we do not get our rights, we will be forced to resort to other methods.

Do you approve of these killings.

Not quite.

Not quite is no answer.

I have to answer according to my choice and conscience and not according to your need.

Silence can be yes and no both.

It is upto you to interpret.

Will you appeal for peace in the state?

We consider violences as a part of aggression. We do not attack, but retaliation is not violence, it is self-defence. It is up to the government to stop violence.

If the police enter the Golden Temple to arrest you, how will you react.

A Khalsa does not believe in surrender, he fights back. It was in Bangladesh that Gen. Shibek Singh made Gen. Niazi surrender, 90,000 soldiers surrender.

That was a foreign army.

That means a Sikh knows how to get people to surrender.

But that was a foreign government. Here it is our own government.

Whose government? It is your government, not our government. If it is our government then why should it take up arms against the Sikhs?

There is a general feeling in the country that ultimately your demands will lead to Khalistan.

Have you read about Khalistan in any of my speeches?

That is not my question. I said ultimately it may lead to the demand for Khalistan.

I have neither opposed nor as yet supported Khalistan. We want to live in India as equals, and it is upto the centre to make the choice whether it wants to keep us with India or not. The centre should tell us whether it wants to live with us or not.

Why should the centre not want you to live here? It is your centre as well. Otherwise you will want Khalistan.

Yes, if they offer Khalistan to us this time, we will not repeat the mistake of 1947. We shall accept it.

Why should the centre offer Khalistan.
If it does not want to offer, it must concede our equal rights.

You have equal rights, you are as good a citizen as anyone else.
I have just now taken my meals, but you have not, and if my taking and your not taking the meals is alright, then will you be happy?

How have you become so intelligent—I mean politically.
By virtue of Guru Granth Saheb. Though I am not educated I teach the educated.

I do not want to provoke you, but I must tell you that you are the most hated person in the country today.
Who hates me? I tell you, it is the government and the press, not the people.
No, the non-Sikh do not hate me, and if the press reports me correctly I would be properly understood even by those Hindus who hate me.

Why are you hiding in the Golden Temple? Why can't you go out and explain your viewpoint to the people.
I have taken an oath not to go out of the Golden Temple unless the Sikhs rights are accepted in toto.

The general impression is that you are a loud-mouthed coward, and that you are afraid of going to jail.
Tell me the name of those who brand me a coward.

I can't name any particular person, but the general belief is that you are misusing the Golden Temple.
You are instigating me, why don't you name people?

Well, the newspapers have written about you like this.
Do you know I was in jail for 25 days, and if they were so brave they could have kept me in indefinitely? I had made an offer to former Chief minister Darbara Singh: I told him I would go to Delhi, he was free to post his army and police to trace and arrest me on the way. If I succeed in reaching Delhi and announced my presence there, all our demands will have to be met—this is a challenge and let them accept it if they have any honour left, I said, Now, tell me, who is a coward, Darbara and his leader Indira Gandhi, or I.

A section of the Sikhs believe that you are endowed with supernatural powers.
Well, cowardice is one thing, and supernatural power is another.

Why do you hate Indira Gandhi so much.
I hate the government, I hate the rulers in Delhi. And she heads the

government which suppresses the Sikhs. I am left with no choice but to hate her.

Why do you call her a Brahmin again and again.

Did she not make the two Brahmins who hijacked a plane MLAs, and didn't she punish the Sikh youth who did the same? Because they were Brahmins she rewarded them politically and made them heroes.

If Indira Gandhi enters the Golden Temple what will be your reaction.

It is a religious place. She can enter it as a matter of right. She will be welcomed if she comes to pray.

Will you get down to meet her.

Why should I? But if she comes to meet me. I would not avoid her.

I understand Prakash Singh Badal wants a reconciliation with the centre and has approached Longowal to urge him to drop the plan to burn the constitution.

Well, it is up to them.

Are you not part of the Akali Morcha.

I am part of the Morcha. So long as this vehicle continues to move I am there. When it stops, I will intervene.

Some people in the Akali Dal seem to be interested only in power.

Who are they?

Badal seems to be one of them.

Why don't you ask him?

You are the leader. You should ask him. Would you like to issue an appeal for Hindu-Sikh unity.

No.

Why.

Let the Hindus first say whether they are in favour of such unity. We have been clarifying our position for the last 36 years, and now it is their turn to clarify their position.

Gandhi would have done it.

He was Gandhi, and I am not even a son of Gandhi, I am a son of Guru Gobind Singh. He is the same Guru who had said that one should go to war only after efforts for a settlement are over.

Do you think all efforts for a settlement are over.

Who says?

Indira Gandhi is in favour of continued negotiations.

She is a clever woman.

No problem can be solved without negotiations. We must sit down and try to find a solution.

We are in favour.

No. You are against it.

No. I am against negotiations in Delhi. They have to be held here in Amritsar. If the centre wants to have a dialogue with me. I will welcome it. But she will have to come here.

Will you agree to any settlement between the Akalis and the centre.

Why not? That settlement must necessarily be that the Sikhs are accepted as a separate nation and their personal law must be separate, and all other demands raised in the Anandpur Saheb resolution are accepted. Until then I will not be a party to any settlement.

Who are you, who do you represent.

I am a servant of the Sikh congregation, the Sikh masses.

This is very vague. The Sikh congregation or the Sikh masses are not an official body.

It is an organisation called the Panth.

The Akali Dal is separate and the Panth is separate.

They (Akali Dal) claim that they represent the Panth. Let us see who represents the Panth.

It means you do not follow the Akali diktats.

It depends. I will accept all those diktats which follow the tenets of the Guru Granth Saheb.

You insist that finally the negotiations will have to be between you and the centre.

This is known to the government. Let it talk to anybody, the real issue is that the problem has to be solved. There are contradictions between me and them (Akalis).

There is obviously a contradiction. How can you deny this after having stated your own position so specifically. You claim mass Sikh support, and there is also a general impression that you carry the Sikh masses with you.

I must make it clear once again. I have no differences with them so far as the Anandpur resolution is concerned. On that issue we are one.

Do you believe Indira Gandhi when she says Pakistan will attack India.

She must know it better. How do I know about such a thing?

Current, 03.03.1984.
pp. (1 + 3 + 21 + 22)

Sikhs must have a personal law: Sant Longowal

If Sant Harchand Singh Longowal is an extremist, he is indeed a very soft-spoken extremist. He emits sweet reasonableness. Having spoken to the fire eating Sant Jarnail Singh Bindranwale earlier in the day I found Longowal a study in contrast. He wouldn't pontificate, he wouldn't raise his voice. He argues, he pursuades . . . .but the difference ends here. As for their demands, the Anandpur Saheb resolution, they speak with one voice—only the pitch is different, Excerpts from the interview:

Exactly what do you want.
What the government, the national leaders of the Congress promised. They had given some assurance to the Sikhs before partition. These should be fulfilled.

What are those promises.
Punjabi Suba.

Who made the promise.
The national leaders—Mahatma Gandhi and Jawaharlal Nehru.

What is your concept of Punjabi Suba.
A separate state for Punjabi-speaking people. That is what the Congress party's resolutions promised.

Linguistic provinces.
The states were to be carved out on the basis of language. But Punjab was reorganised after many agitations.

The dispute is about Chandigarh and river waters . . . .
Chandigarh, river waters and the Punjabi-speaking areas which were left out.

But this demand that you are a separate nation and should not be clubbed with the Hindus, and this particular clause of the constitution . . . .
Punjabi suba was carved out after as many as three committees went into the issue. According to those committees, Chandigarh belonged to Punjab, so also the Punjabi-speaking areas now left out. Our demand is that the claims and counter-claims should be decided on the basis of language, on the principle of one village as a unit and contiguity.

This latest demand for the deletion of Article 25 of the constitution because it clubs the Sikhs with Hindus—this is a new demand.
Before partition the British recognised Hindus, Sikhs and Muslims as separate nations . . . .

I think there is a misunderstanding about the word qaum. Strictly speaking it means nation. Do you use the word to mean community or nation.
We are part of the Indian nation, yet we are a distinct community with a religion of our own.

So far, Sikh and Hindu law was the same under the constitution . That is Article 25. Now the new demand is that the Article should not apply to the Sikhs. And that is why you are burning the constitution .
The main point is that we want a separate personal law. We are burning the constitution to focus the attention of the government on this point. We want a separate personal law as Muslims and Christians have.

Is it a part of the Anandpur Saheb resolution—the demand about Article 25.
Yes, of course.

But why do you want to burn the constitution .
It is a form of protest against non-fulfilment of our demand.

But the constitution is a national document . . . .
The government has not upheld the sanctity of the constitution .

You think a separate treatment in the constitution will save you.
If a separate personal law is enacted our separate identity will be protected.

But my impression was that Hindus and Sikhs are one community, they lived like one family . . . marriages take place between Hindus and Sikhs.
It is true, Hindus and Sikhs are very close to each other. But they are not one, their identities are separate.

But this has created a lot of tension between Hindus and Sikhs and today in the Golden Temple I have not seen a single Hindu.
It is because of curfew.

But Sikhs are coming despite the curfew.
Even the Sikhs are very few.

Don't you think your movement has created a vast gulf between Hindus and Sikhs.
We are fighting for our demands which are based on certain principles within the constitutional framework. The government has created a gulf to kill the Morcha. We are not against any community or religion, we are against the government.

But now it has become an agitation between two communities—look at the Panipat events.

The government is largely responsible for creating these tension. Who is encouraging Bhajan Lal?

You are called an extremist. In that case you are a very soft-spoken extremist.

We are neither extremists nor secessionists. The government wants to malign us, eliminate us.

Bhindranwale is very aggressive and I find a lot of difference between him and you.

You had to ask Bhindranwale on that point.

But do you approve of Stenguns and Brenguns in the temple.

It is in accordance with the Sikh tradition. Sikhs keep arms for self-defence and to fight against oppression.

You want to protect the Golden Temple with your guns or with your faith.

Confidence with faith will go along with arms.

Do you really think Indira Gandhi is becoming an obstacle to the solution of the Punjab problem.

Not only Punjab, she is an obstacle to every problem in the country.

But why.

By her policy of divide and rule she wants to put her son as PM.

She can do that without creating strife.

The majority of the people are not with her. If you count the votes of opposition parties you will see that only 30 per cent of the people are with the Congress. We only want that our problems should be solved and our rights given to us. We are not bothered about Buta Singh. The Sikhs must be satisfied. Buta Singh, Zail Singh, Darbara Singh—these are all puppets.

But if she sends in her police.

We will resist and sacrifice our lives to preserve its sanctity.

She can send 10,000 police.

We will embrace martyrdom. We will sacrifice our lives.

But will it solve anything.

The solution would go out of her control, she won't be able to control the situation.

What if the country demands that the police be sent in.

Since it is the centre of the Sikhs, every Sikh has links. Every Sikh would react, it would create problems for the country.

It will alienate the Sikhs from the other people.
Sikhs are living in other countries, they would go to the UN.

People ask why the movement has been launched from a religious place.
It is the tradition of every movement in this place. We launched the freedom struggle against the British government from this place.

But that was an alien government. This is our own government.
It is another form of alien government.

Why don't you go out of the Golden Temple to preach this.
The Akali Dal has assigned me to stay here.

Do you believe in hijacking, killing, etc.
We want to agitate peacefully.

What is Bhindranwale's position.
He is not a member of the Akali Dal.

But he acts for the Akali Dal.
He is extending support for the implementation of the Anandpur Saheb resolution. The Akali Dal is waging a war for the implementation of the Anandpur Saheb resolution. It believes in a policy of peace and non-violence. Bhindranwale wants to go fast, I want to go slow.

Would all these things eventually lead to the formation of Khalistan.
The Akali Dal never wanted Khalistan, only greater autonomy. But the government was trying to malign us, defame us by publicising that demand.

You want to remain a part of India. Indira Gandhi and her son have one more allegation against you. That the Akali Dal is being financed by a foreign hand, by foreign countries.
Though Indira Gandhi levels this charge, she has herself said there is no foreign hand in the agitation.

If the real problem is one of sharing power and you are given power in Punjab, will the problem be solved.
The government should solve the problem.

But if you form your own government, as they did in Kashmir. They asked Mir Qasim to resign and made Sheikh Abdullah the Chief minister. The problem was solved. Sheikh Abdullah became very friendly with Indira Gandhi. If we make you the Chief minister, we make an Akali the Chief minister, will it be all right.
There are certain problems that can be solved only by the Union government, such as water dispute and territorial dispute. The Akali Dal called two or three times, but the government never listened.

If a fresh approach is made, will you agree to talks.
We have already explained our stand, there is no need for further talks.

How can you have a solution without negotiations, without talks.
We have not raised any new demands, all demands have already been discussed.

Then, what is your next step.
We will continue the struggle peacefully for our rights.

The morcha will continue.
Yes, the morcha will continue.

But peacefully, you don't favour violence.
We won't go for violence, but the youth can get out of our control. We have been able to hold them back so far, but it may not be possible in future.

Bhindranwale talks very much against Hindus, a kind of hatred. Do you approve of that.
Hindus and Sikhs are equal. According to Sikh teachings all are equal. We do not belong to any community, we are all sons of the one God.

Bhindranwale has spoken against Hindus sitting in the Golden Temple.
I can give only my views.

But you are the chief of the Akali morcha. You can talk to Bhindranwale and ask him not to speak against the Hindus.
I won't comment on this.

Current, 17.03.1984.
p. (10)

We can save Punjab—we must, let Indira go to Golden Temple

Punjab can be saved. It has to be saved. And the only person who can save the strife-torn state is Indira Gandhi, none else. She has to employ her enormous moral and political authority to find a solution before it is too late.

The solution can be reached provided there is a will, willingness on her part and on the part of Akalis, of all varieties. The time has come to stop casting aspersions on one another, and the time has come to sit around the negotiating table and take a fresh look at the problem.

Other ways had been thought of and ruled out. Akalis and congressmen are proven pastmasters in complicating issues. Some of them have thrived on strife. Let them be exposed. They will be exposed the day the Sikhs and the Hindus of Punjab realise that it was the politicians who heaped untold misery on them.

What do the Akalis want? They want Chandigarh as the sole capital of Punjab. Give it to them. The city belongs to Punjab. It was meant for Punjab. And if it goes to Punjab, not only the Akalis but all Punjabis—irrespective of religious or political affiliation—will get it. Haryana can be given Central assistance to build its own capital where it likes.

The Akalis want a major share in river waters. Let them have it. After all, it is the sturdy Sikh farmers who have changed the face of rural Punjab and turned the state into a granary. The whole country reaps the benefits and will have more of it if Punjab's golden fields yield more crop. The Sikhs will not drink all the water or eat all the wheat and rice. Let an independent tribunal decide on the sharing of the waters and let its decision be final and binding.

The Akalis want settlement of the dispute over Fazilka and Abohar. Let a boundary commission sit immediately and give its verdict. Its findings should be accepted by all. The heavens will not fall if the two areas remains in Haryana or go to Punjab. They will remain in India all right.

The Akalis want Article 25 to be so amended as to protect their religious identity. Let there be a committee of experts to find out how the Article can be amended. Let the Sikhs have their own personal law if they want it. How and in what way will it harm national integration? It will in fact strengthen the concept of unity in diversity. If the Sikhs want to feel a separate religious unit, let them do it. After all Sikhism was born in India, it grew and prospered in India. And if it wants to grow stronger and more prosperous, let it. It will strengthen and not weaken India.

Akalis want their religious sermons to be broadcast over air. Let it be. Let the rest of the country know how magnanimous and humane the Sikh religion is. Let not only the Sikhs but every Indian feel proud of the teachings of Guru Nanak Dev. Let his message of peace and brotherhood be heard in every home.

This should have been done much earlier. After all, India is a multi-religious, multi-racial and multi-lingual country, and the sooner this fact is realised in practice, the better it is for the country and its unity.

What else do the Akalis want? They want to rule Punjab. They can do so. Let there be a popular government. Let the President's rule go. Let there be peace and let there be elections. The Akalis can come to power to share power only through the democratic process. They cannot grab power, or it cannot be given to them on a silver platter. Let them have power if they have the majority. Why should one fear an Akali government in Punjab? They had it earlier, and it was as bad or as good as any in any of the states.

Peace in Punjab is the need of the hour. The first imperative is immediate end to strife, violence and insensate bloodshed. Peace can be and will be established the moment Indira Gandhi make a pilgrimage to the Golden Temple—alone. She will win the hearts of the Punjabis and earn the gratitude of the country.

"War" began from the Golden Temple and "peace" will also be established from the Golden Temple. Let her go to the Akal Takht and bow her head before the Guru Granth Saheb, the sacred book of India. And I have no doubt there will be peace in Punjab. She is nothing if she is not brave. And today we need bravery, valour.

Nehru would have done it. Why can't Indira do it? This is the solution. The only way.

Current, 05.05.1984.
p. (1)

Nothing is sacred

The Sikhs are indignant that the Army went into the Golden Temple. Even the secular Khushwant Singh and Marxist Harkishan Singh Surjeet are.

And the non-Sikhs are seen going out of their way to say that the Sikhs have every reason to feel indignant. Even those who sent the Army in are apologetic : We are sorry, but we were helpless, is the tenor of their defence.

We have said in these columns before—and said it emphatically—that armed action doesn't solve any problems, cannot. We have said that, having taken the action, which was inevitable, we must all direct our energies towards healing the wounds inflicted by the action, and that the immediate next step should be towards a political solution.

Granting all this, however, there remains one basic question that we all must ask ourselves. That question is: On what grounds do we take for granted that religious places of worship must be kept beyond the pale of the long arm of the law?

There was a time, long ago, when temple authorities behaved as if no secular law could bind them, their possessions and their activities. But law did assert, and secular disciplines were imposed on Hindu places of worship.

This cannot be said about the places of worship of the minority communities—not at least with the same force. They were favoured with a special privilege, and without grudging.

Over the years there have been instances of the responsibility being taken lightly and the privilege misused—the most blatant manifestation of which we witnessed in the Golden Temple.

Equally, we must say those in charge of the places of worship of the majority community have often—indeed too often – transgressed the discipline and when sought to be corrected raised the cry of state interference in their religious practices.

Nobody talks of the so-called religious practices interfering with the secular norms of society. But that is what is happening on a large scale, making a mockery of our secular protestations.

And this is sanctified by the country's leadership, right up to the top, which thinks nothing of exploiting the religious sentiments of the people—in fact inciting those sentiments.

This is the root of the guilt complex one witnesses. Whenever the state is constrained to lay its hands upon the illegalities often perpetrated in the name of religion. To what horrendous limits these illegalities can go was pinpointed by what Bhindranwale and his gang did to the Golden Temple in cynical disregard of the sanctity of the place which they made much of.

Those who defile a place of worship, whether of the majority community or any other, cannot seek the protection of law. This hoax of 'religious sentiment' must be thrown out of our minds, and if it is the devil, not god, that reigns in any place of worship, he must be dragged out.

Current, 23.06.1984.
p. (2)

Popular government first, then talks: Poll in Punjab

The main objective of Rajiv Gandhi in making Arjun Singh the Governor of Punjab was to launch a massive peace offensive, bring back normalcy and prepare the ground for the return of a popular government.

The goal is specifically to hold elections for the Assembly as well as to the Lok Sabha. If nothing untoward happens, elections will most likely be held in the first week of August.

Though Governor Arjun Singh keeps his cards close to his chest, the gist of my hour-long conversation with him is that his brief is to restore democratic rule in the state, and for the purpose take all possible measures. Home minister S.B. Chavan's idea of a package deal with the Akalis may be given up in preference to polls first and negotiations later.

Rajiv feels that he owes it to the people of Punjab to give them peace first, and peace cannot be established with bayonets. The army will have to be withdrawn, and maintenance of law and order will have to be the task of the police.

His first peace offensive was at the Hussainiwala public meetings, where he made certain major announcements, including the establishment of an integral coach factory, wheat bonus to farmers, a zonal arts centre and the Thein Dam.

Arjun Singh is seized of these issues. A high-level committee of the Railway Board was here to locate the site for the coach factory. Earlier Arun Nehru, who holds the power portfolio, came here to discuss with the Governor about the dam. And the outlines have been formulated for the zonal art centre.

Arjun Singh had earlier approached the Prime Minister to use his good offices for citing an atomic power plant in the state to meet the local power requirements. Presiding over a meeting of the consultative committee for industry, he also said that he would urge the centre to include three border districts in category A to make them eligible for higher incentives for industrialisation.

The Cabinet subcommittee headed by Chavan has been touring various districts, ostensibly to elicit opinion on the Punjab problem but really to assess the mood of the people and how they would react to the elections.

The reorganisation of the PCC with Santokh Singh Randhawa as its new president is meant to boost the morale of local congressmen, though in the process Zail Singh's men have been eliminated, including his nephew Basant Singh, who was one of the general secretaries.

The PCC leadership has more or less gone back into the hands of Darbara Singh and his coterie which, most seasoned congressmen feel, had been responsible for the mess in Punjab. Darbara Singh is perhaps the most unpopular congressman in the state. He is a confrontationist. On the one hand, speaks to the Akalis in the language they understand and on the other continues the peace offensive at the official level.

Darbara, guarded by half-a-dozen burly machine-gun toting Sikhs, has been touring the Punjab interior, holding corner meetings and attacking the Akalis: "We will not accept the Anandpur Saheb resolution. We reject it in its totality," he reiterates in every meeting.

But the fact is, Rajiv Gandhi now says that the resolution can be discussed in parts and its rejection is no more a precondition for holding talks. It is obvious that Darabara's speeches are meant for the consumption of the local Hindus, who will undoubtedly vote en masse for the Congress.

However, at the Central level, Rajiv does not want to close all the doors on the Akalis. His remarks on Punjab made at press conferences held as a matter of routine, have been more conciliatory. He has not uttered a word against the Akalis. On the contrary, he has been urging them not to boycott the meeting of his committee.

"Dialogue" he says, "is the foundation of any democratic solution". And how do the Akalis expect to find a negotiated settlement without talking? It is time they stopped believing in a monologue".

The most important thing for Rajiv is to politically isolate the Akalis by pushing them more and more into the lap of the extremists. Though Operation Bluestar has left deep wounds and their ego and vanity have been deeply hurt, yet a very large number of Sikhs now want a lasting and peaceful solution.

They also want a share in political power and that can come only through elections. The Akali Dal, which is divided in more than three factions, will not be in a position to meet the Congress offensive unitedly, and that is the main strength of the Congress.

The strategy is to fan the flames of strife in the Akali ranks. The internal fights among them will inevitably win the contempt of the Sikh masses. The mutual bickerings will take a turn for the worse once Prakash Singh Badal and Gurcharan Singh Tohra are released, which might be any day.

At the moment, the Akalis are under the impression that they will succeed in polarising the voters on communal lines and capture a majority

in the Assembly. In the last Assembly the Akali Dal (L) had 31 seats and Akali Dal (T) 2, in a house of 117. The Congress had 64 seats.

The Congress is sure of getting an absolute majority and forming a government. The Akalis will then be reduced to play the opposition role, not that of a popular movement of the Sikhs. They will most likely boycott the elections as a party. But in that case not all Sikhs will rally behind them.

The large number of mazhabi Sikhs are unhappy at the shocking treatment meted out by the Akal Takht to Buta Singh. Hazara Singh Majitha, chief of the All India Shiromani Baba Jiwan Singh mazhabi Dal, has launched a frontal attack on the Akalis at the behest of Buta Singh.

The national opposition parties too are now realising that the Akali leaders suicidal subservience to the extremists will not give them any leeway to come to a negotiated settlement and they will not be allowed to strike any package deal with the centre.

Intelligence sources also suggest that ultimately the extremists will devour the Akali leaders in order to confront the centre and sabotage Rajiv's peace offensive. Sant Harchand Singh Longowal's recent rigid postures are basically meant to appease the extremists, but he too will soon realise that he would not be able to whet their appetite.

None of their leaders, including Jagdev Singh Talwandi, G.S. Tohra and Prakash Singh Badal, are morally and politically strong enough to fulfill the ambitions of the extremists, who clearly aim at Khalistan and nothing short of it. This fringe will have to be dealt with as a law and order problem. Arjun Singh is getting himself equipped for this.

The extremists may continue to indulge in isolated cases of violence, but the new administration is confident of holding elections with fewer political murders than what the country witnessed, say, in Bihar during the last Assembly elections.

The new team with the Governor, which is called the Governor-in-Council is in fact looking forward to the polls. One of its senior members assured me that except the Akalis not a dog will bark. The people of Punjab can no more be denied their own government. So, on to the polls—in Punjab.

Current, 13.04.1985.
pp. (1 + 3)

We stand for all Punjabis
S.S. Barnala speaks

Sardar Surjit Singh Barnala talks like a professor at the end of his career. He is not only soft-spoken, one has to strain one's ears to hear what he says. He is tall, thin and dressed in a white shirt tucked in his bluish-green trousers. He unwittingly embraced me and I jumped aside. He was wearing a bullet-proof jacket. Can it stop bullets, I asked. His reply: "I really do not know. So far nobody has trained his guns at me. I will face them if it comes to that."

Not Barnala alone but anybody in public life in Punjab lives dangerously. As we sat for an hour-long session, four well-built and very handsome Sikhs stood guard with their fingers on the triggers of the automatic weapons. Such is life in Punjab and Barnala appears determined to restore normalcy to this strife-torn state. Excerpts from the interview.

The Akali victory and Congress defeat have brought jubilation in the Congress camp. In fact the whole country has heaved a sigh of relief in your victory. Why?

I don't know whether the Akali victory has brought jubilation in the erst while Congress camp or not. But certainly some sensible congressmen have expressed happiness. Because the Congress had failed in the state. Even in the President's Rule, the Congress-ruled centre had failed in the state. So naturally they thought where they failed, perhaps Akalis would succeed.

Rajiv Gandhi has described your victory as that of Mother India.

It was very good of him to have said that.

How can your victory be synonymous with that of Mother India.

Because Sant Harchand Singh Longowal had championed the cause of integrity of the country and its amity.

Before the elections, suspicion was expressed that the Congress was interested in the Akali victory. Similar views were expressed in the newspapers and also the Congress had purposely put up weak candidates against Akalis.

This was a wrong notion which was totally denied both by the Akali Dal and the Congress. Rajiv Gandhi paid four visits and toured 16 constituencies in Punjab. Earlier, he had never done so in any other state. It was a vigorous campaign on the part of the Congress. Forty MPs were

deployed. A lot of election material was made available. A lot of funds were made available. I think the candidates were perhaps very good.

Candidates for Parliament seats were good. But the Assembly candidates were weak.

We had got better success in Parliament seats than what we had expected.

Rajiv Gandhi did not speak anything against the Akalis which is an opposition party.

Perhaps it was more appropriate for him to do so considering the prevailing situation in the states. He had accepted all the Akali demands. Could he have said then that the Akali Dal had been agitating.

It appears a large number of Hindus have voted for you which was not the pattern earlier. Did they do so for Hindu-Sikh unity or in a very calculated move to hand over power to the Akalis.

It was a vote for Hindu-Sikh unity. It was a vote for the efforts made by Sant Harchand Singh Longowal and the path he had shown. It was in fact a vote for the accord.

Vote for the accord or was it their sheer desperation—let the Akalis come to power.

No. Not so. They are educated people. Most of them, that is.

But the Hindus have never voted on such a large-scalc for the Akalis before.

This time they knew Sant Longowal had sacrificed his life for a cause. The cause of Hindu-Sikh unity. And Punjabis. So they knew that a Punjab party, if it came to power would champion the cause of Punjabis. They also knew that if the Akalis come to power that would benefit all Punjabis.

The Akali Dal is the only party which till now has championed the cause of all Punjabis. Not any other party. The Akali Dal alone has struggled for the cause of all Punjabis.

You mean to say that the Akali Dal now represents the whole of Punjab and not only Sikhs or the Akalis.

Yes, that is why Hindus voted for us.

So your efforts now will be to consolidate Hindu-Sikh unity in the state. And you will include some Hindus in your cabinet, isn't it.

Yes.

Observers say that the Akalis fought all these bloody battles just to acquire power . . . .

No, nothing like that. We thought all these battles were necessary to secure the rights of Punjab, rights which were denied. Like Chandigarh which

was denied to Punjab for 20 long years. Nobody else fought for it, be Jana Sanghis or congressmen. Even Communists didn't. Mind you Chandigarh isn't a predominantly Sikh city. If there were three or four assembly seats here, Hindus would win them all. Still we fought for Chandigarh because we felt it belonged to Punjab.

You mean the Akali Dal is adopting a secular attitude now.

Yes. Earlier also we did so. But this time we have done it to a greater extent. We invited applications from Hindus also. We received 16 applications out of which six were given tickets. Two of them won on Akali tickets and two with our support.

Does the Akali Dal represent regional sentiments.

I think so.

Like the Telugu Desam.

Yes.

Akali Dal is no more a religious party.

Yes. It represents the sentiments of Punjab.

Will the Akali be more secular in future.

Yes.

Are you delinking Gurdwaras from politics.

Gurdwara politics is part of our life. Gurdwara, for us, is not only a place of worship, it is also a place of community meetings. That includes us also.

Is it some sort of a socio-religious politics.

You see, since the time of our gurus Sikh politics and religion have been together.

You plan to continue the same pattern.

Yes.

Your victory is a gift of the accord. Do you agree.

No, there are many factors. People have realised that it is only the Akali Dal that has struggled for the rights of Punjab. They have understood our sacrifices. Our successful morcha, our voice against Operation Blue Star and finally the sacrifice of Sant Longowal. All these have contributed.

Bhindranwale was completely forgotten in this election campaign.

You see Baba Joginder Singh called for a boycott of the election. The two belonged to the same group.

Have Sikhs discarded Bhindranwale completely.

That was the calculation one had to make.

Joginder Singh has an important segment of Sikhs with him. Did you try to win him over?

We did try to win him over. Through the press I requested them to reconsider their boycott decision. But they did not listen.

Did you meet him.

No.

Would you like to meet him now.

He is a senior man. I have regards for him. But our paths are different. So for the time being I won't like to meet him.

During the elections you appealed to all Sikhs including Joginder Singh to unite.

I didn't get any positive response.

I thought you will work out an accord with him.

No, no. There's nothing like that.

Some of his followers came to you.

No that's not true at all.

What will be his next move.

His move of boycott has failed. Even in those areas where his followers are predominant—areas around the Indo-Pak border—our candidates won.

People have realised that in a democracy they can have better achievements.

Yes, I think so.

What'll be your relationship with the centre, specially with Rajiv Gandhi.

We will have a constructive relationship. We will go for the implementations of the accord.

Will Rajiv Gandhi co-operate with you.

Yes.

Have you established some kind of rapport with him.

I never met him after the accord.

Did you meet him before the accord.

No.

The only time you met him was in the course of the accord.

Yes, first and last time till this date.

Did you approach him through the Governor or through somebody else.

For the accord, yes.

Did he congratulate you personally on the victory.
Yes.

On telephone.
Yes.

What did he say.
Well....

Did he talk in Punjabi or English.
I have the telegram.

What did he say on telephone.
He congratulated me.

What sort of rapport will you have with the centre. Like that of MGR and NTR.
It won't be exactly the same. Because we have big problems here. We don't have enough money right now.

Do you think the centre would co-operate with you and give you the money.
They should.

Lately NTR has adopted a conciliatory attitude towards Rajiv Gandhi. In fact, he has a better rapport with him than most of the Congress CMs.
We won't have any confrontation with him for the sake of confrontation.

Will you again make an effort to bring all opposition parties together.
Our effort will be to bring peace in the state and see that it prospers and progresses. For that whatever is necessary. I'll do.

You are an opposition Party. How will your MPs behave in Parliament.
We have seven MPs in Parliament now. They will behave like opposition members.

Do you think terrorism will again raise its head. In case it does, how do you plan to combat it.
Terrorism is still there because terrorist elements are still there in the state. The Darbara Singh government and President's rule did not make any effort to contain them. But we will try to contain them as far as possible.

In one of your statements you had said that terrorism was a creation of congressmen.
Yes.

Do you have any information on that.
I read about it in newspapers while in Pachmarhi jail. The first conference between terrorists and congressmen was held here. Dal Khalsa was the creation of Giani Zail Singh.

You think this situation was created by the rivalry between the Giani and Darbara Singh.

Yes, yes.

What do you think of Giani Zail Singh now.

I can't express any opinion on him as a Sikh.

What is the Akali Dal stand vis-a-vis the Anandpur Sahib resolution.

The Anandpur Sahib resolution as such contains all the demands. Even Chandigarh, water, etc. are there in it.

You have indiscriminately released a large number of terrorists.

Most of these people are not terrorists. They were involved in false cases. We have evidence for that.

What about army deserters.

I've already said that there was no mutiny as such. They has simply left their barracks. They have not created any trouble either. So they should be leniently dealt with.

What about Simranjit Singh Mann. What's his case. Will he be released.

I don't exactly know his full case. I only know that he is under NSA.

Weren't those 222 whom you released were detained under the NSA?

They were all under NSA. We revoked the NSA.

What about Mann.

For the time being no. Perhaps, in his case it can't be revoked by the Punjab government.

Are there two NSAs.

He was arrested in Bihar and brought to Punjab. Perhaps the Bihar government would have to release him.

Gurcharan Singh Tohra said that if Akalis come to power the Akal Takht would be rebuilt.

I subscribe to his view. It will be demolished and rebuilt. Earlier also, it was not rebuilt. It was repaired. The same thing will happen again. Tohra being in charge of SGPC, he will be able to say about this best. But surely the state of the Takhts was pathetic when I saw it. I cried and cried.

Will you continue to be president of Akali Dal.

The party will decide about that.

Will you allow Haryana to stay in Chandigarh.

For two years, yes. That we will settle among ourselves.

Why have you kept Badal out of the Ministry.

He wanted to relax.

Do you apprehend any trouble from him.
No, he is a good partyman, a good leader.

Current, 12.10.1985.
pp. (1 + 3)

B. The Assamiya Resurgence

Report from Gauhati

I met Assam's super-star Prafulla Kumar Mahanta in a secluded hostel room of Gauhati University where he has been hiding for a couple of days.

The warrant of arrest was issued against him and all the fourteen members of the executive of All Assam Students Union in the first week of April. The police have been able to arrest only four of them. But as I was about to begin my two-hour-long interview with him a student leader informed us that two more had been picked up by the police from the headquarters. Mahanta did not betray any sign of nervousness. "I am ready to be arrested any moment," he said.

I was accompanied by Lalit Rajkhowa, adviser to the AASU. We found a number of police jeeps on the main road hardly 50 feet away, but either the police did not know his hide-out or they feigned ignorance. As the powerful, popular and idolised President of AASU, Mahanta is the most sought-after student leader, and his arrest is bound to give a tremendous help to the movement.

Despite the seven month long struggle which has paralysed the state and enormously damaged its economy, the soft-spoken and unassuming Mahanta's determination to drive out the state's 45 lakh 'foreigners' remains unflinching.

He is not willing to start another round of negotiations either with Indira Gandhi or anybody else unless the 'black acts promulgated by the centre' declaring Assam a disturbed area are withdrawn the arrested leaders released and the warrants of arrest are taken back.

The people of Assam will not permit any compromise on 1951 as the cut-off line. The detection of the 'foreigners' has to be done on the basis of the 1951 national register of citizenship. "It is a constitutional demand and the national leadership is committed to it."

'D' dominates the Assamiya resurgence. The three Ds—desh, deletion, deportation have become the article of faith of the people of Assam origin though the same three Ds stand for degradation, demolition and death for the 'foreigners'.

Mahanta added four more Ds to the impressive list. Two of them are 'dialogue' and 'distribution'. But the centre, he said knows only the other two Ds. One, deployment of the army, CRP and BSF, and two, deadlock.

Though he is the chief spokesman of the movement against foreigners' neither he nor his colleagues have found a solution to the gigantic upheaval that will be caused not only in the north-eastern region but in the whole country if their demand for the first three Ds is accepted.

What do you intend to do with these 45 lakh people if they are declared unwanted." I asked him. A long silence, and then:

"Well, I don't know. Let them go back to the countries of their origin".

Do you have any idea of the explosive consequences of what you just said?

"Yes, I have, Mahanta said coldly without batting an eyelid. "These foreigners are mainly Bangladeshis, Nepalese and Bhutanis.

But these people have been living in the state for nearly 30 years. Don't they have the citizenship rights and are they not voters?

Yes, but all those who entered Assam after 1951 and whose names are not in the NRC have to be detected and finally deported.

But neither Bangladesh nor Nepal nor Bhutan will take them back. They will be stateless people, the worst thing that can happen to human beings.

Well, we are not bothered. It is the centre's headache. Why should Assam alone bear the burden? Let them be distributed all over the country.

Wherever they go they will be stateless.

Again there was a long pause as though he was searching for an answer. I added : "What about their property, their land and their houses?" The answer came promptly.

The land does matter. The government can decide about the property. These people have refused to assimilate themselves with us, our culture, and have refused to learn our language. The movement has no communal overtones. The Bangladeshis whether they are Hindus or Muslims are foreigners and they have no business to stay on the sacred soil of Assam. They are culturally and emotionally closer to the people of West Bengal.

Look, what has happened in Manipur. The Manipuris are in minority. The Bengalis have taken it over. The Bengalis in Assam and other hill

states have refused to mix with the locals, learn their language or mix with them. They live in a world of their own with their own schools and colleges. If we fail to implement the 1951 cut-off line, very soon we will be submerged. Do you know, in the North-Eastern Railway 90 per cent are Bengalis, and Assam and the other six hill states have only 10 per cent?

Mahanta made yet another startling statement: We are not communal though we are branded as such, but there are some areas in Assam which are known as 'Maulana Bhashani areas'. Here the Pakistani flag was raised during the war. All these people who raised the Pakistani flag in 1965 should be declared foreigners and deported.

How would you know who raised the Pakistani flag 15 years ago, and how does it disqualify one from being an Indian citizen.
Well, the CBI should investigate.

How can it be investigated after 15 years.
It can be done. Those people are still there.

Having made the statement, Mahanta tried to wriggle out of it: "The centre has a heavy responsibility in preserving the unity and sovereignty of the country and should not do anything which endangers the integrity of the country. Instead of settling our problems, the government is conspiring to crush our seven month-old movement. The conspiracies are being hatched with the help of the administration and some foreign powers with a view to building a counter movement and to encourage linguistic and communal trouble. Any attempt to break the movement without resolving the problem of foreign nationals will have dangerous portents for the sovereignty of the country. Our movement is a powerful bulwark against the political conspiracy of aliens to separate one state from the country."

Mahanta has no answer to the 'final question' of the detected foreign nationals. They must be deported, but where, he does not know, nor do any one of his colleagues.

"If the government does not agree with us we will continue our agitation as long as there is life in our body. We will not withdraw the agitation, nor will we permit even a drop of oil to flow from the pipelines."

"All the educational institutions including the Gauhati University are closed for seven months—let them be closed for seven years. The movement cannot be withdrawn. It has taken roots. It runs in the blood of our people. We cannot betray our martyrs—we have shed blood."

Mahanta says his movement is not against the Bengalis but against the Bangladeshis and Nepalese. But every Bengali settled in Assam fears he is the target. There is a feeling of insecurity among the people of Bengali origin, both Hindus and Muslims.

The movement leaders also apprehend that the centre may prove mischievous. It may bring an amendment to the constitution declaring all these foreigners as Indian citizens. "In that case what will you do". I asked them. "We shall fight".

You will be fighting against the constitution and the will of the people. "Well, let it be, but we will continue our struggle. We are not going to be cowed down. Do you know what the Home minister told us during our last meeting with him? He said: Well, you let the oil flow and continue the agitation as long as you want. That is how they look at our problem.

The Prime Minister feels that somebody else is guiding our movement. In our meeting at Gauhati she asked us: Who is your leader? We pointed at the photograph of Mahatma Gandhi hanging over her head and said, 'he is our leader'.

There is no doubt that the movement is peaceful and that:

1. Every Assamiya is deeply and emotionally involved;
2. It is non-communal and a large number of Assamiya Muslim youth are in the forefront and it has no foreign connections;
3. It is entirely financed by the people;
4. Every Assamiya feels that he is totally justified in demanding 1951 as the cut-off line, and if that was not agreed he would be reduced to the status of a second class citizen in his own home state;
5. They believe that the Bengalis have an eye on Assam and their design is to take away a large chunk of the state as a part of "greater Bengal". Every Assamiya is aware of the map of 'Greater Bengal' published in some Bengali newspapers;
6. The only way to remove poverty, improve the economy have more employment opportunities and let the rivers of milk and honey flow, they believe is to compel the government to agree to 1951 as the cut-off line and get rid of the 45 lakh foreigners;
7. To them the camp of Jyoti Basu symbolises Bengali chauvinism and they believe that his party's secret plans are to communise the whole north-east through Bengali infiltration. Every Bengali, according to them, is a potential carrier of the red germs; Communism gives him moral and ideological strength to expand and capture other's land.

I have never seen a movement like this. It is a mass upsurge, an

upheaval. I had a glimpse of it on April 28 wnen the people responded to the AASU call for 'marital sound' for an hour and a half from 11 a.m. It was meant to be a symbolic protest against the 'injustice'.

At 11 sharp, the roads of Gauhati were flooded with well-organised and disciplined processionists beating huge drums, *dhols, khols* and blowing trumphets, horns and conch shells. In the churches bells chimed, in the mosques the mullahs gave 'azan', and temples resounded with the sound of various musical instruments.

Women outnumbered men. Elegantly dressed in kosa silk garments, women and young girls marched in twos near the AASU headquarters at the Cotton College it was a sea of humanity—peaceful and dignified. Not a single policemen was in sight. Almost every government servant participated in the procession. The employees of the hotel in which I am staying converged on the spacious lawns and incessantly beat the drum and sang for an hour and a half. How can we live if Assam dies was the one-sentence song.

I spoke to a number of women participants. I got only one answer: Now or Never. The student leaders are the heroes. Mahanta, of course, is the most adulated, but there are others too. Biren Bhattacharya, who won the coveted Jnanpith award is one of them. Perhaps the most influential organisation is the Assam Sahitya Sabha with its 700 branches all over the state. One has to visit Assam to find out how much the Assamiya rever their language.

I asked a ten-year-old boy who was carrying a magazine: Is it Assamiya or Bengali?

Assamiya. It is my language. It is beautiful. I love it.

I met the boy at the AASU headquarters. A primary school student, he serves tea to the student leaders and has not gone to school for seven months. I am serving the 'andolan' and I will go to school only after our demands are met.

I was reminded of an eminent Bengali professor who told me in Calcutta the night before my departure to Gauhati: Assam is finished. It will secede from India and take the rest of the north-east. Assamiya is no language, it is a corruption of Bengali.

Though the Assamiyas and the Bengalis have been living together for centuries they know so little about each other.

Current, 03.05.1980.
pp. (1 + 2 + 19)

Assamiya bent on 1951 as cut-off line

'Assam is burning.' Almost every statement, handbill and booklet issued by the leaders and the organisation spearheading the 'Save Assam' movement begins with this sentence. But Assam is neither burning nor will it burn.

The 'Save Assam' movement has so far been peaceful and its leaders are determined not to let it turn violent.

There are no secessionist elements amongst the leaders of the movement. Though all the national parties have lost their relevance, no regional party has yet taken firm hold of the situation. The Purbanchaliya Loka parishad led by Socialist Nibaran Bora is trying to emerge as a regional party. Bora's main fight is against 'Bengali chauvinism and expansionism'. Neither he nor his party has ever dreamt of being secessionist.

The leaders of the 'Save Assam' movement are nationalists and patriotic. 'We are the sons of Mother India,' they assert.

But Bengalis and, specially the Bengali intelligentsia in Calcutta, unreservedly brand the 'Save Assam' agitation as a secessionist movement. They are convinced that Assam will go the Bangladesh way. This is a misconception. The people of Assam and the whole north-eastern region have certain genuine grievances. The only way to meet the challenge is to understand their problems and solve them.

The people in this region are as good or as bad Indian as the policy makers in New Delhi. It will be a grave mistake to dub them secessionist or condemn them as anti-Indian.

Assam will never go the Bangladesh way but Assam should be saved from becoming a Bangladesh.

Assamiyas live in a world of their own. Few of them have stepped out of their state. They are proud of their language, culture, music, poetry and folk songs. They are now in the grip of a fear complex which can be appreciated or understood only if one visits Assam and talks to its people.

The first thing one has to learn in Gauhati is to pronounce properly the name of the place and the people. Assamese call themselves Assamiya. Assamiya and Ashomiya and Ahomiya. The pronunciation differs from region to region. The Sahitya Sabha uses only 's' for Assam.

Bengalis, Nepalis, Bhutias and Marwaris settled in the state pronounce Assam in their own ways.

Pronounce Assam in whatever way you like, but don't call its people Assami. It means a criminal.

The Co-ordination Committee of the Gauhati Teachers' Association which has been in the forefront of the 'Save Assam' campaign reflects the fear. It not only agrees with the student's demand of three D's—Detection, Deletion and Deportation—but has also suggested measures to prevent any infiltration in future. It has no faith in the Indian Army or the Border Security Force. Its powerful convenor Upendra Nath Das says:

"As an immediate measure to stop infiltration the centre should start the construction of a concrete wall along the 231 km-long Indo-Bangladesh border instead of depending upon the Border Security Force whose commitment to keep the borders secure has not been reassuring. If there is the question of funds for raising the wall, it may be pointed out that it will amount to much less than what Indira Gandhi invested in terms of money and military or administration resources during the liberation of Bangladesh."

The 'Save Assam' movement has entered its eighth month. In this period not a drop of oil has come out of the refineries. The state is losing Rs. 20 crore daily in industrial production. The oil refineries are losing Rs. 4 crore a day. The state will lose royalty of Rs. 24 crore which it earns from the sale of crude at Rs. 42 a tonne. The production of natural gas has come on to a half. It might lead to the closure of the fertiliser factory and the thermal power station at Namrup. Because of the power cut the tea gardens are in doldrums and losing lakhs of rupees every day.

Since most of the government servants have joined the agitation, the administration has come to stand-still. All educational institutions are closed. The prices of essential commodities have gone up by 40 per cent.

Yet the 'Save Assam' movement continues with full fury. The Assamiyas of all classes are getting more and more deeply involved. They do not talk of hardship. Government servants give one day's salary every month to the collective funds of the movement. Businessmen and contractors donate liberally. No dent has been made in the determination of the people to 'save' Assam. The 'foreigners' will have to be detected, their names deleted from the voters list, and they should be deported lock, stock and barrel from Assam. "Any other solution will not be acceptable to the people of Assam", says teachers' leader Upendra Nath Das.

The movement is controlled and led by the All-Assam Gana Sangram Parishad. It is made up of ten constituents:

1. All Assam Student's Union
2. Assam Sahitya sabha
3. Purbanchaliya Lok parishad
4. Assam Jatiyabadi Dal
5. Assam Jatiyavadi Yuva Chatra parishad
6. Young Lawyer's forum
7. Assam Yuvak samaj
8. All Assam Tribal sangha
9. Progressive Plains Tribal council of Assam
10. Co-ordination Committee, Gauhati University Teacher's Association

Their major demand is that the National register of citizens prepared in 1951 should be treated as the basic document for the purpose of detecting foreign nationals living in Assam. Arbitrary cut-off dates such as 1967 or 1971 cannot be accepted as the base year since than dates have no constitutional relevance. The acceptance of any date other than 1951 will open the floodgates of fictitious claims from lakhs of people claiming Indian citizenship.

The Gana Sanghram Parishad has turned down Prime Minister Indira Gandhi's suggestion that the foreign infiltrators should be detected and deported with 1971 as the starting year.

This is not acceptable to the parishad leaders. They say the citizenship of the person should be determined on the basis of the National Register of 1951. Assam cannot be made a dumping ground for foreigners and infiltrators.

The parishad is convinced that Assam has more than 50 lakh foreigners or infiltrators and if they are not thrown out of the state life in Assam would be in jeopardy. It disputes the centre's claim that between 1961 and 1971 over two and a half lakh infiltrators have been deported.

In a letter addressed to Indira Gandhi on April 24, 1980 the Assam Sahitya Sabha asserted that Assamiya should not be punished for the mistakes committed by the Indian leadership.

"It has been claimed that about 2.5 lakh of infiltrators were deported in 1961-71, the letter says, "but we have reason to feel that there is yawning chasm between paperwork figures and actual performance, for the international border has never been sealed to preclude the deportees re-entry. We gather ideas from our discussion with the Governor of Assam on March 30, 1980 that the centre has directed Gauhati to rehabilitate refugees upto 1969 provided they came in the wake of the Indo-Pak war of 1965. This decision remains inscrutable to the people of Assam."

The letter points out that while the centre has given great publicity to the figure of 2.5 lakh deportees in 1961-71, it has also admitted that it has rehabilitated lakhs of refugees during the same decade in Assam. May we ask to which category these people belong and who has been served with deportation orders and who were given a royal reception? It boils down to this: 2.5 lakh Muslim infiltrators were thrown out and some five times the number of the deportees were rehabilitated because they were Hindus.

The centre is, therefore, guilty of throwing to the winds the sacred principles of secularism and also of compromising the trust of religious minorities, which ought not to have been sacrificed in such a hopeless manner. The people of Assam are not prepared to accept one set of infiltrators as Indians and another as foreigners on the consideration of their respective religious faith, nor do they see any legitimacy behind any inscrutable discrimination between two sets of foreign nationals."

The 'Save Assam' movement is neither foreign inspired nor financed by any international agency. It is a people's movement though it has been built up on the basis of fear. The Assamiya fear Bengali domination. When they talk of 'foreigners' they are actually talking of Bengalis both Hindus and Muslims. Parishad leaders are convinced that the governments of West Bengal and Tripura are using all methods to encourage Bengali infiltration into Assam by issuing fictitious citizenship certificates to the infiltrators.

The Assamiyas are convinced that the massive infiltration of foreigners into their state is a planned and organised 'invasion' aimed at over-running the people of the state and reducing them into a politically insignificant minority in their own homeland. The solution of the problem brooks no delay.

The parishad has urged that the centre should implement the 1951 cut-off line on a war footing. The local police and the executive magistrates should be empowered to detect the infiltrators and deport them, with no right to appeal.

Is it easy to detect and deport 50 lakh people? Will it not cause an upheaval not only in Assam but in the entire north-eastern region? What will happen to their property? The leaders have a ready reply. They say: All property, movable or immovable, belonging to those declared foreigners should be automatically vested in the state government. Since they are served with notice to quit India they should be kept in detention camps until they are finally deported out of the country. The maintenance of such detention camps should be the responsibility of the centre.

They also suggest that the people from Bangladesh who have obtained citizenship certificates from West Bengal and Tripura and who have settled in Assam should be sent back to these two states. They are not acceptable to Assam. Indian citizens who have given shelter and protection to these infiltrators should be punished.

One of the demands of the Gauhati University Teacher's Association is that the hundreds of people pouring into Assam from various neighbouring north-eastern states should be asked to identify their citizenship. Even though some of them are found to be Indian citizens, they should not be allowed to stay in Assam since that would lead to the worst demographic imbalance affecting the interests of the Assamese people.

The centre should immediately take appropriate constitutional safeguards for maintaining the majority character of the Assamese in Assam. The National Register should be introduced and all the people living in Assam should be introduced for the state of Assam.

The Assamiya intellectuals and especially teachers and bureaucrats genuinely—fear that the collapse of the 'Save Assam' movement would finally lead to the formation of Greater Bengal. Jyoti Basu is termed as a Bengali chauvinist and it is apprehended that the whole north-eastern region will fall to the communists.

The parishad leaders vehemently deny that their movement is secessionist or separating from India, "It is inconceivable", says Nagen Saika, General Secretary of the Assam Sahitya Sabha emphatically. The ASS whose leaders are in close touch with the All Assam Students Union also assure that the 'Save Assam' movement is strictly based on the Gandhian non-violent pattern. "We will never take to the path of violence", they assert.

Almost all the AASU leaders who accompanied me during my recent visit to Gauhati again and again assured me that they cannot imagine even in their wildest dreams in terms of taking up arms. But they fear that the 'Bengali Communists' who are determined to communise not only Assam but the entire north-eastern region will unleash violence in sheer desperation.

Professor R.P. Barooah who heads Department of Political Science and Journalism at Gauhati University sees a serious threat to Assam and its culture from Bengali chauvinists. An ex-CPI member, he says completely aligned himself with the Sangarsh parishad and its demands. The problems of Assam, he sincerely feels, is "the accumulated result of a multi-pronged attack on Asamiyas for decades by linguistic and theocratic expansionists."

An intelligent and articulate don, Prof. Barooah hands over a nicely printed folder to me authored by him. It says: The idea is to turn Assam into a Bengali-speaking state, and its genesis dates back to as early as

1837 when Bengali was language of instruction and administration in Assam. The second idea is to turn Assam into a Muslim majority state, and it originated with the Muslim League movement in India.

The cause of continuous and heavy influx of infiltrators into Assam cannot be explained by superficial factors like insecurity of Hindus and economic hardship of Muslim in Bangladesh. In the name of employment opportunities and security of life, he says, the infiltrators are serving the ends of a deeprooted political design to create a 'Greater Bengal'.

Current, 10.05.1980.
pp. (10 + 11)

Human life is more precious than democracy: army alone can save Assam

Assam should be handed over to the army immediately. An extraordinary situation has gripped the strife-torn state, the country can ill-afford to let Assam sink in its own blood.

There is a complete breakdown of law and order, the civil administration has totally collapsed, the political parties have run away from the scene, the AASU and AAGSP leaders have been thrown in jails, a vast majority of the people in the Brahmaputra valley are up in arms against the government, and the non-Assamese minorities are facing a holocaust the country has witnessed before.

The massacre of over 2,000 men, women and children all over the state has shocked the conscience of the nation. The threats of more Nellie type bloodbaths hold Assam at ransom.

There is no other alternative but to rush the army and if possible the air force too to bring Assam under control and establish a semblance of sanity. The state has gone beyond the control of civil authorities who should in fact be held largely responsible for the colossal loss of human life and property.

Assam is under President's rule. Governor Prakash Malhotra is the chief executive. His head should roll first. He is guilty of misguiding the centre and his leader Indira Gandhi. He is also guilty of being negligent, complacent and callous.

Despite prepared promises of safety for the people, their life and property during the election period and later, he has not been able to save a single life nor protect a single piece of property. With him the Chief

Secretary, the Home Secretary and the police top brass must be sacked. They are the guilty men.

Assam's most immediate need is the restoration of law and order. It is a state at war against itself. Its people have destroyed in a fit of mass frenzy the communication system, the power installations, the railways, road transport, the roads and the bridges. In the last week alone, over one thousand bridges have been razed to the ground. The local police are on the run, the police stations are in flames, schools and colleges have been shut down for months. Consumer goods have vanished from the markets—milk, sugar, salt, rice, matchboxes, edible oil, kerosene and petrol are not to be seen.

Miles of paddy fields in Nowgong region are littered with hundreds of dead bodies of infants from field to field. The stench of rotting bodies pervades the air. Several reporters who rushed to the scenes of massacre broke down, some of them vomited and a couple fainted at the grisly sight.

Among the Nellie victims, 80 per cent of the dead were women and children. "The bodies of mothers clutching babies. It makes taking a walk across an act of bravery, such is the gruesome carnage," writes correspondent Shekhar Gupta of the *Indian Express*.

But Nellie was not the first nor will it be the last act of mass madness. Assamese and Bengalis have been at each other throats since the announcement of the elections. Passions have been on the rise as polling dates neared, and the visits by national leaders including Indira Gandhi, Atal Behari Vajpayee and Namboodiripad had aggravated rather than mollified the agitators.

Nellie happened despite Indira Gandhi's assurance that the government had taken the responsibility of protecting the life and property of each and every person wishing to participate in the democratic process and that it was fully equipped to hold the elections without much disruption.

Mass violence nevertheless engulfed the state, despite the presence of over 50 battalions of para-military forces. The centre has stationed battalions of BSF, Home Guards, Haryana Armed Police, UP's Provincial Armed Constabulary, Rajasthan Armed Constabulary, and yet the situation went out of control. The local police did not co-operate and the local civil servants in a rare act of defiance withdrew from the scene, ignoring the National Security Act.

The wounds are too deep to be healed in the foreseeable future. The chasm between various religious, linguistic and ethnic groups has become too wide to be bridged without a lasting political solution. Violence has

become the order of the day, the spirit of revenge has taken deep roots. A massive effort will be needed to bring the situation to normalcy. And at the moment only the army can effectively prevent the recurrence of mass killings.

Though the final solution has to be political, the army is the need of the hour. One should not hang on to ego and prestige. What is at stake is human life, not democracy. The elections have undoubtedly boomeranged and tarnished the image of a national leader of Indira Gandhi's stature.

If the elections had become an inevitability because of constitutional requirements, what prevented the centre and the Prime Minister from taking the elementary precautions needed to keep the situation under control?

If Indira Gandhi can spend a month touring Andhra and Karnataka and almost all her Cabinet members could be stationed in those states, what prevented her and her illustrious colleagues from making their presence felt in Assam?

Is Assam less important than Andhra or Karnataka? If half a dozen Central ministers could be sent to these southern states as her party observers with a hotline to 1 Safdarjang Road, what prevented her from taking similar steps in Assam?

The tragedy in Assam would have been less gruesome had some of her seasoned and senior colleagues been posted in various districts of the state, even at the risk of their lives. That would have given them an additional chance to prove their loyalty to their leader, if not to the country.

How little importance was attached to bleeding Assam can be seen from the fact that the Prime Minister spent hardly two days in the state and that too in the predominantly 'immigrant' areas.

The only Cabinet minister who was made to stay on was Abdul Ghani Khan Choudhury for obvious reasons. According to reports this brash Bengali added fuel to the fire by concentrating only on the Bengali and mostly Muslim electorates and making statements like "Muslims will be thrown back into Bangladesh if they did not vote for the Congress". The Congress completely ignored the Assamese in the Brahmaputra valley.

But why blame the Congress alone? The CPM, which has planned to 'communise' the whole North-East exploiting the situation, has been concentrating only on the Bengali Hindus. They have come to recognise the CPM, with its hold on Bengal, as their saviour. The Marxists are definitely playing an opportunist and reactionary role.

They were more keen to hold the elections 'at any cost', as their chief spokesman EMS Namboodiripad declared from Cochin thousands of miles

away from the scene of carnage. He did not have the guts to be amongst his suffering Bengali Marxists followers and was content to remain in the safe sanctuary of Kerala. "The violence in Assam," he said, "is a challenge to parliamentary democracy. Unless the fact that Assam is a multi-linguistic and multi-ethnic state is recognised by the Congress, BJP and the Janata, the basic problem cannot be solved."

EMS cannot deny that the alienation between the Assamese and the Bengalis is largely the contribution of the CPM which has been functioning on a vicious theory that the Bengalis in this region have been its preserve, its vote bank.

It ignored the Bengali Muslims because, despite its efforts to win them over they thought Indira Gandhi can give them better protection. They may have to change their opinion after the Nellie massacre, where the victims were Muslims.

Nellie was not a communal killing. The tribals who hacked them to death in the most merciless manner could have done the same thing to the Hindu Bengalis too had they been within their firing range.

In that hapless state it is pressure on land, on property, on jobs and on the ownership of economic resources. The Bengalis have the best of the land, property and jobs.

The army is immediately needed to prevent further ethnic and communal killing. The 'election' was a farce and the elected Assembly will have no democratic sanctity. And if the newly 'elected' legislators insist on sitting in the House, they are bound to be the targets of the assassins.

The solution lies in the dissolution or suspension of the Assembly and the re-imposition of President rule—but not Prakash Malhotra's. It is the army which will have to administer the state and save from further bloodshed and anarchy. Ultimately there has to be a negotiated solution to the Assam problem. But that is a far cry.

Current, 26.02.1983.
pp. (1 + 3)

We'll implement the accord—Hiteshwar Saikia

Unassuming, polite, urbane and unruffled by the storms which have been blowing over Assam: That's Hiteshwar Saikia for you. Despite having one kidney, donated by his brother, and poor health, he is always on the move and leads a simple, frugal life. Confident of getting an absolute

majority, it was at his insistence that the centre introduced the Citizenship Act which assures the minorities of their full rights, except the right to vote for 10 years. Excerpts from an interview on November 27.

The Congress and the AGP are both contesting with the accord as the major issue. What is the dividing line between the two.
The accord was signed jointly by the AGP leaders, the government of Assam and the government of India in the presence of Prime Minister Rajiv Gandhi. The accord is fully supported by us. We approve of all its clauses. We're sincerely trying to implement it. I can tell you that some of its provisions are to be given by the state government and some by the centre. I made a public announcement about two months back that those of the Assam government would be disposed before the elections.

Before the elections.
Yes. And I'm proud to tell you that 99 per cent of the accord provisions have been implemented.

The centre part is still left.
They are in the processing. Some of it has already been implemented. I hope the rest will follow soon.

Does this mean you are getting full co-operation of the centre.
Naturally.

AGP leaders allege that the Congress is not sincere about the accord, that they will go back on it if they win the elections.
It's impossible. I've just told you that the Assam government's role is already over.

They allege that Ghani Khan Choudhury gave a speech against the accord in Cachar.
Not exactly. What he said was that the Congress government should implement the accord fully, seriously and sincerely as it was meant to give justice to the people of Assam and that only through its implementation could the Congress come to power.

AGP leaders say that in the beginning, you had some misgivings about the accord. You were not happy, has your own view about it.
That's not true. The accord was shown to me long before it was signed. And I had approved of it.

But I think you had some apprehensions about the minorities and spoke to Rajiv Gandhi about making provision for them.
All I said to the centre was that the accord deprived some people who

came to Assam between 1966 and 1971. The Home minister and others told me that they wouldn't lose any rights. I wanted something to this effect in writing from the centre.

Have these been incorporated into the Citizenship Bill.
Yes.

Were you consulted while the Bill was being drafted.
I was informed about it.

The AGP leaders say they weren't consulted and want to know why.
I don't know about that. It's for the government to decide. The Bill is not a part of the accord. In any case, the latter itself says that the people who came to India between 1966 and 1971 will be disenfranchised. But there had to be some provisions whereby they could make out a living here. The accord doesn't say that they will be deported, only disenfranchised. Therefore a Bill was necessary.

By an act of Parliament.
Yes.

So the Bill will help the foreigners.
Yes. They will be able to earn a livelihood, go to court, get passports. It's all so important you see. And they are happy about it.

What about the AGP.
I think they will agree with it as time passes by.

The accord has reportedly given a fillip to communal and regional elements. The AGP is a regional party, the UMF a communal one. Do you agree.
The accord has helped restore peace and normalcy to the state. For me, it has meant a tremendous boost. The misgivings of others could be anything.

Do you think the accord will be followed should, sometime in the future, more people come to the state from Bangladesh or any other neighbouring country.
We won't allow anyone else to come. We are agreed that foreigners who came here after 1971 will be deported.

What are the reactions of the Bengali population.
Initially there were differences, but now they are all right.

Do you fear violence during the polls.
There may be one or two incidents. But there cannot be any large-scale violence. We'll take every precaution to prevent untoward incidents.

Will the Citizenship Bill mollify the minorities.

I'm told they now understand the ramifications of the accord, and are happy.

You say that the minorities are not against the Congress, but against the accord.

They were before the Bill was passed. Now they support the accord.

What about the UMF.

I don't think the Front will pose any problems for us.

Is the Front communal or regional.

It comprises ethnic, regional and linguistic people, so it cannot be called communal. It has Manipuris, Muslims, Bengalis, Nepalis—all are there.

What are the issues aside from the accord.

Development.

Bhrigu Phukan says that he favours a federal set-up under which defence, finance and external affairs alone should be with the centre, the state would look after the rest.

We oppose this.

Some congressmen say there has been massive bungling in the distribution of tickets. Even the PM accepts this. How are you going to retrieve the situation.

There have been two or three such cases. It was inevitable, given the large number of applicants.

Why have you dropped 39 sitting MLAs.

They don't have winning chances.

What about those who have been given tickets.

Most will win.

Who is this person who the PM denied a ticket at the eleventh hour.

One Dr. Bishen Shastri.

Why did he get it in the first place.

His case hadn't been examined.

Aren't congressmen who have been denied tickets discontented now.

I don't think so. There may be a very few such men.

Have congressmen then closed ranks and stopped the infighting.

Yes.

What about the rebel candidates.

I'm told there are only 46 of them in the fray.

What if they win.

They won't.

If the Congress does not get an absolute majority, will it go in for a coalition government.

I can't say anything about that right now. I'm confident we are going to get an absolute majority.

How many seats do you expect the party to bag.

I cannot give the exact number. But we will definitely get the majority.

Current, 07.12.1985.
pp. (1 + 3)

Assam is in trouble

With the explosive situation in Kashmir and regular killings in Punjab, the gravity of the ethnic violence in Assam has almost missed national attention. Reports trickling out of that border state indicate that Assam is another Kashmir in the making. While the brutal assassination of industrialist Surendra Paul by the extremists of the United Liberation Front of Assam, the non-Assamese in the Brahmaputra valley is in great panic and if this kind of selected violence continues it will inevitably lead to a mass exodus of these people paralysing the state's economy.

The sudden spurt in Bodo violence after a lull of four months and a few days before the crucial fifth round of the tripartite talks on the Bodo problem in New Delhi reflects the hardening attitude of Upendranath Brahma, leader of the All Bodo Students Union. The Bodo militants have succeeded in cutting off direct link between the North-East and the rest of the country by blowing up the main road bridge over river Manas. They have been blowing up rail tracks and bridges in upper Assam with casualties rising to 60 innocent lives. Though the ULFA and the ABSU have different aims the mode of their attaining the goal is the language of the gun.

The ULFA is seeking to cut off Assam from the rest of the country and declare it an Independent state while the ABSU wants an autonomous Bodoland. The sources of their arms supply is however the same. Sophisticated Chinese arms are openly smuggled from across the Burmese border.

The ULFA remains a mysterious organisation. It has in a way inherited the legacy of Asom Gana Parishad which now rules the state. Prafulla Mahanta's movement had begun with the slogan of Assam for Assamese

and ended by capturing power after much violence and destruction. As the AGP did in late 1970s the ULFA too has caught the imagination of the people specially in the rural areas. It kills opponents and protects those who support it. Its reformist role is appreciated by the people who without fear give refuge to the ULFA cadre, keep its supply lines open and generously donate money to its organisers.

The ULFA, supported by the people, runs a parallel government in most districts. They admire its reformist activities such, as closing down of the wine shops, running and controlling of the local schools and helping the old and the weak. Its leaders are a kind of local Robin Hoods who fight only against the 'exploiters', the police and the administration. The police turn a Nelson's eye to their activities while the district level *babu*s lend them a helping hand. The AGP cadre too extends its sympathies to them. Central intelligence men posted in Assam suspect heavy Naxalite infiltration in the ULFA rank and file though so far Naxalite leader had identified himself with the movement.

Mahanta's government is plainly ill-equipped to face the grave situation. Its police does not have modern arms and its communication system is not worth the name. With its heavy commitment in Kashmir and Punjab, the centre is not in a position to rush para-military forces to the rescue of Mahanta. He also faces difference of opinion and approach in his government and the party. While he is for firm action against the ULFA and the ABSU, his Home minister Bhirgu Phukan favours some sort of political approach. He has been trying to establish a dialogue with the second rank of the ULFA activists. In the process the government has become less effective and the police and the bureaucracy appear helpless.

The centre will have to come to the AGP government's aid before it is too late. Mahanta had discussed the issue with Prime Minister V.P. Singh during his last meeting with him in New Delhi. He was promised total support after wide-ranging discussion on the eve of the tripartite meet in the third week of this month. The Prime Minister may even visit Assam after the talks for an on the spot study of the situation. He has to act swiftly. He can ill afford another Kashmir in a far off state which is a window to the North-East.

Current, 21.04.1990.
pp. (2)

C. Kashmir—It is a Human Problem

Conspiracy in Kashmir

Violent demonstrations are all too familiar in Kashmir. What happened last week in that valley of unparalleled beauty was a part of a sinister conspiracy hatched by pro-Pakistani elements to sabotage its process of normalisation of economic, political and secular atmosphere. It was instigated by a mauled, frustrated Prime Minister of Pakistan, Zulfiqar Ali Bhutto.

Mr. Bhutto's hirelings in this sensitive state and precious limb of the country were controlled and commanded by Mir Waiz Maulvi Farooq, who thrives on his rabid anti-Indianism. Strangely enough, the main target of Maulvi Farooq and his mentor is Sheikh Abdullah whose explicit loyalty to India and commitment to Kashmir's accession has robbed the Pakistani leader of 'legal, religious and moral' claim over Kashmir.

There is an enemy within. Certain elements in the Kashmir Congress have also launched a systematic attack on Sheikh Abdullah and Chief minister Syed Mir Qasim to pollute the spirit of détente and the successful efforts to bring back the Lion of Kashmir to the national fold.

These turncoats are unwittingly acting as Mr. Bhutto's stooges. They feel that with the re-emergence of the Sheikh as the national voice of Kashmir their synthetic secularism will no more be a paying proposition.

They maintain a close liaison with Maulvi Farooq and provoke him to cut the Sheikh to his normal size. Maulvi Farooq's hired *thug*s had attempted to disrupt Id prayers and prevented the Sheikh from delivering his traditional address to the congregation. They have hurled shoes on the pulpit, fought duels, snapped power connections and tore off the decorations.

The state government should have nipped the trouble in the bud by apprehending the known disruptionists. Maulvi Farooq's complicity needed no further proof and the least the Kashmir government could have done was to show him the way across the border. Kashmir has had too many agent-provocateurs and a time has come when none should be tolerated. The policy of liberalisation is meant for only those elements whose loyalty to the country is unquestioned. But to enable Maulvi Farooq

to misuse this new trend is a gross violation of the very concept of this much appreciated move.

It is beyond doubt that only Sheikh Abdullah is capable of turning the tide in Kashmir. He is the right answer to Mr. Bhutto, his local agents and those Kashmiris who want to bargain with India. His statement that "we acceded" to India after signing the Instrument of accession at "our own free will" and that there was no question of changing the present status of Kashmir should be taken as his final opinion. What the state government can and should do is to strengthen his hands, extend him the political and moral support he needs.

With these forthright declarations the accession of Kashmir is no longer an issue with the Sheikh. The Kashmir Congress policy of isolating him has also boomeranged and the attempts to frustrate Mr. Mir Qasim's policy to restore his honour and national prestige will also meet the same fate. The theory that "surrender" to the Sheikh would mean the end of the Congress in the valley is absurd. In fact, the writ of the Congress in the valley does not extend beyond a few ineffectual individuals. It needs a total overhaul, infusion of fresh blood, and a certain amount of boldness and courage to fight back the quislings.

The Congress position is still worse in Jammu where a handful of congressmen have surrendered to the communalist and fascist forces. They did nothing to prevent the recurrence of violence in this hot-bed of anti-integration intrigues. They lack the moral fibre and political commitment to sustain the forces of secularism. Some of them have been too long in power and it is time they are forced to make way for more dedicated men with larger commitment. They have developed a vested interest in the perpetuation of political tension in the state.

Kashmir is the most heavily represented state in the centre with five members in the Council of ministers. Their paralysis during times of crises is a pathetic commentary on the lack of co-ordination between them and the state government. Issuing appeals for peace from their sanctums of New Delhi proves their tenuous commitment to the problems of the state. It is time they establish greater rapport with the Chief minister in his task of boosting Sheikh Abdullah's moral authority to expose and fight pro-Pakistani *thugs*.

Current, 24.11.1973.
pp. (1 + 20).

Sheikh defends 'black law' we have done the right thing

The Public safety ordinance, branded as Kashmir's Black Law, has raised a storm in the country. But it has not caused even a ripple in the serene waters of Dal Lake.

The valley has taken the ordinance with rare equanimity. It has not made the slightest dent in Sheikh Abdullah's unparalleled popularity. He remains the Sultan, the uncrowned King of the Kashmiris.

His opponents have not yet recovered from the stunning blow of their ignominious defeat in the last Assembly elections.

The local press, with the exception of one or two papers specially the daily AINA (See Editor Shamin Ahmed Shamim's despatch on page 15), has adopted a neutral posture.

The avalanche of criticism in the national press and also by top political leaders including Janata Chairman Chandra Shekhar has almost been ignored in Srinagar's official circles. But some senior ministers including D.D. Thakur admit that his government should have taken the state and the country into confidence while promulgating the Ordinance.

In a private conversation, Thakur took great pains to explain his government's position.

But the Sheikh is unperturbed. He is basking in the glory of his electoral success. The people are behind him.

I drove with him from Srinagar to Anantnag and then to Achhabal. The 35 km route was lined with thousands of people waiting to glimpse the Sher-e-Kashmir who was elevated by President Sanjiva Reddy to "Sher-e-Bharat."

His sky-blue Mercedes was stopped by crowds every few kilometres and showered with rose petals. Men and women jostled one another to kiss his right hand which he extended through the car window. The limousine was flooded with petitions. The common demand was roads, electricity, schools and hospitals. And the Sheikh kept promising to do his best to provide these things.

The whole Cabinet with top officials accompanied him to Achhabal town where he held a day-long court with local representatives discussing the plans and problems of the district. This procedure was new to Kashmir. His lieutenant, Mirza Afzal Beg, called it "taking the government to the people."

Despite a massive heart attack recently, the 74-year old Sheikh appeared as fit as a hatu. He showed no signs of fatigue that evening when I met him and Thakur for our interview lasting nearly two hours. His eyes retained their sparkle and his laughter echoed with the strength of a man in power.

The Public Safety Ordinance has taken the country by surprise. It is described as a Black Law, a mini-Emergency and a draconian measure to curb all freedoms. The national press has attacked it and not spared you. Political leaders including Chandra Shekhar have condemned it. Was it at all necessary?

Yes. The criticism is based on misunderstanding, lack of understanding. There are people who criticise us as a matter of habit. They have eyes but they cannot see. Whatever you tell them they will say they are right. I cannot convince them because they do not want to be convinced.

But I do admit that there are people who honestly feel we have committed a mistake in issuing the Ordinance. But if they come to Kashmir they will understand the situation and agree that whatever we have done is right.

The Ordinance has to be viewed in the context of the peculiar situation existing here. This is the mildest and almost human piece of preventive law issued since 1974. The old laws were harsher and stringent. They existed because the situation needed them. It was necessary to have them.

But was the Ordinance necessary after Emergency and specially after your massive victory?

The MISA was applied to us during Emergency through the DIR. This means Emergency affected us only through DIR. After Emergency the DIR lapsed and with it went the MISA. Kashmir is the only state which has no MISA though the rest of the country still has it.

I'am asking you about the necessity of this Black Law. It is stringent. It smacks of fascism.

(The Sheikh was not provoked: he smiled faintly perhaps recalling his long years of detention.)

After the DIR lapsed we were left with no laws to deal with infiltrators, anti-social elements, spies and saboteurs. There was a vacuum and naturally we had to come up with some legal measure to meet the situation.

[The Public Safety Ordinance was promulgated to replace (1) The J&K Public Security Act; (2) The J&K Security Rules; (3) The Emergency Provisions (Continuance) Ordinance; (4) The J&K Preventive Detention

Act; (5) The J&K Customs Act; and (6) MISA: and (7) Defence and Internal Security of India Act—all of which were inoperative as of either May 1976 or Sept. 1977.

The normal laws cannot deal with the extraordinary situation in Kashmir where "saboteurs and spies are a class of offenders by themselves". The authorities are not interested in merely punishing them but to prove their inks, modus operandi, contacts and channels of communication.

Such probes can be conducted only in secretary. Under normal laws the offenders would be bailed and could continue their anti-national activity.

The new law, according to government sources stands shorn of all the rigours of the old laws. The grounds of detention will be communicated to the detenue except in specific cases where the facts forming the basis of the grounds of detention need not be informed and this conforms to Article 22 (5) & (6) of the constitution .

In Kashmir government had discussed the new enactment with Central officials and they had agreed on the need for such a measure.

Some 40 provisions of the Public Security Rules (1946) are not incorporated in the new law. In several parallel provisions the punishment stands reduced from three years to two months. For insurance, "unauthorised entry using force" would get seven years under the old law but today the same offence gets three months.

Banned periodicals can make a representation to the government within 10 days and the government must take a decision in 21 days. If the petition is rejected they can approach the High Court. On the other hand, the old J&K Customs Act (1901) could ban papers "for any period without assigning any reason."

Rule 34 of the J&K Public Security Rules (1916) empowers the government "to direct the editor, printer or publisher of any newspapers containing any prejudicial report to abstain from editing such paper and deposit Rs. 5,000 as security with the government. "The new law has no such provision. But another clause which exists forces an editor "to disclose the name of any person concerned in the making of any prejudicial report in a prescribed document and to deliver the document to the competent authority. "The punishment for failure to do this has been reduced from three or two years."]

Did you take the centre into confidence?
The Home minister said it was not necessary to consult them.

Was a copy of the ordinance sent to the centre?

No. We are not bound to. But we had appraised the centre of the situation. We had told them that the DIR was about to lapse and that we would have new laws. We tried to introduce the law in the last Assembly session. A draft was tabled but it couldn't be taken up due to some other pressing matters.

The Ordinance came as a bombshell.

You can say whatever you like because you're in Bombay and not in Kashmir. The situation in Kashmir is different. The state has long, sensitive international borders. Ours is the only state which has been in conflict for the last 30 years.

We have seen three wars. Armies are still posted on the borders. Pakistan is obviously interested in our defence installations. There's infiltration.

Have you caught any spies or infiltrators?

Yes, only the other day 14 of them were caught. Now, tell me under what law should I deal with them? We have defence installations and Prohibited Areas. They come to spy on them. Under what law should I arrest them? Under normal law I cannot detain them. They are foreigners.

There's instability in Pakistan and an explosive situation is developing on the borders. They may divert their attention to Kashmir to escape internal problems.

Sheikh Saheb, are you sure these laws will not be used against innocent people?

No. But they will be used against people who spread caste and regional hatred and teach violence. Newspapers which indulge in fanning these feelings will also be kept under scrutiny.

Some other democratic methods can also be used, dialogue or persuasion . . . .

I do agree.

Your curbs on the press appear more draconian than they were during Emergency.

No. That is wrong. The present law is much milder. If we curb a newspaper it has the right to appeal within 10 days and the government has to give a decision in 21 days and if the petitioner is not satisfied he can go to the High Court in Srinagar.

The High Court may take months to decide.

Well, it's upto the High Court.

The impression is that you want to silence the critics.

No. I welcome constructive criticism.

Who is to decide whether the criticism is constructive?

I have to decide that. And if I take action against them they have a right to appeal first to the government and then to the High Court.

But there's total peace in Kashmir. The situation has improved a great deal in your state after your victory. There are no signs of subversion . . . .

There's a section in the Ordinance which deals with militant drills . . . .

Thakur: The RSS. It teaches young boys how to stab. How can we make peace with them?

Sheikh: Yes, they teach them how to stab, to use the lathi. There are Ananda Margis also who teach how to kill.

Thakur: The militants in the RSS and the Jamat-e-Islami can cause a lot of trouble. We have to prevent this. We have to preserve public order. Ours is a border state, a sensitive area and all these things have to be taken care of.

Are you prepared to modify these laws?

Thakur: The Ordinance will be before the House in three months and it has to be passed.

It will be passed because you have a massive majority.

Sheikh: There are certain laws which are repugnant but we have to face a special situation in Kashmir. If you give us any other remedy to deal with situation we'll use it. Give me the remedial measures to deal with the situation. How am I to deal with such things?

Thakur: The ordinary law, the Penal Code can help the government in dealing with the situation to a certain extent. A man is arrested and a bail order is passed by a magistrate within 24 hours. He is again at large to continue his activities.

Some of your cabinet colleagues indicated that they were open to amendments regarding the Press section of the Ordinance.

Sheikh: There are some sections which cannot be amended. Especially the declaration of the source of information. You say that as a professional journalist, it is unethical? Alright, then you must accept the responsibility and take the punishment.

But the source is never divulged in our profession.

Then you accept the responsibility unless you reveal the source.

It is worse than MISA.
Whether it is MISA or not, show me how to control the situation. I'm not here only to defend the small state of Kashmir. It is a question of the defence of the whole country. No government can function without such laws. The centre has not yet done away with MISA. Tomorrow if trouble starts you'll ask me if I was sleeping.
You mean you have taken anticipatory steps?
Yes. Who knows what will happen tomorrow on our borders? We never used or misused MISA. Even during Emergency. We ourselves have suffered long incarcerations. We firmly believe in all freedoms and especially the freedom of the press.

During Emergency I firmly rejected Mr. V.C. Shukla's advice to use censorship and curb the press. Emergency was hardly felt here.

Current, 19.11.1977.
pp. (1 + 2)

The Shiekh is dead...
long live Abdullah

Srinagar: Farooq Abdullah has the makings of a Gaddafi. He is impatient. He is determined. He would brush aside dead convention, appeal to the people directly. Barring the constraints of democracy he would not allow anything to stand in his way. He must act, act fast to give a clean administration to his state.

He has picked up corruption as his Enemy Number One. He wants to begin by rooting it out.

"My blood boils at the sight of them", said the handsome, debonair Chief minister about the corrupt, casting wishful eyes at the grey mountains across the Dal Lake. "They are the main cause of Kashmir's miseries. It's time they are shown their place. They should be handed over to the people."

Do you want them to be lynched?
Not exactly. But they should be punished.

As he was talking to me, a huge crowd waited outside. "It is not possible here. Let us go somewhere else, I must talk my heart out to you."

We drove to the Oberoi Palace hotel. He pulled up two chairs in the lush green lawns. We sat under a chinar tree peopled with chirping birds.

"Ayub, I'm a changed man. I'm transformed. The responsibility has clustered my mind with ideas. My mind has become a storm centre of ideas. I was not able to sleep last night. Look at my eyes. But I shall not take rest."

While he was talking to me in the seclusion of the Oberoi, his ministers and officials were frantically searching for him. Two hours later he had to go to the Raj Bhavan for the swearing in ceremony.

How can you head a Cabinet full of corrupt men? How can you begin your fight against corruption with this rotten team?

Yes, Yes. That's what I've decided while driving to this place. I will have an entirely new team with no black spots. I will shake the government, the party, and root out the corrupt. I will identify them. I won't bother about the courts. I will directly go to the people on television and tell them about the corrupt men. I will ask the people to take them over. God is with me. Nobody can hinder me in this jehad. I cannot rule with the corrupt as my colleagues.

The same evening Farooq threw the bombshell at a huge public meeting held to mourn the death of his father. The multitude danced with joy as he announced that he had decided to do away with the entire Cabinet and form a brand new government of people with absolutely clean records.

"From today my battle against corruption begins. I seek cooperation. May God give me strength." The old are gone, he told the frenzied crowd, "but watch the new ones with binoculars. If you tell me they are misbehaving I will throw them in the Dal Lake."

This was enough to win over the hearts of Kashmiris. Farooq's political future was made at this public meting. It was instant rise to popularity matching his father's.

People kissed and hugged each other when he threw another bombshell. "From today it will be an open government. If I shut my doors on you, come to me through the windows. I belong to you. The Sher-e-Kashmir has given me to you as his amanat." Farooq sang with the mob, his body shaking with emotion.

As though this was not enough to make his audience dizzy with joy, he took away their breath by announcing at the top of his voice: "Anyone who wants to remove Article 370 will first have to remove me." The crowd was choked with emotion.

I was wonder struck. A few hours ago he was telling me. "Please Ayub, don't ask me too many political questions. I am a novice. I am a toddler in state craft."

But at the Iqbal Park public meeting he was an entirely new man, exactly a la Gaddafi. Watch this man.

It is difficult to fill the void created by the death of the Sheikh. You have many qualities of your father and the people in your state and in the country expect that you too would attain a new stature. With the death of the Sheikh an era is over, a chapter of history is closed. Now a new era begins—the Farooq era. How do you assess your sudden ascendancy to power.

Well, it is not only difficult but impossible to fill that void. The void left by Mahatma Gandhi or Jawaharlal Nehru could not be filled, similarly the vacuum left by the Sheikh will also not be filled. But as you know when they look at Madam Gandhi they see Jawaharlal Nehru in her eyes. Similarly here in Kashmir and in the rest of India, people will look for Sheikh Abdullah in my eyes. That will be one consolation the people will have that I will continue the work that he was engaged in since 1931. And I hope that I will be able to come up to his expectations so that when my time comes and I have to go and meet him there, I will be able to tell him. "I have done my bit towards completing the mission you had left for me."

What is your mission.

My mission is to strengthen the legacy of communal harmony which my father has left. Communal elements in the country are raising their heads, separatists are raising their heads. My greatest ambition is to see the India of Mahatama Gandhi's dreams and *Shere-e-Kashmir*'s dream—that people of all religions and also those who don't believe in religion live together in peace and harmony.

Secondly, I am sure the separatist tendencies will die their natural death. But we have to work hard to make every Indian feel that he is very much a part of the nation.

Do you mean the Kashmir nation.

No, when I talk of Kashmir, it is as a part of India. I think it is necessary I talk in terms of India rather than Kashmir alone. I am no doubt a Kashmiri like my father. I love this land, I love its people, its mountains, its rivers, its ups and downs. But I feel at the same time that I am part of a great nation the Indian nation. And therefore I cannot live without India and India cannot live without me.

It has to be an integrated living, is it not?

Yes, it has to be and I hope in my lifetime I will be able to achieve what my father has left me to achieve.

Will you in this process also attempt to foster greater affinity between the people of India. Kashmir and the rest.

Yes, I will. One of the greatest tragedies of our life has been that many did not understand Sheikh Abdullah till his death. But Sheikh Abdullah continued to tell them we are a part of India. We may be Muslims, we may be in majority in the state, but we have Hindus, Sikhs, Buddhists, Harijans, Christians and Parsis living here. We are like a mini India. And let us give them a feeling of security and safety. To all communities and once this security is achieved, the fears which people hold here in the rest of this country will die.

I agree that the Sheikh symbolised secularism and it has taken roots here. But would you also take some steps towards the economic development of the state.

The first task I would like to take up is to uproot political corruption. My lifetime's dream is to see that we have men who can be identified as clean. My ambition will also be to try and expose corrupt politicians and put them on trial before the people.

Politicians in your own party.

Any party including mine. It is not my task alone. It is a task for the entire nation. Here, in a small way, I shall try and see to it that honest politicians are promoted.

Do you have enough honest politicians.

I will try and see. We may have less of them but when honest people are given positions, when honest people are given party tickets, many more honest people will come forward.

How will you identify the corrupt politicians? What will be the process, the machinery.

The people, the people will be the ones who will tell who is corrupt and who is not.

Are you planning to start people's courts.

No. I will receive the complaints of the people and I will have a cell, a sort of anti-corruption cell. I shall investigate in detail where is truth and where it is not. And will dispense justice there and then.

Will you carry your anti-corruption campaign against your ministers also.

I tell you, not only my ministers but my party workers and officials of my government from the smallest to the biggest.

It is a kind of a Jehad you seem determined to launch against corruption. Do you think you will be able to succeed.

Insha Allah!

This is your determination. But when it comes to enforcing it, you will face an entirely different situation. The whole machinery, the whole system has gone corrupt. It is reeking with corruption. How will you be able to fight it? I am not discouraging you, I fear it will be a very grim battle.

There is a saying that if you tread the path of honesty with courage and determination, god himself will guide and help you. That is how I am sitting today in this chair. It is not because of my doing. It is because god willed it. He will send me those men who will be a pillar of strength to me.

I appreciate your trust in god. But the question is of the corrupt official machinery. If you turn out all the corrupt you-will be left with nobody to run your government and your party.

Yes, I will. But for god's sake don't tell me that there are not enough honest men going around.

There may be enough men, but the corrupt would not permit them to come in.

It is for me to root out these corrupt men and get the honest in.

How soon will you begin this process.

Insha Allah! Soon. Very soon.

Will this be your first step.

You will soon start seeing my steps.

The National Conference was single-handedly created by the Sheikh. It was totally identified with the personality of your father. With him no more, what shape will you give to the National Conference?

As the people will look for Sheikh Abdullah in me, similarly they will look up to the National Conference as the creation of that man, and sustain it with their lives.

Will you include fresh blood in the Organisation.

Yes, the doors of the National Conference are open to everyone. When I took over as President of the party last year I announced that all honest, good and hard working people can join it.

Are you also planning to move nearer to the Congress.

It may take me nearer to any party.

I am asking you specifically about the Congress.

Yes, why not.

Will you form a coalition with the Congress when the time comes.

Well, a coalition is not the need of the hour. Understanding is the thing that is needed. They are in opposition. I am in power. If we have an understanding and if I continue to do good, they would support me.

If they want to share power with you.

I do not need them. I have enough. I have 46 members in the Assembly.

I am talking of the future. The process of reconciliation between these two major political parties of the state.

I will have to see how things develop. This is a decision I cannot take alone. I will have to consult my party and the Congress leaders will consult their party and their High Command.

In the Congress in Kashmir there are two factions—one is pro-Sheikh and Farooq led by Mir Qasim and the other anti-Sheikh dominated by Mufti Mohammed Sayeed. Similarly, in your party also there are two groups—one is for reconciliation with the Congress and the other is extremist, that is anti-Congress. How will you be able to create a combination of all these elements?

As you have pointed out, the National Conference symbolised Sheikh Abdullah. I say Indira Gandhi symbolises the Congress. And so long as my understanding with her continues to remain good—she understands me and I understand her—I don't think I have to worry about anything.

I understand you have established extremely cordial relationship with Indira Gandhi.

Yes, I hope it continues and I am sure it will be strengthened further in the days to come.

You also seem to have established good relations with Rajiv Gandhi.

Yes, I have a very good friendship with Rajiv Gandhi.

Do you have proper political understanding.

I have all sorts of understanding with him that one needs for the betterment of the country. Above all, we have family relationships. We may have political difference at some point of time but the family relations remain.

The National Conference also represented besides other things Kashmiri nationalism, what you call 'Kashmiriyat'. Will you like to broaden the precept of the National Conference and introduce some other elements which can make it a part of the national mainstream.

I will continue to work for *Kashmiriyat* as well as what I would call *'Hindustanism'*. I will strengthen bonds between *Kashmiriyat* and *Hindustanism.* And that can be achieved only if I have strength in my

own people. If I do not have strength here, can I stand from Bombay. Can I win an election in Delhi or somewhere else. It is not possible. I have to make my own home strong. It is only when I have my home strong that I can speak with power. So I have to have this strength, the Kashmiri strength.

If I get a quarter of the love and affection that they have shown for my father. I will be able to strengthen the bonds of love and friendship between the people of Kashmir and the rest of India.

In this process of reconciliation between your father and Indira Gandhi, Mir Qasim has played a significant role. He offered his Chief ministership to the Sheikh. And for the last two years he has been promoting the idea that the Sheikh was the real symbol of Kashmiri nationalism and that he should not be disturbed. It has had a positive impact. What will Mir Qasim's role be now.

I think this question should be posed to Mir Qasim Saheb. He is the one who should reply to this. As far as I am concerned, my love and affection for Mir Qasim Saheb will never die. The National Conference offered him the Rajya Sabha seat so that he could represent Kashmir at the centre. And I would have very much liked him to be a Central minister, so he could bridge the gulf between Kashmir and the rest of the country.

Will you now offer him the Lok Sabha seat from Srinagar.

I will offer him any seat that he wants. He is welcome to it. I am open to offer him anything. He has just to say what he wants.

He would not ask for it. He has his self-respect. It is for you as a younger brother to go to him and offer whatever you like.

It is as a younger brother that I had offered him the Rajya Sabha seat last year. The question is not that I won't offer. I think the country needs him and it should use him in a far more important way. I feel his policies are the same as the Sheikh's.

What will be your relationship with your brother-in-law, G.M. Shah?

They will be very cordial, I have always had good relations with him and I will continue to have good relations with him now.

Will you take him back in the government?

Let me form the government. I must have some time to think about it.

You have been taking a great interest in the problems of Muslims in India ever since you became an MP. After becoming the Chief minister of Kashmir will you continue this interest?

Yes. I will continue to hold the interests of the country's Muslims as dear to me. But I will also continue to suppress the separatist elements in my

own state. It is important for me to make all communities in India realise that Muslims too have played a vital role in the freedom struggle. They are Indians first Indians last. Their loyalties are only to India and therefore their rights which are no doubt preserved in the constitution must be respected in deed and action.

Will you fight for their rights.

I shall continue to fight for their cause.

What are the major problems. Can you identify them.

Their representations in services, which is insufficient. Second as I have seen recently in Jabalpur their conditions are depressingly bad. They don't have jobs in factories and public sector organisations. They are neglected in many spheres. They don't have enough education. Now they are worse than Harijans. The Muslims should also feel they belong to the national mainstream. I shall try and fight like my father to achieve these things.

One important contribution of the Sheikh was to give self-respect to the Kashmiris. Will you try to give self-respect to the Muslims of India.

I shall continue to tell them it is only by confidence in themselves and confidence in God that they will achieve what they had lost.

Are you, as a Muslim a reformist or a fundamentalist.

I am a reformist. I don't believe in fundamentalism. It is dangerous for secularism. Yes, I will continue to bring about reforms.

There is a lot of superstition and illiteracy.

Yes, I shall try to remove them. Education itself will bring about change. As you can see the revolution brought about by education now. Today you walk in any village, any city, you will see Muslim girls in salwar kameez going to schools and colleges.

Will you continue to fight against conservatism and pardha.

As a reformist, I will fight against all these evils and which are giving a bad name to Islam. At the same time I will try to bring out the good things in Islam which people seem to be forgetting.

Is there not too much of Islam in Kashmir while economic development programmes have been ignored. I think as a young, dynamic leader, you should give more economic content to your programmes and policies.

Yes, Ayub, I shall certainly work on those lines—industry, roads, etc.

May I say the major thrust of your programmes will be towards industrial development, besides fighting against corruption.

My major thrust will be on the economic and industrial front and also in the field of education because I must take the literacy rate high. Two vital

things for this state are health and education. If the people are more educated all the superstitions will automatically go.

Will you have more budgetary allocation for education and health.

Yes, they were less earlier. Now I will increase them. I would request the centre to give more money for these priorities.

What will be your approach to the controversial Resettlement Bill.

The Bill is with the Governor. It has not yet come back. And when it comes back, and we hear the points raised by the Attorney General and others we will take the next step. My father had already brought in Nani Palkhiwala and since I have just taken over I really don't know Palkhiwalaji's views or the points raised by the Attorney General. All these views I will put before the Party.

Will it be made a prestige issue?

Let me see the points first. The Bill is there. I would like to understand it myself, its implications and then only will I tell people what I want to do.

What will be your Party's attitude to the Bill.

Well, I will see what are their views and then I will project it to the nation. Tell the whole country.

If your people want this Bill, will you insist on it.

If my people want anything my life is theirs. If they want I will stand by the Bill. If the people want me to stand on anything I shall stand like a rock—like Sheikh Abdullah.

What will be your approach to the regional problem—the regional imbalances?

My father tried to reduce the regional imbalances which have been there for a long time. I will see to it these imbalances are completely wiped out.

What will be your attitude towards Dr. Karan Singh.

I have always been very friendly with him.

Do you think Karan Singh will try to emerge as the leader of the Jammu region where he has a great deal of influence.

Nobody can emerge as the leader of Jammu, Kashmir or Ladakh unless he has all the regions with him. I cannot become the leader of this state unless I have all the three regions with me.

Will you make extra efforts to win over Jammu. I feel Jammu was cool to the Sheikh.

I shall make no efforts in any direction merely to win them. My efforts will be to win my god. My god has shown me the path of doing justice to all.

You seem to be relying too much on god.
(Laughter).

Current, 18.09.1982
pp. (1 + 3 + 4).

Rajiv and I will work hand in hand—Farooq Abdullah

Farooq Abdullah is not made of the stuff most of his brand are. He is handsome, immaculately dressed, full of energy, unconventional, totally free from inhibitions. He is fired with the zeal of an evangelist. He lives in style with an English wife who keeps away from his politics. She looks after him "like a child".

Farooq has the makings of a first class politician though he says he is a novice in the "dirty game". He likes Rajiv Gandhi, and his wife Molin has found a good friend in Sonia.

He gave this interview early in the morning, while still in his sleeping suit, with his son Omar, a Senawarian, listening from his bed.

How do you feel being Chief minister once again. A sense of attainment, or a feeling of surrender.
I don't think it's a sense of attainment. Nor is it a feeling of surrender. What we have worked out is an interim arrangement. The final decision will be with the people. I feel when you are Chief minister you are totally alone. And then there is a so much to do it. That's what makes for frustration. One wants to get the things done, but finds it difficult to do.
What are your priorities as Chief minister.
My first priority is to bring about harmony between the regions of the state and between the people belonging to different religions. Then, I must give them the feeling that we are all part of the nation, we have to grow with the nation.
You mean a sense of belonging.
The sense of belonging which has been eroded in the past. I hope we will not have to go through those traumatic experiences again. I want to remove the poverty, the hunger, the disease, and take the light of education to every home. And finally, there must be industrialisation, side by side with beautification of the state, protection of the environment.

Do you have any major projects in mind.
Tourism is the most important. We always had tourism confined to a few months in a year, in the summer only. We want to make tourism a year-round affair. We have planned to encourage winter sports, that will draw more people.

Do you think there can be a permanent solution to poverty, for the time being. Don't you think tourism is a very fragile industry. Total dependence on tourism may not be good.
I agree with you. We should diversify. But we can't forget tourism. Diversification has to be in the Jammu region particularly. Where there is the railway. We can put up major industries there. In the valley we are trying to develop such industries as would not cause pollution. Electronic units, for example. We have some projects in hand.

Don't you think you are a misfit in Kashmir politics. You are modern in outlook, secular. But your people seem to be living in an antideluvian age. They are very religious, very conservative, very superstitious. You have strayed among them.
No. I don't think so. We have to battle against the current. The people may be conservative, backward. But there is also a ray of hope. There are a few forward-looking people also, they have been educated abroad. I think change is in the air.

Do you feel that, besides being a politician, like Shaikh Saheb you have to be an educator of the people.
I think the basic role of every politician in India is that of an educator. You've got to train them, you've got to change them.

Will you show enough courage to do that in Kashmir.
Inshallah. I have shown the courage already.

Will you modernise the education system, change the university and college curricula.
Yes, I must do that in a big way. Ours is the only state where education is totally free right up to the university level. I am going to change that. There should be free education only up to the 12th standard, further on they must pay for higher education. The state will look after the educational expenditure of only those who are brilliant, those who can contribute substantially to nation-building.

Your educated youth are becoming more and more religious, more and more fundamentalist. Look at most of the Jamaat-e-Islami boys, they are educated, intelligent, yet they have gone very fundamentalist and very

conservative. What is the reason.

The system of education has been wrong. They are educated and they have no job opportunities. So they are frustrated. Many of them have come from poor families. Their fathers, mothers have worked very hard, doing menial work as domestic servants to give them education. And today they have no job opportunity, so the frustration has sowed the seeds of corruption, job rackets. Politicians give jobs to relatives, to people they knew, or people who give them money. In this rat race, the poor are left out. These frustrated youth become easy prey to fundamentalism. There are enough fanatics to exploit their frustration, rouse their passions. This is the problem we are facing today, not only in Kashmir but even in the rest of the country.

Are you referring to people like Qazi Nisar.

No, people like Qazi Nisar are emerging not because they have anything to sell. They are mere products of propaganda. They are anti-national and they. . . .

How do you call them anti-national.

They, the Jammat-e-Islami and others, spread the lie that everything is greener on the other side of the hills. And our unemployed, frustrated youth fall for this kind of propaganda.

This word anti-national is very dangerous. How do you describe an anti-national.

I did not mean anti-national, I withdraw the word.

Do you know you were also described as anti-national.

Not only anti-national. Also Khalistani, pro-Pakistani, CIA agent, KGB agent.

You should not use the word anti-national.

I don't say anti-national. I say these people exploit the sentiments of the people by raising bogeys which are not in the national interest. We have done two things. One, we are creating job opportunities for as many people as possible. We are increasing the number of madarssa. We are trying to see that in these madarssas our children are given not only bookish knowledge but also a sense of participation. We are introducing programmes like reforestation around the school. The boys will be involved in that. And we want to interest them in the study of the good in every religion.

The Muslims need it too.

Of course. After the elections we hope the Muslims will understand it.

Kashmiri Muslim boys should know about other religions.
Exactly. And a Hindu should know what Islam is about. And this concept that Islam was spread by the sword . . .

You are not making them religious, you are going to make them understand religion.
Exactly. So that they understand what the other person's sentiments are.

Don't you think there should be a larger cross communication between the Kashmiri youth and the youth of the rest of India so that they can understand each other, they can come together.
This we do by arranging tours. Our students go out. Our NCC contingents have come to Delhi for the Republic Day parade. They will be visiting Rajasthan, UP, etc. This will be a big breakthrough for them to see what the nation is.

I come back to the political question. What is the secret behind your enviable relationship with Rajiv Gandhi. Is he not the same person who had got your dethroned.
Well, let us be clear on one point. Politics is a very dirty game, and those of us who do not know politics . . . .

You are a politician.
No, I don't think so. I am basically a doctor, a medical man. I am trying to see what politics is all about. The impression that I was fighting with the centre, I was creating all the problems, was totally misconceived, interested people spread that gossip.

Around Rajiv Gandhi you mean.
No, no. Around the previous government.

Around Indira Gandhi.
They created rifts between people. Rajiv is dreaming of a new India, a powerful India, with a totally modern outlook and wants to take the country into the next century as fast as possible. The question was if I and he continued on a confrontation course, we would not be able to build a strong India.

Then forces would emerge who would continue to weaken India, as in my part of the country. We noticed that not only Muslim fundamentalism but Hindu and Sikh fundamentalism too were becoming stronger. A puppet government was installed, a corrupt government.

It was installed by Rajiv Gandhi.
Whoever did it, I am not going to say who was responsible for it, I have no idea about it. But that puppet government created a lot of problems. If

we had not taken this turn about, we had not come nearer to each other, his dream my dream or the people's dream of a new India would remain unrealised.

Was it a mutual feeling, or you felt it that way.

No, no. I think we both felt it.

You had long discussions with him. What were the basic points you discussed.

We both felt that by remaining apart we would not be able to solve the problem of my state. And if turmoil persisted in the state, he would not be able to build the India of his dreams.

You think he appreciated your point.

He must have. We both agreed that we should work together for building a strong nation, a better nation, a nation, in which Kashmir comes out of the rut that it is in.

You want to continue the same tradition.

To continue Sheikh Saheb's tradition.

Why do you have to proclaim in almost every speech that Kashmir is an integral part of India and that accession is final. Is it necessary? For the last 40 years every Kashmiri leader has been proclaiming that.

It is not necessary as far as I am concerned. But it is necessary at times because the people of the state are constantly fed on false propaganda, that minorities are unsafe in Kashmir, that there are Pakistanis in Kashmir. I have to disabuse their minds of such propaganda.

Among Kashmiri leaders over the past 40 years, there are very few whose integrity and secularism has been doubted even by the worst Hindu communalists. Why do you then have to carry a certificate about clean intentions.

This certificate was perhaps necessary earlier. I don't think the situation warrants it now.

There is no need to carry a certificate. You are an Indian.

You will not see me carry the certificate any more.

How do you propose to spend the Rs. 1,000 crore bonanza. Was it an ad-hoc decision by Rajiv or a well thought out gesture to woo the people on the eve of elections.

The Prime Minister has been very kind. He has been kind in the sense that he was able to visit Kashmir in winter. We have been having severe snow this year, and this is the first time that a Prime Minister went to

Kashmir when we were in real trouble. And then he himself drove around on the streets. He saw the problems we have been facing. He saw the situation in the valley. He saw the poor power situation in the state. And he announced what the Planning Commission had already considered on the state's requests.

A member of the Planning Commission whom I spoke to only yesterday said the issue never came up before the Commission.

They had discussed it. And the Deputy Chairman of the Planning Commission was there at the Jammu meeting. To say that the Planning Commission has been bypassed is wrong. Some of the projects are on-going and money has been announced for them. Energy minister Vasant Sathe came to Kashmir long before the Prime Minister came. The Prime Minister has only given a thrust. He gave a thrust to Gulmarg also, he suggested the development of winter tourism.

I think out of Rs. 1,000 crore Rs. 600 crore would go to Pulasti. What about the rest.

Twenty-five crore go straightaway to the Uri project.

Something for education, something for roads, and things like that.

No. You see roads have come up.

There must be detailed allocation.

Yes. Some money is allotted for the Srinagar bypass, as also for the Sopore bypass. One of the major projects is in the Vaishnodevi area.

You have some plans for Ladakh.

One is afforestation. Next in importance is the Zojila road, how to make it possible. It remains closed for six months. The problem is to keep it open for as long as possible. Perhaps we need to cut a tunnel. The people of that region, now totally cut off for six months, must be rescued from this isolation.

How do you think this money will start coming in.

It is supposed to come over a period of years.

Have you appointed a committee to supervise the spending.

Yes. There were a series of meetings between central and state officials, including officers of the Planning Commission. Now we have a committee to monitor the expenditure.

Will you also raise local resources in your next budget.

Yes, we have to. That's the only way we can get on with the project.

Now you are almost a part of the Congress. Do you think the National Conference will one day merge with the Congress.

I think, Ayub, we must realise one thing. The Congress is a major national party. Mine is a regional party. There is no question of merger. Mutual understanding is what matters, what is necessary, what has been achieved.

Has the time come for the National Conference to shed its regional colour and become a larger national party.

Time is the only thing that will decide these things. As far as today's situation is concerned and for some years to come, the National Conference will remain the National Conference.

You mean you will be in better position to fight fundamentalism as National Conference.

I think so. It has got to be the frontline party for us. To fight the divisive, communal forces.

The National Conference stands for secularism, nationalism, democracy and socialism. The Congress party stands for secularism, nationalism, democracy and socialism. Where is the difference.

It is not a question of difference. One is a large river, the other a tributary.

You mean the National Conference is a tributary of the Congress.

Not only of the Congress, of the nation as a whole. There are a large number of small tributaries which flow into the vast river that is the Indian polity.

You will make common cause with the Congress in this fight.

NC will be the frontline force. And it will need backup support from the Congress, the impetus to go forward.

What is the reaction of local congressmen to your accord with Rajiv Gandhi.

You see, there are people in my party who are not happy. Similarly some congressmen too are not happy. But I am more concerned with the larger national interest.

There are unhappy groups in both the parties.

When the Accord produces results, removes regional disparities and brings about all-round prosperity, Inshallah, then these groups will realise that we are right.

How soon are you going to have elections?

I think very soon, may be in March. But the Election Commission has to decide.

What will be the shape of collaboration between the NC and the Congress.

We have to sit down and work it out.

Will you concede some seats to the Congress.

It is too early to say. My mind is working in many directions. But which direction is right I have yet to decide.

The impression is that you are not a typical politician. Now that you and Rajiv have become good personal friends . . . .

I think we have been friends all along, like Sheikh Sahab and Jawaharlal Nehru.

There was no personal rancour between them.

No. When Sheikh Saheb went to jail for so many years, he never lost Nehru's friendship. It is the same with me and Rajiv. I'll never lose that friendship.

Will you concede some seats to the Congress in the valley.

Why only the valley, there is Jammu also.

The Congress Party's main problem has been the valley, not Jammu. They have been winning in Jammu.

My problem also has been in the Jammu Hindu areas. If we both work well, I will no longer have any problem in the Hindu areas.

You will have no problem in seat adjustments with Rajiv Gandhi.

No.

Is there a possibility of reunion with Gul Shah.

No, there is no such chance. I rule it out. Because Gul Shah did not betray me, he betrayed the people. I was elected by the people. He was not elected by the people. He manoeuvred those MLAs, bought them up. He was a Trojan horse, true, but the misery he inflicted on the people can never be forgotten.

Why did the centre allow him to do that.

You should ask the centre.

A personal question. I understand Molin and Sonia have become good friends. Are the two foreign wives influencing their husbands.

They know each other they meet. What exactly is the level of their friendship they alone know. I have no idea about it. One thing common to them is that both do not interfere in politics.

Molin does not. What is your assessment of Sonia.

No, she does not either. I think she has got enough on her plate, she has a home to look after, children to look after. And you know, so many dignitaries come to India and have to be received and entertained. It's a big thing, a lot of work.

There is an impression that Sonia Gandhi is a major influence on Rajiv in decision-making.

I do not know, and I won't comment, but judging by my wife's situation, I think Sonia can't be different. Molin has so much on her hands, she has the home, the children . . . and the biggest child, perhaps, is myself, she has to look after me. You see, she has to look after a difficult child that I am. But Sonia has to look after not only her children, Rajiv included, she has to concern herself with the children of the nation as well. She does and I am proud of her.

So is Molin. I think she is a dedicated mother.

Totally dedicated. And the belief that they are conspiring is totally wrong.

But Molin is not always with you. Sonia is mostly with Rajiv Gandhi.

I think they have got to be together.

Comradeship or what.

No it's not. The tragedy is that I have a large family and he has just two children. I have four children and I have daughters. Three of them are daughters and I think the mother's influence is quite great on the daughters. Therefore, my wife feels that this is a difficult age and she should contribute as much to the development of those girls as possible.

Do you plan to play a role in national politics.

Every Chief minister has a role in national politics.

As an opposition leader, you had involved yourself in national politics. You convened the convention of opposition leaders in Srinagar.

That convention was actually meant to discuss centre-state relations. There was no confrontation with the centre.

Are you completely cut off from the opposition now.

They are my friends. But I will tell you one thing in politics, whether in power or out of power, I have one belief—that if you have friends, be they in the opposition or in the ruling party, they are friends. How can I say that Jyoti Basu is not a friend of mine? How can I say Hegde has not been a friend of mine? How can I say that Advaniji or Badal is not my friend or Barnala or N.T. Rama Rao is not my friend?

You have maintained your friendship.

I have always maintained it. I believe these people too realise that we are all working towards the same goal of building a strong India.

Do you still feel that you are a part of the opposition.

I feel I am a part of nation, whether in the opposition or in power.

Current, 17.01.1987.
pp. (6 + 7)

It's Quran vs Accord
Kashmir in the grip of frenzy

Muslim fundamentalism never has had such a bonanza in the valley. Its green flag flies on almost every hut and pole from one corner to the other defying the values, traditions and norms secular India has been trying to establish. It's a phenomenon which can be witnessed and reported if one is on the spot.

The Muslim United Front, which has hurled a massive challenge to the National Conference–Congress alliance, has taken Kashmir by storm.

The MUF is in fact a gift of the Rajiv-Farooq accord. It has killed the Congress with one stone and wounded the National Conference with the other. The Congress flag flies no more in the valley, and Farooq's red flag is being chased by MUF's green inch by inch.

It's door to door fight. The MUF candidates 48 of them—appear wearing a *kafan* with the Quran in hand and ask their Muslim voters to choose between the Quran and the Accord. They speak the language Farooq and his illustrious father Sheikh Abdullah have been doing for the last 40 years. Now Farooq preaches congressism, secularism and democracy. He tells his reluctant listeners: I want to strengthen Rajiv Gandhi's hand. I have buried the hatchet with him and I do not want to fight with the centre any more.

His followers hear him in utter disbelief. Only a year ago he was speaking exactly the language the Fundamentalist rabble-rouser Qazi Nisar is now speaking.

It's a crisis of conscience for the average Kashmiri voter. A storm is brewing in his mind. He is silent, glum, in a dilemma. He does not reveal his mind. But vote he will for whom only he knows. And if he does according to his conscience, we are in for a whale of a surprise.

The Congress flag no more flies over the valley. It is the first casualty of the Rajiv-Farooq accord. The second is Farooq himself. The third is the people of Kashmir. The beautiful valley is littered with political corpses. The weird scene is like a Salvador Dali painting.

It's a mini-Iran. Fundamentalism is sweeping like the plague, almost every young Kashmiri is bitten by the bug. Slogans like Alla-ho-Akbar (God is Great) and Nizam-e-Mustafa (Islamic order) rend the thin, crisp air. Religious fervour has descended like an avalanche on the mountains and the plains. The Kashmiris are a changed people. They are in the grip of fanaticism.

The saner elements have turned tail. They are overwhelmed, overawed. The nationalists, the secularists who can be counted on the finger tips have lost the elan, the will to accept the challenge, to fight back.

The fundamentalists have successfully turned the battle of the hustings into a Quran-Versus-Accord issue. Their 48 candidates appeared on stage at a mammoth Srinagar meeting wearing a Kafan (shroud) and holding the Quran in their right hand. Their young, firebrand leader, Qazi Nisar, asked the crowd: "It's a fight between the Quran and the Accord, whom would you vote?" The crowd shouted in unison: "Quran, Quran".

Qazi Nisar asked again. "Is it an oath?"

Answer: "Yes, Yes."

Each of the 48 candidates put up by the Muslim United Front (MUF), a combine of half a dozen fanatical groups, hopes to win by a big margin.

They may or may not win. All of them may win or most of them may lose. But it surely is a door to door fight, a most unpredictable election.

The MUF is a camouflage for the Jamat-e-Islami, the most fanatical organised body of Muslims with international links. It was crushed by Nasser in Egypt, Hafiz Asad in Syria, Qaddafi in Libya, Numeri in Sudan. King Khalid in Saudi Arabia, Saddam Hussein in Iraq, Ayub Khan in Pakistan. It now exists in no Muslim country. It exists in Kashmir, of course besides Pakistan.

I heard its leader Syed Ali Shah Geelani's election speech in a village near Sopore. He spoke in Urdu for my benefit, the crowd of about 3000 men and women listened to him in absolute reverence with eyes closed as though in a trance. It began to rain and continued right through to the finish—about 45 minutes—but no one left.

They were drenched and the cold winds were blowing from across the mountains. Geelani too stood without an umbrella and the more it rained the greater was his fervour. He is nearing 70. This is fanaticism.

A spell-binding orator, he speaks like an evangelist profusely quoting from the Quran. He raised four points and made it clear this was for the benefit of our friend from India, and he can write and quote me.

First, the accession of Kashmir to India is neither final nor irrevocable. The people of Kashmir are not a party to it and neither Pakistan nor India has a right to decide our fate, the accession was immoral, undemocratic and illegal.

The crowd responded with (Narae Takbir), Alla-ho-Akbar.

Second, we do not subscribe to the democracy they have in India. Islam does not recognise the rule of 51-49 per cent. We believe in Nizam-e-Mustafa. Our guide is the Quran and we follow the rules laid down in

it. We cannot deviate an inch from it.

Third, Secularism in India is a myth. It is fake and dangerous. The Muslims in India live at the mercy of the Hindus. We in Kashmir do not want to live in that kind of secular system.

Fourth, Socialism is the enemy number one of Islam. We cannot accept any other system because we have our own ordained in the Quran.

To prove his points he draws heavily from the Quran. By the time he finished the drenched audience looked as if they were heavily drugged.

In nearby Sopore the MUF's ideologue, Prof. Abdul Ghani Butt, was telling his frenzied election crowd: I love Pakistan, I love Pakistan: and people clapped and danced with joy, but it does not mean I hate India, the crowd stopped clapping.

This is south Kashmir—Sopore, Baramula, Pulwama, Anantnag—and it is known as Qazi Nisar territory. He has changed the name of Anantnag to Islamabad and no one dare call it by its old name. He seems to have mesmerised the younger generation of Kashmiri Muslims. He was an unemployed young man a year ago. Now he is Mirwaiz of south Kashmir and belches fire and brimstone.

When governor Jag Mohan banned the slaughter of animals on Janamasthami, Qazi Nisar defied the order by slaughtering three rams in the main market of Anantnag (or Islamabad). His writ runs there. The lower echelons of the police and bureaucracy in the area kiss his hands.

Qazi Nisar is not from the Jamat-e-Islami but he is the star campaigner. He is the darling of the crowd and a hero of the young unemployed youth.

The valley has 4,000 qualified, unemployed engineers, almost all of whom are Muslims. They have lost all hope of getting jobs and most of them think if Nisar comes to power he will get them jobs. He says if his party succeeds in capturing power it will bring a rule providing for jobs in proportion to the population. The valley has 95 per cent Muslims.

What will they do if he fails to get them jobs? "Then we will turn Kashmir into another Punjab, a young MUF militant shouted to me with clenched fist.

Qazi Nisar says whatever he is saying today had been said, in fact more vehemently, by Farooq Abdullah in 1983 and by his father Sheikh Abdullah earlier. He pulls out newspaper clippings and quotes from Farooq's speeches in 1983 when he was fighting a grim election battle against the Congress and Indira Gandhi.

Qazi Nisar reads out from a Farooq speech: Indira Gandhi is responsible for the tragedy of Punjab. She got the Muslims killed in Bhiwandi and

Assam. If she is not removed immediately India will disintegrate. She wants to change the special status of Kashmir but I will not allow it. I will fight tooth and nail against the centre and her autocratic ways.

Then Qazi Nisar quotes the choice invectives Rajiv Gandhi had used against Farooq at the time of his dismissal in 1984. He says if Farooq repeats all that he had said against the centre and the Congress he would withdraw from the election fray and support him.

Then he warns: If Farooq, his police and his bureaucracy try to rig the election blood will flow. The MUF has a suicide squad of 10,000 men who will not permit any tampering with the democratic process. All we want is a free and fair election.

The MUF has undoubtedly thrown a massive challenge to 40 year-old hegemony of the National Conference and its young leader Farooq Abdullah. Farooq is on the defensive fighting single handed, rushing from one constituency to another in his newly acquired red-and-white Westland chopper. He does draw big crowds but they appear to be like the swarms Indira Gandhi attracted in 1977. Impassive, they hear him, but do not respond as they did in 1983, when he fought and won against the Congress.

He finds it embarrassing when he tells his audience that he is fighting to strengthen the hands of Rajiv Gandhi.

He is overwhelmingly aware of the crisis of conscience among his activists and followers who have been fed on anti-congressism for years.

The Congress has been his party's most formidable enemy and the only body engaged in dislodging not only him but the National Conference itself. The historic animus between the two parties, their leaders and the rank and file remains unmitigated. Farooq finds it difficult to tell his workers to canvas votes for the Congress candidates.

The Congress leaders have completely withdrawn from the scene.

Farooq has conceded only six seats to the Congress in the valley and he knows most of them will be lost. In the Gund election rally he held aloft a poster of the hand, the Congress symbol, and asked the audience not to vote for the plough, his party's symbol, but the hand. "It is Rajiv Gandhi's hand, vote for it. Don't for heaven's sake put the seal on your hand but the hand on the ballot paper. The hand, the hand, the hand."

He went on repeating to the confused audience. At the end he was exasperated. He knew they will not put the seal on the hand.

But hand or no hand, plough or no plough, I must win this election, I am fighting it to preserve the unity of India. Win I will, come what may. Let me come back to power. I will pulverise these fanatics, the religious

bigots, he went on repeating his speech while driving the Gypsy.

The Congress and the National Conference are in a tight corner because the Rajiv-Farooq accord is taken to be between two individuals and not the two parties. The antagonism between their workers is too intense to remain unnoticed. Farooq has pushed aside all those supporters, some of them powerful and influential, who disagreed with him. Rajiv has sidelined leaders like Mufti Sayeed and Maulvi Iftikhar Ansari who refused to work under Farooq's leadership. Mufti was the PCC chief and Ansari was the leader of the Congress legislature party at the time of the Accord. Mufti was removed from the PCC presidentship and Ansari was denied the party ticket.

The result was the Congress collapsed like a pack of cards and its demoralised workers are now actively engaged in sabotaging the Accord.

The MUF is in fact the gift of the Accord. Instead of a triangular fight it is now a straight contest between Farooq and the fundamentalists. The Congress has vanished from the scene. And if it loses all the six seats in the valley it will be wiped out altogether.

Mufti Sayeed, known as a relentless fighter for years against fundamentalist and obscurantist forces, has withdrawn into his shell. He addressed only one election meeting and that too in his home district of Anantnag. And as he said he had come to Anantnag to clarify his position and some misunderstanding, the crowd jeered at him.

He immediately realised the folly and said: sorry, not Anantnag; it's Islamabad. Ansari too was on the stage, but did not speak.

It's gone case. My heart aches. I am seeing the disintegration of the Congress with my own eyes, an edifice which I had built up brick by brick. I fought on the streets, I was maligned, I was socially boycotted, I was branded as an Indian agent. I was humiliated. But I kept the Congress flag flying. Where is it now? The Mufti remarked with a lump in his throat.

Maulvi Iftikhar, who once roared like a lion as leader of the opposition in the NC dominated assembly, appeared like a bundle of bones when I visited him at his Srinagar residence. Lifeless, dumb, crippled with humiliation.

"I do not care whether I was denied the ticket. It was the unkindest cut indeed, but why this (accord) should have happened at the cost of the Congress?"

Like Mufti and Ansari, thousands of congressmen have a terrible feeling of being let down. They feel orphaned, leaderless and rudderless. At the desolate and deserted PCC office, an office-bearer remarked bitterly.

Have you come here to offer Namaz-e-Janaza and walked off.

Current, 21.03.1987.
pp. (1 + 8 + 9)

Kashmir is perched on a volcano

A couple of hours after I checked in at Hotel Broadway in the heart of the city my telephone rang. The conversation went like this: As-salam-elekum, I am speaking for the Kashmir Liberation Front. We have kidnapped Rubia Sayeed, daughter of Home minister Mufti Mohmmad Sayeed. Near his house we hijacked the mini bus in which she was coming home after her duty at 3.45 pm.

I asked him *ap kaun hein* (who are you?)

"I will not disclose my name but I can assure you she is safe and three of her sisters are guarding her. We will not harm her, but we have certain demands.

What are those demands, I asked.

First, all our colleagues should be released unconditionally. They are five: Abdul Hamid Sheikh, Gulam Nabi Butt (younger brother of Maqbool Butt), Abdul Ahad Waza, Noor Mohmmed Kalwal and Mohammed Altaf. We are meeting to review the situation tonight and if our demands are not met, soon the list may be increased. Our area commanders will decide. We will then demand more things in ransom.

How did you come to know I am here in this hotel, I asked.

The thick voice on the other side said Through intelligence sources. We have our friends in the IB, the CID.

What ultimately you want, I interjected.

The voice: Nothing less than an honourable life. The rest can be negotiated. If the government can negotiate with Prafulla Mahanta and hand over Assam to him and if Simranjit Singh Mann can be released and given a chance to be elected to Parliament, why not us? We have not killed hundreds of innocent people. We just want to assert that we also have a right to live as we want.

What do you want me to do, I continued.

The voice: I am an engineer but now I am on the road because the government will not give me a job. And many more things. But we are open to talks. We then will place our demands.

I asked him: Why don't you release that innocent girl? What is her

fault?

The voice: "She is our sister. But she is also the daughter of the Home minister". He snapped the phone.

The kidnapping plan was meticulously executed. The terrorists must have been following Rubia for quite some time. The minibus driver Abdul Majid Butt, who has been arrested, is suspected to have been keeping the militants informed.

The negotiation for her release were made through an intermediary. A police constable jailed for helping the militants came to the government's help. He was flown to Srinagar from a Jammu jail in a special plane to establish contacts with the KLF militants. He confirmed that Rubia was safe but emotionally disturbed. The kidnappers have been insisting on the release of Hamid Shah who was undergoing treatment in a local nursing home after being shot and injured by the police.

As the news spread like fire in the city people were stunned but none of them condemned the dastardly act. No sense of remorse was discernible. Markets were open as usual in Srinagar where shops get closed at the drop of a hat.

The Muslim reaction in India was one of revulsion and a number of Muslim leaders including the Shahi Imam of Jama Masjid described it as an act of cowardice that deserved universal condemnation.

The valley is in the firm grip of the fundamentalists and the militants. It belongs to them. The Governor and the Chief minister have become infructuous. Farooq Abdullah, who is abroad for a heart check-up, is undoubtedly the most hated man. His writ does not go beyond the four walls of his magnificent bungalow on a hill top. Both the National Conference and the Congress have just vanished from the scene. Their leaders are not to be seen anywhere. The Farooq government is in the summer capital, Jammu. No minister has, so far, dared to come to Srinagar. It's a government in absentia.

Last night the Director-General of Police and the Chief Secretary landed at Srinagar. But they were almost in hiding. Kashmir is perched on a volcano. Law and order does not exist. It is rule of the Kalashnikov and the word of the militants called the jungnoos—the fighters is the law. The lower rungs in the intelligence agencies faithfully work for them. The militants are more well-informed than these agencies.

The kidnapping of Rubia took place on December 8 at 3.45 pm but till 8 pm none of them knew anything about it. A very senior police officer in Jammu did not have any idea till 10 pm. The Chief minister was not

contactable anywhere in the US or Europe. Governor Krishna Rao a retired Chief of Army, sat in his palace of a house. He had no instructions and even if he had, he is too wooden headed to take prompt action.

Home Minister Mufti Sayeed's house on the outskirts of the city has been totally unguarded. The simple, three bedroom house has no furniture and a *kacha* road leads to the house. When I went to see his wife and family a wireless jeep were found posted there, unconcerned about the sensational kidnapping. Calm and composed, Mufti's gracious wife sat on a bamboo mat surrounded by her close relations. Her husband had talked to her a few minutes earlier and assured her that Rubia will be safe. "But I want my daughter back safe".

I spoke to Mufti Sayeed on phone from Srinagar. "I will not succumb to pressure, come what may, though she is my darling daughter", he replied in a faltering voice. Mufti is one of the most admired men in the valley, yet it was his daughter who had to bear the brunt of her father's rise to power. He rejected all offers of negotiation and insisted first on her unconditional release.

The Kashmir militants are divided in various groups though their aim is the same. They include the KLF, Jammu and Kashmir Liberation Front, Jammu and Kashmir National Liberation Front, besides half a dozen more extremist outfits such as Al Jihad, Al Maqbool, Hizb-e-Allah, Hizb-e-Islam, Allah Tigers and Al Khomeine. They all come under the influence of Al Fateh which reigned supreme in the valley in the early 1970s.

They do get arms financed from across the border. The government, the police and the military forces have not been able to control the arms flow as in the case of Punjab. The Kalashnikovs come from across the border and the bombs are locally manufactured. The militants have developed their own communication system and their word reaches the valley in minutes. They can paralyse the valley within moments if they want it. I am told it is not fear, but acts of solidarity with them.

Young Shabir Shah is a cult figure. He is the leader of the People's League and today he is more popular than Sheikh Abdullah in his halcyon days. The valley was closed totally for a week on his arrest. And when the news of his death spread it seemed everything there will be on fire. The government had to deny it before the volcano burst. He is in Udhampur jail, caught, incidentally, by the police. His name has mesmerised the Kashmiris, they treat him with awe, respect and admiration.

In Anantnag, Mufti Sayeed's home district, only one vote was cast because his men placed a TV set in the middle of the road with a note saying 'anybody who will cast his vote will get this TV as a reward'. Not

a bird flew that day in Srinagar. The NC candidate was elected unopposed. Such was the boycott.

Shabir Shah asserts he is innocent and he has not killed even a goat, not to speak of human beings. But he wants to liberate the valley from the clutches of Hindustan.

I spoke to a great number of people during my short visit and almost all of them said they want to live an honourable life. They have been treated worse than second class citizens. The rigging of all the elections held so far in the valley, whether by the Congress or the National Conference has hurt them deeply. The conspicuous state terrorism has forced them to take a firm posture of total hostility. On the day of the last Lok Sabha polling the governor ordered a flag march by the army though the city was absolutely calm.

The hatred against Farooq Abdullah is so intense that Sheikh Abdullah's birthday was observed as a black day.

He seems to be the main target of the dreaded militant groups known as 'Allah Tigers'. It's leaders are a group of educated youth who were active earlier either in the National Conference or the Congress. But the massive rigging during last assembly elections turned them into rebels.

The Kashmir Liberation Front is based in Pakistan with Amanullah Khan as their Chief. On December 6 they blew the ancestral house of a relative of another National Conference MP, P.L. Hando. The valley is totally alienated.

Like Punjab, thousands of unemployed youth have joined the militants. The students who see their future bleak have joined en masse either the Islamic Students League or the Muslim Students Federation. Educational institutions remain mostly closed. Thousands of unemployed youth sit at home and either sulk or join the militant organisations. Poverty rules the roost. The valley is an orphanage with nobody to look after it, without even a ray of hope.

There is no power. Power breakdowns are not an exception but the rule. It can be very hard in the winter. Snow will begin to fall any day. Water scarcity rubs salt on the wounds. The city roads are deserted by 6 pm. Tourism, the main source of revenue and livelihood for the locals, has come to a standstill. The hotels and the house boats are empty. Srinagar is a city without a soul. The militants have forced the closure of all the bars and wine shops. They have announced the next step will be closure of cinema houses followed by shutting down of the thriving video libraries. Hotels, including the five star variety, have closed bars and hard drinks are served only in the rooms.

Last week, the bar attached to Vijay Dhar's cinema house was raided and wine bottles broken. He has been told on phone to shut down his cinema house before the end of the month.

The KLF's Zanana wing, which is keeping Rubia as a hostage, is active on the women's front and no Kashmiri woman is allowed to go out bareheaded, no lipstick and no *bindi.* Hindu women are exempted. The Kashmiri pundits have never had it so bad. They live in fear though they have been assured by the militants that they will not unnecessarily be harmed. The militants target is the oppressive government and not the Hindus or the Sikhs, militants leader told me.

During my conversations with a number of Kashmiri journalists and intellectuals I found they have pinned their hopes on the V.P. Singh government. His very successful visit to the Golden Temple and a breakthrough in Punjab has been received with controlled enthusiasm. Their minimum demand is the immediate removal of the Governor and imposition of Presidents' Rule, dissolution of the assembly and fair and free elections. This will improve the situation half way. Then the centre can sit with the newly elected government and talk things out.

The KLF believes in armed militancy but the leader of the People's League, Shabir Shah will most likely be elected to power in the next assembly. The leader then could be the Mahanta of Kashmir. My feeling is that most Kashmiris are pro-Pakistani and anti-India because they have been wronged time and again. Once they get Kashmir as Prafulla Mahanta got Assam, they will be as bad or as good Indians.

But the new government in Delhi must take Kashmir on top priority basis. And delay will further complicate the situation. It is purely political problem and no military or paramilitary forces can solve it permanently. Mir Qasim, former Chief minister, put it most succinctly when I met him before leaving for Srinagar: *By our behaviour and conduct we must reassure the people of Kashmir that their identity and their democratic aspirations expressed through the ballot will be respected in full measure.* It is as simple as that.

As I was about to leave for the airport in the afternoon of December 9, I was told by the Hotel's Front Office manager about another phone call. This time it was a different voice.

The voice: Are you leaving Srinagar?

Yes, I said, but without getting Rubia out of your clutches.

The voice: Listen to this carefully. If she is not released by the evening of December 11 she will be killed and her body will be thrown in the Lake.

I was perplexed. I said take me hostage and leave the child. She is like my daughter. I am prepared to come any time, anywhere. Take me as a hostage. But I will not come unless you free Rubia.

The voice: No. She cannot be released unless our demands are met. The phone was snapped.

Current, 16.12.1989.
pp. (3 + 8)

Kashmir: handle it with care

The whole valley is up in arms against India. The militants have been able to seize the initiative. They proved beyond an iota of doubt that the entire populace is with them. Kashmiri Muslims in the valley, who have witnessed their hopes and aspirations being ruthlessly trampled by successive National Conference and Congress governments, seem to have decided: so far and no farther.

Kashmir could not have been ceded to India without their active support, though Sheikh Abdullah was instrumental in keeping them away from the clutches of Pakistan and its Pathan raiders. But today the Sheikh and his entire family is taboo. Roads, sign boards and anything carrying his name have been tarred. Books on him have been hidden behind the shelves by bookshop owners.

It is Farooq Abdullah and his Congress mentors in Delhi who have to be held wholly responsible for the tragedy of Kashmir. The Janata Dal government has simply inherited the fireball and now it has been called upon to stem the volcanic eruption. It was like a tonne of bricks falling on the head, a situation for which the Janata Dal government was least prepared. Punjab topped the list of its priorities, Kashmir has pushed it aside.

I have been a witness to the simmering revolt in the wake of Rubiya Sayeed's kidnapping and had come back to Delhi with a gnawing feeling that just a spark would envelop the beautiful valley in an inferno. The abduction of Home minister Mufti Sayeed's young daughter was only a symptom of the rushing avalanche of the bottled up sentiments. I could feel it in crowded bazars and lanes and bylanes of Srinagar. I did not meet any worthwhile person who expressed remorse at the dastardly act. All that was there was an enigmatic silence on the pale, unshaven faces with sunken cheeks. The sight was frightening. It was the calm before the storm.

It happened within a week. Nobody knows the situation in the valley better than Home minister Mufti Sayeed himself, a thoroughbred Kashmiri and a victim of Rajiv-Farooq machinations. By abducting his daughter the militants planned to convey their message to the country of the real situation in Kashmir. Their scheme was to deal a lethal blow to wake us out of complacency, after failing to shake us out of slumber. After talking to them on phone I was convinced they would not harm Rubiya. Yet, they appeared determined to extract maximum concessions and also tell the powers that be that their cup of misery had overflowed.

I am pretty sure they will be the last people to opt out of India and go over to Pakistan. Pakistan is being used as ruse to settle accounts with those who have held them in bondage and treated them as second class citizens. If Kanshi Ram can ask his flock to revolt through the ballot against the perpetrators of injustice, it is because he knows the ballot can play a miracle. But what about those who have lost faith in the democratic power of that slip of paper which can make or break governments and Prime Ministers?

The simple question these Kashmiris, now in a rebellious mood, have been asking is, why should we be denied our constitutional rights? While the rest of the country sings paeans of secularism, democracy, socialism, why have Kashmiris been denied these basic rights guaranteed in that sacred book?

Several enlightened youth asked me in Srinagar: When the Tamils burn the national flag, they are appeased and their problems are studied by commissions, but when we burn the same flag, we are branded traitors and pro-Pakistanis. We have been kept in the shadow of guns for forty years while corrupt and immoral Chief ministers ruled over us as *subedar*s of New Delhi.

When the whole populace turns up to rejoice the release of the militants following the abduction of Rubiya, bursting crackers, defying curfews and snatching rifles from police jawans, and does not allow any political leader worth his name amongst them, then we should sit up and think and act. Not that New Delhi had not shown enough guts to act, but it acted in favour of the oppressors, rubbed salt on the Kashmiri wounds, it poured oil on the embers.

I am convinced the situation in the valley cannot, and should not, be handled as a law and order problem. It is far more complex and as Mufti Sayeed has put it, needs short-term and long-term solutions. As it happened in Punjab, every terrorists shot was replaced by 10 others. We have learnt from socialist countries, and now from Punjab, that bullet cannot be the

answer to civil, armed uprising. As it happened in Punjab, the people openly voted for those very terrorists whom we had kept in jail for years. We cannot have two yardsticks for these two problems. The short-term solution is:

First: The Governor's resignation should immediately be accepted and a new Governor broadly acceptable to the Kashmiris appointed. He has to be a senior politician with impeccable record of integrity and with appreciable knowledge of the Kashmiri psyche. He should not be one who could be considered a New Delhi stooge as too much will depend on the new Governor.

Second: Chief minister Farooq Abdullah should be asked to step down soon after the new Governor takes over. Farooq's credibility has touched the rock bottom. He should not only be removed but also 'withdrawn' from the state till the situation becomes normal.

Third: The Governor's first task has to be to restore normalcy by inculcating hope that with the change of the government in New Delhi, fresh moves will be made to heal the wounds. A healing touch is what is needed. The Governor will have to open dialogues that all sections of thinking people since politicians have totally been discarded by the people. The Urdu Press plays an important role in shaping the Kashmiri opinion and some kind of bridges will have to be built with it.

Fourth: These things need immediate attention. This I am adding at the risk of repetition. One: Power, Immediate steps should be taken to arrange adequate power supply. It has to be dealt on a war footing. Water: despite plenty of it in the lakes, Srinagar suffers from water shortage. Water supply can and should be improved quickly.

Fifth: Over a lakh educated Kashmiri youth, doctors, engineers, teachers are unemployed. It is they who make bombs and burst crackers. The Right to Work scheme can be launched from here.

The long range plan should include: the release of all the politically-oriented detenues as was done with the ones in Jodhpur and other places. Adequate compensation to the families of innocent victims of police firings.

The militants should be isolated from their Pakistani connections. The flow of money and arms from across the border will have to be stemmed. This cannot be done easily because the local police and intelligence services are either in league with the militants or inept and inefficient. The Kashmir police and bureaucracy are not less corrupt than their counterparts in the rest of the country. Without a thorough overhaul of the services very little can be achieved. Militants in Kashmir are not feared, they are admired.

The events in the last two weeks must be an eye-opener to all of us. Besides the unscrupulous politicians, it is the police and bureaucracy that have made a contribution in turning the ordinary, peace-loving youth into militants.

Then comes the crucial stage of opening dialogue with the militants. Dialogue has its own lasting value. Prafulla Mahanta, once branded a terrorist, became an asset through dialogue. We may find a lot of Mahantas in the valley too.

And finally free and democratic elections. But every candidate will have to pledge loyalty to the Indian constitution and the flag. I can make bold to say that a government thus elected may even agree to the repeal of Article 370.

Nothing is impossible in the politics of love and peace.

Current, 23.12.1989.
pp. (1 + 3)

Kashmir: time for action, not ad-hocism

The situation in Kashmir is so grave that it needs certain immediate, drastic steps to arrest further deterioration. Ad-hocism and half-hearted steps to meet the mass uprising in the valley have proved counter-productive and alienated even those who would have helped New Delhi to bring a semblance of normalcy.

It must be conceded that the whole population is up in arms. It is a popular insurrection which can no more be taken as an act of terrorism by a bunch of lunatics. Even women and children defy curfew, bare their chests and face bullets. It will be a folly to imagine that the whole populace has been held to ransom by the militants, forced in submission to their diktats. India has never faced such animosity, hatred and anger from a section of its people since independence.

The valley cannot be controlled by retaliation or by turning it into an army camp. History teaches us that bullets are not the answer to mass uprisings. What is happening in the Soviet Union and what has happened in the Socialists bloc and how Gorbachev has dealt with the extremely delicate situation should be a lesson to us. It does not mean we allow Kashmir to secede from India or walk over to Pakistan. Nobody can take away Kashmir from us but the people of the valley have most certainly been alienated. They have to be brought back. They are our own people. It was these people who defied Pakistan and declared their loyalty to India. They have to be brought back not by force by taking certain major

and bold steps—political, economic and administrative.

First, Governor Jagmohan should be recalled immediately. He has failed to deliver the goods. He has not proved equal to the task. He was sent to Srinagar because of his past record in toning up the administration and taking some popular measures which endears him to large sections of people in Jammu and Kashmir. The situation then was different. He had cashed in on the popularity of Farooq Abdullah. This time he has become a misfit. He has erred in his assessment of the situation and almost followed a tooth for tooth policy. Today he is considered the most hated man in the valley and, if that is true, he should be recalled forthwith. He should be replaced by a mature, seasoned politician with some credibility among Kashmiris.

Second, the leaders of the militants, extremists and terrorists should be identified and some well-meaning people should be encouraged to open a dialogue with them. Kashmir is not an administrative or military problem. It's political and every such problem has to be solved through dialogue. The degree and level of dialogue can be decided by the Prime Minister and it should begin on the premise that Kashmir is an integral part of India and its territorial integrity is defined in the constitution . A beginning can be made with the militant women's organisations which have been in the forefront of the movement of *Azadi*. No mother would like her son to be killed and no sister would like her brother shot dead. It may sound strange but it is the Kashmiri women who hold the key.

Third, the talk of reviving the democratic process or reinstating the dissolved Assembly is an exercise in futility. No democratic organisation worth its name exists in the valley. They have all disintegrated and it goes without saying that the dissolution of the Assembly was nothing but a farce. The Kashmiri anger actually began with the mass rigging of elections in 1987. There is no use putting life in a corpse. Kashmiri leaders from Farooq Abdullah downwards have lost their credibility, they are totally irrelevant. We will have to begin with the new leaders, whoever they are.

Fourth, appointing George Fernandes as minister in charge of Kashmir was a thoughtless act. He is a well-meaning and dynamic politician but has his limitations. He is too busy running the railways or his political errands. Kashmir needs the Prime Minister's full-time attention. It is he who should take charge of Kashmir and guide and control the situation.

Fifth, and it is most important. We must immediately seal the line of actual control from where the arms and trained terrorists are smuggled. Do not bother about the cost or enormous human labour but it has to be done if

the valley is to be saved. And if we have a definite proof then we must not desist from destroying the terrorist training centres across the border. Terrorists infiltration is against the Simla Agreement and, if Pakistan is violating it, we must take appropriate measures to put a stop to it.

Current 07.04.1990.
pp. (2)

It's a human problem

One should not expect a political solution from a retired general. Reports speak of how J&K Governor Gen. Krishna Rao has been ordering about the Army, the BSF and the para-military forces to mobilise public meetings for him so that he may speak to the masses about the political process he has decided to launch in the valley. Nothing could be more ridiculous than allowing a stiff-necked army brat to rub salt into the wounds of a people struggling to have respectability in the society.

If New Delhi is really serious about finding a political solution to problem of Kashmir, it should, first, replace Gen. Rao with a seasoned, mature man known for his political sagacity. It means a political governor. He must have a clear and unqualified mandate to begin a political process. He can do it only by talking to all, without exception all, individuals, outfits and organisations involved in the struggle for *azadi*. He should function independent of South Block bureaucrats and report directly to the Prime Minister.

Second the Prime Minister should change both the home minister and his junior and appoint a minister dealing largely with Kashmir in coordination with the governor. He should bring all those militant organisations free from Pakistani influence on one platform and let them take the lead in finding a solution within the framework of the constitution . It may mean granting *azadi* to run the state by the freely elected representatives of the people.

Third, reduce the presence of the army and the para-military forces and rely more and more on voluntary organisations, senior Kashmir citizens, the local intelligentsia and women activists. No political process is possible without the full cooperation of the people.

Fourth, liberal compensation to the people who have lost their property and the near and dear ones. Compensation review of all those people detained in the last four to five years. Their trials in open courts by

independently constituted courts. The detenues should be provided free legal aid and lawyers of their choice.

Fifth, human rights groups in India should be allowed free access to the victims of state terrorism and they should have total freedom to speak out.

Last, but not the least, treat Kashmir as a human problem, it needs a Gandhian touch. Kashmir needs a mini-Gandhi.

Current, 23.07.1994.
pp. (2)

7

Institutionalising a Coalition Polity

A. Search for a National Alternative

Yes, it's a Jang Morcha

"The best course would be that political parties meet all their requirements of funds for their daily running and elections from membership fee and the people at large. Some practical mode of state funding will have to be found in consultation with all political parties to free public life from the tentacles of big money."

On October 2 an alternative centre of power emerged as Vishwanath Pratap Singh launched his Jan Morcha. AICC General Secretary Ghulam Nabi Azad aptly described it as Jang Morcha, (War Front), which it will inevitably become. It was actually an announcement of an organised war against the Rajiv regime, and as D-day draws closer, the battle lines are drawn more and more militantly. It's now a clear and distinct game of power, and soon it will be no holds barred. Whether it will be value-based politics or power-based struggle to grab the *gaddi* will be clear only after the regime will draw up its own strategy to pre-empt the Morcha's onward march.

The choice of Ram Dhan as the head of the Morcha could not have been more appropriate since Harijans constitute the largest and most organised vote-bank in the country. Half the Morcha's battle will be won if Harijans switch their traditional allegiance to the 'new movement'.

Ram Dhan is a mature politician; his integrity is beyond question. He is not only a freedom fighter but also a socialist and an inveterate champion of democracy and socialism. He had left the Congress during the Emergency, joined the JP movement, spent one and a half years in jail, and when the Janata formed the government in 1977, refused to be a minister. He came back to the Congress in 1984 at the behest of Indira

Gandhi, and left it protesting against Rajiv's elitist policies.

By choosing him as the leader of the Morcha, V.P. Singh killed two birds with one stone. He wiped out the stigma of his 'group being dominated by high caste Brahmins and Rajputs and telling Harijans and backwards that in him they have a tried leader. Ram Dhan does not have the elitist look of an Arun Nehru or an Arif Mohammed Khan. He is a Harijan and he looks one. He can be easily identified with what Gandhiji called the *daridranarayan*. His indeed is an indisputable choice, and V.P. Singh has undoubtedly scored a very strong point over Rajiv who does not have a single Harijan worth the name in the ruling echelons.

By adopting the tricolour as its flag, the Morcha has directly communicated to congressmen on the other side of the fence that finally it will be an inner-party struggle despite the Left making friendly gestures and inviting it to join the common struggle against the regime.

In spite of loud protestations from AICC functionaries, the average congressmen is not prepared to believe that the Shuklas, the Singhs and the Khans are not one of them. They are too practical a people and in their hearts of hearts know that if it is not Rajiv it will definitely be Vishwanath. The next Prime Minister of India will again be a congressman and not a Leftist or a Rightist.

The Jan Morcha is born out of the Congress womb and its policy statements and slogans are the one the Congress has been preaching without implementing them. No congressman has ever said he is not against corruption, or against socialism, secularism and democracy. And it would have been disastrous had VP not publicly disassociated his Morcha with the RSS and the BJP. No congressman in his right senses can associate himself with these pariahs of Indian politics. The Rightists on their own can never come to power in this country democratically—the social and economic structure is such that anybody aspiring to come to power will have to adopt socialist and secular postures.

> "If the fruits of development are to reach the last man then our attention has to first and foremost go to the landless and unorganised labour in the villages and to our Scheduled Caste and Scheduled Tribe brethren."

If the Morcha manifesto is implemented in its totality, then the organised Left will lose its relevance because it is as radical as any communist manifesto. If V.P. Singh takes it to its logical and after coming to power, he will not be accused of being a communist or a Soviet agent.

Even Jawaharlal Nehru had talked about workers' participation in management and he never opposed the demand for reasonable prices for the farm products.

The concept of participative democracy, on which the Morcha has set its heart, is undoubtedly a Nehruvian idea completely destroyed by his daughter and thrown to the winds by her worthy son. The other major points, like comprehensive land reforms, maximum wages to the unorganised labour, 18 per cent job reservation to the Scheduled Castes, have been a plank of the ruling party since the Faizabad Congress.

The Morcha has, therefore, not pulled a rabbit from the hat. It has promised to put into practice what the Congress has failed to do in 40 years of its rule. Nehru could not do it because his other partymen were not ideologically with him and he alone could not carry the leviathan of a party with him. Indira Gandhi was too busy in power politics and used socialist slogans to hoodwink people. Rajiv . . . the less said of him the better. The million dollar question is, Can VP be a success where Nehru, Indira and briefly JP failed? Can he perform the miracle?

> "Communalism and casteism pose a serious threat to our national unity. Distribution of party tickets on considerations of caste and religion and thereafter conduct of election campaigns on the same basis entrenches communal and casteist forces in the body politic itself."

The fact, as E.M.S. Namboodripad has succinctly put it, is that he is underestimating his popularity. Vested interests, upper classes and well-entrenched industrialists will undoubtedly not accept him as their leader. The media will begin to denigrate him, but the masses, as EMS has pointed out, have already accepted him as an alternative. Once he has an organisation and a few more able lieutenants to promote him, he will make much deeper dents in the ruling party fortress.

The only apprehension is that traditional sychophants may also get hold of him and try to individualise politics. He may soon be compared with the familiar 'suraj' 'chand' hogwash and promoted as the 'sole' leader. Power had gone in his head when he was Finance minister. One hopes his present postures of humility are not synthetic, and that if he cannot be a Gandhi, he should not be Indira Gandhi when the moment of truth comes.

Current, 10.10.1987.
pp. (1 + 7)

Harakiri, Jan Morcha style

Vishwanath Pratap Singh is making a mistake, a kind of error of judgement which he and his colleagues in the Jan Morcha will regret sooner or later. He gives the impression of being in an unseemly, indecent haste. The tragedy is that he is rushing towards a disaster with his eyes open and knowing fully well what he is doing. It is pathetic that his valued advisers including Arun Nehru, V.C. Shukla, Ram Dhan, Arif Mohammed Khan etc. have done precious little to prevent him from committing harakiri.

Harakiri is a milder word when compared to the blunder. His attempts to find modalities, via medias, norms, etc., for forging unity and floating a front of centrist opposition parties are bordering on farce. Why should he indulge in such a farce? If the so-called centrist parties are made of human beings and if he expects them to guide the destiny of this troubled nation, then he is on the verge of insanity. He thinks he can fool the 800 million people of this country by telling them that he now holds a common flag, symbol, a manifesto and that he should be installed in power. Nothing can be more ridiculous than what he is aiming at.

How can Arif Mohammed Khan and Syed Shahabuddin be the authors of a common manifesto? How can Arun Nehru and Ajit Singh hold a common flag? How can V.C. Shukla and George Fernandes work out a common programme? How can Devilal and Ashok Sen share a common vision? What is common between Mufti Saeed and Shahi Imam? How can Chandra Shekhar allow V.P. Singh to steal the show and lead the nation? Can Bahuguna and V.P. Singh share a common platform and remain physically intact? How can status quoist and anarchist Madhu Limaye be a part of the would be ruling echelon? Can Subramaniam Swamy and Satpal Mittal be put on talking terms and remain unmauled?

The front V.P. Singh is aiming at has to be made up of these people and who does not know these people. He is trying to chalk out a path where angels fear to tread. It will not be a Front. It will be a mad house, a lunatic asylum. It will sound the death knell of democracy. It will give rise to either right reaction or a one man authoritarian rule. The people of this country will not permit a repetition of 1977 nor would they allow any kind of instability at the centre. A non-government at Delhi, as we have these days, is better than a weak government.

Rajiv Gandhi is indeed a disaster. A great let down. He is the main cause of the wave of despondency sweeping the country. He cannot

govern, he does not know how to run a country of India's size and plurality. He has ruined the morale of the people. He destroyed a political party the day it completed its century.

Yet his only, and perhaps the most praiseworthy, contribution is that he has preserved democracy. He has not fiddled with Parliament and its norms and he has not debauched the constitution. He has not meddled with the concept of secularism. Indians rarely enjoyed democracy in its full bloom as they do it today. For all this he should be thanked.

But the nation is in a foul mood. It is realising its mistake of having a green horn imposed on itself. It has to suffer for its folly for a full term of five years. But once bitten, twice shy. I doubt whether the people will repeat the mistake of replacing Rajiv with a Front. Fronts have always been disasters.

Vishwanath Pratap Singh could have avoided all these follies had he shown some patience and continued to guide the Jan Morcha. The Jan Morcha was the other name of the Congress with of course a better image and better prospects. He should have stuck to the Congress flag, the Congress manifesto and the Congress platform. He should have kept the doors of the Morcha wide open for his Congress compatriots. He underestimated his own strength, his pull and his capacity to bring the Congress back to power, a better and cleaner Congress. He has lost that opportunity.

Current, 30.07.1988.
p. (2)

Front—no substitute

A front cannot be a substitute for a party. Democracies survive in an atmosphere of political stability. A weak government and a developing country like ours cannot afford to have government made up of a motley crowd. We have had the very unpleasant experience of fronts. SVDs, Janatas and alliances. The concept of collective leadership is floated whenever warring leaders fail to subordinate their ambition to broader national use. The difficulty with our opposition is that it has too many leaders aspiring for the *gaddi*. The history of their existence in public life is replete with mutual jealousy, petty quarrels and wars of attrition as happened in 1979-80. The night-mare was put to an end by Indira Gandhi. The vanquished opposition leaders have not learned any lesson from the past; they continue their fights despite efforts to reduce their intensity.

The formation of the Samajwadi Janata Dal followed by the National People's Front with NTR as its chairman and V.P. Singh as convenor can only be looked at as yet another *khichdi* floated as an alternative to the ruling Congress. The Front has, among its leaders, the same old faces who had brought disgrace to the art of governance and had pulled down their own governments. People have little faith in their ability to form a stable government and run it for the full term. They continue to work at cross purposes and jockey for coveted positions. Some of them have even thought what ministry they would demand if the people repose their confidence in the Front.

The only qualitative difference this time is that Devi Lal, who has been bulldozing them to unite under one banner, one leader and one manifesto, has no personal ambition. The four men who are at the helm of the NPF—N.T. Rama Rao, V.P. Singh, Rama Krishna Hegde and Ajit Singh—are known for their unimpeachable integrity and mass base. They are trusted and respected. If the four of them tour the country as a team, the ruling party will have to run for cover. The consensus among most Front leaders is that in case it is voted to power. NTR will go to Rashtrapati Bhavan and VPS will become the Prime Minister. At least Devi Lal, who rules the roost, has made it abundantly clear through his public pronouncements and private conversations. "We need a Head of state from the south and that is none but N.T. Rama Rao and only V.P. Singh has qualified to be the Head of the government. That is an unquestionable peoples' desire. People are in fact waiting to install him as the next Prime Minister."

This is Devi Lal's personal wish, though his feeling, that the people want a change for the better, has a lot of substance. He understands the general mood at least in the Hindi heartland and is also aware of the aversion people there have developed for Rajiv Gandhi. And so long as Devi Lal is there with his *danda* none of the aspirants for Prime Ministership will make a public demonstration of their ambition. But how long he or NTR will be able to hold this unwieldy crowd on leash? Some of them have established secret conduits with Congress's top leadership and will bolt at the appropriate time. Not all of those who have been included in various committees in the SJD and the NPF are committed to the cause of an alternative to the Congress. They will soon be discovered though the Congress will find them a liability.

The Front, as I said, cannot be a substitute for a party. If the Congress has to be replaced, it has to be by a well-organised party and not by a group of individuals. It is only possible if the constituents

of the Front dissolve themselves and merge without conditions and inhibitions.

The Front has to be a party with one leader, one constitution, one manifesto and one flag. The trivialities on common programme are raised by those with personal ambition. No party with an objective to come to power can have a programme other than democracy, secularism and socialism as its permanent and ultimate goal. The difference between this programme and that of the Congress is only of degree, not substance.

The most captivating aspect of the Front is that it has V.P. Singh as its leader. This man's honesty cannot be questioned. And corruption will be a major issue in the coming battle of ballots.

Current, 13.08.1988.
p. (2)

Janata Dal: can it be an instrument of change?

It was Chandra Shekhar's day at Bangalore though Vishwanath Pratap Singh was the focus of attention. The 5000 odd delegates at the beautiful city's palace grounds soon became aware of the key he held for the opposition unity.

Has he not been there the Janata Dal would hardly had taken off despite the presence of VPS, Devi Lal, Hegde, etc. He may not be its president but the fact is that the Janata Dal will be at his command so long as he wants it. Its constitution is the carbon copy of his party. 'Samajwadi' was struck out at his behest, the main policies and programmes were dictated by him and the crucial resolution was moved by him.

He refused to preside and suggested Chief minister Bommai's name to take over the proceedings. At the spacious stage Devi Lal, Hegde, V.P. Singh, V.C. Shukla, Biju Patnaik all hovered over him seeking his advice. The delegates, an intelligent lot, mostly made of Janata and Lok Dal leaders, watched every moment at the stage with the attention it deserved.

The leaders too preferred to be overshadowed by him. Even V.P. Singh, as a matter of strategy, sought to be dwarfed by him. Devi Lal laughed and joked with him though he hated him at heart. Chandra Shekhar was in his element. He shot down Hegde's suggestion of announcing the dissolution of all the merging parties on that day.

Hegde asked V.C. Shukla, who was to move the resolution naming the new party to persuade him and agree to the dissolution of the Janata

Party. 'No not now' he told Shukla curtly. His was the most brilliant and frequently applauded speech made while moving the main political resolution.

All other speakers, including Hegde, Ajit Singh and Devi Lal, gave the impression of accepting him as the real leader and when V.P. Singh got up to address the jubilant congregation, he lavished praise on him as the architect of opposition unity.

October 11, which was Lok Nayak's birth anniversary, was also his day. It was the day when a brand new opposition party was founded with Chandra Shekhar at the helm though not as its Pied piper.

The delegates and the leaders on the stage behaved as though they were about to take oath and that Rajiv Gandhi's day of reckoning had come. The sweet smell of power can be sensed, it could be felt. All, virtually all of them, exuded confidence.

The ones from the Hindi heartland were even thinking of shadow cabinets in their respective states. We will form the government at the centre, though the Congress may come back as the single largest party, a Jan Morcha leader sitting next to V.P. Singh confided.

No. We will not try him. We will allow him to leave the country, another Lok Dal leader from Uttar Pradesh remarked when somebody asked him about the fate of Rajv Gandhi, if he lost.

Chandra Shekhar was once again the topic of animated discussion among the new Janata Dal delegates, all senior people. We have made him President because he has the cleanest image, he has caught the imagination of the youth, he is about caste and communal considerations, he can get votes and above all he is not ambitious.

He does not want to be the Prime Minister. He will at least not fight for it. He is the choice of the people, an ex-Lok Dal legislator made no secret of his inner feelings.

But finally it has to be Chandra Shekhar. This time the son of a peasant has to be the Prime Minister. It is his, said an aide who hangs around him, adding we will not compromise on this basic issue.

At Bangalore, it was a gathering of leaders who have been finding it hard to shed their past, their political affiliations, their likes and dislikes. They were afloat. They were in a state of weightlessness, like a cosmonaut in an airless module.

Each one of them has a question mark distinctly visible on his uncertain face. I had never seem so many quizzical faces. This was the position at the birth of a party which aimed at capturing power. They were perhaps aware of the fact that 'collective leadership is a temporary phase". Finally

the new party will have to throw up one leader not only acceptable to itself but to the people also.

At the moment V.P. Singh enjoys an enviable position with unassailable integrity, mass popularity next to none, at least in the Hindi belt, the capacity to carry with him all and sundry, to listen to everyone and to respect even those who dislike him.

At Bangalore he has been unanimously elected President of the Dal, he impressed all with his humility, his emphasis on mass-oriented programmes, his concern for the rural India and the *daridranarayan*.

A senior journalist thought he was trying to do a JP and might soon initiate some mass-based action programmes. So far he has not found an issue with which he might hit at Rajiv Gandhi as effectively as he did when he left the government.

Corruption will, of course, remain a sharp weapon in his hand but just that is not enough. People will not vote Rajiv out only because his image has been tarnished as a 'thief'. People in this country believe, said Ramakrishna Hegde in his opening remarks, that Rajiv Gandhi is a chor and VPS as a chorpakar (thief-catcher).

No, this may not suffice. It may not motivate voters to elect the Janata Dal as the ruling party. Something else is needed and that VPS, Shekhar, Hegde and Devi Lal know fully well. They are seriously searching that something which will persuade voters to delink themselves from the Congress. Mere anti-Rajiv Gandhism will fall flat on its face.

Bangalore was certainly not a turning point. The turning point will come the day Chandra Shekhar, V.P. Singh, Devi Lal and Hegde begin to tour the country as a team with a solid economic programme and with a promise of socio-economic revolution. They should not equate the problems of the 80 per cent in rural India with those in urban areas. It is the village which should rally round them. Water, power, roads, total land reforms, power to the panchayats. And 70 per cent of the investment of the total national revenue in rural India. Something new. Something to give immediate relief to the farmers and farm hands, to the artisans and rural youth.

The Janata Dal will have to be an instrument of change. The people will reject it if it shaped itself as a status quoist group of power grabbers. At the moment Rajiv Gandhi cannot be excelled as a status quoist and in that case people will undoubtedly prefer him over the entire Janata Dal crowd.

Current, 22.10.1988.
p. (3)

We will try them for graft—Devi Lal

Tall and hefty with grey hair and dark glasses. Haryana chieftain Devi Lal gives the impression his Janata Dal nominee would stroll into Rashtrapati Bhavan any day to take oath as PM. He is so sure of the JD victory in the ensuing election. Nothing on earth can deter him from his resolve to be victorious.

He slips on his white socks, puts on white slippers and gets up to go. Where? Well, he is on the move. All the time. One can often see his motorcade of gleaming white ambassadors from the Haryana Bhavan on the Copernicus Road, in the heart of New Delhi, to the airport where his six-seater beachcraft waits for him. The Chaudhry's tiny little aircraft can be spotted in the blue skies winging its way to the remotest areas in the country.

Here is a man with a mission. He is possessed with the idea of dislodging Rajiv Gandhi. "Hindustan", he comes out in his typical Haryanavi drawl, "is not a family property". Gandhiji did not march from one corner to the other of the country to make it a fiefdom of this family.

One has to see him to believe that this muzhik of a man could wipe out the Congress from the Jatland in a flicker. He bagged 86 out of 90 seats in the last Assembly election. And this time if they play mischief, he spreads his long heavy legs on the coffee table, raises his equally heavy hands and mumbles, I will dissolve the Assembly and see to it that the Congress does not get even those four seats.

As chairman of the Janata Dal's Parliamentary Board he has emerged as the most powerful man not only in his fledgling party but also in the opposition camp. For he holds the key to this strange electoral adjustment with the Right on the one side and the Left on the other. "The target" he looks out from behind his dark glasses and says, is Rajiv Gandhi. When both the BJP and the CPM want to remove him where is the dispute?

As simple as that. Arey ideology hi kahan rahegee agar hum hi na hongey where will ideology be if we are wiped out. We are a centrist party and these two have to rotate around us.

He is not much concerned with the storm blowing over his head, the internecine, feuds, the Chandra Shekhars and Shahabuddins on the rampage in the opposition fields.

How could you be so sure of victory? I ask him.

I see it in the eyes of the people. It is the people who want us to win.

These people knows what is good for them and the country. Haryana is a living example. It's almost a welfare state. Haryana to us means peasant. The peasant of Haryana had never been so happy, so privileged. So if we are voted to power we'll do the same thing in Parliament and the states run by us. We will unleash a unique peasant power. We will take power to the hamlets and huts, to the fields and factories.

Devi Lal speaks in fluent Urdu. Mein angrezi nahin bol sakta—no, I cannot speak English—his alert Political Secretary Deepak, who is with him like a shadow, had already kept answers to many questions neatly written also in Urdu. Despite lack of any formal education this 76 years old peasant leader possesses the most precious thing one needs in politics give more place—common sense. He cannot be taken for a ride even by the cleverest bureaucrat. No Chanakya can fool him.

"I am negotiating with the BJP, Atalji is a nice, cultured man and his desire to change the government and the system is as intense as mine. And Vishwanath Pratap Singh is carrying on with the CPM. They get along famously. It was he who broke the ice by declaring the Left is our natural ally. So this is how we plan to share responsibilities."

I first met him at Chandigarh. Large glasses of lassi, his favourite drink, were served regularly. He spoke with a rare frankness, without any don't quote me please drama. He talks straight from the shoulder. Then at Delhi's Haryana Bhavan, from where he rules his tiny but prosperous state.

What will you do with the present Congress high ups if you win? Without batting an eyelid he shot back: We will try them for crimes against the people. We will try them for corruption. We will of course appoint a commission. The money funneled into the foreign banks will have to be brought back. It's our commitment to the people.

What kind of a government you would like to have if you win elections.

We want to have a government which can reflect the aspirations of the teaming millions of this country, which means that we want to fulfil the dreams of Mahatma Gandhi. He had said, that he wanted to wipe out tears from every Indian's eye. We want to have a government which has its roots deep in the villages. It means that the next Prime Minister should be a peasant or of peasant origin and the Rashtrapati should also be from the same stock. The crux of our entire national struggle was to give a rebirth to India and strengthen its social and economic roots, but unfortunately the dream of the nation were shattered after independence

and I hold the Nehru family solely responsible for it.

I have been touring the villages in most of north India for last two years. I have seen unbearable hunger, poverty and squalor. People still now have no clothes to wear, no shoes, there is no drinking water in village after village. There are no schools and if there is one it has no black board, it has no drinking water. Children of poor peasants study under trees and they are taught by emaciated teachers.

How do you have planned to fulfil Gandhiji's dreams and in what way the Janata Dal government will be different from the one by Congress.

I want to take you back to history for a moment. On December 31, 1928, a Congress session was held in Calcutta with Motilal Nehru presiding The session passed a resolution, demanding Dominion Status by next year. Next year in December 1929 Jawaharlal Nehru took over the leadership and declared complete independence as the party's goal in Lahore and he fixed the date of January 26.

Nehru became the first Prime Minister. He was followed by Indira Gandhi, though in the interregnum Lal Bahadur Shastri reigned now her son Rajiv Gandhi is ruling. The Nehru family has been ruling for last forty years and in this period they have not been able to provide elementary amenities like food, clothes and shelter to the people. This is one of the most poverty stricken areas in the country. I was shocked to see that fifty per cent villagers have no shoes to wear and almost seventy per cent of them were unshod. The family has not provided the people their basic need in their home town. What it can do for the rest of the country?

That is why we are aiming not only to change the government but the very system which permitted a single family to thrive at the cost of the rest of the country.

What will be the basic point of the new system that you are striving to bring about.

These kind of points are traded by leaders only to hoodwink the people. Our aim, our thinking and our manifesto is very simple. Every field must have water, every stomach must have 'roti', everybody should have enough clothes and every individual must have a decent roof over his head, the rest is irrelevant. This is the gist of our ideals, and of our manifesto. These are the very basic points which the Congress has not been able to fulfil. This Congress has been printing pages after pages of election manifestos and nobody reads them. I have seen 12 elections in my career. I can tell you nobody reads manifestos. I myself have not read any manifesto in my life.

Strangely, despite all its shortcomings and drawbacks, the Congress has

been winning election after election and it has built up a permanent vote bank of at least 40 per cent voters. Why? How.

I strongly suspect that the Congress, like the British, deliberately kept the people illiterate and ignorant. So it could exploit their sentiments in the name of nationalism and get their dummy candidate elected. The Congress has been playing this game since independence. They exploited the people in the name of the past glory of the party, sometimes they raised the slogan "Indira lao desh bachao", and now they have come out with the slogan Panchayat Raj and Jawahar Rozgar Yojna which in fact is Congress Rozgar Yojna. They have exploited the country so much that the people have lost faith in them. In fact it has been a party of the capitalists. In 1962 the Birlas had 75 members in Parliament, which formed a formidable lobby. When Goa was liberated in 1962, I had told Punditji that you have liberated the island from Salazar, but when will you liberate the Congress from the Birlas? Please save the Congress from Birla agents like Gulzari Lal Nanda, Deshbandhu Gupta, Subhadra Joshi, etc. I used to raise this voice every year at the AICC and I feel happy that now a Birla has to enter the Rajya Sabha by bribing people. It is now different for industrialists and their agents whom I call Paratroopers. They find it very difficult to get elected to Lok Sabha.

What you will do with those industrialists who have been funding the Congress, if you happen to come to power.

It is a hypothetical question. We will decide about that when the time comes.

The Janata Dal policy is to channelise fifty per cent of budgetary allocations for rural India. If the Congress does the same you will be left with no scoring points.

Why? We will make it seventy five per cent. I am already spending 75 per cent of my state's income on villages and soon I will make it 80 per cent. I am not against cities because our cities too are packed with the poor. A majority of them lives in slums. We are against the national wealth being pocketed by a bunch of capitalists, but if we improve the social and economic conditions in our villages our cities will have no slums. If the people could meet their needs in the villages, they definitely will not pour into cities.

Have you formed a committee or cell in your party to study this very vital problem. Because you will be faced with these issues soon after you come to power.

We do not want to give false hopes to the people. We do not have the

heart to make tall promises. We will prove our effectiveness the moment we come to power.

You are playing a crucial role in the negotiations between the Janata Dal and the BJP. Do you think the BJP will come around to a purposeful election understanding with you in North India.

The basic idea is that this government has to be changed. Both the Leftist and the Right parties have no two options on this. We only have to decide the modus operandi. The present government is a five-star government. It is studded with stars like Amitabh Bachchan and Vyjayantimala with K.K. Birla and Ambani and also one star performer like Satish Sharma and Rajesh Pilot, and the whole thing is headed by a TV star. He can be seen only on the TV. He pops out from that idiot box all the time. The electronic media is being misused by the PM. This has become a curse. I tell my people have a TV set only to see Ramayan and Mahabharat and switch it off when that man pops out of it. When it was proposed to me that my government should buy 1200 TVs for the villages and that the centre will meet 50 per cent of the cost I put my foot down. I told my cabinet I will not have TV even if it is given free to us. Why should I have this *dushman* in my villages.

Do you think this kind of exposure of Rajiv Gandhi on TV will help him electorally.

We have created such an awareness among the people that they either make fun of him when he appears on TV or switch it off. This over-exposure will undoubtedly boomerang on him. People have started hating it.

Your party has decided to hand over DD and AIR to autonomous Corporations.

Yes, like in the case of BBC. The government should not control the media.

I was talking to you about the Dal's electoral understanding with the BJP.

The Left's influence is confined to certain regions and the BJP has its own areas of influence. Neither the BJP nor the Left has any seats in the Hindi belt. So what is the quarrel about. We have to distribute and share these seats which do not belong to us. It is as easy as that.

Have you worked out a certain formula for electoral adjustment.

Yes we have, but I will not disclose it.

Don't you think that any electoral understanding with the BJP will alienate Muslims and Harijans.

I don't think it will affect the voting pattern. The Muslims, Sikhs and Harijans will vote for us.

The BJP has been working up the issue of Ram Janambhoomi, and has made it almost a prestige issue. Do you have any solution to the Ram Janambhoomi Babri Masjid issue. Do you agree with the BJP on it.

It is not exactly the BJP. It is some other Hindu organisation (trying to remember the name) I think it is the Vishwa Hindu Parishad. The BJP people have not yet discussed this aspect with us.

What do you plan to tell the people on this burning and crucial issue during your campaign.

I tell them do you want Ram Janambhoomi or bread. What kind of worship you'll have on an empty stomach.

If the people tell you they want Ram Janambhoomi and not bread what you'll do.

Then let them stew in their own juice. Let them die of hunger. I tell them if you want Ram Janambhoomi then fight among yourself to the end. I will tell them if you want your own *raj* then unite and fight against this evil government.

Will you then tell the BJP not to raise this issue till the election.

This is a hypothetical question. Let the time come. Let us first change this government.

Do you think you will have a stable government if you come to power.

We will not repeat 1979. This is 1989. To begin with it was the Neta Dal; it was packed with all kinds of netas but gradually all these netas are realising their proper place in the eyes of the people. The pruning will continue.

Will the pruning also affect people like Chandra Shekhar.

Whoever comes in the way of unity and our ultimate victory will fall by the wayside. Yes, Chandra Shekhar has been feeling uncomfortable for some time.

But he is attacking the Janata Dal these days.

No, he is not attacking the Janata Dal. He is speaking about some individuals.

What is his main grievance. Why is he so unhappy.

Well, he is a political man. He has a stature in national politics and he is entitled to his opinion.

Did you speak to him about his attitudes.

Yes, we discussed certain things and he has assured me he will not leave the party.

The general impression is that his friends like Subramaniam Swamy and Shahabuddin have been attacking the Dal at his behest.

No, no. It is a wrong impression. This Subramaniam Swamy is a different animal. He will come over to this side if we adjust him in some way. They thrive on the crumbs from one table to another. They are rootless people, empty drums. Swamy is like a paratrooper. He has somehow landed in the Rajya Sabha and is playing a game, a dirty game.

You have been saying that if the Dal wins V.P. Singh will be the Prime Minister. Is it your individual view or your party's decision.

This is my personal view. In my view he took the initiative in bringing all of us together. He took very positive steps on forging unity among the opposition and there is a general feeling that he raised his voice against corruption. He has come to the opposition after leaving a very prestigious position in the government. He has kicked power. But ours is a democratic party. It is the elected members of the Lok Sabha who will finally decide who should be their leader. And I am the Chairman of the Janata Dal Parliamentary Board. We all are also members of the National Front which is much larger than the Dal.

How will you deal with the corruption cases like Bofors and the Submarine deal if your government came to power.

Naturally we will punish the corrupt. We will appoint a commission to find the truth and the culprits.

What will you do with the culprits.

I must remind you here of Pandit Jawaharlal Nehru's outburst against the corrupt on the eve of independence. He said that once the Congress came to power he would have the corrupt hanged from the *ghanta ghar* (Clock Tower) at Chandni Chowk. For 20 years that poor *ghanta ghar* waited for the corrupt to be hanged from it and when no one was brought to it fell down out of shame. Do you know the 'ghanta ghar' suddenly collapsed during Nehru's lifetime. It is one of the architectural mysteries. I think it collapsed out of shame.

Current, 10.06.1989.
pp. (1 + 3 + 16)

Caught in a nutcracker

The Janata Dal-BJP electoral alliance is maturing gradually despite EMS Namboodripad's protestations and apprehensions of the Left in general. It has perhaps inevitable in the emerging political scenario in the Hindi heart land. The BJP with its dedicated RSS cadrc is perhaps the most well-organised political party in the north though it is still struggling to have a mass base, essential for winning elections and acceptability among the Hindu intelligentsia.

That it retains a firm grip on the urban middle class was evident on August 30, the day of the Bharat Bandh. Delhi was totally closed while most of the cities and towns in the rest of its areas of influence supported the bandh. What has impressed the electorate is not so much its strident Hindutva but the remarkable lack of factionalism among its rank and file. It has a couple of leaders of stature at the central level and can pick and choose competent leaders for heading governments in the states. Both Atal Behari Vajpayee and Lal Kishan Advani have shown admirable restraint in dealing with explosive political situation. What is even more, the two leaders have the flexibility required for electoral adjustments at the national level.

The Janata Dal lacks all these qualities except that its leader Vishwanath Pratap Singh will most probably turn out to be an amazingly swift vote catcher. Despite vicious attempts to malign him, to tarnish his image and declaring him enemy No. 1 of the ruling party by leaders who thrive on their caste basis. He is not a casteist. Nor is he communal or sectarian. He has a national outlook and he alone in his party understands the country's economic problems and knows, how to tackle them.

But the apprehension is that it will be a bear hug for the Janata Dal. In two most populous states of the Hindi belt Bihar and UP—the Muslims and the Harijans play a decisive role in any electoral battle. The Muslims are thoroughly disenchanted with the Congress and will vote for it only as a last resort, that is if they vote at all. The Janata Dal would have been the choice of an overwhelming majority of Muslim voters had not entered into seat adjustments with the BJP. Though the Muslims attitude has softened towards the BJP over the years, it has not yet become their third or even fourth choice. The BJP and the RSS are anathema to them though Vajpayee as Janata Foreign minister had won their hearts, temporarily. The Janata Dal is, therefore, taking a serious risk, a risk which will drastically affect its electoral fortunes, in joining hands with the BJP. It might prove disastrous

because Muslims in these two states do play a decisive role in sixty to seventy parliamentary constituencies.

The damage to the Janata Dal will be more sever when it comes to Harijans and weaker sections. Harijans too do not trust the BJP. They consider it a party of upper castes, the exploitative classes. There is hardly any Harijan leader among its ranks, nor have the BJP policy makers made any conscious effort to woo this very vital segment of voters. Bahujan Samaj leader Kanshi Ram is sure to cut deeply into the Janata Dal's backward vote bank. By moving closer to the BJP, the Janata Dal is bound to alienate its 'natural ally' the Left, especially the CPM. The CPI does not count much and it will throw its weight behind the Congress wherever it has some following. It remains subservient to Moscow.

The Janata Dal is therefore, caught in a nut cracker. It may not be able to withstand the massive blitzkrieg the Congress has planned against V.P. Singh's running with the Left and hunting with the Right hounds.

Current, 16.09.1989.
p. (2)

B. Emergence of a Coalition state

All eyes on V.P. Singh: The next PM

Vishvanath Pratap Singh has taken the Hindi heartland by storm. Uttar Pradesh and Bihar, which send 139 members to the Lok Sabha, have almost decided to wipe the Congress out of power. And he is the one man who will be responsible for the electoral disaster of the ruling party. I travelled with him to nearly 25 constituencies and at each place he was bodily lifted by the enthusiastic crowds on the stage. I saw young men crying with emotion as he spoke. I have never seen such uncontrollable display of pent-up feelings.

Words come out of his mouth like bullets aimed directly at the target: Rajiv Gandhi. Is that all, I ask him as we race, to yet another meeting a few kilometres away. I have to be like this. In this kind of electoral battle one should not waste energy and time. The aim has to be the head and the heart. The effect he makes on his listeners is intoxicating. It makes them delirious. His is a magic spell and I first saw its remarkable impact in the

sprawling Amethi constituency.

The first stop was a Salaon nursed like a baby by Rajiv Gandhi, Capt. Satish Sharma and Sonia Gandhi, the sprawling Indira Gandhi Udan Academy is a few kilometres away in Fursatganj. At the airport says Sanjay Singh, once the Prime Minister's most trusted friend in the constituency, Two jets are ready in a take-off position, he will run away from here. The electorate is indeed in an ugly mood in this constituency. Raj Mohan Gandhi's is no more a symbolic fight. The grandson of Mahatma Gandhi whose name has now become Asli Gandhi (the real Gandhi) has been making irreparable dents in this fortress of a constituency.

At Salaon V.P. Singh climbs the roof of a half built building to address a fairly large crowd. He has developed a new, unusual style. He does not speak, but enters into a dialogue with the audience. Aap logon mein kitne berozgar hein, zara hath uthaiya. (How many of you are unemployed, please raise your hands). Almost everybody raises his hands with shouts *Rajiv ne hum ko nokri nahi di.*

This is the situation in Amethi and, turning towards a group of journalists he says "please note this". Then like a magician, he once again throws his spell. *Kerala mein Congress hari ya Jeeti? Hari*, the crowd responds full throatedly. *Karnataka main*? *Hari. Aur ab Amethi mein kya hoga?* The crowd by now jumps with joy and an uproar comes *Haregi, Haregi.*

A beaming V.P. Singh remarks *to ab faisla ho gaya. Zara hath utha kar is faisle per mohar lagaye.* Then he lifts the hands of a shy, bespectacled Raj Mohan Gandhi sitting next to him, and asks the crowd *yeh kon hein?* The response: *Yeh asli Gandhi hein.* And then he asks them once again *Aur woh kaun hein.* The response *Woh naqli Gandhi hein.*

He raises his voice and asks *to phir vote kisko jayega?* By this time the entire crowd shouts in unison *asli Gandhi ko.* The meeting is over. In the next one nearly the same dialogue is repeated.

Raj Mohan Gandhi is no more a non-candidate, "Had my grandfather been alive" he tells the audience "he would have done the same thing. He would have fought against social injustice, corruption and deceit. Rajiv Gandhi has tarnished the image of his grandfather, Jawaharlal Nehru. One cannot separate Gandhi and Nehru but in this battle against corruption I am dictated by my conscience. If the country has to be saved, Rajiv must be defeated. I say this because the blood of Mahatma Gandhi runs

in my veins", he tells a small group in Jais.

Sanjay Singh, who walks with the help of a stick, assures me that Rajiv will lose from Amethi. "Two thousand per cent. Take it from me. You can quote me. Amethi is my bhoomi, not his. He was planted here by me and I will uproot him". There is too much bitterness in the air in this region. V.P. Singh uses some very harsh words against Rajiv but the harsher the words, the greater is the response. He draws huge crowds wherever he goes and people wait for him for four to five hours.

The Janata Dal activists have already hailed him as the Prime Minister. *Sirf shapat hi to dilwana hai. Ye hogaya hai to woh bhi ho jayega 27 tarikh ko*—only the oath taking ceremony has to be done and that will take place on November 27. They firmly believe in his destiny. A booklet *agle pradhan mantri* with V.P. Singh's picture on the glossy jacket is selling briskly-voters in UP and Bihar who have made up their mind to vote for the Janata Dal do it with this single factor in mind. They are voting for the next Prime Minister. As he climbs on to the stage, the announcer on the mike says: *shant ho jaeya ab hamare agle pradhan mantri aa gaye hein.* He is so confident of the victory that for the last one week he has been refusing to share the platform with the BJP candidates. He will not allow the Janata Dal and the BJP flags to fly together." It is a seat adjustment and not a joint campaign. There is nothing common between us and them (The BJP)". In Aligarh a massive crowd of 50,000 waited for him for over five hours and when he noticed the BJP candidate for the Assembly and its flags, he refused to speak and it took Satpal Malik, the Janata Dal nominee for the Lok Sabha, to persuade him to come to the stage. He went up only after the BJP flag and its candidate were removed.

It's not only in central UP but even in the western fringe in Aligarh, Hathras, Mathura, Khurja and Bulandshahar an anti-Congress wave is sweeping the region. Congressmen are fighting the battle with their backs to the wall and most of them have honourably retired from active campaigning. So great is the popular pressure. VP's recent policy of distancing himself from the BJP has been paying rich dividends.

A very large number of Muslims have been flocking to his public meetings and at Aligarh thousands of university boys lifted him shoulder high and carried him to his Contessa. The university has been closed down because most of the students would like to go out in the field and work for the Janata Dal's victory. Over a hundred professors have issued an appeal in support of the Janata Dal. His public meeting in central UP,

including Kanpur from where CPM candidate Suhashni Ali is contesting, were much larger than that of Rajiv Gandhi's.

In Kanpur while Rajiv Gandhi addressed a meeting of barely five hundred people including the plain clothes men, V.P. Singh had addressed a massive public rally of 30,000 in Moti Jheel, in the heart of this industrial city.

Rajiv Gandhi and his party managers have been terribly upset at the poor—very poor for that matter—response from the people all over the state. The situation has been worsening everyday specially after the *shilanyas.* They first antagonised Muslims who, within moments, decided to vote the Congress out of power and then the Hindus were annoyed because the Faizabad district magistrate would not allow the VHP volunteers to go ahead with digging. The whole shilanyas thing was a fiasco for the Congress. The anti-Congress wave developed into a tornado after Home minister Buta Singh committed some blunders at Ayodhya.

The chief *poojari* of the Ramjanambhoomi, Swami Lal Das has gone on record that he considered the Congress responsible for messing the Bhoomi-Babri Masjid affair. He was incensed when asked him what will be his next step. "I will vote for the Communist candidate from Faizabad Lok Sabha seat and the Janata Dal man from the Ayodhya seat. Every Hindu who believes in clean public life must vote the Congress out of power. The whole Bhoomi-Masjid crisis is the creation of Rajiv Gandhi and Home minister Buta Singh. They must pay for it", the Swami says with considerable bitterness.

Dozens of Ayodhya swamis and mahants have gone to Amethi to canvass against Rajiv Gandhi though it appears simply impossible to upset the Prime Minister's apple cart. So well protected and well groomed is the constituency. More than Rs. 5,000 crore have been invested in the area. The first fertilizer plant at Jagdishpur has brought prosperity but the benefits have not percolated to the common man. Capt. Satish Sharma, Sonia Gandhi and daughter Priyanka have been going from village to village braving dust and heat. It is the real battle field. While V.P. Singh was storming Amethi Rajiv Gandhi was in nearby Fatehpur. The next day VPS was in Fatehpur to undo the damage though the public response to the PM in VP's citadel was very poor. As Rajiv jetted his way to Andhra NTR was in Amethi telling his delirious listeners *Nehru ne desh ko banaya per afsos hai ki unka pota paise ke liye desh ko bech raha hai.* He said this in chaste Hindi.

If this is the situation in Amethi one can understand what must be happening elsewhere in UP. All the opposition stalwarts are apparently

on safe wickets. In Bhillaur, a rural constituency adjoining Kanpur, Arun Nehru is treading on velvet. His opponent Jagdish Prashad Awasthi, who had won the seat for the Congress with a margin of over one lakh votes has already conceded defeat.

Nehru has organised his campaign on a grand scale with more than two lakh brahmins switching sides with him. Bhillaur Muslims have already declared their support for him. His is perhaps the most well organised campaign in the opposition camp with a fleet of jeeps and cars speeding across the constituency spread over 100 kilometres.

In nearby Kanpur city, CPM's Suhashni Ali, wife of film maker Muzzafar Ali, has become a cult figure. Petite and pretty she is the daughter of Netaji Subhash Chandra Bose's two lieutenants Lakshmibai and Gen. Sehgal, who was rescued from the gallows by Jawaharlal Nehru in the famous trial at the Red Fort. The whole city seems to be running after her. Her corner meeting draw ten to fifteen thousands people. As I was passing through the Phoolbagh area of the city at well past midnight she was addressing a massive rally.

Kanpur is virtually red with her thousands of young supporters. She is pitted against a veteran congressman, Naresh Chandra Chaturvedi, former AICC general secretary and sitting MP from the city. The only sign I saw about him in the city was a chappal hanging in the middle of a thoroughfare with the message: *Mein Kab se aap ka intazaar kar raha hun. Zara is taraf bhi tashrif laiye.*

Yet another pretty one is Reshma, Arif Mohammed Khan's wife who is seeking an assembly seat which falls in Suhashni's Lok Sabha constituency. Reshma is on the Janata Dal ticket but both she and Suhashni have been campaigning jointly. Both will win hands down. Reshma's father Ishaq Ilmi is the editor and owner of an Urdu daily, *Siyasat*, and held in great esteem by both Hindus and Muslims.

Her husband Arif Mohammed Khan has emerged as the uncrowned king in nearby Baharaich constituency. He is simply adored by his constituents, both Hindus and Muslims. He cannot be defeated. Gonda is next to Baharaich where Raja Anand Singh of Mankapur, sitting Congress MP, is in trouble. His daughter is married to Ajeya Singh, son of V.P. Singh. VPS visited this constituency but appealed to the people to vote for Fazlul Bari, a Muslim Majlis leader, contesting on the Janata Dal symbol. It is a Brahmin dominated area and such is the Janata wave that most of the Brahmin leaders, including Deep Narain Pandey, are actively campaigning for him.

Faizabad comes next where Nirmal Khatri, once Youth Congress leader

and sitting MP, is facing CPI's Mittersen Yadav. The BJP has withdrawn its candidate in Khatri's favour but Yadav is hopeful of romping home. Both Faizabad and Ayodhya are likely to be captured by the opposition. The BJP, supported by the VHP, is likely to have a bloody nose in this land of Lord Rama. I found no signs of communal tension in the twin cities. Hindus and Muslims live in total communal harmony. It is more pronounced in Ayodhya. It has hundreds of mosques and over 4000 big and small temples. I was pleasantly surprised to meet Meer Ansar Hussain who is the keeper of one of the most sacred Sundar Bhavan Mandir. This 83 year old Muslim was born in Ayodhya and has been serving the Mandir for the last 40 years. He keeps its key and opens it every morning. When Meer Hussain fell sick some years ago his life was saved by the chief Mahant of Hanuman Garhi Swami Ramkaran Das by donating his blood. So the Meer has the Swami's blood and the two live happily in Ayodhya. "It is the RSS and the VHP," says Swami Lal Das, keeper of the sanctum sanctorum, "which has sowed the seeds of communal hatred. We will not let them succeed."

The bumpy road from Faizabad goes to the easternmost corner of UP, Ballia, the seat of Chandra Shekhar who is expecting to avenge his defeat this time by a margin of over two lakh votes. The Chandra Shekhar wave is cutting across the caste and communal combinations and almost the whole constituency has rallied round this Janata stalwart. He is facing Jagannath Choudhri of the Congress in a straight contest. The Chandra Shekhar wind has completely damaged the chance of the loudmouthed Union Power minister Kalpanath Rai in the Ghosi constituency. The Janata Dal has taken the bull by its horn and is confident of trouncing him.

A common complaint against the sitting Congress MPs all over UP is that they seldom visited their constituencies after they were elected. The comforts of Delhi, the cosy air-conditioned bungalows and patronage from Bombay's industrial houses completely spoiled them. Even now most of them have Contessas and NE-118s fitted with air conditioners and stereo music systems. The overwhelming majority Rajiv Gandhi received in 1984 went to their head like wine. Now they are facing the music. They are being received with garlands of chappals.

In Pratapgarh where Commerce minister Raja Dinesh Singh is pitted against Abhey Singh, son of former UP minister Ajit Singh, the situation is no better. The two Rajput leaders are traditional rivals but here too the word of V.P. Singh carries more weight than all the Thakur leaders of the area placed together. Dinesh Singh is involved in the grimmest electoral battle of his long political career.

Portly Hari Krishna Shastri, eldest son of Lal Bahadur Shastri and a Union minister is cursing the day he chose Fatehpur. He conceded defeat the day VPS reached this sleepy town to file his nomination after being delayed at Delhi airport. "The delay itself cost me over 50,000 votes," laments Shastri. Fatehpur is easily a one-man show and VPS need not spend his time here.

He is, in fact, more interested in Allahabad, a few kilometres away. Here Kamla Bahuguna is pitted against Janata Dal's formidable Janeshwar Mishra. Kamla is the daughter of the soil, her father Prof. Tripathi was a noted historian in Allahabad University. But her strongest support comes from Hemavati Nandan Bahuguna who is fighting for her from the grave. Allahbad will never forgive itself for defeating Bahuguna against Amitabh Bachchan who finally let down the people of this historic city. Now Bahuguna dead is more powerful than Bahuguna alive and Kamla never has had it so good. Janeshwar Mishra is not a weak candidate either. An ex-Socialist he is quite capable of pulling a rabbit out of the hat. It's a neck and neck race Allahabad and even VPS will have to work hard for Janeshwar.

Uttar Pradesh does not easily let down its heroes. Narayan Dutt Tiwari is one of them. He is the one man against whom the opposition has not uttered a word. The people, who are visibly angry with the Congress, too graciously spare him of their ire. The wrath is heaped on Rajiv Gandhi who would not allow Tiwari enough elbow room. Had the state been left to him the ruling party would not be facing ignominy. Though the Congress is on its way out, he remains the beloved of the masses. He has been drawing much larger crowds than his Prime Minister in separate meeting held by him. He is clearly a victim of circumstances and the whims of his Prime Minister. Had he not been there the ruling party was in for a much more inglorious rout. His worth is recognised even by V.P. Singh, who does not say a word against him in his acid tongued campaign. His only mistake is that he lumped the assembly elections with that of the Lok Sabha.

The situation in Bihar is equally bad. Chief minister Satyendra Narain Sinha has already conceded 24 out of 54 seats to the opposition when he said that the ruling party will get at least 30 seats. A group of journalists visiting Patna and North and South Bihar came back with the impression that the Congress may not get more than fifteen seats and that too if the adverse trend did not continue.

Rajiv Gandhi was possibly aware of the deteriorating situation for his party when he addressed a moderate crowd at Patna's Gandhi Maidan,

on November 13. The crowd was impassive though he was perhaps at the best of his oratory attacking the Janata Dal. The gist of his speech in which he announced the handing over of Bhagalpur to the army was that the Janata Dal is made up of a bunch of traitors who are in league with Pakistan's Benazir Bhutto. "We will not allow Benazir to dictate terms to us".

He branded I.K. Gujral without naming him as a friend of terrorists because no terrorists group has put up a candidate against him in Jullundhar. He snubbed Chief minister Sinha for not allowing him to speak from the stage and instead placed BPCC chief Jagannath Mishra to conduct the proceedings. His son Rahul Gandhi neatly dressed in khadi kurta pyjama stood behind him all the time as he addressed the rally. The local Congress bosses bowed before him with folded hands.

The ruling party is facing stiff competition on each and every seat. In Patna CPI's Ramnath Yadav is far ahead of his Congress rival Dr. C.P. Thakur, while in the adjoining Barh constituency Ram Lakhan Singh Yadav is pitted against Janata Dal's Nitesh Kumar who fears large scale booth capturing. In Muzaffarpur George Fernandes, the Janata Dal secretary, is most likely to trounce Union minister L.P. Sahi while in Gopalganj Mafia don Kali Pande, who joined the Congress barely a month ago, is facing Janata Dal's Raj Mangal Mishra. Pande has specialised in terrorising voters who are against him. Both the contenders are local Bhumihar leaders and the caste vote will be split evenly. Mishra is expecting Rajput, backward and minority votes in this straight fight. The Congress is facing 22 straight contests all over Bihar. And in most of these constituencies it is likely to lose by narrow margins.

The Indian People's Front made up of Naxalites is the dark horse. It has put up 11 candidates mostly in South and Central Bihar. It is emerging as a powerful factor in the state politics and though it may not fare well in the Lok Sabha election, it will give a tough time to any party in power. A large number of Harijans, backwards and lower class Muslims have been joining its rank and file. Because of the presence of its candidates in these constituencies booth capturing will not be possible.

The shadow of Bhagalpur looms large over the state. The killing of innocent Muslims in this district, which produces fine silk has shocked most Biharis. It has undoubtedly antagonised Muslims who have been

traditional Congress voters. Like Uttar Pradesh, in Bihar too Muslims play a decisive role in many of the 54 constituencies in north Bihar about ten seats have Muslim majorities, including Kishanganj, where former *Telegraph* editor M.J. Akbar is locked in a bitter contest with former Congress MP Israrul Haque. Akbar is trying hard to maintain his secular image but local Hindus are in no mood to come to his rescue. Muslims constitute nearly 60 per cent of the electorate and he does not expect to get even ten votes of his community.

The situation is reversed in Bhagalpur where former Chief minister Bhagawat Jha Azad is facing the ire of Brahmins who suspect him of protecting Muslim criminals. In Janata Dal's Chunchun Yadav he has a formidable opponent. And if the election is not countermanded he will find it extremely difficult to win. In North West Bihar our own K.K. Tewari, the walking thesaurus, is having the run for his verbosity, Tej Narain Singh of the CPI is improving his position hour after hour. Though BJP's Kamal Singh is also likely to take away a big chunk of opposition voters K.K. Babu, as he is popularly called, has been a special target of Shatrughan Sinha who has held two massive rallies and vowed to eliminate him.

During his election tour two weeks back V.P. Singh drew unprecedented crowds from Gopalganj to Hajipur. He will once again storm Bihar a couple of days before the poll. He is as popular in Bihar as in UP and every Janata candidate has requested him to visit his constituency at least once.

Most observers in Patna and Lucknow do not give more than fifty seats in both the states. A senior journalist in the Patna editions of the *Hindustan Times* walked out of the local coffee shop in protest when a fellow journalist refused to reduce the number of seats any further. Journalists in both the capitals did not give twenty and fifteen seats in UP and Bihar respectively for the Congress.

The most optimistic congressman I met in Lucknow was Makhan Lal Fotedar. "The Congress", he claimed while puffing his 555, "will get not less than fifty seats. Take it from me and I can be quoted". He gives only fifteen seats to the opposition. "Your friend V.P. Singh will lose his deposit. If he does not, I will quit politics. You can quote me," he pronounced with disdain.

Current, 25.11.1989.
pp. (1 + 2 + 3 + 6)

V.P. Singh is reluctant to wear a crown of thorns

I have never seen so much post-election gloom in this cheerful city of politicians who are always laughing, joking with one another. A sense of shock prevails in both the camps. The victors are as much worried as the vanquished with big question marks looming large over their heads. The congressmen were as much sure of their defeat as the Janata Dal leaders of their victory. Now uncertainty runs like a laser beam from one camp to the other.

This election has killed two birds with one stone, the Congress as well as the opposition, with the electorate having the last laugh. Vishwanath Pratap Singh who waged a relentless battle against Rajiv Gandhi and pulverized the Congress in the North, the West and the East was perhaps the loneliest figure in the victorious crowd of the Janata Dal leaders. Reluctant to take over the reins of power he was pushed around by senior as well as junior colleagues to wear the crown of thorns. The Prime Ministership of the largest democracy was being offered to him on a platter and he seemed to be scared of it. Incredible! I met him several times in these crucial days and I had a feeling that he was not mentally ready for the job. He was persuaded, cajoled and finally mildly threatened to wear the mantle for which more than half of the country stood by him like a rock—"It is not an offer", a visibly shaken Arun Nehru told him, "but a mandate from the electorate and it cannot be refused".

In fact, the real cause of his worry is not the Prime Ministership, he is quite capable of handling it, but the men who manage the Janata Dal and the two diametrically opposed allies who have decided to limp on the road of power with their crutches on either side: The BJP and the Communists.

The Janata Dal is still in the process of integration: Devi Lal and Ajit Singh continue to be at loggerheads. It's a fragile truce, and V.P. Singh has been acting as a one-man peace keeping force. The Lok Dal (A) and the Lok Dal (B) are very much alive and kicking. Both have been pressing him for their pound of flesh. His cabinet has to be evenly balanced.

Ajit Singh is more interested in the Chief ministership of Uttar Pradesh than a berth in the Central cabinet but Devi Lal has staked his fortunes on the little man of UP, Mulayam Singh Yadav. Ajit Singh has also been hitting hard at the Haryana supremo's dynasty—the Chautalas and the Ranjit Singh. In this he has the moral support of most of the erstwhile Jan Morcha leaders. "Look", they ruefully point out, "what happened in Andhra." One of the opposition charges against NTR has been his

unabashed promotion of his sons and sons-in-law.

When I spoke to V.P. Singh in the Central Hall of Parliament, he appeared hopeful of wading through the murky sea of factionalism. My impression is that once he takes over command and fully in control of the situation he will be able to deftly handle the warring Lok Dal factions. Both need power and it may be the first and the last chance for them. They are also overwhelmingly aware that they have ridden on the crest of a popular wave whipped up by this unique leader of man. He will come across a lot of pressure while forming his cabinet but here too he seems to be sure to manage the hurdles.

The erstwhile Jan Morcha men are fully with him though they are keen to have a major share in power. Arun Nehru, Arif Mohammed Khan, Mufti Mohammed Sayeed, Satpal Malik, Rampoojan Patel, Manvender Singh, etc., are the pillars of the erstwhile Jan Morcha and also the Janata Dal. They are perhaps the most experienced men in running a government. Most of them have the reputation of being able and efficient administrators. Their claims can be ignored only at the risk of giving a weak and inefficient government. Both the Lok Dals have ex-Socialists like George Fernandes and Purshotam Kaushik, both of whom have romped home with huge margins from Bihar and Madhya Pradesh. Sharad Yadav too is an ex-Socialist and Devi Lal's blue eyed boy. There is no dearth of talent in the Janata Dal and it will depend on V.P. Singh how best he will make use of it. He is personally least interested in any group or faction and as leader of a party like the Janata Dal he has to be above petty considerations. A great degree of his success will depend on the kind of team he selects and the kind of assignments he gives to it and the kind of advisers he picks up and the way he strikes a balance among all these teams. He will undoubtedly take a leaf from Rajiv Gandhi's book of failures. The ex-Prime Minister did have a mind of his own and made the worst of the bad gift by choosing absolutely selfish, greedy and corrupt men around him and packed his council of ministers with equally corrupt men with sycophancy as their main qualification. He has to avoid sycophants like plague and keep his doors and windows open to all kind of currents and cross-currents. The impression that he can be pushed around has to be done away with a very simple fact in mind that the job of the Prime Minister is to run the country despite the painful reality that his is a minority government. This is a new experiment and an art can be developed of maintaining what Lohia had called an equidistance.

Both the BJP and the Communists will pull him in their own direction

exert maximum pressure on him and may even try to blackmail as they have been doing all along. Not so much the Communist but the BJP with its predominant position will develop the habit to dictating terms as they did before they lent their support to him. But the BJP stalwarts are no fools. They know that he enjoys an overwhelming mandate of the people and if the BJP has bagged an unexpected number of seats it is also due to the pro-V.P. Singh wave. The Hindu wave was assiduously whipped up by the VHP and the RSS and it is most likely to ebb in due course of time. It was created for a limited purpose while VPS fired the imagination of the people and gave them hopes of a clean government, a free society with equal status to all religions and economic groups and classes. He has given them a hope. He has shown them a dream though not a fabulous one. The hope of a government sans commissions and Swiss bank accounts. He can go down in history if he can fulfill these very basic desires of the people. Much bigger problems of removal of unemployment, boost to the rural sector and taking the benefits of the economic progress to the poorest of the poor are matters of detail and will need some time to be tackled at the base level. His foremost task is to put an end to corruption what he had been saying at the high places. Bring the country's money stashed in Swiss banks back and also stagmatise the guilty as a lesson for future rulers.

What I feel is that the BJP and the Communists will not do anything which might lead to the collapse of the government. The BJP will now be more interested in getting the Assemblies in Rajasthan, Gujarat and Madhya Pradesh and form their own governments if possible or enter into coalition with the Janata Dal if it becomes unavoidable. Its next step will be to consolidate its position in the newly acquired power centres and also to increase its influence in UP and Bihar where it is poor second to the JD. It will continue its ideological battle with the Communists but avoid actual clashes. The two have their distinct areas of influence.

In the long conversation the BJP supremo L.K. Advani made it clear that his party's main political task is to put end to the Nehru dynasty for ever. "It has become a curse and Rajiv used it more as a commercial product nicely packed to promote his own ambitions". In his view the Nehru dynastic rule has done more harm to the national fibre of the country than anyone else. This attitude will inevitably cause tension among the erstwhile Jan Morcha leaders who remain admirers of Nehru and his daughter Indira Gandhi and who too would have remained with Rajiv Gandhi had he not antagonised them with his skullduggery.

The Communists have the intention of playing on an entirely different footing. They are aware of their shortcomings in the Hindi belt and will push VPS hard. They will be happy if he can satisfy them with his actions against corruption and also carry on certain economic reforms especially in the rural sector. Their first priority will be comprehensive land reforms which Jyoti Basu has done in Bengal. They expect from him to put up a stiff fight against communalism and also weed out communal fascist elements from the police and the paramilitary forces. They genuinely feel that they are his "natural allies".

Most Janata Dal leaders are very unhappy with the tactics the BJP adopted during the election. At least 30 seats were lost in the North because with the BJP candidates in the fray a triangular fight disturbed the one-to-one strategy, especially in the assembly election in UP. In the Faizabad Lok Sabha constituency, the BJP withdrew its candidate and Rajmata Vijay Raje Scindia made an announcement saying the BJP followers should instead vote for the Congress candidate Nirmal Khatri. Despite this obvious treachery, the CPI's Mitter Sen won with a thumping majority. Though it may take time, the real fight for power in this country will ultimately be between the BJP and secular elements in the Janata Dal, the Congress (without Rajiv) and the Left. The battle ground will be the Hindi heartland.

The Janata Dal's alliance with the Left will most likely firm up because the Communists are now aware of the mass base of this party and its recent winning over of Muslims. The backwards were already with it. Muslims are totally disenchanted with the Congress, especially Rajiv Gandhi, and it will be very difficult for him to win them over. They have been receiving blows after grievous blows in the Congress-ruled states. The combination of Muslims with the backwards, along with Thakurs and Gujjars can be very formidable front for the Janata Dal and the Communists will only be too happy to be a part of it. Not the BJP. It can never expect an unconditional Muslim support, come what may, and in future it will most probably give up its stance of having a sprinkle of Muslims like Sikander Bakht and Arif Beg.

Rajiv Gandhi's mistake was that he tried to be a greater Hindu than the VHP diehards but launching his election campaign from Faizabad and declaring he will usher in an era of Ram Rajya, he was misunderstood not only by Muslims but also Harijans. The tragedy was that the VHP thought he was arrogating himself the right to do what they had planned—the establishment of a Hindu state. In the process, he lost both the Hindu and the backward votes. The MAJGAR—(Muslim-Ahir-Jat-Gujiar-

Rajput)—therefore got a shot in the arm and swept the Hindi heartland. He was left with the most unusual Brahmin, Harijan combine. With Buta Singh, Mani Shanker Aiyer and Fotedar as his advisers what else could be expected from the wonder boy who became Prime Minister? It take quite an effort to destroy an organisation like the Congress.

I am a witness to scores of voters voting against him with tears in their eyes. An elderly lady in Delhi constituency came out from the pooling booth virtually crying and muttering "I never voted against the Congress but this man (Rajiv Gandhi) forced me to do so. Rajiv Gandhi not only destroyed the Congress but the dreams and aspirations of millions of Indians who took the Congress as part of their family. He has split this historic family, but hopefully, not for long".

Congressmen in the Janata Dal and the Congress will come together; if not today, tomorrow. It is difficult to tear off a genuine congressman from his mother party. He invariably comes back, you could call it the home-coming. Soon the congressmen in the Janata Dal and their former party colleagues on the other side of the fence will cast wistful eyes on each other. The one group is in power while the other has just lost it. "Time is a great healer and if Siddharta Shanker Ray, Vengal Rao, Das Munshi, S.B. Chavan, K.C. Pant, Dinesh Singh, Gundu Rao etc., who hurled the choicest invectives at Indira Gandhi and her son, could come back with a bang what will prevent yet another reunion? It will come sooner or later," a very senior ex-Congress minister in the Janata Dal remarked. "But, minus Rajiv Gandhi". He is totally unacceptable to this group. "The pipeline between us and them has always been open. But then it was on different footing. Now it is a matter of sharing power and saving the country from the communal and fascist monster." This leader was quite candid about the shape of things to come. "But the fight", he continued, "was against Rajiv Gandhi, his corruption, his arrogance and his authoritarianism. We have defeated him. He is no more the Prime Minister."

"He is gone but the Congress is very much there and what we are bothered about is the Congress and the future of the country, not that of Rajiv Gandhi. The ball is in their court. Let them get rid of Rajiv Gandhi and the ball from this side will get rolling". He stopped short of saying that a new phase of splits and counter-splits will be the order of the day.

At the moment, the Congress stands solidly by Rajiv Gandhi, especially Congress from the South. But the North-South divide is becoming discernible. Those who have had a drubbing in the Hindi belt are ill at ease with Rajiv Gandhi and will strike when the iron gets hot. Strike they will and some of them at the behest of their former colleagues now in the

Janata Dal. The talks are at an initial stage but it has a lot of substance. congressmen in both the camps feel that it was an anti-Rajiv wave and the electorate was actually not against the Congress. Rajiv too is not unaware of this factor and his intelligence sources have been feeding him with information of the possibilities of a move to have a Congress without him. The Left will, in all probability, support such a move. It would align with a new Congress, with a new determination and a new objective of a democratic, socialistic and secular plan (not like the happening when Gulzari Lal Nanda stepped in).

It is too early to predict what will happen in the coming two to three months but if the Janata Dal fails to give a clean stable government to the country, the electorate will this time write off any alternative to Congress for years to come. The stakes are very very high and Vishwanath Pratap Singh is most aware of this single most important factor.

Current, 02.12.1989.
pp. (1 + 3 + 8)

Man of destiny faces the Nation

Vishwanath Pratap Singh, India's new man of destiny, has been under close scrutiny from the people of India since the moment he took the oath of office. The vigilant electorate has set its eyes on the helmsman who is expected to put in superhuman efforts to rise to their expectations.

He most likely will, as I have known him from very close quarters. He is totally committed to whatever he has promised and if he is not made a punching bag by his own partymen and the two allies, he will set the ball rolling. Nobody expects miracles from him but everybody expects that he will fulfil the promises he has made and that too not only the long range economic and social reforms but also those concerning the purely administrative and legal steps to set the things right.

They are specified in the Janata Dal manifesto and reaffirmed in his hundreds of speeches during the election campaign.

First: His party is totally and unconditionally committed to eradicate corruption at high places. "Our resolve," it says, "is to dismantle the nexus between politicians and vested interests and to eradicate the all-pervasive corruption. It will track down the kickback funds generated by the Bofors

and other deals stashed away in foreign banks. The funds will be restored to the nation and the guilty will be punished."

The implementation of this one resolve alone will make him invincible till the next scheduled election. For this one act alone he will go down in our democratic history as an inveterate doer.

In this crusade he need not touch Rajiv Gandhi or any of his colleagues suspected of the crime but he merely has to ask the head of Bofors to come to the Capital and disclose the names and amounts his company has paid and where the money has been stashed.

Since V.P. Singh has promised an open government, let the Swedish gentleman hold a press conference in Delhi and tell the nation who actually is involved with substantial proof. The Prime Minister then should allow the law of the land to take its own course.

If the Bofors chief refuses to disclose the secret the contract should be cancelled and Bofors blacklisted. But the money has to be brought back because it belongs to the millions of emaciated and hungry people of this country. The Swiss government should be approached according to their and our laws.

Similar steps should be taken in the deals concluded in the past five years. This is an absolute must if the government of Vishwanath Pratap Singh has to survive with dignity and honour.

Not only this. All those industrialists who have taken the money out by evading taxes and using other reprehensible methods should sternly be scrutinised and, if found guilty of the charge, should first be asked to bring that money back and handed over to the legal authorities as common criminals.

The nation will applaud such moves since it has given V.P. Singh the mandate to take these steps. The slightest faltering on this major promise will bring the wrath of the people upon him and he will never be forgiven. It will not be considered vendetta and will be a very big step in providing a clean government. It will also set at rest the suspicions and rumours that certain important members of his party have accepted 'donations' from such individuals whether they are NRIs or Bombay based.

Corruption at governmental, middle and lower levels will be drastically reduced. The nation had got used to corruption. But it had not capitulated to the crime. It is only on this issue the nation reposed its faith in him and I repeat he has to justify it.

Second: He has promised to arrest inflation and the price rise in essential commodities. His party's manifesto says: "The worst hit are the rural

poor as is obvious from the escalation in the cost of living Index for the agricultural labour. It considers price stability as crucial for removal of poverty and steady growth of economy.

If the team of his ministers is made up of honest people he will have no difficulty to take "stringent action against hoarders and black-marketeers. Black money, black market, tax evasion and corruption could not be stopped in these forty years of Congress rule because most of its ministers were neck deep in reprehensible acts of corruption.

The Congress Prime Minister, excluding of course Nehru, not only encouraged corruption among their ministers but themselves became part of these dirty, unpardonable crimes. The price rise has been a by-product of this system.

The system has to be changed and if V.P. Singh cannot do it nobody, in the near future will be able to do it. Janata Dal's pledge to the nation was not only to remove Rajiv Gandhi and his corrupt regime but "an alternative model of governance" committed to liberate the poor from misery and starvation.

The new Prime Minister who has seen abject poverty in rural India during his campaign will have no right to rest until he took major steps to eradicate poverty. It can be done and I am hopeful he will do it. He can do it single handedly. If there is a will, there is a way.

Third: Our problems of poverty cannot be solved unless we shape our rural economy. Janata Dal's promise of deploying 50 per cent investible resources for the development of rural economy will have to be reconsidered. The entire banking system and the might of the huge financial institutions has been directed in making the urban rich richer and creating monsters out of footpath pygmies who gobbled billions of rupees by floating mega issues and the debenture rackets. The Congress created a system in which a few individuals played havoc with the country's economic morale. The funds cannot be channelled to rural India unless these frauds are exposed and the money they had amassed in our banks is taken away and employed in rural bonds and in rural schemes. Men in important position and those in the pay rolls of these mega issue-giants will kick up, shindy, but he should ignore them with the contempt they deserve. It is not the economists who solve the problems of poverty. Take away their air conditioned cars and offices and perks and fat salaries and they will come down to earth. In his crusade against poverty he can be his own best economic adviser. He does not need egg-heads. The Planning Commission has become totally redundant, irrelevant. It should be packed off. It is not worth its name if it has failed to remove poverty in

forty years. The only alternative is to implement ruthlessly the poll promises and make the bureaucrats work round the clock. They have enjoyed too much power and too many perks over the years.

If they fail to work then an entirely new set of people from public life and private companies should be brought in. This comes close to V.P. Singh's promise of "an alternative model of governance". His government should be emancipated from the tyranny of greedy and sycophantic bureaucrats. They have been one of the major causes of Rajiv Gandhi's failure and ultimate fall. Most ministers tend to get scared to these woodenheaded, in most cases corrupt, bureaucrats. The New Prime Minister should remove fear of these overbearing civil servants and attain the idea of free government.

Fourth: Free and open government. The Prime Minister and his team of minister has no right to keep any secret, unless it pertains to delicate defence secrets. The curse of secret, top secret and utmost secret should be done away with one stroke. Even the budget should no more be secret. What secret can there be in budgetary proposals? An open government means an open government though most of the keepers of these secrets in South and North Blocks will faint.

They are not used to their weaknesses being exposed to the people. They have been used to making money in the name of secrets. It was not surprising when the notorious black bonds were sold most in Delhi. If an investigation is made they will be found to be the largest depositors of black money. It is not necessary to honour these bonds. How on earth can V.P. Singh reconcile to the conspiracy of turning billions of rupees into white, untaxable money. Some way will have to be found to bring this money into the government coffers. After all the number of these depositors of black money would not exceed even one per cent in the whole country.

It might shake this microscopic minority of criminals but will send waves of jubilation among the people. This will be a first and most effective step curbing black money and help strengthen the concept of open government.

The idea of taking away the Radio and TV from the clutches of the government and turning them into autonomous corporations has to be done without loss of time. The draft is ready, it has only to be finalised and implemented.

Fifth: Janata Dal would not have been able to form a government at the centre and Rajiv Gandhi would have continued as Prime Minister with a comfortable majority had Muslims not voted for it almost en bloc.

For the first time after independence they threw the yoke of loyalty to the Congress and made it possible for V.P. Singh to smash the cult of the Congress.

Over 12,000 communal riots have taken place since independence and almost all in the Congress-ruled states. Thousands of Muslims have lost their lives and property worth hundreds of crores destroyed, reduced to ashes. This time Muslims have voted out Muslims contesting on Congress tickets and opted for Janata Dal, BSP and even the BJP. It was a truly secular vote all over the country. They have only one demand their lives and property should be protected. All they want is do not kill them and do not burn their property.

There is no other Muslim problem which cannot be solved amicably. Muslim Personal Law, Urdu, Babri Masjid, etc., are the handiwork cf selfish, megalomaniac Muslim intellectuals and leaders and of course a large part of the Urdu press.

It injects communal poison among Muslims in the most brazen manner. This is not freedom of the press but a misuse of the constitutional provision.

Janata Dal has made specific promise of protection to minorities who will enjoy the fullest protection and opportunities to pursue their modes of worship and their religions beliefs and practices and develop their institutions, whether religious, cultural educational or welfare-oriented.

The tragic episode of communal violence has to be brought to an end by taking stern measures and giving exemplary punishment to the guilty, irrespective of religious and caste loyalties. Janata Dal's promise is that it will create a "mixed anti-riot force" so as to enforce totally impartial conduct from them.

Full compensation to victims of communal and caste riots will be provided and action will be taken against officers who fail to control riots. Special courts will be constituted to try cases relating to communal and caste riots. Justice will be done to the victims of November, 1984 riots in Delhi and elsewhere and those responsible will be punished." These extraordinary declarations of faith in communal harmony have yielded rich dividends to Janata Dal and it will suffer a grievous blow if it failed to live upto them.

Sixth: Yet another gigantic promise is about the Right to Work which will soon be incorporated in the constitution by amending it. Every citizen of India has a right to work and lead a decent life. The social and economic policy of Janata Dal has to be geared to realise this fundamental right. Janata Dal has to strike very hard to meet this challenge. The framers of

the policy have not left any ambiguity in this regard when they came out with the idea of a new Employment Guarantee Scheme all over the country. It meets a very simple demand of the have-nots whose number turns into crores—*Roti, Kapda, Makan.*

If V.P. Singh can achieve this in the stipulated time he will usher in a silent, bloodless revolution with no parallel in world history. Imagine at least five hundred million people who live below the *chapati* belt having two meals a day. The million dollar question is can a party with minority in Parliament and with a Right and a Left group watching its performance attain whatever it has promised?

My belief is, it can. Neither the BJP nor the Left has any dispute on these six crucial points. The government will not fall but it will survive and thrive if V.P. Singh leaves the job of mending Dal's political problems with the Right and the Left and busy himself in implementing the promises.

One of the reasons of the two Congress Prime Minister's failure was monopolistic attitude in holding power. Both Indira Gandhi and Rajiv Gandhi believe in absolute power. They were Prime Ministers as well as party chiefs. The result was disastrous. V.P. Singh should leave the inner party and intra-party problems to his colleagues assigned to do this specific job.

He is a leader. His charisma has begun to work and he should make maximum use of it and in the absolute right direction. I remember he had added the following lines at the end of the Manifesto: "The National Front reiterates its commitment to the policies and programmes set out in this manifesto. Burdened by the price rise, hurt by violence, fractured by communalism and shamed by corruption at the top, the nation longs for relief. At last the hour of change has struck. It is for the people of India to ring it in with their votes."

The great people of India have done their job. Now it is for V.P. Singh to rise to their expectations.

Current, 09.12.1989.
pp. (1 + 3)

A fresh mandate

The country is gradually but inexorably moving towards a mid-term poll. Whether Vishwanath Pratap Singh is ready to face the electorate at short notice and whether the fast-moving political developments favour

his return to power is immaterial, the compulsions of the situation are such that a fresh mandate from the people has become inevitable. He can no more hang on to the prime ministership and the more the delay, the greater will be the loss in his popularity and credibility. He should strike before the situation goes completely out of hand. The equations he formed on the eve of the last poll have gone haywire. In his own party his position is no more unassailable. His moral authority to rule is being questioned all over the country. His government has lost the sense of direction. It is being accused of inefficiency and ineptness. The popular feeling is that a regime which is busy twenty-four hours in the game of survival is incapable of providing a government that works. The strategy of crisis management can be feasible only for a short period and cannot work if crises become a permanent feature and political fortunes swing like a pendulum. He has done a commendable job in keeping the government and party intact in an enormously precarious situation and he may have nerves of steel but the people will not agree to live on tenterhooks day in and day out. The lack of stability at the top can be a nerve-shattering experience, the national mood is therefore in favour of a fresh mandate.

Such a mandate is necessary for four reasons: First, the Janata Dal is no more a cohesive party. One of its main architects, Devi Lal, is out to do maximum damage to VPS and his image. He cannot and should not be ignored. His close ally Chandra Shekhar, who never accepted VPS as leader and prime minister, strongly feels the party is not with him and as long as he remains Prime Minister, he and his supporters will continue to work for the government's fall. The prime minister does not also command the unstinted support of three of the four Janata Dal chief ministers. At the moment only Laloo Yadav seems to be standing by him.

Second, the BJP is no more an ally. It may not have withdrawn its support but it has been indulging in a blatant game of blackmail by flinging threats of withdrawing support two to three times a day. Instead of behaving as an ally, the BJP hangs like the sword of Damocles on the government's head. Its out of proportion victory has gone in its head like wine and now it is dreaming to capture at least 200 head seats in the north. Every party has a legitimate right to aspire to come to power, but the ways and means the BJP has adopted to attain its goal has shocked even the most pious, god-fearing Hindus. Lal Krishan Advani's Somnath-Ayodhya *rathyatra* purely to incite Hindu passions and consolidate its vote bank has shaken the faith even of its most ardent admirers. The BJP will not be the same after Advaniji's vote *yatra*. In its desperate attempt to polarise the country on religious lines, it has done great harm to its

own image as a 'party of the future'. It has misunderstood the Hindu psyche by assuming that all those people who flocked to have a *darshan* of the rath will become BJP voters. Just as congressmen are feeling that the huge crowds gathering to see Rajiv Gandhi during his Sadbhavna *yatras* are his potential voters. It is therefore absolutely necessary that the BJP should be allowed to test its electoral strength before it does more harm to the country's secular fabric.

Third, a mid-term poll is the only way to expose the Congress duplicity on every national issue—Mandal report, Bhoomi-Masjid dispute, Kashmir, Punjab, Assam, etc. Rajiv Gandhi has been running with the hares and hunting with the hounds thinking that he would once again hoodwink the people, the Congress has never been on such weak wicket and in the new political situation it stands to lose rather than gain. Its Muslim-Harijan base has been knocked off, the backwards have gone with VPS, it will have to share its upper caste voters with the BJP.

Fourth, the bureaucracy whose role in running the country cannot be underestimated is not in tune with the government for the simple reason that it thinks the minority government may collapse any time. The prime minister's writ does not run at the bureaucratic level. Nothing moves in the government and nothing will move so long as the stalemate continues. It's hung government, a product of a hung Parliament.

In this situation, the prime minister, whose integrity remains beyond question, should take the nation into confidence and once again seek its mandate. He might emerge in a much better and stronger position. Let him prove he is not a limpet.

Current, 27.10.1990.
p (2)

Death of democracy

November 10, 1990 will go down in the history of the Republic as a black day not because an honest man genuinely concerned for the poor, weak, deprived and the minorities was removed from office by manipulations, intrigues and the vulgar use of money power but because a government led by men of doubtful character was installed in power. The whole country felt sad that the bunch of opportunists and crooks surrounding Chandra Shekhar who split their own party at the behest of a few industrialists will now lord over its destiny. For the first time in the

post-Independence history of this country, the loyalties of members of Parliament were openly traded in a brazen manner. Some who crossed over to Chandra Shekhar's camp has reasons to feel hurt by the former prime minister's failure to carry his colleagues with him. He did not know how to run the party and had little time to control the government; so involved was he in the game of survival. He also could not create a team of political managers or trouble-shooters who could work at his behest. He has paid a heavy price for his failures.

In the wake of V.P. Singh's fall, the Congress, of course, has suffered most. Its opportunistic role in promoting a government of defectors has enormously damaged its image in the public eye. The argument that it did so to avoid a fresh poll and the violence it may have generated is nothing but hypocrisy and a ruse to hide its own sins. Bofors was indeed a major factor in its ceaseless efforts to oust VPS. He was about to lay his hands on the main culprits though he could have accelerated the process of uncovering the truth. Nobody disagrees with the fact that bribes were given and there is no doubt about who received them. However, this fact had to be proved with the support of unassailable documents. Had it been done, the Congress party and those in its ranks who had received bribes would have been permanently exposed and punished. But VPS was either too slow or too much under pressure from a group within his own party not to proceed in the right direction. As suggested, he should have placed all the relevant Bofors papers on the table of the House even on the day he faced the confidence motion but he did not do it. Why? He should take the nation into confidence if he has to vindicate his honour.

Rajiv Gandhi's opportunistic posture in supporting a government of detectors has caused great discomfiture among the rank and file in his own party. His plea that his party did not wish to form the government since it did not have a mandate from the people stinks of immorality. Why then did he lend his support to a group of people who were elected on a particular symbol and manifesto but betrayed the people's mandate? The support is unconditional, he insists, and adds that the only condition is that Shekhar should not enter into an alliance with the Bharatiya Janata Party and that "we expect him not to do anything against the Congress ideology and policies". Could there be harsher condition placed on a prime minister?

Shekhar is aware that more humiliation will be heaped on him by his newly acquired bosses. When a man is thrown into the sea with his arms tied, it amounts to killing him. In this case it means political death. The

tragedy is that he has walked into the Congress trap with his yes open, so consuming was his lust for power. As if humiliation was not enough, Rajiv's spokesman Vithal Gadgil made clear the fate that awaits the puppet prime minister. When asked what his party would do if Shekhar was found working against the Congress, the reply was "No one can reply to such questions . . . tell me, suppose the ceiling of this building collapses, what would you do?"

With the temporary advent of Shekhar, the political turmoil in the country is worse confounded. The Janata Dal has been shred to smithereens, the Congress with the stigma of riding on the back of bunch of crooks is facing a virtual revolt from its rank and file. A split at the top is inevitable. The BJP is caught between two stools with the Hindutva wave receding fast. Small parties like the Muslim League, the Bahujan Samaj Party and the National Conference, engaged in a game of one up manship, are trying to extract maximum mileage from a beleaguered prime minister. The ugly side of every political party is there for all to see. The electorate, which will have the final say, is confused. The process of polarisation is derailed and in these anarchic conditions it is each one for himself and no politician can absolve himself of the charge of stabbing democracy in the back.

Current, 17.11.1990.
p. (2)

V.P. Singh spells strategy: 'Rajiv will finish Shekhar'

The loss of his gaddi has not changed Vishwanath Pratap Singh even an iota. He is as usual cheerful, in no mood to look back and remains a man in a hurry. He looks forward to the battle ahead with confidence, determination and the zeal of an evangelist.

"Last time I fought against corruption in high place, for a decent public life, an open society and an egalitarian system", he says with a glint in his eye. "This time my crusade will be for a just society—a system which will have the participation of those who have been denied a say in chalking out the destiny of the nation. My struggle will be for the 75 per cent have-nots who were kept out of the decision making process. It will need major economic and social changes to make them equal partners in the power

structure".

The last time he faced just one foe—the Congress—in alliance with the BJP. This time round he is up against an array of adversaries. The Left parties, of course, are fully with him and "that gives me a great sense of relief". In the last elections he could not give much attention to the South, but in the next one he is sure he would 'gain much more beyond the Vindhyas".

Though he wished Chandra Shekhar success on every issue including the Masjid-Bhoomi dispute, he thinks whatever Shekhar does will be at the behest of the Congress and its leader Rajiv Gandhi. His failure will be Rajiv's too. VPS wonders how in any case the Congress will allow Shekhar to succeed as that would be a threat to Rajiv's position.

In his first interview after his resignation, VP Singh spoke to Ayub Syed. Excerpts:

Now that the Janata Dal has split and further division is bound to take place, do you think it will have its repercussions on the Congress Party also, that is, in the immediate context?

I see it like this: The Congress cannot afford to see the present government succeed. It is against its political interest. Chandra Shekhar's success will mean the annihilation of Rajiv Gandhi. Chandra Shekhar's success will obliterate Rajiv Gandhi's future. So I don't see how Rajiv Gandhi will accept him as a successful prime minister. He will ensure that Shekhar fails. On the other hand, Shekhar knows that if he does not make it, it will adversely affect his political future.

Who will get the better of whom?

I would not be surprised if he makes inroads into Congress itself. But the moment such an attempt is made, Rajiv will have to react. So the possibility is that this love-hate relationship will continue so long as the Congress wants to keep the opposition divided. Whatever be the case, we are not going to have any truck with the BJP.

Your policies have already led to confrontation though I think it was inevitable. What will be your next step?

Now basically it will be of approaching and also mobilising and organising the economically and socially deprived people and making them conscious of their rights and at the same time not taking them on the path of confrontation but appealing to the better judgement of other sections, of society. They are your own brethren, I would like to tell them. All of us

run our families by denying ourselves something. That is the approach we should have.

Are you aiming these policies individually or will they be part of your new manifesto?

No, as a party. Individuals don't count. We have to carry not one section but the whole society with us; not 80 per cent versus 20 per cent. Everyone should participate in making a more equitable and just social order. The party too has to be strengthened. That is one thing we could not do because on January 1 last year I announced the office bearers and within 10 months came the elections. Then all the office bearers came into the party. Now we have Bommai and I have very good relations with him.

Do you plan to make the Janata Dal an instrument of change?

It has to be, but in this we have to broadbase it when it comes to social changes. And the party has to do pioneering work in organising the masses.

What was the main cause of your failure?

There was no question of failure. The decision was to jettison the government. The choice was either to compromise on basic principles or try to save the government. Deciding to sacrifice the government was the success of our pursuit of the principled line. It is not the failure of the government. For those who wanted to remain in power it is a failure, for us it is not for in a struggle the government is only a means to an end. And if the means itself, that is the government becomes an obstacle, then it too has to be removed. And the struggle has to go on.

There is a feeling there was a communication gap between you and your colleagues . . .

We used to have cabinet committee meetings almost everyday.

But on Mandal, some of your cabinet colleagues were not fully with you.

Mandal was in our manifesto. Everyone said from the platform that they were going to implement it. Then the question was raised in every parliamentary party meeting and all the MPs used to ask for it. All the ministers, too, concurred. It was in the President's inaugural address to the ninth Lok Sabha.

In the cabinet, various aspects were discussed—whether the Mandal list, the state list or the common list should be taken; whether it should be extended to educational institutions; whether it should be extended to the defence services or atomic energy department. All these aspects were fully discussed.

So the allegation that it was a unilateral decision by you is wrong?

All the aspects were discussed and then only the decision was taken and that was how a common list was adopted. The full cabinet was involved in it; it was a collective decision.

It seems this time and the last time you were made to relinquish office there was a conspiracy against you.

In my opinion, there was no conspiracy. I see it this way: when I was chief minister of Uttar Pradesh, I resigned on my own because my credibility with the people was the issue. But on the second occasion when I was finance minister I tried to disturb the economic status quo and had to move out. Then I disturbed the political status quo when I was defence minister and for that reason I had to quit and later thrown out of the party.

After becoming prime minister I had challenged the social status quo. So the present struggle is much bigger than the struggle against the party or trying to form a government.

What kind of social and economic forces are you trying to regenerate and how will it affect the country?

In this respect, if you see the social curve and the power curve, tney coincide. If you are on the lower rungs of the social curve, you are also on the lower rungs of the power curve. The social curve and economic curve may not exactly coincide but the social curve and power curve coincide. In the power structure I include the bureaucracy also. The role of the bureaucracy should be seen in a different light. It is not merely the question of holding a job; it is the question of decision-making. By the term power structure I do not mean merely the game of power but the involvement in decision-making, involvement in fashioning the future of the country and sharing its objectives and goals. This is the essence of my commitment.

Why didn't you spell out these commitments much earlier? I think there was a communication gap between you and the people.

No, I would put it like this: In the present dispensation, the majority is deprived from participating in decision making. This is not a happy state of affairs. In a family, every member participates—for example, in determining the future of the family. This is decision making. Till now our approach has been to dole out benefits to the deprived sections through the treasury alone. That certainly will not do. For instance, if a certain member of a family is given everything clothes, goods, food etc.—he will not be involved in the family's affairs. Similarly, a large number of people in the society feel isolated from the decision-making process. So their involvement is necessary in the power structure. I don't want to

make the relationship confrontationist, but I want to settle the issue as an elder brother in the family's affairs.

Now that you are no more the prime minister, how do you feel?
It doesn't make any difference. Public life is a continuous process I have been in and out of office so many times that it makes no difference to me.

Current, 17.11.1990.
pp. (1 + 3)

C. Mandal Commission: Policy Vindicated

Mandal, at last: A revolution unleashed

The stench of upper caste bias in edits and front page articles has exposed those 15 per cent who have been an obstacle in the way to the progress of the 85 per cent have-nots.

If a social change does not cause an upheaval in the society, it is nothing short of a fraud. We have played many such frauds on the country since independence with the poverty stricken millions waiting with bated breath to share the manna. The last fraud played upon them was by Indira Gandhi when she floated the slogan of *garibi hatao* and thrived on it until she was defeated and removed from power in 1977. For 43 years the society, tightly controlled by the blue-bloods of the upper castes, has been shedding crocodile tears on the miserable, pathetic socio-economic conditions of the Scheduled Castes, Scheduled Tribes, the Harijans, the weaker sections and the backwards who constitute almost 70 per cent of the population without allowing any significant changes in their lives.

The situation would have continued unabatedly for another half century had the bull not been taken by the horns. The stagnancy in the society had to be shaken by root and branch and Vishwanath Pratap Singh and his government exhibited rare courage in deciding to implement the Mandal Commission Report. As expected, it has sent shock waves throughout the country. The privileged classes and castes led by their editorial writers in the big business press have hit the ceiling. They have been spitting fire and brimstone giving the impression that the heavens are about to fall.

'Catastrophic,' 'disastrous,' 'ruinous,' and much more hair-raising editorial headings have hit their edit pages.

The Mandalisation of India, one of the upper caste's editorial egg-heads screamed, will destroy the very ethos of the society and lead to an internecine caste war at the national level. The stench of upper caste bias in these edits and front page articles has exposed those 15 per cent who have been an obstacle in the way to the progress of the 85 per cent have-nots, the silent majority which has been groaning under the weight of Manu. The government was aware the de-Manu-isation will raise storm in the tea cups and knowing the consequences it took the plunge. The plunge was a necessity, a commitment, a duty and fulfillment of a sacred pledge.

The Report was submitted more than a decade ago and the then ruling Congress endorsed it in its AICC and later Working Committee sessions. Had the Janata Dal government not lived upto its Mandal promise, it would have been accused of going back on its election promise and the millions of deprived people and the Backwards would not have forgiven the 'treachery.' Before announcing the decision V.P. Singh has foreseen and warned his Cabinet colleagues of the countrywide repercussions and the massive backlash from the upper castes and classes. It is indeed a decision with long-range consequences and which ultimately give justice to the 75 per cent people who were denied the fruits of freedom for long. A wrong has been righted though after much delay.

Had V.P. Singh not given the gift of Mandal to the nation, he would have betrayed his own conscience and violated the promise made in his party's election manifesto. While announcing the implementation of the Mandal Report he neither took Parliament, nor his allies nor the Congress into confidence. Apart from this in his election speeches he had made it emphatically clear that he would implement it without delay if voted to power. His allies, BJP and the Left, must surely have read the manifesto and heard his speeches and the editorial writers who are now casting aspersions on his intention were undoubtedly not ignorant of it. It certainly did not need an amendment to the constitution nor a 'full-fledged debate' in Parliament, nor did it need a national consensus or a Round Table Conference, as suggested by Atal Behari Vajpayee.

A cursory look at the lower, middle and upper echelons in the Central government, the public sector undertakings, state government secretariats, specially in the north, financial institutions, customs, excise, railway, health services, defence, police, etc., is enough to convince an unjaundiced upper caste eye that an unpardonable sin has been committed by the 'blue

bloods' in denying millions what rightfully would have been theirs.

It all has been done in the name of 'efficiency', 'aptitude', 'mental deficiencies', 'social backwardness', etc. It's balderdash. The upper castes should now reconcile to the new drastic, basic turn in the socio-economic fabric of the country.

Current, 01.09.1990.

p. (1)

Communication gap

Mandal has created the expected turmoil among the upper castes concentrated in the urban areas of north India. In the anti- and pro-reservation polarisation, the ultimate victory will surely be of Mandal. Those who are opposed to this inexorable process will have to come to terms with the reality of the situation. The prime minister made it clear in his remarkable speech at the mammoth public rally at Madras that the clock can be put back only at great risk to national unity. His forthrightness stunned even his admirers when be said raising his voice: "We will be firm like a rock on the August 7 declaration of reservation. We are ready to face the consequences even if it means destruction of the government. It would not matter how long the government lived, but how it lived and for what." This kind of determination streams from the realisation that an overwhelming majority of the people have endorsed what he has done and also from the confidence that if he goes to them, their mandate will be in his favour once again. This time his adversaries will be roundly trounced.

Those who believe that Mandal has vertically divided the country and that VPS will be solely responsible for the cleavage are victims of hypocrisy motivated by sheer selfish ends. A decision which benefits nearly 70 per cent of the people cannot be wrong. It cannot break the unity of the country and it cannot promote casteism. Even those upper castes which feel disturbed at the idea of being denied jobs should know that in the selections in the fields of science, technology, medicine, army and admissions to schools and colleges, the 27 per cent formula is not applicable. Merit will prevail here and merit to a very great extent will also prevail in competitive examinations. It is a baseless fear that in a few years the upper castes will be thrown down the ladder and nincompoops will rule the roost, that it would turn society upside down if

27 per cent from among the 54 per cent get a chance to serve the nation in various capacities. Mandal will not churn out doctors, engineers, nuclear scientist, pilots, technicians overnight and place them at the head of great institutions. What it is seeking to do is to break the upper caste nexus which did not allow the backwards more than 5 per cent jobs in the last 43 years even at the lowest levels.

A lot of anxiety among the upper castes and the violence in some north Indian urban centres was caused due to the prime minister's and his government's assumption that the affected people would automatically understand the issues involved and appreciate the government's position. But it was precisely this lack of communication which caused the turmoil. The prime minister should have utilised the vast and effective radio and Doordarshan network to explain to the people the main points and taken the nation into confidence. Instead, Mandal was explained by him and his government in bits and pieces. This kind of slipshod attitude in carrying such a monumental decision to the people is not only unpardonable but also positively harmful. Even now much has not been lost. The prime minister will be within his rights to address the nation on Doordarshan to mollify the sentiments of those who feel hurt. The communication gap has to be bridged and I am sure the people will lend an appreciative ear. The idea is to heal wounds, not rub salt in them.

The total hostility of the media is understandable. The big papers are owned by the big business and most of the medium and small papers are run by men from the upper castes, yet this unbridled attack on Mandal can be taken care of if the government and ruling party spokesmen try to mend fences with the media. It does play a significant role in moulding public opinion though it may be a small segment of the population. A self righteous attitude at this moment will not serve the purpose. The prime minister should also make himself available to his Right and Left allies and must have a heart-to-heart talk with them. This may appear unsolicited advice, but if the flames have to be put down, only an extinguisher can help.

This issue of *Current* is a small effort in this direction. We are the first journal in the country to bring out a special issue on the question. Though we are committed to Mandal, we have thrown open our pages to all shades of opinion. Besides politicians, we are also carrying the views of a number of distinguished columnists who are read with respect by newspaper readers. The crux of democracy is debate, free and frank expression of divergent opinions. We also carry the views of some common people and we will give enough space in future to all those who wish to carry on the

debate for and against Mandal.

Current, 22.09.1990.
p. (2)

Children of a lesser god

One year ago this week, the most ignominious episode in the country's history took place. Rather than contribute to the country's march to a more just and equitable social order: Rajeev Goswami, a college student, tried to immolate himself in protest against the implementation of the Mandal Commission Report promised by the then Prime Minister V.P. Singh from the ramparts of the Red Fort during his Independence Day address. And along with the misguided fool, the whole country went up in flames as it were. The upper-caste dominated Press went into a frenzy. Frothing at the mouth, the likes of Arun Shourie attacked VPS for taking the country to the brink of civil war. And the votaries of Hindutva led by L.K. Advani unleashed a rabidly communal campaign, beginning with the infamous *rathyatra,* to divert the nation's attention from the issue of social justice which has been hanging fire for millennia. Eventually, the forces of status quo succeeded in stymying V.P. Singh's resolve. The National Front government fell and could not return to power. The upper-castes heaved a sigh of relief. Mandal had been marginalised. Hindu society could return to normalcy.

One year later, we are indeed back to 'normal'. On the morrow of Independence Day this year, Ambadas Savne, a police kotwal who happened to be a Dalit, was stoned to death for seeking shelter from the rain on the steps of his village's Hanuman temple. Last month the upper-caste inspired massacre of Dalits in Tsunduru village of Andhra Pradesh hit the headlines. And Jehanabad, Madurai, Nathwara, Arwal and memories of hundreds of other instances of caste-related atrocities are still fresh. Not a day passes when Dalits in this country are not sacrificed at the altar of the 'Chaturvarna' by caste Hindus in an effort to keep them shacked in subordinate positions in the social, economic and political hierarchy—constitutional promises of an egalitarian society not withstanding. A recent survey shows that in large parts of Maharashtra, supposedly a 'progressive' state, the Dalits are barred from entering temples while outfits like the Vishwa Hindu Parishad burn copies of the proposed Places of Worship Bill which, it is argued, interferes with the individual's right to worship.

If one goes by the book, the country has a powerful law protecting the democratic rights of Dalits. Article 17 of the constitution declares the practice of untouchability a crime, going one step further, the Scheduled Castes and Scheduled Tribes (Prevention of Atrocities) Act 1989 which prescribes the death penalty, no less, for certain caste-related offences. Yet the laws are not worth the paper they are printed on. Between 1981 and 1986, 4,200 Dalits were murdered in the 1,15,055 crimes committed against them. Given that many such crimes go unreported or are abrushed under the carpet, the number of offences will certainly be higher. But except for an unlucky few who were more often than not scapegoats, no one has been brought to book—leave alone hanged—for murdering Dalits.

Be that as it may, when V.P. Singh took up 'social justice' as a cause, he was openly derided by the so-called intelligentsia. He was accused of fomenting caste-conflict by political parties as varied as the Congress and BJP. The national Press sniggered—'don't fool with the old Mandal wine in new bottles, weighty editorials chorused.' One editor went far enough to proclaim in a headline, on the eve of elections, that 'A vote against Mandal is a vote for the country's integrity'. Tripe aside, the bottomline in all instances was the same; the upper castes will fight to the last man in preserving their social, political and economic hegemony. So what if a few Dalits are killed in the process.

Now that Ambadas Savne is dead, our platitudinous pen-pushers are expressing 'shock' that such barbarity is still practised in this country forty-four years after Independence. A judicial inquiry has been ordered but don't let that fool you. Once the furore peters out, the case will be closed till other innocent Dalits are murdered occasioning another round of breast-beating and do-gooding. This, of course, will not improve the lot of the Dalits. Only a thorough-going social revolution, an unlikely eventuality in the near future, can achieve that. Till that time, the Dalits will be condemned to be the children of a lesser god.

Current, 14.09.1991.
p. (2)

Mandal is here to stay

For those who believe that Vishwanath Pratap Singh, and by extension the Janata Dal, would dump Mandal once it ceased to be a burning political issue which could rake in the backwards votes are in for a surprise. Last

week, after long and careful deliberation, the Janata Dal national executive formally decided to reserve 60 per cent of party offices for members of the Scheduled Castes and Tribes, other backward classes and minorities. True, the decision is nothing new. In fact it was first taken at the party's convention at Puri in 1991. But at that time V.P. Singh had conjured the proposal out of thin air and it was adopted with much back-slapping and tub-thumping but without a meaningful debate and discussion on the far-reaching implications of the move. No wonder at that time there were a lot of sullen faces in the leadership who found themselves in a minority and did not have the heart or will to voice their objections. That V.P. Singh did not press for the implementation of an important party resolution for over a year gave rise to the belief that the proposal had been given a quite burial.

The Janata Dal national executive's decision last week makes it obvious that V.P. Singh had not put the scheme on the back-burner. In fact, it underscores the point that since Puri the leaders of the party have put their heads together and considered the implications of the reservation formula at length. The announcement was made only after the organisational committee headed by Ramakrishna Hegde vetted the proposal with a fine tooth-comb before putting its seal of approval. So those opposed to Mandal cannot dismiss the Dal's resolve to practice what the party preaches as mere tokenism. And if one cares to examine how other parties, including the ruling Congress, are undergoing through a political metamorphosis, it will be quite clear that Mandal today occupies a very important position on every party's agenda and that it is here to stay. Witness the manner in which candidates were chosen by all parties for the Rajya Sabha elections or Professor G.G. Swell's candidature for the office of President which even the BJP was forced to endorse, and how Prime Minister Narasimha Rao has to willy-nilly field a Harijan, K.R. Narayanan, as his party's candidate for the post of Vice President despite opposition from a section of the Congress. That Narayanan was supported by all parties speaks volumes of their perception of the shape of things to come in the political life of the country.

While one may dispute the contention that caste should be the only criteria for determining social backwardness, there is no denying the fact that all political parties have woken up to the reality that times are changing and if they have to remain politically relevant, they will have to reorient themselves. Unsurprisingly, even the epitome of brahminism, Narasimha Rao, knows that the Congress will become irrelevant if it does not have in its frontline leadership representatives from the depressed sections. At

the other end of the political spectrum, the BJP has had to install Kalyan Singh, a backward Lodh, as the chief minister of Uttar Pradesh, the most sensitive state in the country, to prove its pro-backwards credentials. In the days to come, Mandal will be moving ahead like an unstoppable juggernaut and a much-delayed social revolution would have begun.

Current, 31.10.1992.
p. (2)

Future belongs to backward classes—Vishwanath Pratap Singh

Former Prime Minister and Janata Dal leader Vishwanath Pratap Singh is convinced that the only way the country can achieve peace and prosperity is through Mandal. At first everyone tended to laugh at the very idea but recent election results, and the government's hesitant moves to take the Dalits too in their stride, has changed the scenario.

His suggestion is that Mandal forces, now in different camps, should come together. The process should begin at the grass roots level. If that is not done so as to fulfill the aspirations of the people, nobody can stop new parties and new leaders coming up to do that.

In this exclusive interview to Current, Singh also laid stress on the need to give equal education to all, without any discrimination. That can be done only if 75 per cent of the budget for the purpose is rightfully spent on 75 per cent of the people, that is backward classes. Whatever the case he says, "you can be sure that within the next 4-5 years the country will have a prime minister from these sections. At that point of time, 85 per cent of the chief ministers would also represent the backwards". Excerpts:

It will be a more appropriate if we can bring in social equality. Till now in India only political and economic realities have been discussed. Nobody has bothered to highlight the social realities.

How potent will the Dalit-OBC-Muslim alliance be in the future?

It is going to play a very determinant factor. They have now become conscious and are coming together under their own leaders. The dalits, who have till now been a passive vote bank, have become active players. And the minority (Muslims) which after December 6, 1992 didn't know where to go due to the BJP's hostility and the Congress, had let them down, have now seen that aligning with the Dalits would ensure their

security and make them more politically relevant.

The Dalits too have realised that by joining hands with them they can achieve power. The process of establishment of Mandal raj has started in very concrete terms.

How do you plan to articulate it?

A year back I had clearly stated that this combination can take two to three forms because it is a historical process, a process of social forces themselves. Parties and individuals are just incidental to it.

At the moment social forces of Mandal are in different camps. Either their leaders should have the political sagacity to come together, like the Left has come together and if not, then the people are bound to make their own choices.

Unity will take place from the grassroots. This was proved amply by the recent elections to the UP Assembly where the voters made a choice for the SP-BSP combine because the JD-BSP couldn't come together.

If none of the parties come up to the mark of people's aspirations, there is no doubt that new parties, new leaders would come up. But the historical process will complete itself. You can be sure that within the next 4-5 years the country will have a prime minister from these sections. At that point of time, 85 per cent of the chief ministers would also represent the backwards. While the remaining will keep on harping about *Mandal-Bundle.*

This is how I visualise the process will complete itself.

Do you think this combination would be potent enough to counter communal forces in the country?

Yes, it will be. It has already proven to be. In Bihar we have seen that the combination under the leadership of Laloo Prasad Yadav has effectively contained the BJP in that state. So was the case in Uttar Pradesh. And now everywhere else this combination is bound to checkmate the communalists. This is the one and only way to combat communalism in the country. In fact, secularism without social justice is like a tiger without teeth.

How do you interpret Kanshi Ram's new slogan, 'Jaati Todo-Samaj Jodo', which he gave at the recent rally he held in Bombay?

This slogan touches the core of the problem and also suggests what its aim would be in the future, that is *Samaj Jodo.* In reality, it is the caste system that is the government. Parties and individuals are just its peons.

We go on changing the peons but this government will always continue.

It's time we changed this government. Those who could not find a slot in society because of discrimination just by birth, because of their caste, should be able to live a life of dignity. And that is *Samaj Jodo.*

Where do you think the upper castes would fit in such a system?

We do not want hatred against the upper castes. In fact, I invite them to join this movement, just as they joined in the freedom struggle. If they could come forward to free India I don't see why they should not help us in forming a fraternal India. Otherwise, the direction of social justice could take different courses, for instance the Naxalites in Hyderabad who have taken up arms to fight injustice.

I ask, do we have the political sagacity to see now and give justice to the downtrodden? If the upper castes also joined this process of social transformation it will be much faster and smoother. If we give them their due share, it goes without saying that conflicts too would be reduced. And that will be the real Samaj Jodo.

All these years after independence we have said that they (backwards) have no merit, have no education. But the moot question is why are they not educated? After all, we have been governing this country for almost five decades. How long should they be made to wait.

In your scheme of things, what would the definition of India be like?

The backward sections today comprise 75 per cent of the population. It will be a more appropriate if we can bring in social equality. Till now in India only political and economic realities have been discussed. Nobody has bothered to highlight the social realities. The moment someone tried to do it, he was invariably labelled a casteist or a divisive influence as we were called.

In India, because of the caste system, political and economic power has followed the contours of social power. Reservations have been practised for thousands of years. We are against these reservations.

Do you think a combination of Dalits and backward classes will emerge to form the next government in Maharashtra, on the lines of SP-BSP combine in UP and Janata Dal in Bihar?

It is quite within their reach. This has been the land of reformists such as Shahu Maharaj, Mahatma Phule and Dr. Ambedkar. The Marathas have also accepted the social changes taking place. Hostilities against Mandal and social justice are much less. Besides, a large section of the Marathas are also beneficiaries of Mandal. This is psychologically a good place where this transformation can take place.

What sort of trend do you foresee, specially in the light of the recent

success of this combination in the Uttar Pradesh elections?

To me, this success is a matter of great personal satisfaction. When I tried to implement the Mandal report in 1990, everybody derided it. The sky virtually fell apart. They called me anti-national, divisive, casteist. When we lost the elections it was said that this plank had become redundant. After the Supreme Court judgement in 1992, for the first time, there was grudging acceptance and after the UP elections everyone is appreciative of it. Within three years my stand has been fully vindicated.

So, when the Mandal forces are winning, where is the scope for despondency. We were the first row of attacking soldiers to be mowed down. The flag of social justice has been triumphant.

Yet, the fact remains that your party was not able to make any dent in the recent elections. In fact, in UP it was marginalised completely . . .

The point is that the Janata has won, Dal has lost. Deprived sections have been victorious.

Do you foresee an alliance with the BSP? Was this topic discussed when you held talks with Kanshi Ram recently?

It's too early to say anything about this, specially on the political front. One has to be cautious about it and not rush. Basically, the idea was that those involved in bringing social justice, though we may be politically different outfits, should come together to fulfill people's aspirations. They must start communicating and making links even though there may be contradictions and difficulties in the path. So, one should not be over optimistic.

But the very fact that realisation has dawned towards this direction is indeed a good sign. I have no immediate solutions. Unless these contradictions are removed, to go up in a hurry and then later to turn back would not do any good. It is better to be cautious.

Don't you think the Janata Dal has failed to built itself up as a strong movement? That it suffered because among other things, it lacked a dedicated cadre?

There is no doubt that there is need of dedicated party workers to build a strong cadre and to carry on the movement. A cadre which would be committed to the party's ideology. The movement is bound to suffer setbacks if the people involved are interested only in electoral politics and power games.

I am not saying we are not bothered about electoral victory, we do want to form the government. Had we not come to power we could not have raised the Mandal issue. If getting power is the aim, it should be on

the basis of ideology.

It won't be easy to contain the communal forces. They are bound to put obstacles in your chosen path . . .

Communal forces will be totally marginalised because they are not catering to the basic interest of the larger sections. The BJP which has been considered casteist also happens to be the party which has reduced politics from consensus to census. For them, it's a number game where the majority is Hindu by census. Using that same yardstick the dalit-backward form a clear majority, hence ideally they should rule.

The irony is that BJP, which originally started this game, has now started accusing us of dividing society.

When do you propose to return to Delhi . . . that is, in the light of the vow you have taken?

As long as the first student is not selected in government central service under Mandal. During the elections the government harped about it. Now when it is over, it has stopped talking about the topic. So the pressure will have to be maintained. I will also soon be touring states which have not yet implemented the Mandal recommendations.

What strategy would you adopt to achieve the set goals?

The strategy is to bring social justice forces together in a movement. Our sight is no longer just job reservation. The aim now is to rule. The point is *Raj karna hai ki naukri karni hai.* Reservations have gone in the background. That will happen anyway. Nobody can stop it. It has receded because it has been achieved.

A change in government bureaucracy, leaderships of political parties, economic system through labour participation and media through education are five instruments of the Mandal *raj*. Job reservations was just the needle which activated the gramophone record. The real song will now be played. I want the downtrodden to be in Delhi before I decide to go there.

Do you think the present education system discriminates against the poor?

The present system is totally lopsided. It supports the dichotomy and the inequity of the social system. With commercialisation of education, decision making concentrated in the hands of those who can afford expensive education. The poor and backward are just excluded from this decision making.

The fact is only a very small fraction of education budget goes for expansion of educational facilities, especially in the rural areas where conditions are downright pathetic. How does one expect such students to compete with convent educated students. Therefore our slogan *Saman*

Siksha, Subko Siksha (equal education for all), with special arrangement for Dalits so that they too are helped to come up. Our demand is that 75 per cent of the education budget should be committed to this 75 per cent of India. The whole system of education has to be reconstituted. Unless we do that, social justice will elude us.

With fragmentation gaining ground, is there any party which can describe itself as a national party? In such a situation can you foresee what the future holds for the country?

In future every party will get regionalised. A party may operate on the national level but its pocket of influence will get regionalised. In future, I see a politics of coalition. The National Front and Left Front axis will be having the largest number of states. For instance, West Bengal, Tripura, Bihar, Orissa. We have good prospects in Karnataka. In Andhra, NTR is still a force to reckon with while the Left is powerful in Kerala. So you see no other political combine will be having this sweep of influence.

Do you still hold the view that the NF-LF alliance can provide a viable alternative?

The alliance of NF-LF has been stable till now and it could provide a viable alternative in the future.

Current, 29.01.1994
pp. (VII + VIII)

8

Congress back in the saddle

A. Rajiv rules by proxy

Caught in a nutcracker

The cold war between Rajiv Gandhi and Chandra Shekhar has made a snap-poll imminent though neither is eager to face the electorate. While Rajiv's future is at stake in the next battle at the hustings, Shekhar is hopelessly mired in the ignominy of being a 'bonded' prime minister. He know that neither he nor his party has the remotest chance of even retaining whatever strength the party can boast of now. But in this battle of wits, Shekhar is apparently on a stronger wicket as he has succeeded in establishing a better image as a go-getter politician, a down to earth man ready to take risks despite his untenable position. He met Mann despite stiff opposition from Rajiv but his willingness to initiate a dialogue with the militants has won him popular support.

To his credit, he has so far not yielded to the unceasing pressure from the Congress to dismiss the Karunanidhi government. He has also refrained from publicly criticising the BJP and its leaders or crossing sword with Jyoti Basu and the CPM. Similarly, he has also desisted from launching a frontal attack on both the Right and the Left despite Rajiv's advice to do just that. Interestingly, he is yet to utter a word against V.P. Singh after assuming office. This has led the Congress camp the suspect that he may be aiming at either a national or a coalition government. The suspicions have gained strength after Vajpayee's call for a national government and Vasant Sathe's insistence on a coalition set up. Rajiv detests both propositions. If he has to return as prime minister, he can do so only as the leader of the single largest party enjoying a comfortable majority in

the Parliament. That, congressmen feel, is not even remotely possible.

While Shekhar's image is on the upswing, Rajiv's has taken a beating in the past three weeks, especially after his inept handling of the anti-Mulayam Singh Yadav and Pawar campaigns. He gave Narayan Dutt Tiwari the go ahead to have a unanimous resolution passed in the UP Legislature Party to withdraw support to the Mulayam Singh Yadav government, but developed cold feet when both Yadav and Shekhar threatened a mid-term poll in case the JDS government was pulled down. As a result UP congressmen have lost faith in Rajiv's leadership with most of them on the verge of switching their loyalty to V.P. Singh whose stock has gone up with each mistake that Rajiv has committed. Given a choice they would opt for VPS. The Congress base in this crucial state has eroded and according to local leaders, it may not win a single seat if it continued to support Yadav. The general feeling among the UP congressmen is that basically it will be a fight between VPS and Advani with Bahujan Samaj Party's Kanshi Ram coming third. Rajiv may not win even the Amethi seat, it is forecast. Rajiv should, therefore, be ready to face an exodus of congressmen to the VPS camp. Shekhar's JDS is bound to be routed.

Rajiv's stupid move to humiliate and remove Sharad Pawar also has come a cropper. It is well known that the plot to dislodge Pawar was hatched at 10, Janapath. People like Sushil Kumar Shinde and Ramrao Adik, who cannot even sneeze without Rajiv's consent, would not have raised the banner of revolt had he not given the go-ahead. In this case too, he underestimated Pawar's maneuverability. His resignation was undoubtedly an exercise in stooping to conquer. Rajiv should have realised that unlike in the case of Karnataka and Andhra, his minions had no chance of garnering support among the 121-odd MLAs who stood by Pawar. Congress does not have absolute majority in Maharashtra Assembly and only Pawar can manipulate to run the government by keeping the JD, the Shiv Sena and the BJP at bay.

The Congress government would have fallen like a house of cards had Pawar been removed. Pawar may have remained in the Congress but is no more Rajiv Gandhi's man in Maharashtra. No one can predict what will be the Maratha leader's next move.

Having lost the game in UP and Maharashtra, Rajiv is now busy working up some sort of combination and permutation to go in for a realignment of forces and make attempts to split the two JD factions. He is aware that Shekhar has not accepted him as his leader. Having fulfilled his ambition of becoming prime minister by hoodwinking Rajiv, he is in

no mood to play second fiddle to the man he detests.

In the ensuing battle he will rather go down fighting than capitulate. The JDS will split if some of its members like Chand Ram, Ranjit Singh, Manphool Singh, Dhankar and even Devi Lal are assured plum posts. Former Jan Morcha men like Manvinder Singh and Ram Dhan also seem to be sitting ducks. Dhawan and Fotedar have also been making efforts to rope in Ajit Singh with his 12 or so supporters in Parliament but the growing popularity of VPS has struck fear in their hearts. They know that if they let VPS down now they may not be elected again.

Current, 02.02.1991.
p. (2)

Puppet on a string

The responsibility of pulling down a democratically elected government in Tamil Nadu rests entirely on the august shoulders of President R Venkataraman who succumbed to the pressure exerted by Rajiv Gandhi and his puppet, Chandra Shekhar, and signed on the dotted line. The deed was all more dastardly—because Governor Surjit Singh Barnala stubbornly refused to capitulate to the centre's diktat and submit a report concurring with the lies propagated by the Rajiv-Shekhar-Jayalalitha gang. The whole of Tamil Nadu is incensed by the move and the democratic people of the country have expressed revulsion at the cowardly act. The body-blow dealt by the Rashtrapati Bhavan to the concept of federalism and the electorate's right to have a government of its choice is bound to have an adverse repercussion all over the country.

The day Shekhar hijacked the prime ministership through chicanery with Rajiv Gandhi's connivance, Karunanidhi knew his fate was sealed. It was not a question of not whether but when he would be ousted. His instant reaction to Shekhar's skullduggery was that the "dismissal of my government is an effort on the part of the prime minister to save his own government." In fact, the dismissal of the Karunanidhi government and the dissolution of the Tamil Nadu Assembly is a case of outright deceit and treachery because during his two visits to Madras, Shekhar had publicly declared that he would be the last man to dismiss a legitimately elected government. The turn around once again proved that he is not his own prime minister. The strings are pulled by Rajiv whose authoritarian

streak is a genetic aberration.

Having lost power in a democratic election last year, Rajiv Gandhi is still not reconciled to the fact that he and his party do not have a monopoly of power any more and that he will have to put in much more hard work in order to stage a comeback than rely on midnight coups and gross misuse of the constitutional provisions. The first subversion of Article 356 after Shekhar's swearing-in took place when the AGP government of Assam was sacked. It was obviously done to make the Congress's return to power in that state less difficult. Shekhar's lust for power remains unsatiated and Karunanidhi was axed to please Jayalalitha's 11-member AIADMK group in the Lok Sabha whose support to Shekhar is crucial for the survival of the JDS government. The charge of a ULFA-LTTE-DMK nexus has yet to be substantiated. Compared to Punjab and Kashmir, where extremists cock a snook at the centre, Uttar Pradesh, which has been rocked by communal violence for the past few months, and Andhra Pradesh where Naxalites rule the roost, Karunanidhi's Tamil Nadu was a well-administered state, a haven of peace and completely free from the communal and caste strife which is sweeping other states. If the puppeteer Rajiv hopes that the removal of Mahanta and Karunanidhi will pave the way for the return of the Congress to power, he couldn't be more wrong. In fact, both moves are gross miscalculations. It has been proved in such cases that the people do not take any attack on their democratic rights lying down and it is bound to prove right in all cases, be it Assam, Tamil Nadu, Punjab or Kashmir.

The really disturbing factor in this sordid episode is the attitude of the President. He is the custodian of the Constitution and is expected to use his discretion in such cases. He does not have to be a mere rubber stamp especially when the government of the day lacks legitimacy and when Parliament has lost the moral authority to enact laws. This prime minister and the present Parliament have become totally irrelevant and nobody more than the President is aware of this aberration. It is a pity that he did not listen to his own governor nor did he make any direct attempt to find out whether the allegations against the DMK government were based on facts. It is his job to find out the truth and his duty to the nation, which has placed him as its head, is to see that no injustice is done to any segment of society and that no institution created by the Constitution is subverted. He is to remain above petty politics. Indeed, such acts bring the President's office into disrepute.

The damage can be repaired only by ordering fresh elections in Tamil

Nadu as soon as possible. If the events of the past week are any guide, the people of Tamil Nadu appear ready to re-elect Karunanidhi and send him back to Fort St George. The Constitution does not permit the abrogation of people's fundamental right to have a government of their choice. Any delay in this process will only create a law-and-order problem and will add insult to the injured psyche of the proud Tamils.

Current, 09.02.1991.
p. (2).

End this farce

'How long will your government last?' Is the first question journalists ask Chandra Shekhar at every press meet. Amidst laughter he replies unabashedly: 'As long as Rajiv Gandhi wants.' That laughter is shared by the whole country. The prime minister's Sancho Panza, Om Prakash Chautala, goes a step further. 'Our government lives from minute to minute; whenever my telephone rings, I fear that it may be a message announcing the demise of the government.' He told press persons recently. Unable to run the show, the prime minister flits between his South Avenue house, his official residence at 7, Race Course Road, his South Block office and the Bhondsi farm 50 kilometres away attending lunches and dinners. In the 100 days he has been in office he has dined out mostly at the homes of his 'personal friends' including an impressive number of tax-evaders and mafia dons—for 87 days.

For all practical purposes, today the country is without a government. While governance has been reduced to a farce, the prime minister has become the laughing stock not only of the nation but also of the world. And an Opposition leader is behaving as though he was the prime minister. Parliament has been shorn of moral authority—the current budget session is not debating a budget and the country's coffers are empty. The bureaucracy does not know who to take orders from, for the government is rudderless. The fact is that Parliament has outlived its mandate. And in situation like this the only way out of the mess is fresh elections. The longer the delay in allowing the people to elect a new Parliament, the greater will be the frustration at the national level. The present Lok Sabha was elected in the wake of an anti-Congress and anti-Rajiv wave, but what we see today is that a party which was rejected at the national level

is indulging in governance by proxy. It is clearly a subversion of the mandate. The people had elected Shekhar and his gaggle of 50 odd MPs on an anti-Congress platform under the leadership of V.P. Singh. These people have entered the Parliament calling Rajiv a 'thief' and the recipient of kick-backs in various international deals. By licking the boots of the same Rajiv they have betrayed the people's faith. They do not deserve to be in Parliament let alone the government for a minute. They do not represent the will of the people any more. A mid-term poll is therefore necessary not only to undo this aberration but also to restore to Parliament its lost honour.

But a fresh poll does not suit either Rajiv or Shekhar. Therefore Rajiv is making desperate efforts to engineer a split in the Janata Dal. His strategy is to kill two birds with one stone—snatch the prime ministership from Shekhar and emerge as the leader of the centrist forces in the country. But Shekhar is equally determined not to allow him to pull down his government by manipulation. He would rather have the Parliament dissolved than be voted out. And there is no gainsaying the fact that he is a much better manipulator and a shrewder politician than Rajiv. Whenever he feels Rajiv is trying to outsmart him, he holds out the threat of a poll. He says it openly that when he captured power, he knew his reign would be even shorter than that of V.P. Singh. "When Tenzing Norgay climbed the Everest, was he planning to build a house there?, is his rhetorical question when asked about the transient nature of his government.

In this situation both Rajiv and Shekhar will serve the cause of parliamentary democracy if they decide to save themselves from humiliation and try their luck with the people. The situation is no more tense and explosive as it was, when V.P. Singh stepped down. The law and order situation has improved and the communal situation has cooled down. The people seem to be ready to exercise their franchise. The BJP, which whipped up a communal frenzy, has also realised that only Ram cannot place them on the *gaddi* and that much more is required to win the people's confidence. It is keen for a trial of strength, but so is V.P. Singh and his Left allies. The situation could not have been more ideal to restore the democratic dignity to our system which fortunately remains intact.

Current, 09.03.1991.
p. (2).

Think of the future

In the ninth Lok Sabha no party enjoyed a clear majority. This gave birth to V.P. Singh's majority government. VPS's fall, in turn, led to the formation of a rag-tag government which had only 50 odd members in the House. The next election too is not going to produce a decisive result. Once the results are in, we may find that we are saddled with another nasty stalemate at the centre. A number of reasons can be forwarded for this muddled state of affairs. First, not a single person capable of commanding the confidence of a large number of people has emerged on the national scene. The electorate is convinced that the present lot of politicians are a bunch of scoundrels who cannot be trusted. The voters feel that promises are made only with a view to hoodwink them. This appalling lack of faith on the part of the voter is the main cause of the prevailing apathy. Barring a few exceptions, our politicians are a confederacy of charlatans which deserves to be consigned to the dustbin of history. Second, all the three major contenders for power—the Congress, Janata Dal and BJP are merely trying to regain lost ground instead of presenting fresh ideas to solve the country's social and economic ills.

Of the three contenders for power the Congress, though more platitudinous, is not sure of what it wants to do. Stability cannot be a winning slogan because the people have ceased to believe in such rhetoric. No wonder the Congress party, with the largest number of members in the eighth Lok Sabha, managed to get a thumb's down because the people discovered it was unfit to govern the country. Besides corruption at the highest levels which brought about its abject fall, instability was another factor which swayed the voters. There is no denying the fact that during Rajiv's five years in office, state governments were reduced to a servile status and chief ministers became doormats. This lamentable emasculation of the democratic set up is still fresh in the minds of the people. And this factor alone has made the voter chary of the Congress. Moreover even when it has a brute majority of 412 members in Parliament, it exhibited only contempt for the people who had put them there.

Unfortunately its successor, the Janata Dal, was unable to emerge as a convincing alternative because in his enthusiasm to bring about social justice and strengthen secularism, V.P. Singh failed to provide leadership to the country. Mandal has undoubtedly yielded him rich dividends. His unequivocal stand on Babri Masjid has won over the Muslim voters, enabling him to build a formidable vote bank. But it is evident that a

number of VPS's senior party colleagues are not in tune with his politics. Though his faith in the rapid progress of what Gandhi called the *daridranarayan* cannot be questioned, he is without an organised party which is tapping to his tune.

The situation in the BJP is not dissimilar. Its politics and slogans have created bad blood because its main plank is baiting the minorities, especially Muslims. One cannot build a national edifice in a diverse country like India with hatred for fellow Indians as building blocks. A political party seeking state power in the name of religion will be resisted not only by the minorities but also by all other political parties from one end of the country to another. The BJP's attempt to form the government by dividing the country on religious lines is bound to boomerang because the people will not permit more bloodshed. This is where things stand at this juncture.

But given the maturity of the Indian voter, I am confident that in the days to come each one of us—men, women and youth—will decide that we do not want to be quagmired any more; that we have to put the country back on an even keel. It is obvious that we cannot continue to live with the past. We have to think of the future.

Current, 13.04.1991
p. (2)

B. Narasimha Rao: The Consensus PM

At the crossroads

Never before has the country faced such a grim situation, on almost all fronts, as the one obtaining in the forty-fifth year of our independence. The Congress which reigned supreme all these years is in a shambles. There was a time when Congress rule was synonymous with stability. During its halcyon days the Nehru-Gandhi factor has a stabilising effect on the party. They remained its pillars of strength despite internal wranglings, factionalism and splits. The Congress, obviously, has lost its moorings. The reasons are not far to seek. The party fell into a rut because the ruling family never allowed a second line of leadership to develop. Nor did it permit the rank and file to think beyond 'Panditji and Indiraji'. Today the party's imposing headquarters, known as Jawahar Bhavan, give the impression of being a palatial orphanage for none among the left-overs has the confidence to fill the vacuum. If Narasimha Rao was

installed on the *gaddi* it was because he was the oldest and weakest among the aspirants and because the slain leader's widow dropped enough hints in his favour to the shell-shocked, working committee members. So, this prime minister is her nominee as will be the next one if PV is replaced. The lady's power to make or break prime minister stems from the fact that she is the widow of the last Gandhi. This slavishness has led to the total moral collapse of the century-old party which led the country to freedom in 1947.

The situation in the party is more than grim. It is pathetic, Partymen are missing the golden chance of liberating themselves from dynastic rule. They are succumbing to the temptation of building political careers on the cult of personality. Instead of putting its house in order and devising ways and means to regenerate the Congress, its lilliputian leaders are desperately pinning their hopes on Sonia Gandhi. The importance attached to her is evident from the statement of TNCC chief Ramamurthy, who recently resigned from the central cabinet, that had Soniaji been persuaded to intervene there would have been no difficulty solving the Cauvery problem. While PCC chiefs like Jagannath Mishra and Mahabir Prasad touch her feet in public and beseech her to take over as the 'supreme leader' of the party, the whole Council of ministers led by Narasimha Rao, Arjun Singh and Sharad Pawar regularly meet and 'brief' her about the state of the nation and the party. The prime minister has admitted that he calls on her regularly and gives a detailed briefing on how his government is functioning. Today, 10, Janpath attracts larger crowds than the residence of the prime minister and against all expectations she spends hours meeting all of them. The Opposition is obviously intrigued at the rise of this extra-constitutional authority and is sure to launch a broadside once she agrees to contest the by-election from Amethi. Once formally in politics she is bound to be exposed to the most horrendous campaign of calumny. The ruling party and its leaders will have no choice except spend most of their time and energy defending her. The pro-Sonia elements in the party have oversimplified the situation. They are building castles on the sympathy factor which cannot but boomerang on the party.

If the cult of the family, right-or-wrong, continues it will sound the death knell of a democratic, egalitarian and secular India. The Congress kept the country on even keel all these years by uniting the centrist and leftist forces under its umbrella. But the party's downslide resulted in many right-thinking people opting out of its fold with the result that today other centrist parties have emerged as a clear alternative to the Congress. However, this 'split' in the ranks of the secular forces has enabled the

rabid Right to grow at a phenomenal pace. So the coming together of the Congress, Janata Dal and Left parties as a united force against the rabid Right, symbolised by BJP, will be in the interest of the country's democratic ethos. However, the opportunity to bring about the unity of the centrist forces will be lost if Sonia is in charge of the Congress. The BJP will inevitably win the day if Sonia chooses to lead the party but if she decides to abstain from active politics, that will be the signal for the centrist forces to join hands to face the challenge from the Right unitedly. The coming months will unfold what is in store for the country. At the moment it is at the crossroads, unsure of what lies ahead.

Current, 17.08.1991.
p. (3)

'I am a Consensus Man'
PV Narasimha Rao

Like old wine, Prime Minister P.V. Narasimha Rao is—in stark contrast to Rajiv Gandhi—mature to the last drop. He sits on the prime minister's gaddi as though he has been on it for years. A philosopher, he takes a cosmic view of the storm raging around him. He has ready answers to the most ticklish questions, even those concerning Sonia Gandhi.

During a two-hour interview, I found him cool and composed, a picture of serenity. He gives the impression that he will not cling to the prime ministership like a limpet though he seems to have devised ways and means not to give it up easily either.

Prime Minister, do you feel confident of the stability of your minority government or will some sort of coalition help you avert another mid-term poll?
I believe in consensus. I believe in issue-based support. I do not think that numbers are all that important we may be 10 or 15 short but the critical question is; are we doing the right thing for the country? Are the people with us? Can we rally the people from different parties around causes which are common and interest that converge? I believe we have been able to do this so far.

I am firmly of the opinion that if political parties sit down and talk coolly and rationally with one another, we will discover that the area of agreement is much larger than that of disagreement.

There is a group in the party which is constantly trying to embarrass you. What's the main grievance of this group?
I really don't know. I don't even say that any one is deliberately trying to embarrass me. The Congress Party has always been expressing its views within the Central Hall (of Parliament) and in private. If it's happening on a larger, wider scale now, I can understand. The point is that today the Congress is in no position to make it self-decisively felt. We are 15 less in Parliament which makes all the difference.

Though the Congress Party is in a minority, it is still a secular, socialist democratic party, it should not lose heart. That's what the common people feel. They feel its regeneration is necessary.

Absolutely. Not many people remember what used to happen in Indira Gandhi's time. What happened then led to a split. Compared to that, what people are talking in Central Hall today is not as serious a matter. I would say a congressman feels a little irritated that we should be functioning as a minority government. As a result of which he finds fault. You see, fault-finding occurs when you are weak.

They are not holding you responsible for this state of affairs. The elections were held when you were not the party president or PM. They were held during Rajiv's time and he's no more. So, obviously, you are not the scapegoat.
The point is that it is a general irritation that is being expressed. And may be everyone thinks someone else is responsible. This is also one of the common features of the weakness. If you are inherently strong, then you feel confident. I am feeling confident because I do not think that being less by 12 or 15 votes going to affect the stability of the government.

Some members, it is possible, feel that we are not acting as strongly as we should. This feeling has been expressed. But the members today are mostly new. They are not those who were in Parliament in 1967 or 1968. This is a new experience in their lives. This phenomenon will, I think, dissipate with time.

Some congressmen have been raising the issue of one man one post. They say the time has come when one person should be AICC president while someone else should be PM because in today's circumstances the PM, running a minority government, needs more time to manage the affairs of state. Sharad Pawar also supports the one man one post idea. What is your opinion?
I have no problem, I am in the hands of the (Congress) working committee, in the hands of the party. I've no particular wish to keep both posts. That

is why I have not reacted. I have left it to the party. I am keeping my mind absolutely open on this and I have no difficulty in doing whatever the party says.

But there is no consensus in the Congress party itself over the policies the government is adopting....

There will be people who have reservations. That has always been the case. From policy to policy there have always been people even in the Congress who had reservations. In fact, some of these reservations snowballed into splits. You know that. Therefore, I have nothing to say except the Congress has been an open forum and in this ideas have been crystallising from time to time. This has been the greatest strength of the party. I very much welcome all these discussions in the party and I'd like them to continue.

As Congress president, are you planning to convene the AICC to deliberate on the new policies?

The new policies have been debated and discussed. I am sure more discussion will be held.

How soon do you plan to hold organisational elections? Do you plan to retain the two posts till then?

A special group has been set up to plan for organisational elections in the Congress Party and it is my intention that we hold these organisational elections.

How soon?

Actually, we are going to decide about all the details of the elections shortly. That's why I have called on the PCCs to find out how much membership has been completed and what the position in regard to the electoral process is.

Do you think the AICC will endorse your elevation to the party presidentship ?

No, there is no need for endorsement. It is only a ratification. The AICC will ratify my appointment and the election process will go on.

There seems to be a concerted move to replace you and make Sonia Gandhi the Congress president. In fact, it has been suggested that you should, on your own, quit and make way for her.

This is a question that only people who you (Press) feel are making the moves can answer. It is true that people from UP and Bihar are insisting that she take up the party leadership. And right from the beginning my approach has been to leave the matter to Soniaji. She is already a member

of the Congress. We look upon her not in the formal sense, but in the sense that she is a part and parcel of this party and we feel very strongly about her bereavement. And the whole country has seen the reaction of the masses about what happened.

Therefore, how she would like to help the Congress, what she would like to do is something no one should pressurise or advise. Though we meet and discuss party affairs, we should leave the matter to her. That has been my approach.

How often do you meet her?

I met her now and then, to discuss politics though not in detail. Her wish is that the Congress should be united and what her husband and family did for the Congress should not be set at naught. She is very categorical about this and that gives us added courage. We are happy Soniaji also expresses her firm opinion about what the Congress should be and how it should be united. Beyond this we have not gone into the nitty-gritty of Congress politics . . .

Is she politically inclined? She meets 100-200 people everyday.

I think she gets various reports of the weaknesses of the party. They had come into bold relief during the elections. So she is expressing her concern that the Congress should not become weak and should remain strong and united. She is very much alive to the role of the Congress.

Is she thinking of contesting from Amethi?

That again is left to her. I do not know what she is thinking. But I know that she is very much interested and concerned about the way Congress functions, the way it gets strengthened. I have no idea right now (of her plans) and we should leave it to her (to decide) the timing and how she looks at her role vis-a-vis the Congress.

But isn't there a question of propriety also? Two PCC chiefs—Mahabir Prasad and Jagannath Mishra—have urged her to take over the presidentship of Congress. Did they go to her with your consent?

I have not been consulted. It's a question of individual thoughts. I would not hold it against anyone if he thinks in the manner he does. But the fact is that they did not consult me. And there is no need. That's how I look at it.

They are PCC presidents and you are AICC chief . . .

They did not go on behalf of the PCCs. Even if they went . . .

They went in a delegation.

I wouldn't like to comment anything more than that except that I had nothing to do with that.

The post-Rajiv political scenario in the country has changed. New forces have come up. The BJP has suddenly increased its strength in Parliament from a couple of seats to 117. And it has a long-term programme to capture power. Any political party has a right to capture power but the manner in which it is trying to capture power—I think you share my view—will disturb the national equilibrium, the national ethos. I see a polarisation of forces. One side is the BJP, on the other side are the centrist parties like the Congress and JD and, of course the Left parties. Do you welcome the idea of all these forces coming together? I am not saying merger, not even a coalition, but surely some kind of ground level co-ordination of centrist forces has to take place on policies and programmes.

What I have been saying is that I'd like to have issue based support from parties. Apart from government, we would certainly like to face the issues, solve the issues with the cooperation of those who are like-minded, so what you are suggesting is very well subsumed in what I am saying.

In what way would you like to take the initiative?

I am taking the initiative in all important matters. At the party level we have not yet come to that stage but once we initiate something on specific issues which have already been thrown up, then we will have some confidence to approach and sit with other parties on more and more common areas. I am sure this will happen.

There are move in the Congress and also in a section of the Janata Dal to strike some kind of ground-level co-ordination between the two parties.

My effort has always been to search for a common ground and operate upon it in the national interest. I always welcome co-operation and sharing of ideas.

Do you think you and the Congress alone will be able to meet the BJP challenge at the national level? Is there any dialogue between you and the Janata Dal leaders, including V.P. Singh, on a joint strategy in this direction?

It is Congress alone that will meet the BJP challenge. That is because it is only the Congress whose philosophy is broad based and is such that it includes all sections of society. The Congress alone embraces all of India and all Indians and it alone can meet the challenge of divisive tendencies.

How serious, do you think is the challenge from the BJP?

It is serious. Whereas we had thought their strength would go down from the 88 MPs they had (in the ninth Lok Sabha), you find that they have gained in strength. And they have got seats in areas where they never had any seats. The point is that for some reason or the other, more voters,

seem to be influenced by it. Well, you'll have to go into the basic question why is the BJP approach appealing to the people.

They have mixed religion with politics. How you are going to delink Ram from politics?

Today you find the BJP very strong. But its strength depends on only one factor—religion coming into political thought. Now I consider this difficult and easy at the same time in the sense that if this factor is removed then it collapses. In the case of other parties it's not one factor, but many. What is the performance of the Congress party? Now that would be judged as one of the factors. No government can satisfy all the people. There would be some dissatisfaction which some other parties can cash in on, but in this case once the two elements that do not mix, and should not be mixed, are not linked in the minds of the people, the BJP would lose its appeal.

Do you think it's an easy task?

That is what I'm saying. From the point of view of education, it's not going to be easy. From the point of view of totality, we don't have many things to explain. You have only one things. So, from that point of view it's easy, only that the first breakthrough should take place. Whichever way you look at it, it's a single issue. No party can continue to remain strong for too long. For one election yes, for a second yes, but not for all time to come.

The Janambhoomi problem is going to be solved one way or the other. We have said there has to be an amicable settlement. All of us have to try for it. What the BJP will do, we don't know. But the other parties are more or less agreed that the temple should be built without destroying the mosque.

An amicable settlement without the BJP's co-operation?

There is something like public opinion. The issue loses its forces after some time. There is also the question of other issues and other elements taking centre-stage and it becoming a peripheral issue. All these things can happen. If for the next five years the BJP thinks that it is the only issue it should keep alive and that they will succeed in doing that, it is mistaken. On this issue you cannot have a continuum.

You have a BJP government in UP which supports the Mandir issue. If the UP government decides to demolish the mosque what will be your . . .

We will not allow that.

Will you dismiss the government?

Well, don't ask me all these questions.

How will you prevent it at the party level or the government level?
Both levels.

You can't intervene in the law and order situation. It's state subject. Have you thought of this eventuality?
We are thinking. We are constantly in touch with others. In fact, I don't want to say anything about what we are going to do. Our manifesto is clear. We should not allow and we will not allow the dismantling of the mosque. This is very clear. And the Congress party, the Congress government and Congress workers, everyone, will have to be involved in this and I am sure we will succeed in saving the mosque.

Are you thinking of mass mobilisation?
I really do not know. Whatever is necessary would have to be done. I do not know what the other side is proposing to do. My own hope is, having come to power, they will not go to an extent where it becomes totally uncontrollable. Any government which is ruling the state will have to think a hundred times before doing anything. I don't say they will not do it. But I am saying anyone will have to think twice before creating a situation which may lead to an uncontrollable situation. We will talk to them, tell them not to do it, mobilise public opinion. Other parties will do likewise.

There is a difference again. Advani and the BJP were against Rajiv Gandhi but they don't have that antipathy against you. It was difficult to hold a dialogue with Rajiv as PM. I don't think they will find the same difficulty with you. Do you feel you will give a healing touch and have them reconsider their stand on the issue?
What I am aiming at, hoping to do, is to create an atmosphere where whatever bitterness has come abates and a peaceful solution acceptable to all emerges. If it emerges, I don't think the BJP will have any difficulty in accepting it. The point is they have been saying different things at different times. It is not as if they have been sticking to one issue. And their leaders are also speaking with different voices.

From our point of view, in the prevailing scene I would expect the BJP also to fall in line. But if they don't, and if the extreme elements have the upper hand, that is the situation we have to watch. In any case one thing is clear: we will implement what we have said in the manifesto.

You have said that the court decision is final. Now if they prepare for a confrontation, as they did during V.P. Singh's time are you prepared to face it?

That's what I am saying. You see, whatever is necessary to fulfill our positive statements in the manifesto will have to be done. We are bound by it.

When you wrote the manifesto the situation was much different.
Whatever is the situation, the point is the objective there. I am not bothered about the situation. Naturally the situation makes it easy or more difficult. But the objective remains the same. It doesn't change. That is why I am saying that we are going to talk to other parties. Sometimes more needs to be done. Some more homework. We are undertaking to do that immediately.

Don't you see this as an opportunity to issue an appeal to the centrist, secular, democratic forces to come together on this issue and co-ordinate with them as Indira Gandhi did in 1969?
Well, first we will decide in the party itself what our approach should be. After that we will take whatever line the party wants. It wouldn't be proper for me to say anything now. We have to consult the party, the Cabinet Committee on Political Affairs. There have to be lots of deliberations. Then we will adopt an approach.

The point is that we've never had a political confrontation on religious issue. We always had clear political confrontation or competition. Now for the first time we have run into a problem which is not political. It is mixed up with religion. And that is where we are at a disadvantage. Merely to say that these two should be delinked is not enough.

It needs a much greater effort to educate the people as to how these two things should not be mixed up in my view, we've not succeeded in doing that. We have not gone to the grassroots. We have failed. This is the real measure of what we have to do sitting in a village *chaupal* and telling the people what this means, how the BJP is exploiting Ram for its own political ends and how this is not going to be beneficial to the people themselves. These are things which our Congress workers will have to do. Thousands of villagers in thousands of meetings.

But the Congress workers are totally demoralised . . .
That is the point. The Congress workers are demoralised because the acknowledged leader who led the party is suddenly gone.

The party has to be regenerated. The rank-and-file congressmen feel that after the drubbing in the last elections, the party programme has been given the go-by. The workers have not been taken into confidence on the future plans of the party. The party, they feel, is taking decisions of far-reaching importance unilaterally. They feel they are not being consulted.

The difficulty is that if we had not brought about changes within those three or four days, things would have been so horrendous by now, the country would have become a defaulter. I explained all these issues and no one had any doubt about these. The time factor, for example. Suppose the election process had got over two or three weeks earlier, we would have had the time to do all these things. Tragically, we lost Rajiv Gandhi and simultaneously we lost so much time which would have been very necessary in between. Therefore, we could do nothing except go ahead.

We are going to convene meetings of the party. The CWC has met over two days. It has come up with some suggestions on the subsidies and so on and we are looking into those things. The party's opinion is always important from the point of view of the government will gain nothing by bypassing the party. I am absolutely sure about that.

I believe in taking the party and Parliament into confidence. I have never done anything behind the back of Parliament. I have always asked for more and more discussion for the last 10 –11 years I have been in Parliament and my approach has always been that the Parliament has a right to govern and we have a duty to govern. In the first place I am consulting other party leaders on issuing like Mandal.

Did you consult V.P. Singh on Mandal?

I am going to do that. In fact, in Parliament also I said that I will have such consultations with other parties. I am sure something like a consensus will emerge out of that. This is not a party matter at all, it goes to the very root of the Indian polity and society. We cannot have social disharmony at any cost.

Mandal very much remains a national issue. Some senior members in your party and the government are of the view that the Congress should take an unequivocal stand on Mandal.

There is no question of the Congress taking an equivocal stand on Mandal now. Long before the current spate of interest in Mandal, the Congress governments had implemented reservations for backward classes in states like Tamil Nadu, Karnataka and Andhra Pradesh.

Mandal has been politicised and made an instrument of political manipulation. That is what we object to. How can we object to what Mandal says or the spirit with which it is said. The Congress has always stand for the same. We want social justice along with social harmony. Apart from reservation, the Congress believes in the whole package for backward classes which includes education, economic assistance and social uplift.

There may be differences on modalities but generally congressmen, especially Sitaram Kesri and other senior leaders, feel Mandal has to be implemented in toto.

The word Mandal doesn't really reflect the whole opinion of the Congress party. The Congress has brought in the concept of economic backwardness. The Congress is wedded to reservations for backward classes. We have brought in an idea wherein the poorer sections among the backward classes should have some priority.

So all these ideas are being woven into our approach. All this will emerge as a particular approach to the policy to the backward classes. It will require some homework. At the same time, it is possible to bring a consensus on this.

I don't think it is possible because the main argument of the Mandal militants in the Janata Dal is that for the last 43 years the Congress has been talking of elevating the poor and backward classes, yet nothing has happened. They have their facts and figures. That is why V.P. Singh found it suitable to pick up the issue politically.

The Congress party has given backward classes reservation in many states, particularly in the south, without difficulty even before Mandal came into existence.

But the Mandal concept is here to stay . . .

Whether it is Mandal or non-Mandal, the essential question is what do you do for the backward classes, especially the socially and educationally backward classes. The elément of economic backwardness has also been brought in.

Actually, there is a school of thought which strongly believes that even in the socially and educationally backward classes the element of economic backwardness must be built into it. The other day, V.P. Singh himself said so. I told him if that were the case, it shouldn't be difficult to incorporate the economic backwardness criteria in Mandal. Later on, after 15-20 days or one month, he came up with the idea that some reservation should be given to the economically backward also.

Earlier the issue was not looked at in a holistic manner. It was looked at only as a political point for the moment. But if it had been gone into greater detail—whether there was any lists of backward classes in all parts of the country for there are some states where there is no list of backward classes. All these anomalies had been there and even the Janata Dal had in its manifesto said it was going to appoint another commission to look into these anomalies. If they had really looked into this first before

making it an issue, then all this would not have happened.

My approach is going to be absolutely positive, constructive. I'll talk to the other parties. I am sure they will agree with me. They may have some differences on how to do it, but we can remove these.

Since you have accepted Mandal as a national issue, would you like to hold a round-table conference with the Janata Dal, CPM and other parties? Such a conference can create a broad consensus.

When I said in Parliament I'll hold wide consultations on this, I think I've said enough. That is my approach. I am also saying that I want a little more time because we are so busy with Parliament, Budget and other matters.

You can fix a time-frame.

I would not like to postpone it because as long as this is postponed, the issue will keep simmering. We will not have peace in society. The issue must be clinched.

Do you think there is a possibility of a split in the party on this issue because some senior congressmen are not in favour of it?

We have all opinions in the Congress. But when there is a decision, everyone falls in line. I am sure whether it's X or Y there will be no differences. There may be people who may hold the opposite view also, but that will not make any difference. This is what Rajivji wrote in the manifesto and this is what we are going to implement.

Notwithstanding the promises in your manifesto, do you feel you will be able to bring the prices under control in 100 days as Rajiv claimed?

The economic situation has certainly improved. We have restored the confidence of investers, both domestic and foreign. The flight of capital which could have taken place did not take place. There is a new confidence in the Indian economy and industry—both Indian and foreign businessmen are looking to India for new business opportunities.

As far as prices are concerned, I might say that the price rise in the first fourteen weeks of this financial year has been 2.6 per cent, as opposed to 4.5 per cent during the corresponding period last year. We have kept our promise of rolling back prices to the extent that we could, given the extremely tight fiscal situation.

Will the new industrial policy ultimately lead to the gradual elimination of the public sector or de-nationalisation of the core sector? Many Congressmen feel it is a deviation from the Nehruvian policies.

I do not think that the New Industrial Policy negates the Nehruvian

policies. It is wrong to think that Nehru championed the cause of inefficiency and low productivity. Efficiency and planning have necessarily to go with each other. The 1948 Industrial Policy Resolution talked about creating wealth as a precondition for equitable distribution. The 1956 Industrial Policy Resolution talked about the public sector being run on business lines and about according a significant role to the private sector.

What the present industrial package does is to recognise the challenges that the Indian economy has to face, consolidate on the strengths that have been built and take action in areas where weaknesses have crept in.

You will find that all that we have done is to put into operation the ideas contained in our manifesto. The Congress manifesto talks about improving international competitiveness of Indian industry, about opening all manufacturing activities to competition, about obtaining foreign investment and technology to increase exports and expand the production base, about making the public sector more efficient and about emphasising efficiency and production in our economic activities.

The manifesto has also said that the Congress would tackle the problem of the present exchange rate crises, inter alia, by establishing an appropriate mechanism. None of these ideas clashes with the Nehruvian line. The Public Sector is not sought to be disbanded. On the other hand, it is to be made more efficient as it has to play a pioneering role.

Though you have denied the role of the IMF in the framing of the new policies, the impression persists that it does play a decisive role in shaping the economic trends.

There is no role for IMF in the framing of our policies. All the critics said that the IMF is recommending reduction of food subsidy. The Budget increased the food subsidy. The critics said that the IMF wants India to slash import duty rates. The Budget did no such thing. The things that we are doing are based on a consensus that exists amongst a wide cross section of people on what requires to be done to restructure Indian economy. They are based on our own assessment and judgement. Prominent economists have welcomed the measures that we have taken and have said that there is, on the whole, a clear consensus among them.

A very personal question—your relations with Chandraswamy . . .

I have said I know him for a number of years because we belong to

Hyderabad. When I was there, he was there. I know some of his family members also.

Will you maintain relations with him now that you are prime minister?
There is no relationship as such. The point is you meet a person in a meeting or in dinner or some place, it's like that. We meet all kinds of people. There is no special relationship.

Does he come to see you often?
No.

Of course you are above board but his record or involvement.
I have to come into contact with many people. It is not possible to institute an inquiry into their antecedents before granting an interview.

After coming to know his activities . . .
We certainly keep it at the back of our minds. Actually we have all sorts of people coming to us . . .

Do you allow him to interfere in the government or party affairs.
Not at all.

The impression is that he and his men wield considerable influence in your government . . .
I have said before and I will say it again that I have known Shri Chandraswamy since both of us belong to the same place. Beyond that, no one wields any extraneous influence on my government.

Current, 17.08.1991.
pp. (4 + 5 + 6)

Give them their due

The Adivasis of Bihar, Bengal, Orissa and Madhya Pradesh must be given a state of their own for obvious reasons. They are the original inhabitants of the region—they were there much before the Aryans settled in the sub-continent. After their subjugation by the plains people, their social, cultural and economic exploitation has continued uninterruptedly through the centuries. In fact, even after Independence, they are considered sub-human by their exploiters. Their culture,

languages and aspirations have been ignored by the successive governments of these states.

Though billions of rupees have been spent on their 'upliftment', no perceptible change has come in their daily lives for the money sanctioned for the umpteen projects, plans and other schemes has gone down the drain due to rampant corruption. Even after forty-five years of grandiloquent projects in education and social welfare, the number of qualified men and women among them is infinitesimal. One has to search for an Adivasi with a magnifying glass in the central or provincial civil services, in our armed forces, or in other service sectors. How many Adivasi ambassadors, heads of public sector units or ministers in the Union or state cabinets do we have? And there is not a single Adivasi who is the governor of a state.

The Adivasi belt is the richest in mineral wealth. Bihar alone gets 70 per cent of its revenue from its Adivasi region. The country's largest steel plants are located here. The Tatas have thrived in this region. But the original inhabitants of the area are victims of ruthless exploitation. They live in poverty, hunger and primordial conditions. Instead of suppressing the Adivasi movement for a home state, our rulers should hang their heads in shame for their sins of omissions and commission and concede their demand for a separate homeland with grace. They are part of our flesh and blood and the industrial backbone of the country.

The centre should take the initiative in undoing this unpardonable injustice to them, invite the chief ministers of the four states and persuade them to carve out an Adivasi state. Nothing will be lost because it will remain an integral part of India and a feather in our democratic cap. Let the Adivasis rule themselves, let them chalk out their destiny and establish their ethnic identity. After all India was their land before we converged on it and confined them to the jungles and made ourself rich and prosperous by sucking out their wealth. We should not be concerned with their greed for loaves and fishes. We have to be magnanimous. We have to give them their own home and we should go out our way to make this new state a viable unit of our federal system. The Adivasis are the finest and the noblest citizens of this country: Their only fault is that they trusted us. We should rise to their expectations.

Current, 26.09.1992.
p. (2)

No, Prime Minister

Citizens of the country who are watching the non-performance of Prime Minister Narasimha Rao with dismay took the statement - issued by 46 of his party MPs last week—that he is the "most decisive Prime Minister we ever had" with a fistful of salt. It did remind us of the days of dynastic rule when such edicts were frequently issued singing paeans of the 'only leader' to bolster the moral of the ruling clique. The present statement has suddenly raised a pertinent question: Why did the prime minister need such a sycophantic pat on the back by his own MPs? With a comfortable majority in Parliament, Rao is safely ensconced as prime minister. So far no one from within his party has openly challenged his official position. The two contenders for power—Arjun Singh and Sharad Pawar—have merely been struggling for the No. 2 position, knowing fully well that so long Rao is perched on the *gaddi* the party will not make any move to dislodge him; never mind his shortcomings. Congressmen in general have no choice. The people, too, do not seem to be in a mood to let him go fearing that the devil they know is better than an unknown rascal.

There is no threat to Rao from the Opposition parties either. Their performance in the last few sessions of Parliament was not only lackluster, it was pathetic. Leader of the Opposition L.K. Advani openly praised Rao inside and outside the House while the Left and centrist parties failed to mount a meaningful attack on Rao or his policies. None of them want him to be replaced. They dread the very thought of a mid-term poll. Rao's low profile suits his admirers as well as detractors. Roa is also aware that he is merely a prime minister and first among equals, not a leader of stature. True to form, he has not shown any ambition to be such. He cannot be authoritarian even if he wished for the situation does not allow it. Furthermore, nobody seems to be opposed to him. Only age is against him and that is not his fault. He did not struggle to be prime minister, the post was given to him by nervous partymen who did not have any choice. So he is there and will remain there unless he is struck by lightening, in manner of speaking. Rao is our Hamlet. He is rightly being accused of indecisiveness but he conveniently camouflages the handicap as a consensual approach to ticklish problems. It is his style of functioning. He lost his chief ministership way back because Indira Gandhi found him to be too ineffective. In fact, he has never been effective at the centre where he headed some large and prestigious ministries. A man used to a snail's pace should not be flogged to run like a race horse. The discontent

is more within the party than among the people. The party which did brilliantly in the south is now in a shambles. Rao could have nip the trouble in the bud in Andhra and Karnataka had he acted on time. The power struggle in Maharashtra between Pawar and Naik has its epicenter in the PM's house and the faction fight in Kerala too is beyond his control. The AICC has not met after Tirupati, nor has he nominated the 150 members from the weaker sections, Scheduled Castes and Tribes to the body as he promised. The CWC, the party's most important policy making body, remains incomplete and the Congress Parliamentary Board, the supreme decision-making organ, does not exist. To compound matters, almost all the party cells remain headless. The PCCs are paralysed due to lack of direction from the so-called High Command. Worse still, the leadership is caught in a web of confusion on the most thorny issue of Ayodhya. The Union Cabinet remains incomplete with Rao himself bearing the burden of half the government. Dozens of ministerial aspirants are agitated because of his non-functioning and the Opposition, which is the direct beneficiary of his consensual approach, has a stick to beat him with in the coming winter session of Parliament.

Current, 07.11.1992.
p. (2)

Three wrong steps

Prime Minister Narasimha Rao has made three grievous mistakes in a short span of a week. First, the arrest of L.K. Advani and other extremist Hindu leaders, second the banning of the RSS, VHP and other fascist outfits and, third, the decision to build the mosque. All the three insensate steps are fraught with dangerous consequences. They will have an adverse, long range impact on the social and political fabric of the country. Its political ethos will not be the same and nobody in his right senses can foresee in what direction the country will move in the coming months. The most disturbing aspect of the faux pas is that the government is too weak and fragile to carry on along with such acts. It certainly does not enjoy the democratic will of an overwhelming majority of the people. It is headed by an old, indecisive, decrepit Prime Minister and an effeminate Council of ministers whose writ does not run beyond Palam. It reminds us of the last days of the Mughals. It cannot be saved because of its own death wish.

The arrest of Advani and his cohorts on flimsy grounds at a time when he was at the peak of his 'popularity' among the vast section of Hindus has made him a hero among his admirers whose number now runs in legions. A dithering Prime Minister first allowed him to whip up the mass hysteria to a crescendo and let thousands of frenzied kar sevaks raze the mosque to the ground in the presence of battalions of armed men and then put him behind the bars. Had he shown the courage of Laloo Yadav he might have saved himself the ignominy and the country from a blood bath. The courts are sure to come to his rescue and he will come out of jail as a real challenge to the powers that be. Politically speaking, the arrest of the leader of opposition does not go well with the democratic norms. He has to be fought politically. But the ruling party reduced into pulp can hardly stand up to face such an adversary.

The ban on the RSS, VHP, etc., is bound to boomerang. In the past three years these organisations have become mass movements. They are no more a bunch of die-hards representing what was called a lunatic fringe. Not to recognise this major development amounts to running away from reality. The ban may also not stand judicial scrutiny. Their followers are in a hostile, menacing mood, no administrative measures can subdue the avalanche. The past two weeks have abundantly proved, if proof was necessary, that the police and the bureaucracy have gone over to the other side. There is a danger of its refusing to carry orders and that will be the end of this fragile democratic establishment.

Lastly, the decision to build the mosque was unquestionably a panic reaction. Who is the government to build a new mosque when it was not able to save the old one. It is not the job of the government to build mosques and temples. Its duty is to protect them and if it fails to do so it should quit. Quit must the Prime Minister and the Home minister on this grave issue of letting the country down and plunging it in a holocaust.

The Hindus are keen to build a Temple at Ram's birthplace. Let them do it. The question as to who will do it and in what manner can be decided by a consensus among themselves. The Babri mosque no more exists and the Muslim psyche has been deeply hurt on its demolition. The wounds will take time to heal. The fact is that it was not the mosque which they wanted to die for. The struggle was for the preservation of their identity as a minority community. The mosque merely was made into a symbol of their dignity by their sectarian leadership. Islam does not reside in mosque. It resides in the hearts and minds of the people who have faith in its principles and teaching. There was nothing sacrosanct about the Babri. It was neither Mecca nor Medina nor was it Al Aqsa. But to millions of

Hindus, Ayodhya is the Ramnagri and they can and should have a temple in his memory in this holy town. Let the Muslims have their mosque away from the spot if they wish to have one. But the government should not be allowed to build either temples or mosques.

Current, 19.12.1992.
p. (2)

A darker shade of saffron

The Congress party's after-the-event secular bravado notwithstanding, it is clear that the ruling party has hitched its fortunes to the Hindutva bandwagon. Events over the past week clearly indicate that Prime Minister Narasimha Rao is seeing political merit in becoming a born-again Hindu. The mercenaries running the country have come to the conclusion that since the Muslims have 'turned against' the Congress after the December 6 outrage, the party has no choice but to become more Hindutva-oriented than the BJP if it wants to recover lost electoral ground. Indeed, short of claiming credit for the destruction of the mosque, the ruling party's propaganda machine has started saying that the high-water marks of the mandir saga were reached when the Congress was in power at the centre. At the same time, by allowing *darshan* at the disputed site and simultaneously indicating the government would permit a mosque only at a site away from the makeshift structure that stands over the Babri Masjid's rubble, Rao has given a clear signal that the ruling party's political strategy has undergone a sea-change.

The mercenaries in New Delhi, who have already mortgaged the country to the IMF World Bank combine, are of the view that by mortgaging their secular credentials and offering a diluted saffron solution to the nation may give them electoral mileage in the mid-term poll which no one wants but which is inevitable in the short run. Rao is not embarrassed that in the bargain his party has been reduced to a pathetic sideshow of the Hindutva offensive. Nor is he worried that by allowing *darshan* in Ayodhya he has conferred legitimacy on the December 6 outrage and that his action is tantamount to doing what the BJP has been demanding all along. It seems Rao gives a damn to the observation that his position is indistinguishable from the BJP's stand on many issues. He is out to woo the militant Hindu voter.

But will such a blatantly cynical move convince anybody? It is true

that the Congress has time and again managed to make a comeback after reneging on its principles, but hitching a ride on the Hindutva horse may come a cropper. There are many reasons for this. For one, the religious minorities are already questioning Rao's secular credentials. Secondly, the Dalits, the mainstay of the party for so long, cannot be expected to remain in the Congress fold once the ruling party aligns itself to the upper castes. Thirdly, even the secular voters—including Hindus who form the biggest chunk of this segment—who have traditionally supported the Congress are certainly not going to vote for a party which debunks secularism just because the mercenaries running the show see political advantage in turning a deeper shade of saffron. Fourthly, fundamentalist Hindus are most unlikely to desert the Hindutva combine which has succeeded in putting a medieval issue on the agenda of a polity which, until recently, had legitimate aspirations of modernity.

By his inept handling of the situation before the demolition of the mosque and his subsequent opportunistic pronouncements in order to remain attached to the *gaddi* like a limpet, Rao has put the country in a situation which remind one of the Weimar Republic. With the Congress tailing the Hindutava combine and other parties failing to come out of political paralysis, the sound of goose-stepping on Vijay Chowk has become a distinct, fearsome possibility.

Current, 09.01.1993.
p. (2)

A tribute to Bombayites

When Bombay was rocked from one corner to another by a chain of powerful time bombs last week, the people of the city exhibited a remarkable sense of equanimity and courage. The first explosion took place at 1.28 p.m. in the basement car park of the 28 storied building of the Bombay Stock Exchange. Dozens of people were killed on the spot, bodies and limbs flew in all directions. People splattered with blood rushed out of the building, dazed and asking for help. Within minutes others from nearby restaurants, offices and shops threw a cordon around the dead and the dying, requisitioned private cars, taxis and even a BEST bus to rush the bodies to the nearest hospital. Several taxi drivers voluntarily picked up the bodies and rushed to hospitals. Two young men ran around shouting 'first aid, first aid!' While the fire brigade busied itself in dousing

the flames and the police did the *bandobast* the victims were removed for treatment.

Hundreds of young men belonging to all castes and communities lined up at the gates of the hospitals to donate blood. The doctors, nurses, ward boys and staff members at the JJ, St. George and other hospitals, their white robes soaked in blood, did a magnificent job in saving many lives. Nurses cried in silence while washing blood, collecting the severed limbs or stitching the wounds. Young men rushed from hospital to hospital carrying cartons of medicines. Bombay rose like one man to face the adversity. Within minutes the police and ambulances were rushing in all directions in Juhu, Dongri, Dadar, Zaveri Bazar, Worli, Bandra and Santacruz. Citizens in the affected areas immediately organised themselves to help the victims and rush them to the hospitals. No cabby or private car driver said no to the help sought. People who will faint at the sight of blood were seen carrying dead bodies and placing them in ambulances. One college boy fainted while helping the victims near the Century Bazar, the worst affected area, and was rushed to a private nursing home.

The indomitable spirit of Bombay to live and let others live in peace would make India proud of its sons and daughters in this megapolis. This is same city which was engulfed in an unprecedented communal carnage only two months ago. The scene was most heartening at Nariman Point where a powerful bomb exploded at the ground floor of the magnificent Air-India building. Thousands of men and women who work in this most affluent complex of high-rise buildings for the rich and famous of the country panicked momentarily but betrayed no signs of nervousness. Life was absolutely normal with smartly dressed office girls quietly waiting in queues to catch buses and share taxis. They were tense but quite determined to keep Bombay going. The terrorists who aimed to tear the city into pieces or shatter its morale failed. The message was; we will keep the commercial heart of India intact and also not let the country fall into pieces.

Current, 20.03.1993.
p. (2)

No mosque, please

Narasimha Rao is once again playing politics with the sensitive Mandir-Masjid dispute. He is using the notorious Chandra Swami to create a rift

among the VHP dominated Sadhu-Sant Samaj and also holding discussions with a number of Muslim fundamentalists. He is anxious to float the promised trusts and start work on the construction of the Mandir and the Masjid before the ensuing elections in the four BJP dominated states. He is having a dialogue with only those Sadhus and Mullahs who insists that the Mandir and the Masjid should be built at the same place. Neither is prepared to withdraw the claim. When he meets the Sadhus he assures them that the Mandir will be built at the sacred place and sheds copious tears on the demolition of the Masjid when he meets the Mullahs. Both sides, interestingly, are aware of the old man's duplicity and neither of them trust him. He tells the UP Congress leaders to ignore the Muslim vote bank as Mulayam Singh has already hijacked it and concentrate on the majority voters by playing the 'soft' Hindu card. Having written off Muslims he plans to meet the BJP challenge on its own ground. He spoke a great deal at Surajkund on the construction of the Mandir and did not bat an eyelid when somebody from the audience shouted "what about the mosque?"

But he is ignoring a very serious opinion among Muslims that the Masjid should not be built anymore, not to speak of the same place. It is only a handful fanatic Mullahs led by members of the Muslim Personal Law Board and the two discredited Babri Masjid committees which insist on building the mosque at the same place either by the trust to be formed or by Muslims themselves. These so-called Muslim leaders are living in a world of their own ignoring the fact that a Mandir at Janamsthan is a matter of faith to millions of Hindus while the place where Babri stood is neither sacrosanct nor desirable. It's time Muslims gave up the claim in the larger interest of national unity as Maulana Wahiduddin Khan has been assiduously advocating. As an economically and socially weak minority which carries the stigma of dividing the country, Muslims will have to come to terms with the reality. Maulana Wahiduddin has had the courage to warn his community that "most of the time we are faced with a reality that is less than ideal. But we have to make do with it." Muslims must recognise the fact, that Ram existed aeons before the advent of Islam. In fact, one cannot conceive of India without Ram. He is the very being of this great country. The sooner they reconcile to this reality, the better it will be for them.

The warning against confining Ram in a ballot box has to come from Hindus like eminent journalist Prabhash Joshi who is convinced that the real aim of the BJP is to "establish a Hindu Rashtra and use

Ram to achieve this ambition. Ultimately, it is only the citizens who can help expose the fanatics and what they really are." What he meant to say was that Ram is not the personal property of the BJP, that he belongs to India, the whole world. A magnificent Mandir in his memory at his birthplace is the minimum we can do to honour him, to own him. The mistake Narasimha Rao is committing is to make Ram a pawn in his factional fight. It is not only the Congress party or the BJP which should raise this memorial but the whole nation should be involved in it. Forget about the Babri. It's gone. The minority has to be magnanimous. It has to win the hearts of the majority for its own survival.

Current, 10.04.1993.
p. (2)

The soul survives

December 6 last year shook the nation as never before. An overwhelming majority of Hindus was appalled as thousands of lunatics were let loose to demolish a dilapidated mosque. Their leader LK Advani praised them as "kar sevaks" who had avenged the humiliations perpetrated on the Hindu nation for centuries by the followers of Islam. It had to happen one day, and he was happy it had happened during his lifetime. The despicable act supposedly put the last nail in the coffin of pseudo-secularism, heralded the era of cultural nationalism and laid the foundation of Hindutva. December 6, he thought, would catapult him to power at the centre. He fired the imagination of the kar sevaks with the slogan *aaj panch pradesh, kal sara desh.* He hailed the Ayodhya vandalism as, 'a civilisational catharsis' and his eyes sparkled with inane hope whenever he was referred to as the future prime minister. He mounted such a sharp-edged ideological offensive against minorityism that even hard-core secularists lost their sleep. His predecessor Murli Manohar Joshi thundered at a New Delhi press conference that not even an earthquake could prevent them from unfurling the saffron flag from Red Fort.

The Hindutva brigade took the country by storm during the recent elections to the five Assemblies. The electorate rubbed its eyes in disbelief at the massive flow of money. The bullock-cart party was suddenly airborne. Advani and dozens of saffron leaders were airdashing in private planes and helicopters from one constituency to the other. No one knew

the sources of the funds. December 6 was a winning card in Advani's eyes. The elections were sought to be turned into a referendum on what had happened that day in Ayodhya. But the socially and economically oppressed electorate who constitute the backbone of our democratic fabric refused to be taken in by his divisive, aggressive rhetoric and took this rampaging bull by the horns. Advani's diabolical gimmick has fallen on its face. He may not again, if he is an intelligent man, take the electorate for granted. They have reiterated their faith in the country's secular, democratic order. Advani's defeat is the victory of the soul of India.

By giving a decisive demonstration of his power and preference, the common man has once again shown that he is not taken in by the hollow saffron promises of Ram rajya and perpetual peace and prosperity. It is in the fitness of things that the barbaric demolition of the masjid which they had thought would be their stepping stone to the Delhi *gaddi*, has come back to haunt them. It is this one single act that has alienated even former supporters from the Hindutva cause. No wonder the BJP got the drubbing it deserved.

But it is also imperative that his unexpected electoral bonanza should not make the ruling party complacent. What it has been given is a temporary reprieve, a chance to mend its ways. One more instance of the indecisiveness and inaction it displayed when the kar sevaks were dancing on the ruins of the masjid, and it will be swept aside in the same manner as the BJP.

Current, 11.12.1993.
p. (2)

Unite they must

Despite its defeat at the polls the BJP has emerged as the main ultra-rightist outfit with an anti-Muslim gospel as its *force majeure.* It may be down but not out. It may have lost its elan but will once again try to divide the country between Hindus and Muslims and capture power. It has a very meagre chance of taking the South for a ride but the Gangetic belt will undoubtedly remain its favourite battlefield. The forces opposed to the BJP are also identified—the Scheduled Castes, the Scheduled Tribes, the Backwards and of course Muslims and Christians. They make up over 80 per cent of the total population of the country but the unity displayed by them in the recent elections

seemed to be temporary rather than permanent posture, except in the case of Muslims and Christians.

The BJP is down but not out. A line of thinking represented by its umbilical chord, the RSS, will always attract the upper caste intelligentsia and the mercantile class. What is the viable alternative to the BJP? History has offered a chance to all those elements that have been striving to preserve the country's liberal, secular, egalitarian and democratic norms and prevent it from becoming a pawn in the hands of lunatics. Which are these forces? First and foremost the Left, which resembles the Nehruvian Congress, the various Janata Dals, not all but half of the Congress, and regional groups like the DMK and the TDP. These can be broadly termed as the centrist soul of the country. Indira is basically a centrist country. It has never taken to extremes, religious or otherwise. It has pursued a middle path since time immemorial. Authentic Hinduism, which has guided its destiny for millennia, is and should be the guardian angel of our democratic system. In fact only Hinduism as interpreted by Vivekananda, Gandhi and Radhakrishnan can save our constitution from being subverted by the saboteurs of Dharma.

The centrist forces will therefore have to bury the hatchet of personal egos and come together. Their ideologies, if there were any, have coalesced. The only individuality which remains is the size and colour of their flags. Even their slogans have a commonality. Their opponent is one. Their goal is one. But their methods and ways are divergent. The common man who views the BJP designs with apprehension is their friend, teacher and philosopher. In the recently held polls he has given them the message to sink their artificial differences and come together under one umbrella. Come together they must, unite they must.

Current, 18.12.1993.
p. (2)

The battle against corruption

Everybody agrees that corruption should not be allowed to flourish and that if this virus is left unchecked, India is in danger of becoming a collectively immoral nation or just another banana republic, where everything, including national honour, is available for a price. Nevertheless, it is doubtful whether the few upright and honest men like G.R. Khairnar, T.N. Seshan and Anna Hazare can cleanse public life of corruption, no matter how hard they try.

Khairnar's so-called campaign against corruption, for instance, focuses on just one politician whom he calls the most corrupt, he does not have an iota of proof and is just playing footsie with the public sentiment. And by fixing his sights on Pawar alone, he is only helping Pawar's detractors, who are no less corrupt. It therefore follows that the fight against corruption has to concentrate on cleansing the system, and not against one individual.

Ever since the jeep scandal which tarnished the Jawaharlal Nehru government, corruption has been a part of the system. Rajiv Gandhi, the so-called Mr. Clean of Indian politics, saw the Bofors scandal bring his government down, and V.P. Singh, who claimed his political foe's mantle, could do little to unravel the scam. Even if there were no kickbacks, it does not follow that there was no corruption during his tenure. Even Prime Minister, P.V. Narasimha Rao has been able to ride the pay-off accusation by Harshad Mehta, and the multi-crore securities scam has yet to make any tangible progress.

It is common knowledge that crores of money is funneled into winning elections and politicians are forever devising means to raise the required sums. And yet, it does not stop the people from casting their vote for the politicians who are corrupt to the core. Even if Seshan were to correct a few distortions in the electoral system, it is doubtful whether he will be able to cleanse the electoral system of all its flaws. In fact, the disenchantment with V.P. Singh set in when he glossed over corruption and concentrated instead on the Mandal report and its implementation.

What has to be understood is that while the politicians themselves did not create corruption, they are themselves a part of it, even as the people themselves are. This system is continuing and will, at least in the near future, continue to thrive, despite the Khairnar's, Seshans and Hazares.

Current, 30.07.1994.
p. (2)

9

Communalisation of Indian Polity

A. Hindutva—Emergence as a Political Trend

RSS chief Bala Saheb Deoras expounds: who is a Hindu

The Rashtriya swayam sevak Sangh, will once again play a significant role in consolidating the Rightist forces specially in the Hindi belt. It has already captured the Janata and has designs to control some of the northern states through its political wing, the Jana Sangh.

The split in the Janata has positively added to its strength and prestige. Stalwarts like Jagjivan Ram and Chandra Shekhar have become its chief spokesmen and though they have not unequivocally defended the RSS ideology they are left with no choice but to totally depend on this organisation.

On the eve of the most crucial Parliamentary elections, the country is divided by the politicians into 'authoritarian' and 'communal' camps. How superficial and fragile this battle line is will be proved by the people in January 1980.

The RSS Chief Bala Saheb Deoras has emerged as a decisive force in the Janata camp. He has been intensively touring the country with an eye on the polls, though he says RSS is not political. He also says RSS is not "communal", it is an association of nationalists.

Though we have been its strong critic we would like our readers to know and understand the RSS views through its chief spokesman as we highlighted the views of the Shahi Imam Abdullah Bukhari recently.

What is the ultimate goal of the RSS?

Our only aim is to promote the development of the nation based on the time honoured values of our ancient culture. To attain this the RSS shall preserve the glorious traditions of our motherland. It will struggle all along to bring national integration.

We shun petty discrimination, communalism, provincialism, linguistic chauvinism and sectarianism but we strongly hold that we should evoke a sense of respect and pride towards our ancestors. There is no another organisation in the country which can match the spirit of discipline and dedication of our workers.

If your final objective is so noble why the RSS has been controversial since its inception?

The people are well aware of our activities and what we had been able to do in the last 54 years. We have pledged to make India a great nation but our achievements have not been properly publicised.

Our reputation is sought to have been tarnished by our critics on the baseless allegations against us. Now there isn't a day when our detractors do not spit out poisonous propaganda against us. Your own paper has been doing this.

We have been stating facts?

You keep on harping on the same baseless allegations. We do not forbid you to do so but you should at least ascertain which company has manufactured the 'record' and whether the company is genuine or fake. What we mean to emphasise is that you never bothered to check the facts. Did you ever try to find out about these allegations from an ordinary RSS worker, not to speak of crosschecking them from some of our senior members. Obviously your attacks on us were biased and onesided.

This is exactly what has prompted us to approach you. Why the impression has gained ground that the RSS is a communal and authoritarian organisation. You believe in turning this country into Hindu Raj which will mean that the minorities would have no place.

This is entirely wrong. Let me explain to you my concept of Hindu Raj. Hindu Raj is a cultural concept to which every Indian citizen can contribute irrespective of his religion. But the condition is that he should have a feeling of love and dedication towards the motherland and our ancestors. The concept of theocratic state is entirely different. Those who associate such a concept with that of a Hindu Rashtra are grievously mistaken.

What is your concept of a theocratic state?

A state which is run under the leadership of a priest on a religious perspective.

Do we have any example of such a rule in India?

No one has ever been discriminated against on religious grounds in the long history of our country. We have always given asylum to the

oppressed and rejected people from different parts of the world. We embraced those who sought our protection. We welcomed refugees irrespective of their religion, caste or creed. Where then is the question of discrimination on religion grounds.

Why then is the RSS subjected to such a malicious propaganda?

There is one and only reason. The RSS believes in Hindu Rashtra. Are we defining terms Hindu. Hindu Society and Hindu Rashtra for the first time. This country has been known as Hindustan from ancient times. Our ancient historical records confirm the existence of the maps of Hindustan.

The expression 'Hindu Rashtra' has been used by great Indians like Swamy Vivekananda, Maharshi Arvind and Lokmanya Tilak in their writings as well as speeches. Would you accuse them of communalism and narrow mindedness. To stigmatise Hindus as a community of casteist communalist and sectarian is nothing but an attempt to humiliate them.

The issue is not making the choice between the words 'Hindu' and 'Indian'. The problem is effecting a physiological transformation. Why don't you opt for 'Bharatiya Rashtra' in place of 'Hindu Rashtra'.

In our concept the expression Hindu, Hinduism, Hindu Rashtra and Bharatiya Rashtra are all synonyms. If you ever attend our daily prayers you would observe that we hail victory to Mother India—*Bharat Mata Ki Jai.* We conceive India in its geographical dimensions. These words crystallise a concrete image of our nation. Our concept is similar to one enunciated by Dr. Radhakrishnan in his treatise—"Indian Culture".

But you have been accused of being anti-Muslim and anti-Christian.

When Delhi, Andhra, Gujarat and Bengal were reeling under storms and flood we rushed relief to the afflicted people without any discrimination. We never thought what religion the victims had of these natural calamities. In the flood stricken areas of Andhra we built houses for Muslims and Christians. It was the RSS workers who helped over 4,000 Muslims in Morvi.

Last year when Bengal was facing floods Muslims youths wore the RSS badges and carried the relief work with the help of our swayam sevaks. You study the speeches of our workers and you will not find any derogatory remarks against any religion or community. We have never uttered a word of disrespect to Islam or Christianity or against their revered prophets and Gods.

The Shahi Imam has accused the Janata government of placing a double edged sword in the hands of the RSS.

Our motto is: *'Sarvesham Avirodhena'* which means obstruction to none

and everyone marching on the path of progress. This is what we preach.

The traditions glorified by Ramkrishna, Vivekananda, Guru Govind Singh, Rana Pratap, Shivaji and others are the very basis of Hindu culture. It also confirms the base of the Hindu Rasthra. Hindu culture brings about harmony between different sects and systems. Our belief is that this concept of culture if exposed in right perspective will bring about our Muslim and Christian brethren to reconcile with our concept of Hindu Raj.

There is an impression that the RSS leadership is obscurantist and it prefers people with antediluvian ideas.

What is wrong in this? Is it not necessary that those conventionally known as Hindus should be organised. Doesn't the Hindu society constitute the backbone of this nation. I must tell you that this country never had a communal rule. *Upasnanam Anekta*—unity in diversity is the essence of life here.

Those who accuse us of anti-secularism do not understand the meaning of the term. To them, everything pertaining to Hindus is anti-secular. Muslim League and Christian Missionaries and their institutions—are they entirely secular. Is it an anti-secular act to look after the interests of the Hindu society. We have accepted the fact that all religions are equal and that is secularism. Branding us anti-secular is nothing but puerile talk.

Secularism has been the basis of our society. Secularism is not there merely because it is guaranteed by the Constitution. I must tell you frankly that secularism in this country is guaranteed by the Hindu community which has deeply imbibed the concept of religious equality. Remember, the day the Hindus are reduced into a minority in this country it will herald a communal rule. The sooner we realise this the better.

The RSS is considered a para-military organisation. Is it necessary to have this kind of training.

If we say that it is necessary to bring about union of steps and meeting of minds people call it semi-military organisation. It is ludicrous. To impart training for self-defence is necessary.

Is the demand of 20 per cent reservation in the government services for Muslims raised by the Shahi Imam motivated to create a separate communal identity and feeling of separatism amongst Muslims.

I am not anticipating that. You better direct this question to the Shahi Imam. I can say that there has been men of great distinction like Dr. Zakir

Hussain, M.C. Chagla, Sikander Bakht and Samuel Mathai and many others who have paid glowing tributes to us from the RSS platforms and from many other forums.

Many Muslim brothers who were detained during Emergency along with us and who had the chance of understanding our viewpoint have praised the RSS. A good number of leaders have come into power with the support of swayam sevaks. But they are out to malign the RSS the moment they realise that we no more support them in their struggle for power. Some of our critics confined to me: "Accusing Sangh is a part of our politics. Please don't take it too hard." It only proves that the entire campaign of calumny is motivated.

Does that mean Hindu culture?

Yes. How you can be averse to the word Hindu or Hinduism. This aversion betrays narrow mindedness and smacks a foul thinking. We protest against these accusations.

Why have you delayed entry of Muslims into the RSS?

I went to Aligarh which is a big Muslim centre. A number of professors and academicians from the Muslim University came to see me. We were together for about two hours. We discussed many problems threadbare and frankly but we did not reach a situation where they would ask us to be admitted in the RSS or would invite us to be members of some Muslim organisations. I meet people everywhere in Hindustan but so far we have not been asked by Muslims to join the RSS. We discuss various aspects of our national life which more often than not lead to the elimination of misconceptions and differences. I would not claim that Muslim brothers have realised that there cannot be Hindu-Muslim unity unless they join the RSS.

JP had suggested to you that Muslims should be allowed to join the RSS and Hindus be invited to join some Muslim organisations.

I have a friend in Nagpur Sriman Kanitkarji. He is a Gandhite and believes in Sarvodya and is a confirmed opponent of the RSS. He is the head of the Gandhi Chair in Nagpur University. During a debate on the Muslims admission into RSS he wrote an open letter to me with a copy to JP. In that letter he suggested that I should not agree to the admission of Muslims in the RSS but advised that I should keep on meeting the Muslim leaders as often as I can and try to remove misunderstandings. He said that Muslims joining the RSS and Hindus becoming members of the Muslim organisations would create misunderstandings. There is absolutely no

need for such a thing.

During my meeting with JP in November 1977 at Patna while assuring that I would give serious thought to his suggestion about opening our doors to the Muslims I also apprised him of Kantikarji's views. I don't claim that JP completely agreed with his views but agreed that his suggestions carried weight and merit consideration.

Therefore I cannot make a final statement regarding Muslim admission into the RSS. Whether such a gesture is needed, remains to be seen.

Would you like to meet the Shahi Imam who has used extremely harsh words against you.

My doors are open for anyone and everyone. We have not put up any sign board at our door declaring who is welcome and who is not. Our doors are open to anyone who lives in Hindustan irrespective of his faith and religion.

During the last Lok Sabha elections the RSS raised a huge fund which sparked lot of controversy. It ran into crores.

It is just to malign us that they have dragged *guru dakshina* in this controversy. You must understand the significance of *guru dakshina.* It is different from other organisations. The swayam sevak's spend their own money on uniforms, transport and boarding and lodging whenever our camps are held. I am in Bombay to participate in one of such camps. Nearly 2000 sevaks from different parts of the state are participating in the camp. This is a typical characteristic of our functioning. We do not collect funds or spend money in transporting our workers to Delhi for demonstrations.

We were in jail for almost 20 months but we never lost our nerves. When the decision to launch a passive resistance was taken, our swayam sevaks constituted 50–80 per cent satyagrahis. It is because our education system is different. We are organised. The same holds good about *guru dakshina.*

Doctor Saheb (Dr. Hedgewar) told us: Look brothers, when a marriage is held in the family, do you go out to collect funds? When a child falls sick in the family, do you go out to collect alms for his treatment? No. You bear all the expenses. Why then should we beg for donations?

Since then the great tradition of *guru dakshina* began. Our swayam sevaks contribute liberally on the day of the guru. The offerings are substantial that prevent us from seeking outside favours. Even then people accuse us of being financed by traders and the CIA.

Current, 10.11.1979.
pp. (1 + 2 + 19)

We may break but we won't bend—Balasaheb

"We consider politics as an inseparable part of life, yet that is no end. We are equally concerned about other aspects of life. Our Constitution provides that a swayam sevak, who does not hold extraneous allegiance and eschews violence, can become a member of a political party. It does not mean that every swayam sevak has to join one or the other political party. He exercises his own choice, declares RSS boss Balasaheb Deoras in the second and concluding part of his exclusive interview to 'Current'.

People feel that the RSS is an anti-socialist and pro-capitalist organisation.
In our country slogans have become a fashion. We have been shouting hoarse slogans of socialism, secularism and democracy. Socialism has been a mask for the charlatans. Everybody calls himself a socialist. If you mean by socialism exploitation of none but equal opportunity and progress for everyone, then who will not oppose it?

Does the Sangh believe in untouchability and, is it anti-Harijan?
On 16th September 1947 Mahatma Gandhi addressed a rally of swayam sevak in Delhi and praised the Sangh that it was devoid of any 'feeling of untouchability, right from the very beginning. As far back as May, 1939 Dr. Ambedkar addressed a Sangh camp organised at Poona and observed, "the swayam sevaks of the Sangh are not conscious of their own caste, what to say of untouchability".

It was the result of the constant efforts of our ex-Sar Sanghchalak revered Guru Golvalkerji, that the heads of different sects declared that there is no place for untouchability in our religion. At the World Hindu Council Session held in Udipi, in 1969. R. Bharnaiya, IAS, a Harijan member of the Karnatak Public Service Commission, who presided over one of sessions, was so overjoyed that he embraced Guruji and said, "In you we have discovered the true friend of the Harijans."

As a follow up of declarations at Udipi, Guruji spelt out his guidelines for the Sangh: "We should seek inspirations from our inner conscience, and should inculcate this into our daily lives. We have to work at all levels, spiritual, moral and social. I, earnestly, believe, spiritual morality is not wrong. There is nothing in it which could be called wrong."

The RSS has a big mass base. It is based on communalism.

In our country the word communalism has assumed different connotations, that is to work against the interest of another community.

Hindus society has always been liberal towards the followers of other sects and faiths. How can the Sangh which has developed and been nurtured in such a traditional environment ever be communal.

What were your reasons to oppose the appointment of the Minority Commission.

Yes, I did say that there is no necessity to appoint a Minority Commission. Such an act perpetuates a tendency of separatism. The minorities begin to feel that they are being persecuted and the commission would not remain immune. What has never happened appears to be perpetually happening to them. My suggestion was based on the consideration that such an action would infringe the process of natural integration. As an alternative I suggested that a Human Rights Commission be instituted in place of this cases of discrimination language, caste, community or sex can always be brought before such commissions.

It is a general impression that the RSS instigates communal disturbances. It is also felt that behind all communal troubles Sangh's involvement is almost certain.

Morarji Desai, as Prime minister, categorically rejected the insinuation that the RSS was involved in the Aligarh disturbances of 1978. Out of five members of the Minority Commission four members absolved the RSS of even an indirect involvement in Jamshedpur disturbances as was alleged. Only one member, M.A. Ansari, remarked that the RSS was covertly involved in sparking the trouble.

The other members accused Ansari of being a victim of a vicious propaganda carried out by the Muslim bigots and the hostile Urdu press. There is no truth in Ansari's assertions, they were based on heresay.

The Shahi Iman makes a different interpretation of this. He says although no commission of enquiry instituted to probe into the causes of communal troubles, has found RSS guilty of involvement. One has to bear in mind that a thief would never make a declaration before embarking upon his thieving mission.

That apart, no court of law has ever found a swayam sevak guilty of indulging in a violent incident. Indira Gandhi has also said that no enquiry commission appointed during her rule even has found the RSS guilty of inciting communal disturbances.

Is the RSS a fascist and an authoritarian organisation?

In a fascist system the authority of state is concentrated in one man with

which he commands allegiance of the people.

A voluntary organisation like the Sangh, which has no authority to force a member of remain in it, can never be a fascist organisation. This very fact was communicated to the government of India by a liberal leader, the late T.R. Venkatram Shastri, in July 1949, in one of his letters.

During Emergency, the Sangh became the bulwark of a struggle successfully carried out against Indira Gandhi's authoritarianism. This is the reason why the Sangh has gained the status of a bastion of democratic forces in the country. Hindu philosophy teaches many a system for attaining truth, and all these systems are correct. It does not believe in the imposition of one faith over the other. Hindu philosophy seeks to maintain the state power under the discipline of the moral authority of the people. How can, therefore, an organisation like the RSS which conforms to such a discipline, be accused of having anything to do with fascism where all powers of the state are concentrated in one individual which he uses to destroy all contending systems.

Nation builders like Vivekananda, Aravind and Tilak used the word Hindu to convey its natural character, since a Hindu has remained the life force of the nation for thousands of years. This goes to prove that the RSS could be a nationalist organisation, and not a communal body.

Leading social reformers like Rajaram Mohan Roy, Madan Mohan Malaviya, Mahatma Phule, Ranade, and Mahatma Gandhi who sought to banish social evils of casteism, untouchability and dowry in life-long efforts, kept in view only Hindu community. No one accuses them of fostering communalism, then how can they call the Sangh a communal organisation.

What pattern of Hindu Rashtra do you have in your vision, what kind of parliamentary system do you have in mind?

The RSS believes that parliamentary democracy is a system best suited to this country, with a condition that elections are held in time. The Sangh is one of a very few organisations in the country which qualifies in such a test. Every third year it organises elections at different levels as laid down in its constitution.

What do you mean by different levels?

That means upto the Panchayat level. The Sangh is a votary of decentralisation of power.

You have claimed that the Sangh has helped some political elements to attain power and they turned into your enemies because you did not support them according to their designs. This proves that the RSS does

participate in politics.

We consider politics as an inseparable part of life, yet that is no end. We are equally concerned about other aspects of life. Our constitution provides that a swayam sevak, who does not hold extraneous allegiance and eschews violence, can become a member of a political party. It does not mean that every Swaym Sevak has to join one or the other political party. He exercises his own choice, but the Sangh does not believe that the welfare of the society can be accomplished through pendent of other parties.

The RSS members support the Jana Sangh only. Can you cite an example of a Swayam Sewak supporting any other political party? Why don't you make the RSS a political organisation independent of other parties.

We have no such constraints. The swayam sevak could be a supporter of any political party, but that exclusively depends on his free will. I have already explained that the Sangh does not consider political power as the only agency to perform social welfare. Therefore I reiterate, that the Sangh can perform social service without entering into active politics.

What do you say about the dual membership?

An unnecessary controversy has been build up by certain politicians by raising a scare of dual membership. We continue to assert that some members have connections with other organisations. But let me tell you that this scare is completely an anti-secular stance.

Is the Sangh undergoing a transformation?

Yes, they say that the Sangh is transforming. And it should change. Any living organism changes through a natural process of transformation. This only points out the state of evolution. Change is a gradual process. A thing that does not change is dead wood. It is a lifeless object. But this transformation cannot occur in isolation of the fundamentals of life. I say, therefore, it will continue to change. We are seized of the expanding dimensions of the word Hindu Rashtra. We are desirous of accommodating our brothers of various religious denominations. But such a change will come up only when the swayam sevaks realise that this is meant for the national well being. Any amount of criticism, opposition or threats by the political parties can not force us to change.

What are the reasons that the swayam sevaks of the Sangh are so dedicated? What powers do you possess?

The swayam sevaks are the product of a special system of education. Other organisations raise an army of workers only to fight elections or carry on publicity campaigns. But this mercenary army suddenly disappears at the time of national crisis. We have no magic wand to attract

the workers. It is the education of the Sangh which builds the character, self-discipline and a spirit of brotherhood. This is the only mystical power if you profuse to call it so.

Balasaheb, camps of the Sangh are organised in a number of states in December. People are saying that you are organising such camps only to instruct the volunteers of the Sangh from the taluka to state level and to give guidance as to what role they have to play during the electioneering time.

It is entirely wrong to think like this. We are organising camps because we think December would be very near to the elections. The camp in Maharashtra which was scheduled to be called in December was organised recently.

We never thought of any directions of guidance in respect of the elections. But I know for certain that the press and the so-called critics of the Sangh will call these camps as pre-election exercises.

Raj Narain has taken a pledge to destroy the RSS. How do you react to it?

There are many people who criticise the Jana Sangh. But there are some, who having understood the purely nationalistic role of the Sangh, has changed their viewpoints. But yes, there are others who have taken it upon themselves to oppose and create misunderstandings to serve their political interests. Even 'Brahma' cannot convince them, what of me a mortal. "Brahma, Pitam Naranm Na Ranjayat", there goes the saying. You can awake a sleeping man but no one can awake a man who pretends to sleep.

Why does the RSS shun publicity? Why are the activities of the Sangh conducted in isolation? This is what leads to misunderstanding.

Some ministers or leaders go on extensive touring. But do they ever touch this soil or would they smrich their feet in mud? Yet they will manage to get photographs of these tours published in the press with the help of their journalist friends. What is the result? Obviously a big zero. Barring a few exceptions don't you think it is a cruel play with the public life. On the other hand the swayam sevaks go to the remotest areas and stay there for a month in selfless service. But who takes notice of that?

What do you mean by exceptions. In the Janata government there were many ministers from the Jana Sangh constituent who owed their allegiance to the RSS. Does this not apply to them?

I am not talking of any constituent in particular. I am talking about all. Whosoever does not follow a proper code of conduct should be

condemned.

You said that the RSS played a leading role in bringing victory to the Janata. Why such a vast organisation could not keep the Party united? Why did it disintegrate? In fact the real cause was the RSS again.

We have not supported anyone in the rat race for power. The reasons for this is because we have our own politics, ideals and principles. We may break but we shall not bend.

Current, 17.11.1979.
pp. (12 + 13 + 23)

Bala Saheb was interviewed by our staff correspondent Ramesh Nirmal in Hindi. It was translated into English by Mahavir Adhikari, editor, Hindi *Current.*

—*Ayub Syed*

Thackeray: formidable challenge

The victory of the Shiv Sena in the Aurangabad civic polls has sent a wave of jubilation among thousands of Maharashtrian youths all over the state. The Sena rules Bombay, nearby Thane, and has now captured the largest town in the Marathwada heartland. Sena supremo Bal Thackeray's plan is to first storm the urban citadels of Maharashtra and then win in the rural areas. According to his plans the Sena will emerge as the major opposition party to the ruling Congress by the time the next Assembly election is held, at least in 20-odd major towns and cities. There is every likelihood of Bal Thackeray realising his dream. In one year the Sena has spread its tentacles to almost every town in the state and its flag flies at every village in Marathwada and Konkan.

Bal Thackeray, who launched his crusade against the South Indians in Bombay city some fifteen years ago, has now trained his guns at the Sikhs and Muslims. He plays the Hindu card, has been making the most virulent communal speeches and daring the government to take up his challenge. His speeches in Aurangabad and earlier during the Vile Parle Assembly by election were noteworthy for their virulent communal tone and despite complaints from sensible congressmen to the government, no action was taken against him. The spreading of communal hatred is an offence under the election law, but Chief minister S.B. Chavan turned a Nelson's eye towards him. Even when he threatened the Sikhs with social boycott, no political leader worth his name or any of the local newspapers

reminded him how great a damage he is doing to national unity.

The ruling party, which could have taken up cudgels against him, has most abjectly capitulated before him. The other day, Chavan told local reporters that in his party he "alone was speaking out against the Sena and you know about the others." The MPCC or the BRCC have turned tails while the so-called Leftists find themselves too weak to stand up to him. The other secular parties in the state have been shrewdly avoiding a confrontation with him—something they ought to have done. Strangely the BJP is the only party which feels the threat from the Sena. Thackeray has been making inroads into its Hindu following and most of the Maharashtrian boys who had earlier flocked to the RSS now feel much more secure under the Sena flag. Thackeray has not only been restoring a sense of pride in them but also getting them jobs wherever possible. In Aurangabad it was the youth who deserted the RSS and accepted him as their new messiah.

Secular Muslims are in trepidation. Communal Muslim leaders have turned into collaborationists. The Sena could not have won the Mayors' election in Bombay last month had it not received the Muslim Corporators' votes. Muslim League and Shiv Sena leader are on the friendliest terms in the civic body. The stiffest opposition comes from the Dalits but no political party patronises them.

The fact is that the youth in Maharashtra have begun to look up to Bal Thackeray as their genuine leader who symbolises their aspirations. Thackeray and his Sena have thus emerged as a formidable challenge to the Establishment in Maharashtra.

Current, 30.04.1988.
p. (2)

Hindutva is the name of the game

The Bharatiya Janata Party put up a grand show of unity of purpose at its annual convention in Bombay and told the nation that it was fully geared to face the election with its brand new slogan of Hindutva as its main plank. It is apparent that the BJP leadership, in its anxiety to improve electoral performance, has again taken the Hindus for granted. It is so keen to whip up Hindu sentiment that it deleted even the word secularism from its manifesto. In the last manifesto it was 'positive secularism' but it has disappeared. Not that the plank of positive secularism had brought it some minority votes in the earlier elections but its absence did reflect the

new mood of militancy.

In the surcharged communal atmosphere on the issue of Ramjanambhoomi Babri Masjid, the BJP policy makers thought fit to take a few more steps forward to appease the Hindu electorate. In the new manifesto the old chapter "National Unity and Positive Secularism" has been replaced with "National Unity and National Integration". It says it is not against the minorities but is opposed to the appeasement of this section of the population because it forms a solid chunk in the ruling party's vote bank. "It is the duty of the state" the manifesto says, to guarantee justice and security to all minorities. The BJP considers that it is imperative to national integration that minorities do not develop a minority complex."

It cannot be denied that the ruling party's policies all through these years have been to create a sense of insecurity among the Muslim minority and keep it tied to its apron strings. The social and economic conditions of Muslims have deteriorated since independence, specially because of the Congress party's policies of keeping them weak deliberately so as to exploit their backwardness and capitalise on it electorally. Hindu-Muslim riots take place in the Congress ruled states at the drop of a hat, and invariably the police and the administration fail to make steps to prevent communal violence. Maximum communal riots have taken place in the Congress ruled states in the last forty years and the strange phenomenon is that Muslims, knowing fully well that the Congress has been the cause of their miseries, have been voting for it election after election except in 1977.

The non-Congress states like Bengal, Tamil Nadu, Andhra and Kerala have proved that communal violence can be curbed within minutes if the government wants it. In Jyoti Basu's Bengal communal violence is a rare phenomenon whereas in the same Bengal earlier communal flare ups were common.

The BJP has also contributed a great deal in pushing Muslims towards the Congress. By its strident anti-Muslim posture towards them it pushes them to the lap of the Congress. Muslims, it has been proved are neither pro-Congress nor pro any particular political party. They are pro security. Their major problem is protection of life and limbs. They are the main, and in most cases the only sufferers in communal violence.

Though it is mostly the administration and the local Congress MLAs and MPs who fail to intervene effectively at the time of a communal flare-up, Muslims somehow get the impression that the BJP and the

RSS play a leading role in senseless destruction. It is this BJP attitude that has permanently antagonised the Muslims against them. It wants Muslim votes and has showboys like Sikander Bakht and Arif Beg. Yet it has not found a way to win them over. The slogan of Hindutva, may not bring in bagful of Hindu votes but it will undoubtedly antagonise minority votes.

What useful purpose can the Hindutva slogan serve in a country where 85 per cent people are Hindus. The tragedy of the BJP is that, despite this antediluvian method, not many Hindus go for it. A majority of Hindus have been committed to vote for the Congress as we have seen in the past. If not for the Congress, they vote for the regional parties or the Communists but never for the BJP or the RSS. Do we, therefore, understand that all those Hindus who do not vote for the BJP are not good Hindus. It means the majority of the Hindus who do not subscribe to the BJP brand of Hindutva are not pure or good Hindus. The sooner the BJP decide to give up the outdated slogans, the better. It should, instead, talk of nationalism, unity of the country and above all modernising our old, rusted society so that it can take us into the age of technology. It should not, of course, be at the cost of our cherished traditions, culture and history. It is not necessary for this party to propagate the Congress brand of secularism but at least it can stop preaching hatred and animosity among various communities. No party in this country should expect to come to power if it does not adopt a national outlook. People have rejected narrow, communal, sectarian poll planks and this time too they will opt for those parties which promise to keep the country's unity and integrity intact.

The BJP has a large number of leaders with impeccable image and the country will gain if they get a chance to guide its destiny but not if they hold the divisive views as part of their philosophy. The Nehrus have been ruling this country since independence with a brief interruption because of their total commitment to the communal harmony and national integrity, though their party has had a big number of members whose views were as anachronistic as those of the BJP's. Hindutva may therefore pay the BJP in a short-term but not to the extent of capturing power at the centre. For coming to power next time they will have to find a much more dynamic national outlook.

Current, 07.10.1989.
p. (2).

Ayodhya is not for sale: says Swami Lal Das

While the Hindi belt, especially UP and Bihar, was the victim of communal violence, peace and tranquility prevailed in Ayodhya. Here, the Hindus and Muslims lived in remarkable amity and camaraderie.

I visited the site of Ramjanambhoomi-Babri Masjid in the third week of November and was welcomed by the chief poojari, Swami Lal Das, with open arms. He made a number of amazing statements during a long conversation, ruthlessly exposing the designs of the VHP. Excerpts from the interview:

Who do you think is responsible for the worsening situation in the country.
None other than the Vishwa Hindu Parishad which started this senseless Ram Janambhoomi agitation.

It all started with their *Tala toro* campaign immediately after Indira Gandhi died. As chance would have it, the government of Uttar Pradesh, under orders of the court, opened the lock on February 1, 1986. Till February 5, the VHP kept quiet but thereafter they took out a *pradarshan rath* and gave the highly communal and dangerous slogan of *Babar ki santaan se khoon ka badla lena hai* and *Ayodhya humko pyari hai, Mathura ki taiyari hai* (We have to take revenge on the children of Babar and Ayodhya is dear to us. We are preparing for Mathura).

This greatly affected the Muslim sentiments and naturally led to communal riots. So many people were killed in Kashmir. Mandirs were razed to the ground. Calcutta, Moradabad, Aligarh besides other places in the country too witnessed large scale communal conflagration. In all, I am told 4,600 persons lost their lives in these riots. This situation was created only by the VHP.

What was the motive of the VHP in bringing about such a situation.
As I have been saying, Ram Janamboomi was not at all the issue in the minds of the VHP leaders. The aim of their agitation was nothing but extortion of money from religious Hindus, to mislead them.

How could they do this.
But this is what they have done. They collected a lot of money in the Rath Yatra. Then they started circulating the brick all over the country against all religious principles there is absolutely no tradition which sanctions this circulation of the bricks. We Hindus have the religious rite of performing puja whenever any development work or new construction starts. We do *shilanyas,* rather *shila pujan,* which is a religious rite. But

circulating the brick all over the country is not at all there in our religion.
Are you against this.
Of course, I am against this. There is no land, a case is pending in the court, the concerned department has not passed the building plans, what does all this mean. There is no consensus between the parties to the dispute. So why have they gone ahead with all this *tamasha* of circulating the brick and performing the *shilanyas*. What was the need for this? And do you know where they have performed the *shilanyas?*
Tell me.
The place belong to the Nazul, that is the government.
Has the government given them this land.
The government gave the land to defuse the situation. The land had been allotted earlier to the Nirmohi Akhara. Interestingly, the chief of the Akhara is not with the VHP.
Has he opposed the VHP.
Oh, yes. He has filed a land case against the VHP and it is pending in the court. Again he had filed a case on the question of *shilanyas* against the VHP.
Who is the head of this Akhara.
He lives in Gujarat and his name is Ram Chandra Acharya. He has been opposing them consistently . . . nobody is with them. That is why they had to "buy" two sadhus from Ayodhya.
Who are these.
One is Gopal Das and the other is Ramchandra Paramhans. Gopal Das lives on commission collected from the Pandas while Paramhans is a government stooge who does whatever the government wants him to do. These two have been bribed by the VHP. Then there is Ashok Singhal, general secretary of the VHP . . .
Who is this Singhal.
He owns a big computer factory at Delhi. . . Then there is Dau Dayal Khanna. He is a congressman. He has been a minister in UP. Then there is Dikshit, former Director General of Police U.P. . . Then there are Srinath Katju and Deoki Nandan Agarwal, retired judges of the Allahabad High Court. So all combined they are a motley group of comfort loving government stooges and two sadhus on hire *(kiraye ke sadhu)*. Together they have misguided the people of India to such an extent that the nation is paying the price for their mischief . . . and will continue to pay for times to come.

How much money must they have collected?
Forty five crore coupons were printed by the VHP at Delhi. And no coupon was worth less than Rs. 5. I get letters from all parts of the country. I meet hundreds of people every day. I am told that there is not a single hamlet from where they have not collected money.

What will they do with this money.
They have gobbled it up . . . and now are using it in the elections for the BJP . . . In one of my interviews I had pointed out that while Shahabuddin is trying to become the 'neta' of Muslims, the VHP is trying to capture the leadership of the Hindus. Actually both are misleading the people. Both the communities are not with them. The Babri Action Committee is going in one direction while Shahabuddin is pulling in a different direction. The same is the case with the VHP. The Hindus are not with them. The people who are with them are the same who are members of the Bajrang Dal, Rashtriya Janata Yuva Morcha, Mazdoor Sangh, RSS. The common Hindu is not with them. The intelligentsia saw through their game much earlier and identified their true face. It is the common people that they are misleading. First they did it by saying that we are going to make the Ram Mandir, to have the *shilanyas*. Earlier they had collected tons of money circulating the Rath and by misrepresenting that they had got the lock on the mandir opened. The fact is that it was done under orders of the court. They took the credit for a thing that was not at all done by them. Now that they know that they cannot construct the temple they are threatening to launch a *jail bharo andolan.*

Why is it that they will not be able to construct the temple.
They have no land to construct the temple and they have swallowed the money. Moreover, question of Ram Janambhoomi-Babri Masjid is pending in court and is sub-judice. How can they then construct the mandir. The only solution to this dispute is either a court verdict or a compromise worked out by the two warring sides. How can anyone else build a Ram Mandir here. One should not even think of doing it.

Were you here when the shilanyas was performed? Did you oppose it?
Yes, I was here and I opposed it. I pointed out that the place where the *shilanyas* was being performed was a public urinal. Being such an unholy spot nobody could even think of having a mandir there. But these people were in a hurry to justify their actions that they just dug a pit, put four bricks there and announced that they had performed the *shilanyas.* Now *shilanyas* is not done in this manner. *Shilanyas* is performed after a holy spot is identified. *Puja* is then performed and *havan* done. A raised

platform is then erected and only then that the *shila* is placed on it. What they have done is that they have just dug a pit. In fact, they have dug up a grave . . .

Was there a grave there.

Yes, of course, there was a grave underneath. Even bones were found. A lot of graves are there. This one was a *pucca* grave. In any case, it is treated as inauspicious to start construction at such a site. But the VHP has done it. Their main idea was to convince the illiterate and the gullible people that they had done the *shilanyas*. They were only misleading the people. When I opposed it, I was attacked.

By whom.

By the *goons* of Bajrang Dal. About 25–30 *goondas* surrounded my mandir and then almost strangled one of my men. First I ignored it but then I had to get up to face these anti-social elements. The CRPF was there but the government played dirty and removed it on the day of the attack. The district magistrate Srivastava is their old 'chela' and he played a very dubious role in the whole affair. He replaced the CRPF with the PAC and the latter you know how bad they are. We were almost killed but luckily a constable of the civil police pressed the alarm signal and the DIG rushed in with reinforcements. This is how we were saved in the nick of time.

Has any case been registered.

No, nothing was registered by the authorities.

Did you report it to the police.

Earlier also there was an attack on me but then . . .

The people of Ayodhya didn't take any action.

If the people of Ayodhya were not with me do you think these VHP people would have left me alive. If I am here today it is because of the people of Ayodhya. It is the VHP which is without any support of the people of Ayodhya. That is why they have had to requisition the services of hirelings. What these people do is to hire some *goondas,* make a lot of noise and then go away. The only people they have with them are those two hired sadhus.

Are you in favour of communal harmony.

That is what I want exactly in fact, there is no communal friction here. Both the parties to the Ram Mandir-Babri Masjid dispute go together to the court, with one another, have tea together, share their meals. I also go to Lucknow sometimes. Hashim Mian and Ikhlaq Mian (of Babri Masjid

Action Committee) go with me and return with me. I go to the Muslim areas like Saadatganj and all people of all religions. Yes, some Hindus did come and tell me not to go to the Muslim areas as the Muslims may attack me since I am connected with the Ram Mandir. I have always said that I have nothing to fear from the side of the Muslims. It is only the VHP people against whom I have to be on guard. Why should the Muslims attack me? I go all over the state and never, not even once, have I been attacked by the Muslims. Whenever I am attacked it is the Vishwa Hindu Parishad who have taken pot shots at me. When the mandir was ravaged, it was the handiwork of the VHP, when the mandir was robbed, it was again these people. In fact, a case of dacoity has been registered against Dharam Das who is a VHP leader. So whenever any attack is there, it is from the side of the VHP. I am most safe when I am among Muslims . . . the mischief has been done by some, but the entire population is suffering . . . and mind you there are elements in both the Hindu and Muslim communities who want the people to fight one another.

What has been the role of the government in all this.

The government wants the Hindus and Muslims to fight amongst themselves. . . . if you ask me one man responsible for this imbroglio it is Buta Singh. Whenever both the Hindus and Muslims are quiet he comes out with some provocative statement, ignites the whole atmosphere, leading to trouble. His only aim is to make both the communities fight so that his party can remain in power. This is the basic point.

Why don't you appeal to the people to ignore Buta Singh.

I can only appeal to the people who can hear me and see me. Sitting here I cannot appeal to people in Calcutta . . . now see what they (VHP) do. They send a small group to raise slogans like *Hindustan mein rehna hai to Vande Mataram Kehna hai* and *Babar ki santaan se khoon ka badla lena hai* in sensitive areas. What will be the result of this? Naturally there will be trouble . . . the intelligentsia knows their true character, so ignores them. The same is the case with peace loving people. It is only the anti-social elements which enjoy all this.

No religion wants this flak. Would Ram have appreciated this kind of hatred.

No, never. No religion says that. The real nature of this fight is really stupid. In fact, to me it appears that this is fight for money . . . both the

sides want money . . . otherwise tell me why Shahabuddin is always there at every meeting of the VHP. On October 29, Union Home minister Buta Singh, Chief minister N.D. Tiwari, Ashok Singhal, Mahant Gopal Das, Advaidnath and Ramchandra Paramhans were there and Shahabuddin was there. Why is it that the Babri Action Committee people are not their. Why is Shahabuddin taking the lead? On one hand he is there with the VHP at the latter's meetings and on the other belches fire against Hindus, gives inflammatory speeches. The Congress gave him some support so he started forming his own party. Insaf Party.

Where will it all lead to? What is the solution.
The only solution is that VHP and Shahabuddin should leave the Ram Mandir-Babri Masjid issue alone. Leave it to the people of Ayodhya to solve it. The Muslims of Ayodhya are fighting for the last 40 years and they have been fighting peacefully. There have been no riots. The fact remains that a new mandir cannot be constructed as there is no place. The Nirmohi Akhara would like to construct the mandir itself. Why will it allow the VHP to do it. They have already filed a case against the VHP for performing *shilanyas* on its land.

Why did the government allow it.
The government allowed it only to defuse the situation, that's all.

Where will the Hindus of Ayodhya and Faizabad cast their votes.
I think they will cast their votes for the Communist candidate. There are two lakh Muslim votes in Faizabad and about one lakh in the Tanda region. They will also vote against the Congress.

Whom will you vote for.
To the Janata Dal and the Communists.

Why did Rajiv Gandhi tolerate all this.
He wants cheap publicity.

Swamis are now going to Amethi to canvas against Rajiv.
They would be beaten up there.

Then why have they gone.
May be somebody told them you will be paid Rs. 11 per day, free food and dakshina, etc. Now they are swamis, they are free to go anywhere. That's all Swamis too can be misled.

Current, 02.12.1989.
pp. (6 + 14)

Babri demolition—'over my dead body'

Swami Lal Das holds the key of the Ram Janambhoomi. This diminutive chief poojari seems to have nerves of steel. His unflinching faith in communal amity is to be seen to be believed.

As an appointee of the court, it is his duty to protect the sanctity of the Masjid and the Bhoomi. "The mosque," he says emphatically, "cannot be demolished. The VHP can do it over my dead body. I am against the desecration of any place of worship."

The swami fears for his life. Last week he met home minister Mufti Mohammed Sayeed and briefed him on the explosive situation in Ayodhya.

What is the current situation in Ayodhya like?

Very bad. Communal feelings have become so insidious even the administration is influenced by it. For example, DIG Pradeep Kumar Sharma is an out-and-out communalist. He takes his cues from Baikhunth Lal Sharma, head of the Delhi-based Vishwa Hindu Parishad, District magistrate R.N. Srivastava is a disciple of Swami Chinmayananda and along with S.P. Joshi is deceiving Mulayam Singh Yadav and is totally guided by the VHP. Yadav is unable to make out who his people are.

Isn't the chief minister aware of this?

No, because the local CID is in league with the VHP and is feeding him with wrong reports. That's why I say no one knows what will happen there.

Have you met the Home minister and informed him what's going on?

Yes, I have told him everything—how the communal situation persists there, how the people are harassed, how I am kept on tenterhooks, what the administration is doing. He also gave me an assurance for full protection.

Why do you think the VHP is after your scalp?

The Vishwa Hindu Parishad sees me as the only impediment in their path to success. They know that if they manage to kick me, they can occupy the temple. But since they cannot do anything directly, they are harassing me through officials.

You were appointed to this position by the court, is not it?

Yes, in 1982. Prior to that, the city magistrate had appointed me. I've been there for ten years. Only the High Court can remove me.

Have you ever been attacked?

Yes, four times on August 5, some five or six people entered the temple

premises with revolvers when the *jhoola utsav* was going on. There were a lot of people there and they managed to nab two of the goons and took them to the kotwali. But instead of questioning or arresting them, the cops released them. I didn't tell anyone about it.

Not even the Chief minister?

No, because long before this (incident). I had cautioned the CM about such possibilities. Earlier, they had taken away the temple flags. Whenever I informed the police, they said I was lying. That's why I say the police are with them.

What is the scene you foresee on October 30?

Where is the place to construct the temple? There is only six acres of land available and that to away from the janambhoomi. It's near Sakshi Gopal and Manas Bhavan. Fronting it is the Kalahari temple and on another side the Janamsthan. It is surrounded from all four sides. Where is the space to build the temple?

What about the six-acre plot?

Raja Ramdasa of the akhara will not give them the land. He has already filed a case against the VHP. The latter announced that it has taken the land from the Raja and they started an exhibition there. The district officials supported the VHP and did not take any action. It was then that the Raja filed a case—one in the Faizabad court and another in the Allahabad High Court. There is another six acre plot comprising the kabrastan (cemetry). The VHP wants to put up the temple there also.

Where will they erect the temple then?

There's no place at all. There's some land which belong to barijagah, owned by Raghubir Prasad Acharya. It is only two or three acres but he will not allow them (to build the temple there). There are some houses on half of this and a portion is with the post office. What is left is less than a fourth of an acre. How can a temple be constructed there.

What is the way out then?

They want to demolish the mosque and construct the temple there. This will naturally create massive disturbances all over the country.

What is the area of the land where the mosque is situated?

Less than half an acre enough for 8 to 10 rooms.

Do you want the mosque to be demolished?

Why should I want that, I want all concerned to await the court decision, then abide by that.

Given a choice, will you favour demolition of a religious place?

Not at all. I am never in favour of any such things ever. I'm totally against the demolition of the mosque.

Does it mean you are against the construction of the temple?

No, I am in favour of having a temple but not as big as they want it to be. Even if they demolish the mosque, they can't achieve their goal.

Where are the shilanyas bricks?

They are two kilometres away. There's no place to keep them near the Janamsthan. Lakhs of them are lying on the banks of Saryu (river).

Where had the VHP performed the shilanyas?

They had first forcibly occupied some portion of the land belonging to Sakshi Gopal and tried to do the *shilanyas* there. When objections were raised, they shifted to the cemetry, kept two bricks there and announced that they had done the *shilanyas*.

Is it proper to have the temple in a cemetry?

Not at all. You see, a temple can never be constructed on *kabrastans* and *shauchalayas* (toilets) which are *apavitra* (unholy) places.

Then where will the temple be constructed?

They have collected million of rupees from all over the world. Now there is a lot of breast beating about the temple to show the people they are doing something.

The VHP claims there will be more than 20 lakh people there to support them on October 30?

That's the time of the Kartik mela. Lakhs of people come to Ayodhya at that time of the year for a holy dip in the Saryu and to do puja. After this they go away. So, it can't be said the devotees are coming to support the VHP, though such a claim is being made.

At a given time, how many people can be there at the Janambhoomi?

Not more than 500.

How will the widely projected, massive structure come up then?

I myself don't understand. Its an astute ploy to cheat the people. I don't understand how one temple will be demolished and another one will be built in its place.

Will you try to prevent the demolition of the mosque?

Yes, to the fullest of our capacity.

What if they beat you up?

As long as I am alive, I'll continue to prevent them. They can do it only over my dead body.

What about the people of Ayodhya? What do they want?

They don't want this. The VHP has literally bought over two or three sadhus. One is Ramchandra Paramhans, who has always been a broker of the police. Another one is Nitgopal Maharaj. The third is Ram Vilas Vendanti, but he has no credibility with the people.

What about the local MLA?

He is Jai Shankar Pandey of the Janata Dal who defeated the VHP candidate. In fact, the entire Faizabad district has no BJP or VHP representation.

What is the attitude of the Congress?

They're with us. They're against the VHP. Even former Congress MP Nirmal Khatri is with us.

And the Janata Dal?

They are also with us.

The Muslims?

They also don't want any *danga-fasad.*

Do you apprehend trouble on October 30?

Yes. Local people are against it but elements from outside Ayodhya will come here and create trouble.

How did the chief minister react when you met him?

He assured full co-operation, but unfortunately he continues to be misguided. I'll meet him again.

How many temples are there in Ayodhya?

About 8,500. And at none of these places is there any such problem.

How many temples had Sirajudullah given?

150. The biggest among them is Hanumangari, built by Nawab Sirajudullah.

Actually Hanumangari was a small temple. Since the land belonged to Sirajudullah, he gave it for construction of the temple. He also gave land for the Barijagah, Janki ghat, Raj Gopal, Naranachari and many other places for construction of temples.

What the VHP is doing is selling Ram. Since a lot of money is coming in the name of Ram they are bent on extorting more out of the Janata.

Current, 15.09.1990.
pp. (1 + 3)

Hey Ram!

I am convinced that Lal Kishan Advani's Rath Yatra was launched with an eye on the mid-poll and the BJP's ambitious plans to capture at least 200 seats in the Lok Sabha. He has been saying "we are the party of the future and if we can jump from two in 1984 to 88 in 1989, it should not be difficult to get at least 200 in the next election." The Advani Yatra is, therefore, a desperate attempt to capture power and not the Ramjanambhoomi. It is being used as an instrument to attain a purely political goal, though the course Advani has adopted is fraught with danger. It has already vitiated the communal atmosphere in the country and polarised a certain section of the Hindu opinion in favour of the Yatra. He is becoming more and more belligerent in his statement which are pushing the country to the brink of an explosion. This soft-spoken, urbane intellectual, who began his career as a journalist, is spitting fire and brimstone with least concern to the catastrophic consequences.

It is wrong to apprehend that the Advani Yatra will lead to a Hindu-Muslim confrontation. A barely ten to twelve per cent population spread all over the country cannot afford to be confrontationist, and if it does it will be at an incalculable loss to the community as a whole. All those Muslim leaders who are taking the Yatra as a challenge to their religious existence and adopting threatening postures are playing with fire, entering a lethal process of self-annihilation. All these leaders who meet in New Delhi's cozy atmosphere are charlatans, phantoms, fakes. They are giants with feet of clay. They are living in a fool's paradise if they think they are the only defenders of secularism and that secularism is the sheet anchor of their faith. Let me tell them their secularist pretensions are only skin deep. They are dyed in the wool communalists, sectarian and obscurantists. A statement issued by them last week at Delhi says: "In case the centre fails to restrict and ban the rath yatra of Mr Advani by October 12, we will be compelled to chalk out our strategy and programme to stop the yatra." It sounds like a suicide note. What "strategy and programme" can they possibly chalk out? How can this bunch of discarded, discredited 'leaders' stop an avalanche except by provoking poor, innocent Muslims to become sacrificial goats. It is time these Muslim leaders realised that secularism in this country cannot survive a day if the Hindu majority decides to do away with it. They should damn well know that modern secularism is not a contribution of Islamic thinking and that in no Muslim country in the world secularism is the order of the day. It is an alien concept to them. In fact, secularism as enshrined in our Constitution is

India's gift to humanity. The less these Muslim leaders talk about secularism the better, and stop misguiding their Muslim brethren.

If secularism has to be strengthened and defended, it can and will be done by the Hindus and Hindus alone. If the *rathyatra* has to be stopped, it can be done only by people like Vishwanath Pratap Singh, Mulayam Singh and Laloo Prasad and not by a few bearded Mullahs and clean shaven Muslim fanatics. The Singhs and Yadavs are not less Hindus than Lal Kishan Advani. It was only a few months ago that millions of Hindus reposed their trust in them and even today they are the tallest Hindu leaders who have thrown themselves onto the battle ground in defence of the values for which Mahatma Gandhi laid his life. They are the true inheritors of the Father of the Nation, and had he been alive, he would have been the first to lay down his life. National unity and secularism will survive and thrive so long as these leaders are on the forefront. And they are not alone. Millions of Hindus are behind them and many more millions will come forward to save the values and ideals they stand for.

Lal Kishan Advani has grossly miscalculated the Hindu or the Indian psyche. Had it not been so, the BJP would not have got two out of 524 seats in 1984 and had it been so it would have got at last 300 seats in 1989 when it had gone to the electorate for votes in the name of Ramjanambhoomi. To imagine that all those people flocking to have Advani's Rath *darshan* will in no way become his voters also. Had it been so the BJP would not have lost to socialists and communists in Ayodhya and Faizabad and Nagpur and Pune which had been the RSS strongholds for over half a century. The experience of the past 43 years teaches us that the Indian electorate chooses only those parties which promise to keep the unity and integrity of the country as their highest goal. Otherwise a secularist, socialist, democratic party like the Congress would not have ruled the country all these years.

And if Advaniji fails to reach Ayodhya on October 30 and build the temple as he has promised, it will be disastrous for him and his party. The only way left to him is conciliation and compromise. India has survived for thousands of years because it kept its heart and mind open to mankind, its windows were kept open to all kinds of winds which blew from north to south and east to west, because it thought it was not a country but a world, because it thought it cannot be contained in a narrow mind and because it thought it was the creator, not the created, not a piece of land, but cosmos. How can Advaniji confine Ram to a ballot box?

Current, 12.10.1990.
p. (2)

I want raj not Ram: Laloo Prasad Yadav

Laloo Prasad Yadav has taken Bihar by storm. This pint-sized, frail chief minister with crew-cut grey hair has proved his detractors wrong on every count.

A rare discovery among corrupt, degenerate Bihar politicians, this scion of a poor Yadav family—his two brothers continue to work as peons in a local college—seems determined to change the socio-political face of a state wallowing in poverty, disease, hunger, superstition, casteism. Corruption, nepotism and greed among its politicians and bureaucrats, which became a way of life, appear to be on the run. He takes decisions on the spot and wield the axe mercilessly.

Laloo's commitment to secularism, socialism and public accountability emanates from his faith which he inherited from Ram Manohar Lohia. That maverick socialist leader seems to be guiding the destinies of the people in the Hindi heartland.

Lohia's spectre haunts Bihar and looms large over neighbouring Uttar Pradesh where another Yadav, nicknamed by his VHP haters 'Maulana' Mulayam Singh, is shaking what Gobind Ballabh Pant once described as the sacred land of Ram, Krishna and Shiva. The two Yadavs together are performing a phenomenal task which has few parallels in our history. Recently addressing a Sadbhavana rally at Raghopur in Vaishali Laloo warned Advani that he would not spare any efforts to maintain communal amity. Agar zaroorat hui to hum sampradayikta ke rath ko usi tarah pees denge jaise roller sadak par kee gitti ko pees deta hai. (If need be I shall crush the rath of communalism in the same way as a road-roller crushes the pebbles). Those who are saying let us see how Mulayam Singh Yadav copes with it should first see how Laloo copes with it, he added.

Laloo is a man in a hurry. In his unique style of functioning he moves as though the whole government is moving with him. He issues orders while cycling from his home to the secretariat. Mighty bureaucrats shake in front of him like leaves and heads roll in dozens when he thinks they come in the way of progress.

I spent a day with him in Patna and am convinced that Bihar will not be the same if this man continues. Excerpts from a free-wheeling interview:

You are about to face a great challenge on the Bhoomi-Masjid issue. Lal Kishan Advani's rath will soon be entering Bihar?

I know he will be entering my state and we are fully prepared to face the challenge. I will tell him we do not want Ram, we want Raj. It is with Raj

in our hands we remove the difficulties of the people. We have been worshipping dozens of gods but we have hundreds of ailments and drawbacks in society. These gods have not helped us to remove poverty, hunger, illiteracy, ignorance, superstition. Biharis worship Saraswati but the largest number of illiterates are to be found in this state. The Bengalis worship Shakti, Kali in a big way but the most physically weak people are found in Bengal. Shakti is not worshipped in Haryana and Punjab but these states have healthy and sturdy people.

What will you tell your people about the rathyatra?
I have been telling them the BJP has been using them to pull the rath while opposing reservations. This is hypocrisy of the first order. It cannot work. There is very little response to the *rathyatra* and we have launched the Sadbhavna campaign in a big way. You must know that 99 per cent of Hindus are secular. They are least concerned with these *'sharyanths'*. We have been telling our people to keep off these divisive forces and we have also assured the minorities not to worry, not get provoked. The might of my police and government is with them.

Do you fear any communal flare-up?
No, not at all. I will face the situation as it develops.

What you will do?
Well, it is my commitment. I will not tolerate communalism for a moment. I will chase communalism out of my state. I will not allow any disruption and any break-down of law and order.

Will you try to stop the rathyatra?
The question has yet to arise. Let the *rathyatra* enter Bihar and we will face it.

If Advaniji's speech disturb communal peace will you arrest him?
Time will tell. Wait and watch. I will not compromise on the issue of communal amity. I will appeal to people to remain in their homes and perform the Puja. Ram is in every house, in every heart. Why drag him out on the road?

What in your view is the solution to the mandir-masjid dispute?
Status quo till the verdict of the court. My message to my people is to wait for the court decision. There is no other way.

The VHP and BJP insist they will not abide by the court decision.
Let them say what they like, but they cannot ignore the Constitution and the judiciary.

The BJP has threatened to withdraw support on this issue.

Let them do it. We will not compromise on principles. We do not love the chair. We have come after a very stiff, very long struggle. We cannot be intimidated. We have not come to power to stick to the chair. We have come to power to change society. We will be happy to face the people again.

Are you in favour of a mid-term poll?

Let that bridge come, we will cross it. But I must tell you if the mid-term poll is held. V.P. Singh will sweep the polls. We will be the single largest party and this time we will be in a majority. All these leaders opposed to the Mandal Commission and trying to misuse the mandir-bhoomi issue will be wiped out. People will throw them in the dustbin.

It means in the next election the BJP will not be your ally.

All these parties are disintegrating. Mandal has broken them. It is a typhoon. They will be blown off the earth. V.P. Singh has given such a turn to the country's politics that all these people have become irrelevant.

No compromise, no going back.

No. No. No, even if the heavens fall we will not look back.

How are you facing the post-Mandal situation in your state?

Vishwanath Pratap Singh has taken a historic decision. After thousands of years the backwards and weaker sections have now got real freedom. Do you remember the slogan we used to raise. 'Raja Nahin fakir hai,' Bharat ki taqdeer hai' has become a reality. We are totally committed to him and Mandal.

Some people including Devi Lal and Chandra Shekhar are suggesting economic criteria as the base line. Do you agree with them?

No. I do not. They are fooling the people. The Constitution has no such provisions. Mandal is the final word and there is no compromise on it, come what may.

Devi Lalji has asked the prime minister to go slow and enter in a process of consultation.

No. I do not agree with him. We will not slow the process. We will not go back on our commitment.

Chandra Shekhar is also making similar suggestions.

All those MPs who are making these suggestions should first resign from the Lok Sabha membership. They should be removed. It means they are sabotaging the Janata Dal manifesto. We will launch a move that they should be thrown out of the party. Because when elected we take a pledge

that we will be loyal to the Constitution. Those who are opposing the Mandal Commission are violating this pledge. Reservation for the backwards is our pledge to the people and those who are trying to water it down are betraying their conscience.

Reservation for the backwards is not in the Constitution.

It is. The Mandal Commission was appointed according to the constitutional provisions and its report is binding on the government. The constitutional provision is that we must remove social and economic inequality and that's what we have done. As Dr. Ram Manohar Lohia used to say, if we have to protect the unity and integrity of the country, then we will have to remove disparities in society. We will have to create special conditions to remove these inequalities.

Then why is Chandra Shekhar trying to sabotage the process?

I do not know what he wants. I do not know why he is doing this. He is immaterial so far as our commitment is concerned. We are committed to the nation and nobody can reverse this process.

The prime minister is under tremendous pressure on this issue from within the party.

Don't be under such an illusion. He is a very strong man. His moral fibre can't be destroyed by such pinpricks. The whole country stands behind him. No prime minister in the past had such an opportunity to destroy the fortress of inequality. Today the backwards, Harijans, Scheduled Castes and minorities stand behind him like a rock.

Are you not worried about the loss of life, the self-immolations and the police firings?

What can we do if somebody wants to put an end to his life? The Congress is 100 per cent behind these inhuman acts. These Congress leaders drug these young boys and girls and ask them to burn themselves. Some of these young men who are indulging in acts of violence specially in Delhi are the same who murdered the Sikhs, burned them alive and put their property to flames. You think I do not know who these people are. These are the same 1984 people. The same NSUI and the same congressmen who were found to be behind the 1984 riots.

Who organised these riots in Bihar?

The same people. Dr. Jagannath Mishra is opposed to Mandal and is behind this unrest. He is financing it. He has opened his purse strings. But strangely the backwards in the Congress are with us. Ram Lakhan Singh Yadav, Sidheswar Prasad, Sitaram Kesari, Lahtan Choudhary—*ek*

ek Congressi Backward *hamare sath hai.* This party is vertically split. It is gone. It has been reduced to a party of upper castes.

Do you expect them to create more trouble for you on this issue?

Nothing. They are rats. They come like thieves and set fire to public property. They are traitors. This is no fight. We can crush them. *Fauj to VP Singh ke Sath hai.* The message that V.P. Singh is with them has reached the people in every nook and corner of not only Bihar but the whole country.

What are your priorities? How do you plan to implement them?

I started functioning an hour after I was sworn in as chief minister. My first priority was a war on corruption, bureaucratic lethargy, inefficiency, nepotism. These were the banes of Bihar. I would not have moved an inch had I not taken the bull by the horns. And the results are there for everybody to see.

Have you been able to combat corruption?

Corruption is on the run. I have transferred hundreds of officials who had made it their privilege to occupy plum posts. The screws have been tightened to such an extent that they no longer seek these positions, specially in the irrigation and public works departments. Honest officers will now be publicly recognised and adequately rewarded. Honesty in my government will not be ignored. It will be rewarded.

What will be the criteria? Who will judge honesty?

Every officer in a sensitive post will be given a task and time to complete the work. We monitor his work and then reward him if he comes up to our expectations. The chief secretary monitors the performance of senior officers and prepares their CRs. The cabinet too regularly reviews the work and progress. There is no dearth of money. We have decentralised work and delegated power.

Has corruption been reduced?

Drastically. The *looteras* have been identified and packed off. Now they do not seek plum posts. They had thought no government will touch them, so resourceful had they grown. I have found there are a lot of honest officials but earlier they were ignored and bypassed. Now I have brought them up. I am either closing down sick industries and giving compensation to workers or handing them over to private enterpreneurs. I have also decided to privatise power.

I have suspended nearly 60 engineers and hundreds in other fields against whom there were bad reports.

What action have you taken against the mafias?
First I tackled the land mafia. I have taken away land from landlords and distributed it to tillers. In two districts alone in Purnea and Giridih Swayam Sevak I have distributed 2,000 acres land. The process will continue in other districts. I have warned that even if one man is dispossessed of his land I will take it that I was dispossessed. The punishment will be sever and exemplary. The collector of that district will be held responsible and punished.

Are you planning comprehensive land reforms?
Complete, without any compromise and with a degree of ruthlessness. This is a major issue and I will not rest until I succeed, until I break the backbone of the landgrabbers. Bihar's poor and landless have been told that soon their days of misery will be over. Our anti-poverty revolution has begun from the land. Land must go to the tiller.

And the coal mafia?
I have broken it. I have issued licences to 15,000 local people, specially Adivasis, and asked banks to give loans to them to buy trucks. The main source of mischief were the transporters. Now these Adivasis will own and run these trucks, and once they pay off the loans they will become their owners. Every such truck owner will also employ four people to assist him. It means 60,000 new jobs and it also means the end of the mafia hold on transport of coal.

What about the co-operative mafia?
I am going to smash it. The Biscoman Bhavan has been raided. All its files have been seized. I cannot arrest the cooperative mafia chief; Tapeshwar Singh, because he has taken anticipatory bail. But rest assured I am not going to leave him. He will be booked and all his wealth disgorged I have also smashed the road mafia. The engineers and the contractors who used to mix sand with bitumen have been thrown out. All those mafia touts who used to buy and sell chief ministers have been bundled out. Their entry in my house has been banned.

Are you getting enough time to undo all those evils?
I am enjoying the game, place the national flag on my bicycle and go among the people.

What about your officials?
They also follow me on bicycles. I say you also lose some weight. You have become too used to the cozy life. Now cycle your way, walk to your office. You be healthier and not suffer heart attacks. I have banned all

officers from using cars on Mondays and Tuesdays. They are given only three and a half litres petrol per day and no officer is allowed to use cars for private purposes. If an officer is found violating these rules his official car is taken away and a new car is bought from his salary. I will thus save crores of rupees and use it for development work.

Current, 13.10.1990.
pp. (1 + 11 + 13)

Message from Ayodhya

I spent a day in Ayodhya last week. No place in the country today is so peaceful, so serene, so full of love and compassion as this city of the temples. With me was Jaishankar Pandey a hardcore Lohiaite who trounced his VHP-BJP-Congress rivals in the last Assembly election. This short, gutsy man is deeply religious, knows the Ramayana by heart and does pooja every morning before sunrise. We were joined by Swami Lal Das, the official keeper of Ram Janambhoomi and an ardent devotee of Lord Ram. We first visited the Babri Masjid which houses the idol of Ram and where the Pooja was being performed. I asked the young poojari offering *prasad*: Would you like the masjid to be demolished? *Kadapi nahin. Yeh nahin ho sakta hai. Hum dharmic log kisi dharamsthan ko nahin torte*. He was firm in what he believed.

Next to the masjid/janambhoomi is a cute little temple of Sakshi Gopal. We went in to be welcomed by Mahant Ram Kirpal Das who also offered me *prasad* and let me have the *darshan* of the deities. Mahantji, I asked him, would you like the masjid to be demolished? *Hare Ram, yeh pap kaise ho sakta hai. Koi hindu yeh pap nahin kar sakta. Hum yeh nahin hone denge*. This led me to put the same question to a number of mahants, swamis and lay devotees. Almost all affirmed: *Koi dharamashthan nahin tutna chahiye*. But all added: *iska koi shantipoorvak hal nikal aaye to achcha ho*.

Ayodhya is a part of Faizabad parliamentary constituency which encompasses nine Assembly seats. In the last Lok Sabha poll, a hardcore communist, Mitrasen Yadav, defeated his rival—backed by the VHP-BJP—by a huge margin and all the nine MLAs won their seats by defeating this combine's nominees. The issue even then was the same. One of the MLAs is a Muslim who trounced his BJP opponent even though his constituency does not have more than five per cent Muslim voters.

This is the bare, stark profile of Faizabad Ayodhya, an Island of peace and communal harmony. The people of these twin cities told me very clearly and firmly: "we must be allowed to find a solution to this problem. We have been living here for centuries like brothers. We never had communal riots and we do not want any communalisation of life here." Those who want to see how the two communities live in peace, honour, respect and dignity should visit Ayodhya. If proof was needed, it was there for all to see at the stupendous welcome the people of this holy place gave Rajiv Gandhi. They opened their hearts to him with only one slogan—we want peace. He was so much overwhelmed by their desire for communal harmony that he walked on the dusty, unpaved roads for more than 10 kilometres in the blazing sun. An old bearded Muslim presented him with a copy of the Ramayana and a Ramnama with Ram written on it a thousand times. A respectable Mahant gave him a copy of the Koran. All this happened only last week even as Advaniji's rath is rolling towards Ayodhya to 'liberate' Ram Janambhoomi on the one hand and amidst the Shahi Imam's jingoistic cry of *hifazati dasta* on the other.

I had driven to Ayodhya straight from Mulayam Singh Yadav's public rally at Lucknow's La Martiniere College grounds. It was the largest public gathering the city has ever experienced and one of the biggest I have ever witnessed. This mammoth assemblage of men and women from all parts of the state gave Yadav a standing ovation when he shouted at the top of his voice: *Mein masjid nahin torne dunga, magar mandir bhi banega.* Who can be a better Hindu than me. I have been reading the Ramayana from the day I opened my eyes and I know Hanuman Chalisa by heart. But my Ram has taught me to respect all religions. I am a Hindu of the highest order and am one who will lay his life to protect those whose faith is not that of mine. That's what Gandhiji, JP, and Lohiaji have taught me. The millions of people of Uttar Pradesh reserved their most thunderous applause when Chandra Shekhar told the rally: I am a Hindu, but I have not been taught to hate any religion. My Ram is the Lord of compassion. In his *rajya* not even a bird was hurt. He was the symbol of love.

Lucknow's was the 48th public rally addressed by Mulayam Singh Yadav. Never has a man held so many public meetings in such a short period with unprecedented crowds flocking to them. His rally at Faizabad-Ayodhya was second only to that of Lucknow's in terms of turnout. In all he has addressed over a crore people. "But now I feel suffocated. The people in Delhi who ought to have decided the course of events by now have done nothing. Let them meet as soon as possible and find a peaceful solution. I plead with folded hands to Advaniji to save the country from

a bloodbath . . . to stop the rath and find a path strewn with flowers of love and amity." The 140 km distance from Lucknow to Ayodhya is a road of peace. Dozens of towns and villages on its side are a picture of communal harmony and peace. People at tea shops and *dhabaas* repeat only one sentence: "We want peace; our greatest worry is to make two ends meet, we do not want quarrels, we have lived together for centuries and would like to live like this for many more, please leave us alone. If we can live together, why not Ram and Rahim?" This is the message of the people of Faizabad-Ayodhya and all the roads leading to Ram Janambhoomi.

Current, 20.10.1990.
pp. (2).

Face to face with Advani

I had a two-hour talk with Lal Krishna Advani on Saturday, a day before he left for Ayodhya, at his Pandara Park residence. Incidentally he had been to the Ramjanambhoomi only once, and that too very briefly, years ago. Most BJP leaders have never been to Ayodhya and they are not religious in the traditional sense of the term. Purely political Hindus, their main aim is to attain power and then shape the country according to their dreams. What these dreams are they do not know exactly. Advani is perhaps the only person among them who knows what he wants. He is suave, polite, courteous, erudite, articulate and most profound in a face-to-face conversation. He chooses his words carefully, using them effectively. We have been good friends and respect each other. He knows his ideology is not mine and nor would I ever approve his politics of mixing religion with politics. Yet we often meet and discuss even the most controversial issues coolly, not allowing our blood pressure to shoot up.

I am giving this personalised account because in the next poll, whenever it takes place, he will play the most crucial role in the Hindi heartland. In the coming month four men will dominate the scene at the national level, because unfortunately it is this region which has been deciding the course of events in the country since Independence. The south is contended with itself, its leaders hardly show any ambitions at the national level. So the field this time will be left open to Rajiv Gandhi, Advani, Vishwanath Pratap Singh and Chandra Shekhar. Advani among them will be the only man who will be able to hold public rallies with the police and the

bureaucracy swooning over him. He will be the only man backed by the most well-organised force made up of RSS-VHP- Bajrang Dal storm-troopers with the Hindu sentiments at its peak. To his advantage, his three adversaries will be facing the electorate with lots of explanations for their failures and acts of omission and commission. Advani will go with a clean slate. He talked a great deal about Hindu psyche and an overwhelming feeling among his co-religionists of being taken for a ride by a minuscule 12 to 15 per cent Muslim minority.

But he had no plausible answer to my question as to why 85 per cent of the Hindus had not reposed their trust in the BJP or its earlier *avatars,* the Jan Sangh, the Hindu Mahasabha, the Ram Rajya Parishad and the Shiv Sena or any political body claiming to reflect the Hindu thinking. Why is it that invariably the centrist, leftist or regional parties with secularism, socialism and democracy as their plank have always got the better of Hindu communalist parties. Why did the Congress always get anywhere between 38 to 45 per cent votes and manage to rule this predominantly Hindu country for over 40 years. All the seven prime ministers were votaries of secularism and whatever we may think of Chandra Shekhar, his secular credentials are beyond question. None of them used or misused Hindutva and yet ruled the country for decades. None of them came to power riding the crest of a Hindutva wave. Why the BJP got only two seats out of 524 in 1984 and I am sure had there not been seat adjustment with the Janata Dal it may not have got the impressive 86 that it did in the last poll.

"I am not for Hindutva. That is the Shiv Sena slogan. I am for nationalism which has no place for minorityism or pseudo-secularism". Like Laloo Prasad Yadav he almost said that he was for Raj and that Ram would be used only as a vehicle. " I did not have the portrait of Ram on the Rath, it was the Lotus, my party's election symbol". Surprisingly, he is not sure whether the mammoth crowds which gathered for the *Rath darshan* will keep the Lotus in mind while deciding the fate of the country. In fact, he had originally planned to do a *padyatra* from Somnath to Ayodhya but the announcement of the acceptance of the Mandal report by the VPS government made him opt for the *Rath*. Mandal thus became a decisive factor and he thought the *Rath* would manage to pull down the caste barriers. It did, momentarily, but finally the electorate, especially the 75 per cent Mandal beneficiaries, will remember Kabir—'bhuke bhajan no hoi Gopala' (one cannot worship God with an empty stomach) once things cool down. But astute politician that he is, he realises that in the coming battle both Rajiv and Shekhar will be irrelevant at least in UP and

Bihar—the two most decisive states in the battle of the ballot—and it will ultimately boil down to Mandal vs Mandir. And here too V.P. Singh will mix Mandal with Mandir. He is not opposed to the Mandir, he is against the demolition of the mosque. 'I too would not like to demolish the mosque. No Hindu in his wildest dreams would ever think of desecrating any place of worship, especially a mosque, but I would like it to be shifted elsewhere brick by brick if Muslims agree to such a proposition. I felt hurt when I saw the picture of the boys on the top of the mosque's dome. No, this is not my way', he was precise.

Yet he is aware that if the spirit of 'nationalism' has to be kept up till the elections, there would not be any place for this *Rath* business but extensive propagation of 'our brand of nationalism". The main attack will be on what he calls the 'Nehruvian' fortress. "The media, especially the English one, is still in the grip of the cult of Nehru." But he has no explanation why millions of illiterate masses do not opt for his brand of 'nationalism'. Are all those people who refuse to accept his approach to national unity and integrity anti-national and only a mere 7.5 per cent who voted for him 'nationalist'? He has perhaps a wrong notion of the 'Hindu psyche'. This time, despite the *rathyatra,* the BJP's percentage of votes may not cross the 10 per cent mark which would mean that 90 per cent of the voters will remain unconvinced of his concept of 'nationalism'. In Delhi itself where it bagged all but one seat, the BJP might face a tough time and even Advani will find the going rough in his constituency.

Current, 24.11.1990.

p. (2).

Stop this lunacy

In one of his poems Rabindranath Tagore said: 'Whenever a child is born it brings the message that God is not yet disappointed with humanity'. We Indians have come to hate ourselves so much that we have begun hacking infants to pieces. The communal fire raging in the country has turned human beings into animals. Reports from the communal battle grounds reveal that not even infants are being spared. Blood-curdling reports of children being decapitated, maimed, burnt and thrown out of running trains by religious zealots have horrified the nation.

What religion is this? Which Ram or Rahim has taught his followers

to shed the blood of innocent men, women and children. A normal human being having faith in God, any God, cannot just pick up a knife and pierce it through the heart of a child. For this, first he has to lose faith in his God, reject his religion, turn into a beast and then act. A normal human being cannot kill a fellow human being, let alone a child. Those indulging in killing and roasting their fellow beings are not normal. They are committing a crime abhorred by every religion, law or code of ethics. What is the remedy? How can it be stopped? We had failed to stop it in 1947 and paid the price by sacrificing the noblest son of India—the Father of the Nation.

If a section of our people (or do we call it the lunatic fringe?) have decided to live by the dagger or come to power after swimming in a river of blood or after mounting over a pyramid of corpses, then we have to decide here and now whether we will permit ourselves to be ruled by a blood-thirsty marauding mob of dagger-wielding lunatics or put our faith in law abiding citizens. How does it matter whether the victim of the dagger is a Hindu or a Muslim. Once we permit the law of the dagger, faith and religion are blown to smithereens because no faith or religion can sustain itself or be guided thus. It has never happened in the history of human civilisation and cannot be allowed to happen in this country. The dispute is whether the mosque should remain or be razed so that a temple can be built on its ruins. If the demolition of the mosque can save a single life, let it be torn down. Human lives are much more precious than bricks and stones. The pro-mosque Muslims should ask a mother, whose child has been cut into pieces in front of her eyes, about such a mosque. Will any of these pro-mosque leaders allow their kids to be slaughtered if they are asked to choose between the mosque and the lives of their dear ones? I do not wish to indulge in the academics of Islam, Hinduism, religion, language, holy books, modes of prayer, culture, Mecca or Ayodhya. To me, the sweet smile of a child is worth millions of religions and if a child is sacrificed on the altar of faith, that faith is not worth following.

In a war of faiths nobody wins. And if somebody feels he has won, even that feeling cannot be permanent. As Krishna said, no victory is permanent and no defeat is permanent. By slaying a child if a fanatic feels he can establish the supremacy of his religion he is not only wrong but is inflicting a grievous injury on himself. The holy land of Ayodhya is soaked in the blood of hundreds of Ram *bhaktas* and the temple will come up there because millions of faithful desire it. It could have come without shedding a drop of blood. And I want the temple to come up

without any more blood shed. Let it be a most beautiful, magnificent temple, but it's foundation should not rest on the graves of the innocent. Let the fanatics from both the Hindu and Muslim communities sit together and resolve that in the struggle for supremacy of their faith, the dagger will have no place. The rest will be taken care of by the people of this great country who detest the murder of the innocents.

First stop killing, looting and arson. Do not go back to the dark ages. Let's not barter our civilisation for barbarism.

Current, 22.12.1990.
p. (2).

The BJP's soul-searching

The thousands of BJP delegates who had assembled at Jaipur's sprawling Sawai Man Singh stadium for the party's plenary session were stunned to hear their idol—outgoing president Lal Krishna Advani—announce that too much of Hindutva will harm the larger cause of the movement launched by him from Somnath. "The *Rathyatra* has achieved its purpose but the party will have to go to the people on much broader platform, the question of *roti* is equally important." India does not comprise the Hindi belt alone but stretches from Kashmir to Kanyakumari: the party cannot come to power on mere slogans, it will have to win the hearts as well as the minds of the country, he told them. He chided those who raised provocative slogans aimed at the Muslims. "We are not against Muslims, we are opposed to the minorityism and pseudo-secularism." He followed up his speech with a series of interviews to the Press to push his ideas in a more articulate manner. In an interview he emphasised: "I do not want to mix religion with politics but there is nothing wrong in a politician being religious." He was loath to see India as a theocratic state but a secular state does not mean an irreligious state. In a bold exercise to refurbish his party's image, replying to a questioner who asked him whether the sectarian tag disturb him he said: "it does, it has been disturbing me all along. I have instructed the BJP governments in the three states where we rule that if there are riots anywhere, see that they are firmly dealt with. Whether he is Hindu or Muslim, a rioter is a shame and a disgrace to the country."

His successor Murli Manohar Joshi took a step further when he said that the parties opposed to the BJP turned the Mandir-Masjid issue into a

Hindu-Muslim dispute which is far from the truth. "These parties made it appear that the Hindus want to build a temple by demolishing a mosque built by Babar. There can be no bigger lie. The BJP considers this as a matter of national self respect. The birth place of Ram is a symbol of national glory. It was from this point of view that the BJP suggested the reconstruction of the temple and the respectful shifting of the structure in Ayodhya to another site." Joshi's soft-peddling of the Mandir-Masjid controversy left nobody in doubt when he dropped Vijayaraje Scindia, Sardar, Angre and a few other die-hards of the VHP from the party's apex bodies and inducted 'liberals' in their place. He thought Ram can play a role in galvanising votes to a certain extent but the issue of *roti* can be ignored only at the party's peril. The BJP has not openly opposed Mandal, it has merely objected to some technical details and the way it was imposed on the country all of a sudden, as a political gimmick.

In yet another very bold effort to enhance the party's 'secular' credentials, seasoned politician Atal Behari Vajpayee was brought to the fore. He too, in a number of interviews, made startling statements including the one to the effect that if the VHP-BJP were to demand the demolition of the mosque he would oppose the move and if the two communities cannot reach a mutual agreement, the issue should be referred to the Supreme Court. It is undoubtedly a major departure from the BJP stand. He also made it clear that it was a wrong impression that the VHP was calling the shots and added: "If the BJP agreed with the VHP line, one could not blame the VHP for the impression created." In this revealing interview to a Bombay magazine he said he was against "invoking the name of Ram for electoral gains." Departing from the VHP line he said a distinction should be made between the invaders and those embraced Islam on their own free will or were converted at the point of the sword. The present generation should not be punished for the deeds of their fore-fathers. At his Jaipur press conference he made it clear that he had reservation on Advani's *rathyatra* which roared like a lion. Where is the lion, he was asked. "It has been enchained. It is lying there outside the conference venue". What is it doing there, he was asked, again. "It is eating grass," he remarked.

The BJP leaders were in an introspective mood in Jaipur and the process seems to continue in its inner circles. The debate has assumed serious dimensions. The question is whether the party can capture power—it is very serious about attaining this goal—in the name of Ram alone or has to add a larger dimension to its national image. After all, India is not confined to the Indo-Gangetic plain only. An India also exists south of

Vindhyas. The results in the recent District Council elections in Kerala, where the party contested over 400 seats but won only two have made the process of soul-searching all the more agonising. In the north too, it is most unlikely that almost every Hindu will vote for it for there is no such thing like the Hindu vote bank. The backwards, Scheduled Castes and Tribes and Muslims put together make up more than 70 per cent of the total electorate. And they largely remain unconvinced of the BJP's strident Hindutva deal. The Congress may have been defeated but it is not, by any stretch of imagination, down and out. The Janata Dal and the Left are developing their own pincer movements which have encircled the BJP heartland. The party is likely to wilt under the multi-pronged attack from all the non-BJP forces in a no-holds-barred battle. The realisation that it will be the main target of attack from all these forces has forced the Advanis, Vajpayees and Joshis to cultivate a national constituency.

Current, 16.02.1991.
p. (2).

A most dangerous game

Two days after assuring the home minister that it would do nothing to add new complexities to the Babri Masjid Ramjanambhoomi dispute, the BJP government of Uttar Pradesh, taking advantage of constitutional provisions, has acquired 2.7 acres of land surrounding the disputed site in Ayodhya in a devious manner and asked the district collector of Faizabad to take physical possession of the tract in the 'public interest'. By doing so, the Kalyan Singh government may have cocked a snook at the centre, the judiciary, the minority community and secular opinion in the country but that does not mean that the BJP's insidious plan to rekindle the mandir campaign to gain political mileage in the forthcoming by-elections will go unchallenged.

To begin with, the acquisition has no legal basis as the notification violates the Allahabad High Court's injunction to maintain status quo in the area. Furthermore, the government has brazenly thrown to the winds the provisions of Section 5 of the Land Ceiling Act which provides for consultations with parties in the dispute before acquiring the land. Not only has the government not observed even minimal procedures, it has taken recourse to lying when asked to explain the pressing urgency for the acquisition. The notification states that the land is being acquired to

'promote tourism', yet the UP Tourism Development Corporation has no inkling of the plans afoot to attract more tourists to Ayodhya. And to deliberately compound confusion, the notification does not pin-point the actual acreage taken over by the government—it is still unclear whether the numbers of the plots mentioned in the order refer to the two revenue settlement maps of 1861 and 1937 or pertain to the nazul map—and the mandatory requirement to place the site map in the Faizabad collectorate for public inspection has been dispensed with.

The BJP's gameplan is obvious. The Kalyan Singh government has failed miserably on all fronts in the nearly four months it has been in office and will be facing the electorate once again in the by-elections less than a month from now with no evidence of having done anything. Having tested the efficacy of the Ram card in the summer, it is hoping that the voters can by swayed again on the same ground. The hasty acquisition of the land surrounding the Babri Masjid is supposed to demonstrate the BJPs resolve to make good the promise it had made in its manifesto to remove all obstacles in the construction of the Ram Mandir. But in the present circumstance there is every possibility that such posturing will not cut much ice with the voters, for other issues, especially the back-breaking price spiral, will dominate the elections. Moreover, the BJP will, in all probability, face one-to-one contests all over the state. Already there is talk of seat adjustment between the Janata Dal and the SJP, with the left parties throwing their weight behind such a move. It was precisely the split of votes between the Janata Dal and SJP—the Congress having ceased to exist as a political force in the state—which had enabled the BJP to record a spectacular victory in the summer election. In the coming by-election it will not reap the benefit of a split of non-Congress votes.

By any yardstick, Kalyan Singh has bitten off more than he can chew. His decision will not only further alienate his party from the rest of the political class, it will also create tensions between the centre and the state. At the same time, the UP government faces the possibility of contempt proceedings by the Allahabad High Court. Moreover, affected parties like Babri Masjid Action Committee will certainly take to the streets to contest the government's decision which, in turn, will galvanise Hindu organisations like the Bajrang Dal into retaliatory action and the state will be plunged into communal strife on a scale not witnessed before. This will not be in the BJP government's best interest. Kalyan Singh may be under tremendous pressure from the VHP to go ahead with this hare-brained scheme so that work on the Ram Mandir can start even before the court has delivered its verdict or before the dispute is resolved amicably,

but he should see beyond the end of his nose if he wants to avert chaos and anarchy in the state he rules. If he does not, the centre must intervene decisively and nullify the notification. If that is not done the repercussions will be severe, bloody and dangerous.

Current, 19.10.1991.
p. (2).

Lying in Ram's name

There are many ways for political parties to come to power. Adolf Hitler adopted a particular path but the price that humanity had to pay was very high. Conversely, democrats have chosen to win the people over to their side. In a democratic country like India, where the ballot has ruled supreme since Independence, a smooth transfer of power has been the order of the day—even an authoritarian leader like Indira Gandhi had to bow to the will of the people in 1977. Unsurprisingly, the methods the BJP and its cohorts like Shiv Sena, Vishwa Hindu Parishad and Bajrang Dal chose to employ as a short-cut to power distinctly smack of fascism at its worst. The obnoxious attempt to single out Muslims as their main target and to whip up a nation wide campaign of hatred smacks of a Nazi ploy to unleash a pogrom against a minority community. In 1989, the BJP and its allies rode piggyback on V.P. Singh and managed to place themselves in advantageous positions in the country as well as the Parliament. And a year later they hoodwinked the nation in the name of Ram to increase their strength even though their dream of capturing power in New Delhi was shattered by a vigilant electorate.

Be that as it may, last week's events must have shattered the hopes of the vote bank L.K. Advani had consolidated in the wake of his *rathyatra* when the votaries of Hindutva were caught in their own trap. The construction of the Ram Mandir in Ayodhya has not yet begun and the possibility of that happening in the near future is remote because of the opposition to the BJP's diabolical scheme from half-a-dozen local mahants, including Swami Swaroopanand Jagatguru Shankaracharya of Dwarkapith who has challenged Kalyan Singh's move to demolish the Shakshi Gopal and various other temples on the acreage acquired by the UP government in a devious manner. "Is it really necessary for the BJP-VHP to demolish the Hindu shrines for the construction of a temple," the venerated sage asked them in anguish.

It will be remembered that Hitler rose to power on millions of dead bodies half a century ago, though in dissimilar circumstances. 1991 is not 1933; India is not Germany and Indians are not Germans. India is a country with a tradition of tolerance and Hinduism is undoubtedly the most unique gift of this fertile land to the world. Unlike Islam, Christianity and Judaism, the history of Hinduism cannot be defined or confined to a certain period—it is cosmic: it begins with the beginning of human thought and is not the personal property of a few power-hungry politicians. India is too big to become a fascist state to be ruled by religious bigots. Indians will not allow the BJP to hijack Hinduism and take the real life out of it. Hundreds of Hindus have spoken against what the neo-Nazis have been doing in Ayodhya in the name of Ram, the greatest son of India.

What the Jagatguru said in anguish reflects what an average Hindu feels. And what Madhavrao Scindia said also reflects the mood of modern Indians and millions of Hindus who do not subscribe to Advani's definition of the country and its ethos. "Who has given the BJP the right to decide which temples should be built and which destroyed? As a Hindu I am proud of my religion because of its philosophy of tolerance and its glorious past which, through the centuries, has never been tainted by an attack on a religious place of worship. Temples and mosques are places of worship and not pawns in a political game," he says. Advani may dismiss Scindia as a politician but what about Mahant Lal Das, the keeper of the sanctum sanctorum and the chief *pujari* of the Ramjanambhoomi? "The BJP will not be allowed to demolish the structures and if it does it will do it over my dead body," he has warned. Is Mahant Lal Das a lesser Hindu than Advani?

The question is not the Babri Masjid or the construction of Ram Mandir. The Babri dispute has been aggravated by Hindu lunatics like L.K. Advani and Muslim maniacs like Syed Shahabuddin who want to establish their supremacy over the gullible masses. Shahabuddin by his utterances and asinine antics has done more harm to his community than any other Muslim communalist since Independence. The question is, if Advani cannot be allowed to hijack Hinduism, then Shahabuddin too should not be allowed to play havoc with the sentiments of the Muslim masses. It is the duty of enlightened Muslims to show Shahabuddin his place and expose him as a fanatic. He is a paper tiger, a creation of the media. The moment he opens his mouth he makes hundreds of enemies for his community. The tragedy is that he does not speak for Indian Muslims. A mandir has to come and must come in the memory of Lord Ram and it must come up at Ayodhya, his birth place. But should it be the monopoly

of a political party or the cherished dream of million of Indians including Muslims. Ram is India and India belongs to all of us—not to Advani alone.

Current, 09.11.1991
p. (2)

Mandir wahin banega

The BJP is slowly but inexorably moving towards the demolition of the Babri Masjid. Its latest act in razing some ancient temples including Shakshigopal to the ground reveals its real intentions. This follows the removal of the Bhoomi's chief pujari, Swami Lal Das, who has been proving himself to be a major roadblock in pulling down the mosque. Now the general apprehension is that the moment it completes the Ram Diwar it will turn its wrath on the Babri. It has naturally shocked all level headed people who would not like the country to be plunged into a communal holocaust. The ferocity with which the BJP has moved took the centre by surprise and forced a stunned Home minister S.B. Chavan to tell an agitated Parliament: "I could never imagine at the time of bringing the religious shrine bill that people could demolish the shrine belonging to their own community." But, asserted BJP's Sikander Bakht, "We have come to power in UP on the mandate of temple construction." Chavan was so taken aback at his vehemence that for a few seconds he even fumbled for words but finally succeeded in making his government's policy clear. "I have no objection to the construction of the temple," he said and added, raising his voice, "because I am also a Hindu and a religious person. But the temple cannot be constructed by demolishing the mosque."

The BJP has tightly shut all the avenues for a legal solution claiming that the court cannot decide on a matter of faith. Neither does it want any negotiated settlement. For the BJP it is out of the question as it does not want to waste any of its "precious time on confabulations since that phase is over." VHP's Ashok Singhal does not mince words nor does he ape the BJP's forked tongue. He is explicit: "the Ram Diwar is the beginning. By the time we reach the shrine, where the sanctum sanctorum will be built, our fervent hope is that the Muslims leadership will agree to shift the mosque." They are in a hurry because the feeling in the inner RSS circles is that P.V. Narasimha Rao may go in for a fresh mandate by the end of this year and possibly succeed in making deep inroads into the BJP

fortresses in UP, Rajasthan and MP. They know the Congress is improving its electoral prospects with an unexpected rapidity and that it will not allow them to continue to capitalise on Ram's name to grab power. It may have succeeded so far but not any more. If their opponent was a cosmopolitan Rajiv then, it is a highly religious Narasimha Rao now. He is much more religious and a better Hindu than most BJP leaders.

The newly revived, highly aggressive BJP stance has to be seen in this context. Now even a 'liberal' like Vajpayee is compelled to equate its brand of Hindutva with nationalism. The minatory tone is obviously borne of the fear of an uncertain future as also the anxiety to hold on to whatever it had managed to grab. Perhaps the BJP leadership also knows that the electorate in their strongholds have begun to see through the vicious game they have been playing and the chances are that they will be more circumspect this time. The BJP-VHP is undoubtedly poised to launch yet another 'movement' to whip up mass frenzy, possibly under the leadership of Ashok Singhal who has already warned that if the Babri fanatics do not give up their unequal fight "other means will have to be devised. Hindus will have to use their clout to fulfill their sacred mission."

Current, 28.03.1992.
p. (2)

Let people decide

The mosque, as apprehended, has been razed to ground. The kar sevaks have taken away pieces of bricks home as souvenirs, the BJP-VHP-Bajrang Dal leaders have patted each other's backs for having wiped out what they describe as the 'symbol of shame', the police and the para-military forces have, as expected, allowed the job to be finished without interference and the prime minister and home minister have, earned the gratitude of the forces of Hindutva for keeping to their promise of a smooth operation. A grand show indeed. A bewildered nation watched the destruction of the monument, which was first a mosque, then a temple and finally a structure in awe. Lal Krishan Advani has come back from Ayodhya as a hero, an uncrowned chieftain of the great Sangh Parivar, poised to grab Delhi *gaddi.* It is his for the asking and Narasimha Rao is there to offer it to him on a silver platter. The next step, logically, is a mid-poll, a national referendum on Advani's agenda to turn the country into a BJP fief. He and his parivar are in high spirits. They are convinced,

as never before, that they will get an overwhelming mandate from a grateful nation. The destruction of the mosque has brought them closer to power as never before. A magnificent mandir will now be built on the very ground where the mosque stood, may be even before the nation is asked to decide whether what Advani did was wrong or right.

It will be Advani versus the rest. The rest does not mean UP alone. It means the whole country. The issue was the same in the last election also and the country decisively voted against Advani and his parivar. Coming as it did soon after the mind boggling *rath yatra,* he was convinced he would be taken in a flower bedecked rath to hoist the flag at Red Fort. But he had misjudged the mood of the masses. Had the Janata Dal not split, his party could not even have dreamt of getting half the seats which it has now. The situation was such that he had to run away from his home constituency to far off Gujarat. His challenger was a cine actor from Bombay. Time alone will show what fate awaits him and his parivar in case of an electoral battle. But I am convinced India's soul and mind is intact, its acumen to judge the bad from the good is not daunted and its vision to distinguish nationalism and fanaticism is not blurred. The collective wisdom of the people will not allow our constitutional democracy to be a victim of narrow-mindedness, hypocrisy and deceit. They will not fall prey to vandalism, as President Dr. Shankar Dayal Sharma has aptly put it. The people will ultimately find a way to save the country from falling apart and are sure to rescue it from the avarice of a bunch of leaders who have arrogated to themselves the role of saviours.

The ruling party has failed us. It has betrayed the nation. But the eighty per cent of the electorate, which voted against the BJP in the last election, will once again establish supremacy over the ballot box. It's time Narasimha Rao went to the people. He has no choice.

Current, 12.12.1992.
p. (2)

Death of a city

Can India live if Bombay dies? This city of ten million people died several times in the last one week. Death stalked it from one corner to another, talking away in its wake hundreds of innocent men, women and children. Dozens of dead, burnt and half-burnt bodies lay on the haunted roads, lanes and by-lanes. Hospitals were packed with slashed bodies

and decomposing corpses with doctors and nurses falling on each other with exhaustion. The loud wails of women and children pierced the eerie silence. Cries for help came from one thickly populated Muslim basti to another while policemen watched the dance of death with nonchalance. They were there not to protect the victims but to patronise the killers and arsonists who came in hordes and pounced upon the terrorised, the hungry, the unarmed and the helpless.

The hoodlums, armed with swords, pick axes and petrol bombs, instigated and led by local Shiv Sainiks indulged in killing, looting and burning with impunity. The police was on a picnic and when it did train its guns, the targets were old, emaciated Muslims who could not run more than a few yards. They fell on their faces, their blood flowing in the gutters.

It was an absolutely preplanned attack on Muslims, their houses, shops, bakeries and industrial establishments by thousands of lumpens with the police turning a blind eye and in many cases assisting them. It looked like the Nazi pogrom. Muslim youth were dragged out of their ghettos and shot and burnt alive as the Nazis did with the Jews in Germany. Thousands of them have run away with only clothes on their backs, leaving behind their ghettos to be taken care of by the hoodlums. Over 50,000 of them crowded VT and Bombay Central railway stations.

Even in the posh localities of Malabar Hill, Carmichael Road and Cuffe-Parade, hoodlums invaded the flats and demanded protection money. Name plates of Muslim residents in all these flats were removed. The house of Haroon Rashid, editor of Urdu *Blitz* was torched. His desperate pleas to the CM, police commissioner and even the fire brigade went unheeded. For three days and nights, trapped people from Bandra, Andheri, Jogeshwari, Worli—in fact from all over Bombay—called constantly. But the chief minister did not come on the phone, the police commissioner showed no concern. The DGP, Ramamurthy, completely shaken by his inability to discipline his force, was found responding to appeals for protection.

This was Bombay—the jewel of India, the economic backbone of the nation, the city of glamour, the abode of millions of working people, the bastion of the freedom movement. It is also the city of Bal Thackeray who held it to ransom. The government of Sudhakarro Naik collapsed, it capitulated to the Shiv Sena. The police saluted him, held him in awe. His word was law. His newspaper *Saamna,* whose circulation shyrocketed, was the bible of policemen on duty. They held a gun in one hand and *Saamna* in the other.

In the first round of communal frenzy, soon after the Babri demolition, the trigger happy police ran amuck in the narrow *gullys* of thickly populated Muslim bastis Bharat Nagar, Andheri East, Shastri Nagar, Nirmal Nagar, Navpara, Bahrampara, Govandi, Kurla, all over north and north-west Bombay and moved down around 200 Muslim youth in the age group of 20-25 and left the bodies in the hutments, near the gutters and on the lanes. The killing continued for another three days. Answering to agitated reporters Police Commissioner S.K. Bapat remarked, "the bullets do not ask names."

In the second round of violence which began in the first week of January, the same police lowered its rifles and extended full protection to the rampaging hoodlums. They allowed looting and torching of the hutments all over the megapolis. People running like rabbits were shot in the back. The chief minister did not stir out of his air-conditioned bungalow. He remained incommunicado and refused to meet people. He had all three meals, puffed his pipe and slept well. Home minister Shankarrao Chavan who 'airdashed' to Bombay parked himself comfortably in the Raj Bhavan, consulted a few politicians and officials and went back to Delhi leaving the city in flames. A senior Maharashtra minister was found holidaying at his farm house for three days while frantic calls to other ministers, senior bureaucrats, police officials and the fire brigade were met with stony silence.

Former Chief minister A.R. Antulay, who has an excellent equation with the chief minister and the home minister was not available either on the phone or at his residence though he was very much in Bombay. The South Bombay MP and BPCC boss Murli Deora did respond on the phone but expressed his helplessness. The other influential MP, Sunil Dutt, ran from pillar to post beseeching for help but he was treated by Naik and all his subordinates in the cabinet, bureaucracy and police with contempt. He resigned in sheer desperation and went on hunger strike along with some of his film colleagues with tears in his eyes. Concerned film actors, actresses, musicians and directors did make desperate attempts to save the city from carnage but they too were asked to keep quite and remain indoors. A smug chief minister played deaf when a delegation of senior citizens pleaded with him to hand over the city to the army. They rushed to Defence minister Sharad Pawar, who had camped in the city, imploring him to order the army to take cver and control the inferno but he too did not get any co-operation from the chief minister. Left with no choice, with their heart bleeding, they went on hunger strike led by the seniormost citizen of the country, JRD Tata.

In the wake of the unprecedented mayhem, only Sharad Pawar was seen moving across the length and breadth of the city splattered with blood, burning shops and hundreds of dead bodies strewn all over the metropolis. He was the only politician who exhibited exemplary courage, fortitude and a human heart. He did order his army to accompany the police, asked General Shively to go on TV and appeal to Bombayites to help the army restore peace. It did not have much effect. Next day he himself rushed to the TV station and appealed to the people to help save the city from destruction. He perspired and breathed heavily, his face ashen with anxiety. Pawar was also the only man who personally responded to each and every telephone call. He was on the phone whenever I rang him and he explained in detail the steps he was taking. He would have perhaps acted in a more decisive manner had his hand not been tied. Yet, whatever could be saved it was due to him. He rose like a gentle giant and the city enveloped in smoke did feel his presence.

The magnificent, hard working, law abiding people of Bombay, who have made the city the pride of the country, were dumbfounded by the fury of the violence. For ten days the commercial capital of the country was totally defenceless. I saw hardcore industrialists, bankers, office goers in a state of stupor, they were gripped with fear. Their city was under siege. Courageous reporters from the local dailies and weeklies were under attack. Some of them were lying in hospitals, slashed by swords and knives. Young Manmohan Bharti of a local daily was lying in an ICU ward with stab wound inflicted on him by the RSS marauders. Another half-a-dozen are battling for their lives.

Bombay is a wounded city. It is being bled white. Its soul hangs on the tip of a dagger held by a hoodlum. Can India live if Bombay dies?

Current, 16.01.1993.
p. (2)

Living with lies

Hitler's propogandist Goebbels believed that a lie repeated over and over again becomes a truth. India is witnessing an era of lies told with such sanctity that people have begun to believe in them just as what happened in Nazi Germany. The Jews were made the target of such an intense hate campaign that when Hitler sent six millions of them to the gas chambers, Germans were so convinced of the Jewish evil that very

few protested while the whole of Europe, including the Vatican, the torch bearer of the Christian civilisation, watched the holocaust in horror.

Similar lies are being dished out in India with such regularity, ideological gusto and religious fervour that it takes lot of guts and moral courage to call a spade a spade. The media has gradually begun to submit to them and the government-controlled Doordarshan has conveniently adopted a policy to ignore them. These lies are not only damaging our secular, democratic fabric but also paving the way for a fascist takeover. All these lies are told and spread by the Sangh Parivar with a halo attached to them if spewed by man like Arun Shourie.

First lie: That hundreds of temples in the Kashmir valley have been desecrated, pulled down, burned and razed to the ground. This lie has been repeated so often in the media and from public platforms by L.K. Advani, Kedar Nath Sahani, K.R. Malkani, etc., that an average Indian started believing in them. This lie was first investigated by former *Hindustan Times* editor B.G. Verghese who visited all these 'damaged' temples and reported that almost all of them are intact with the pujaris offering regular puja. He was not believed even by his colleague Arun Shourie.

Last week *India Today,* whose credibility cannot be challenged by anybody in the great Sangh Parivar, sent a team of reporters and photographers headed by old Kashmir hand Harinder Baweja. She visited each and every temple supposed to have been demolished at great personal risk and revealed that they were very much there. She even produced photographs to nail the lie. The lie was nailed but the Advanis and Shouries continue to repeat the canard.

Second lie: That Delhi is infested by over three lakh Bangladeshis. Delhi MP Madan Lal Khurana was so incensed by the presence of a lakh of them in his constituency that he almost invaded Okhla, the Jamia Millia. The threat did not materialise because, the citizens of the capital in an exemplary show of solidarity frustrated his diabolical plan of making Bombay out of Delhi.

Last week Khurana, Shourie and Jagmohan held a seminar in Delhi with Atal Behari Vajpayee in the chair under the auspices of Ghuspaith Abhiyan Samiti. Shourie thundered amidst the shouts of Har Har Mahadev: If the government did not take action against the infiltrators, it might end up facing a Ayodhya-like backlash and the situation could easily spawn a Bal Thackeray in Delhi. Vajpayee saved the situation realising that Shourie had gone beyond his brief. 'We don't need another Thackeray. Nor do we want to create problems in Delhi. 'Unke jaise

politicians sulag rahe hain', we don't want flames'. It was Shourie, not Vajpayee, who was the hero indicating that the BJP stalwarts may soon become a cry in wilderness. The problem is not that complicated. If Delhi is infested by the Bangladeshis, let the government identify them and send them back across the border. Incidentally, The *Pioneer* did send its reporters to find out the truth. Their report was that only 22 Bangladeshi families were found in Khurana's constituency including Okhla.

Third lie: That shiploads of sophisticated arms are being unloaded all along the Bombay coast. One paper said even rocket launchers have been smuggled into the country. That the don Dawood Ibrahim has placed all his ill-gotten wealth at the disposal of Bombay Muslims and soon the city will be turned into another Beirut. The reports in certain local newspapers and rumours are so persistent that the Bombayites have begun to believe them. The government has done nothing to refute these lies.

If the reports of smuggling of weapons on such a large scale are correct then the authorities should swing into action immediately. The Bombay Police is known for its efficiency and it can seize the shipments if it wants and if the arms do exist. If the reports are not true, the least the Police Commissioner can do is to scotch these rumours and nail these lies. Defence minister Sharad Pawar, with his armada and coast guards, can beat the hell out of these gun runners.

More than the government, the police and the defence forces, the media can and should rise to patriotic heights and prevent the advent of the holocaust. If *India Today* and *The Pioneer* can do it why not the thousands of newspapers across the country. The media enjoys more credibility than the existing establishment.

Current, 27.02.1993
p. (2).

The BJP's final solution

The saffron brigade is in turmoil. Even party president L.K. Advani wants to resign his post because the BJP fared miserably at the polls. Indeed, the debacle in the assembly elections in the four northern states and Delhi could not have come at a worse time for the Sangh parivar. Not only have the trishul wielders' hopes of a triumphant return to power in

the four states they ruled till December last year been belied, their boast of being a government-in-waiting has come a cropper. It is not surprising then that the party leadership is now clutching at straws and trying to find the reasons why it was rejected by the very people who brought it to power only a few years ago. One of the reasons now being touted for the humiliating defeat, for it is precisely that, in the four northern states is the party's limited social appeal. This was only to be expected, for there is no other way to explain the victory of the Samajwadi Party-Bahujan Samaj Party alliance's victory in Uttar Pradesh and the Congress successes in the other three states.

But if there is one thing the parivar leaders are totally ignorant about, it is the social dynamics of this vast and great country. Indeed, any post-graduate student would have informed them that it is well nigh impossible to 'unite' Hindus, the majority community, on the basis of religion alone. Still, the parivar's geriatric patriarchs in Nagpur believe this can be done. However, the younger trishul bearers believe this is poppycock. As Govindacharya, a RSS worker on secondment to the BJP, was quick to admit in a television interview, that the person for the electoral setback was that the BJP had failed in its task of 'social engineering'. Coming from someone who is perceived as an ideologue of the party, this is indeed a startling revelation. For, if he is to be believed, a section of the party leadership has come to the conclusion that the Ram card alone is not enough to win votes. The party can appeal to a Hindu electorate only after the minorities, both ethnic and religious, have been obliterated.

The social engineers believe this can be done by putting the weaker sections on guard against the perils of their possible dismemberment from the main body of Hindu society if they join anti-Hindu religious groups through conversion. As is well known, the largest number of religious converts today are the Dalits who have renounced Hindu caste society in favour of Buddhism. This is not a bit of saffron gobbledegook we are familiar with. The new buzz-word has its ideological roots in similar experiments elsewhere. It is worth recalling that Adolf Hitler tried his hand at social engineering to make Germany a Reich that would last a thousand years and Stalin's nationality question was supposed to create the Soviet man. Since then the Idi Amins, the Pol Pots and the Radovan Karadzics have tried their hand at the same science, with disastrous results. The BJP's perception is of a piece. Indeed, the party's younger leadership which is now under the influence of neo-Nazi ideologues, thinks only a Hitlerian 'final solution', for that is what social engineering is all about,

can help the party capture power at the centre. This dangerous development, which has been overlooked by the media, can soon become a reality. And when that happens, India will certainly become another Bosnia.

Current, 01.01.1994.
p. (2).

B. The Muslim Question and Electoral Politics

The Imam roars: whoever wants us must pay the price

The Shahi Imam emerged as a powerful spokesman of the minorities and specially the Muslims. His importance has grown out of proportions and in the past few days leaders of national stature had been dancing around his little finger.

He has discarded and dumped the Janata. The Lok Dal is 'dead and the sooner it is buried the better for the country'. Bahuguna, yes. He is the hope. But the great Muslim patriarch has suddenly developed a soft corner for his once tormentor Indira Gandhi. "Yes, she visited me along with her son Sanjay Gandhi. It was a preliminary meeting. Her son kept silent and somebody asked me to bless him. I refused. The time for blessings has not come yet."

The national attention is however focussed on the parleys between him and Indira Gandhi's Ambassador extraordinary and plenipotentiary Abdul Rahman Antulay. I will not divulge the nature of the talks. They will remain secret unless I decide to disclose them. The time has not come yet. It may come soon Insha Allah.

Myself and Mahavir Adhikari spent an evening with the massive Imam in the suite of a five-star hotel during his visit to Bombay last week. The Imam is a man to reckon with. He is blunt, straightforward and ruthlessly outspoken. The 'niceties' of politics or the vulgarities of today's political life are beyond his comprehension. He looks at things as they are.

He exudes confidence and the very fact that national leaders and parties wait for a few crumbs from his table has gone to his head. He does not speak. He roars. He talks to you as though he is addressing a public meeting.

It was not exactly an interview, a conversation which he strove to

dominate, to make it into a monologue. But we succeeded in cajoling him and converted it into a trialogue.

Imam Saheb, is there a possibility of a pact between you and Indira Gandhi? In fact there is an impression that you two have already reached an understanding.

What pact? I am not aware of any pact. The negotiations between me and her representative Antulay Saheb are in progress. We have already met four times and I am deeply impressed at the keenness and desire shown by them to understand our problems. They have atleast cared to go through our demands and discuss them threadbare, point by point. The fifth meeting may be decisive. It may succeed, it may fail.

Will you reach an agreement with Indira Gandhi over the head of your dear friend H.N. Bahuguna?

How it is possible? Myself and Bahuguna are together in our political mission. The Shahi Imam will not take any step which harms Bahuguna. We are on the same wavelength and our ultimate goals are similar.

Though Bahaguna is not a participant on your negotiations, are you proceeding with a view to have an honourable place for him in the new schemes?

Of course, I cannot conceive of any agreement or alliance with any of the parties without Bahuguna. Though I am conducting my talks with her emissaries on principles, issues and certain fundamentals, Bahuguna's inevitability as a part of my plans will not be ruled out.

Imam Saheb, why you are so much given to Bahuguna? Why you two are so closely associated. What is the secret of this affinity.

There is no secret. I like him and admire him because he is the one person who understands our problems and who has done much for the Muslims and the weaker sections.

Did you advise him to keep out of the Lok Dal?

He has done good by not joining the Lok Dal. Why should he trade his life with death?

You didn't wish him to join the Lok Dal?

Whether I like it or not, he himself didn't cherish the idea.

Will you advise him to keep the CFD independent and chalk out his own course of political action?

This can be a possibility. God may guide him to go in that direction. He already has an organisation. If no alliance takes place then he will be left

with no alternative but to go it alone.

Will you also go along with him?

I would wish to be with him. But if there is some diversion in our ways and if the interest of my community are jeopardised then. . .

I don't think Bahuguna will ever be inclined to take any step which goes against the interests of the minorities.

I hope so. But I must tell you that to me my community is more important than my friendship with anybody.

Do you visualise a time when you, Indira Gandhi and Bahuguna will share the same platform?

Why not? Anything is possible in politics, if she agrees to the demands of the Shahi Imam, and if she sincerely promises to implement our programmes, then there can be no obstacle.

But don't you remember Turkman Gate and what happened during Emergency?

(The Imam suddenly lapsed into a meaningful silence, threw his head back and began with a deep voice).

I am nothing if not magnanimous. The tradition of Islam teaches us to forgive even the worst enemy. The prophet had forgiven Hinda who had chewed the heart of his uncle Amir Hamza. But when she accepted Islam, the Prophet said: "Hinda, you are one of us. But keep a step back so that you may not remind me of the gory Incident." My heart is open to anybody who show the willingness to sincerely serve my community and the weaker sections of the country.

Then we can also contemplate the possibility of Balasaheb Deoras and you making common cause.

You are talking of the Qatil (murderer)? Yes Even that Qatil is welcome though his hands are dripping with the blood of innocent people.

Why do you call him Qatil now. It was you who joined hands with the Janata which was dominated by the Jana Sangh and the RSS. Don't you realise at that time the real character of your new found Janata friends?

Yes. Now I realise it was a mistake. But it was an imperative. The situation at that time was such that all the past enemities were forgotten. We marched ahead with the single objective and against a single person.

I had thought that the long years of wilderness and the harsh treatment given to the RSS may have changed them. That they may have realised the futility of making one community fighting the other. But alas, they have not changed a bit. It was I who had demanded the lifting of the ban

on the RSS immediately after Emergency. I firmly believe that you cannot eliminate an evil by ostricising it. You have to deal with it at a different level.

In these circumstances do you think it advisable for Muslims to form a party of their own?

It is very important question and I have explained it in detail in my 15-point manifesto. I have said that I'm not interested in the Muslim problems alone. I consider the problems of all weaker sections and backward communities as my problems and I am striving for their solution.

It's my desire that the minorities and the oppressed people should be brought together under one flag. Their rights should be safeguarded. I am not in favour of communal alliances. I divide India into two classes. The poor and the rich. One is the exploited and the other the exploiter.

But you would agree with me that at the moment Muslims constitute an oppressed and deprived community and I have to fight for them.

You are talking of Muslims all over the country or of certain pockets? There are affluent and rich Muslims too. There are Muslims who enjoy lot of privileges and cosy life. What I mean to say is that all the Muslims are not oppressed.

I'm not talking of Muslims alone, I am talking of the oppressed people to whatever religion or caste they belong. But the question is that for Harijans there are reservations in services, in Assemblies and in Parliament. And I am glad that our Harijan brethrens could come up because of these reservations. But what about us—the Muslims. A deliberate attempt has been made since Independence to keep us backward economically and socially. We were hoodwinked. And they tried to please us by giving us lolly pops, by making a few individuals President, Vice President and Governors. We don't want precedence or these honours. Give us jobs. I will prefer being given 10,000 clerical jobs to some Muslims than being made a President.

My question remains unanswered. What I have asked you is whether it is necessary for the Indian Muslims to form a separate party.

Yes, I understand your question. There is democracy in this country and everybody and every community has a right to form a party whether on communal lines or non-communal lines.

But I am personally against any political groupings on religious lines.

Don't you want the Muslims to come on one platform?

The Muslims should come on one platform meant for the poor irrespective

of religion.

How do you view the efforts by the leftist parties including the CPM and the CPI to organise the have-nots?

I agree with their economic approach. I have been to the Soviet Union several times and I admire their economic equality but as you know, India is a deeply religious country. Though I appreciate the economics of socialism, I should tell you that India's main diet is spiritualism. This country cannot go atheist. I am opposed to their atheism.

What are the basic reasons for communal riots?

I can refer to my manifesto. I have analysed the causes and also suggested solutions. There have been numerous communal riots since independence and the main reason for their occurrence and perpetuation has been the attitude of the ruling parties, whether at the centre or in the states. But the most important reason has been the partisan and thoroughly communal attitude of the law and order machinery.

I am of the firm conviction that Hindus and Muslims want to live like brothers and sisters in this country and they don't fight on their own. They are made to fight by greedy and avaricious politicians to serve their own ends. I had asked several Chief ministers who have been coming to me to take preventive measures but some of them, including Karpoori Thakur, told me that the communal riots are being fomented with the active connivance of the centre. It's Morarji, they told me, who is interested in communal riots.

But when Jamshedpur happened, I went to Bihar and asked Karpoori: "Thakur Saab, you are the Chief minister here. Now why can't you control Jamshedpur: There's no Morarji in Jamshedpur".

What are you suggesting to prevent them?

My suggestions are:

1. The centre should immediately agree to recruit 20 per cent Muslims in the police, Army and other central Services.
2. It's beyond doubt that in almost all the communal riots the police and the PAC sprinkled fuel on fire. I don't call them communal riots. I call them police action. I therefore suggest that the government should not use any armed force to curb communal riots.

   Instead, it should immediately establish a new armed and trained force—a peace force—in which at least 65 per cent people should be from the minorities and weaker sections and in this 65 per cent should be Muslims.
3. This peace force should be under the central government and trained

to curb communal riots.

4. The district civil and police officials should be immediately suspended the moment a communal riot takes place in a district.
5. There should be special courts to try the criminal caught during communal riots.
6. But even then if a communal riot takes place the central and the state government should give adequate compensation to the victims irrespective of religion and caste.

This is my solution to prevent communal violence and I will not enter into any alliance with any party which does not agree to these suggestions.

You have been blaming the RSS for communal tension and riots. But the RSS spokesmen vehemently refute your allegations. They say that so far nobody has been able to prove the RSS involvement including several commissions set up to probe the causes of communal riots.

The fact is the thief always tries to make his effort fool-proof. The thief would never like to be caught and when a theft is committed with the help of the police who can catch him?

The Janata leaders, including Chandra Shekhar, have been approaching you. What was your answer to them?

Not only Chandra Shekhar, even Jagjivan Ram has sent dozens of emissaries but how can I support them? It's simply impossible.

Is it because of the RSS? Will you consider to support them if they disassociate themselves from the RSS?

Yes. Minus RSS there can be a possibility.

In that case you should support Charan Singh. He has completely disassociated themselves from the RSS.

Yes. Charan Singh wants to possess the diamond without paying its price. How he can lay his lands on Kohinoor? It's impossible (The Imam laughed vigorously. His bulge shook like a jelly).

What's the price?

Everything has a price in the 'market' but this jewel is priceless.

Your Jewel may be priceless, but I am sure you must have put some conditions.

Yes, Conditions are there, you know about them.

If Charan Singh concedes your demands?

Who.

Charan Singh.

He will not accept even if he dies.

Why?

He possesses the 'Bania' mentality.

But he is a Jat?

I am talking of mentality, not the caste.

Indira Gandhi is the highest bidder for this diamond.

No. She is not alone. There is a line of fabulous bidders. The winds are blowing from north to south and from east to west. It's difficult to gauge the direction of these political winds. Some of them change their course even before they pass through you.

This time the election is for the Prime minister. All the candidates in the field are known to you. They have been seeking your help. Who do you think can be the Prime minister of your ideals?

I cannot say that. It depends on the situation and the individual. Anybody who becomes the Prime minister in alliance with us must fulfill our promises. Otherwise he will have our wrath. Our 'danda' will be on his head. We will not spare him.

You are considered as the Khomeini of India. (His laughter reverberates in the low-ceiling suite and everything shakes.)

You may call me Khomeini, you may call me Mohammed Ali Jinnah. Once Gandhiji asked Jinnah how he should address him. Jinnah replied: "You may address me in anyway. The rose remains a rose". You may call me anything but I am a simple man with no ambitions. I am a Fakir. Call me whatever you like.

Do you agree with the happenings in Iran?

I agree with it fully.

And do you also appreciate the development in Pakistan?

What is Pakistan to us? To us, India and its problems are much more important. Pakistan is an independent country and let them do whatever they like. It's none of our concern. But I would be happy if there is democracy in Pakistan and the people are given their rights.

Imam Saheb, you are considered a leader of the illiterate and backward Muslim masses. Your acceptability among the Muslim intelligentia is very low.

I don't know that I myself am an illiterate person. I do not care for a few rich, literate elite. I belong to the poor and I take great pride in speaking for the have-nots.

Current, 27.10.1979.
pp. (1 + 2 + 10 + 11 + 14)

Who lives if India burns

Communalism poses the greatest danger to the country's unity, integrity and stability. Let there be no doubt about it. It grows in the minds of people and no force can purge it unless the whole attitude, the whole thinking, the whole education system changes. The authority, the police and the army can put it down when it erupts into violence but that is no solution. It's a temporary measure, communalism continues to destroy the very fabric of our secular society.

Communalism continues to threaten the unity and oneness of the country though. Mahatma Gandhi laid down his life to root it out, Nehru fought it tooth and nail, though Lal Bahadur Sahstri was an apostle of communal harmony, though Indira Gandhi treated it as the main dark force and paid with her life.

And Rajiv Gandhi, whatever his shortcomings as Prime minister, is the symbol of India's secularism. He too considers it a cancer to be removed with a hot iron rod.

"Nothing—I repeat nothing—is more damaging to our nationhood, our composite culture, and our future than the cancer of communalism. India would survive as a secular India or not at all." These words can come only from a man with abiding faith in the secular destiny of the country.

He is undoubtedly in a unique position to protect and promote the country's secular heritage. He is far above the narrow religious, caste, regional, linguistic barriers. He is nurtured in secular traditions. He is the section of a family which laid the foundations of a modern, secular India.

And if he fails to instill the spirit of secularism among the people, if he fails to change the outlook of those who have conspired to compartmentalise India on the basis of religious loyalties, if he fails to introduce an educational, social and cultural system which fortifies the values the fathers of our Constitution had envisaged, then no one—I repeat no one—can succeed.

Communalism is not a temporary phenomenon. It has a historical background. It has seeped into the minds of many people. It results in mutual hatred, in a mutual desire to annihilate each other, to treat a person belonging to another faith with contempt, suspicion, hatred. Our democratic system gives the licence to the fanatic to stoke the embers of communal hatred, it allow the textbooks to teach our children to hate their classmates belonging to other religions, it allows mosques and temples as platforms spreading the poison, it allows our electoral system

to divide the people on the basis of their religious and caste loyalties, it allows the worst communalists to be elected to Parliament and assemblies, and some of them become policy makers.

The cancer of communalism, fanaticism, fundamentalism cannot be eradicated with a bullet or a bayonet. If you control one Meerut, it will pop its head somewhere else. It's hydra headed. You can extinguish the flame but the powder keg is very much there. It is that powder keg which has to be destroyed. It's indeed a long-range process but not insurmountable. If India is to live, it cannot live perched on a powder keg.

What Rajiv Gandhi has to do as a secular Prime minister is to begin to remove this powder keg brick by brick. Change the education system, withdraw all those textbooks which poison the minds of our youth, change the electoral system which breeds narrow feelings, change the recruitment policy in police, army and government services and provide adequate representation to qualified men of all regions and communities, ban all political and social organisations which thrive on fanning communal passions.

Religion and its profession should be declared a private affair. No religion teaches hatred. All religions teach love and respect for fellow human beings. Nobody should be allowed to distort these basic tenets, and if he does, the firmest action as Rajiv Gandhi put it should be taken against him. No communal force should be allowed to hold the nation to ransom.

The initiative will have to be taken by the ruling party and its head. It should be taken without loss of time. The Prime minister should reconstitute the National Integration Council, it should be trimmed and only those who have a passion, a commitment and vision and a stake in India's nationhood should be associated with it. The committee should not merely be a deliberative, toothless body. Its recommendations should be considered as official policy and implemented in right earnest, with vigour, with zeal. The Prime minister should be totally involved in the execution of its recommendations.

The Committee should be given a statutory status. Ministers responsible for carrying out its decisions should be answerable to it. Parliament should sanctify its decisions and rules and regulation should be amended accordingly.

Rajiv Gandhi should rise to these expectations as the head of the government. He will earn the gratitude of the nation if he builds a truly secular India whose foundations were laid by his grandfather.

India must be saved from the impending holocaust. Who lives if India burns.

Current, 30.05.1987.
pp. (1 + 2 + 8)

Meerut a city at war against itself

Meerut looks like a war-ravaged city. The wounds inflicted by the communal carnage on its poor, innocent people will take long to heal. Had the army not been rushed in and given control, the damage in human life and property would have been incalculable. The army saved the city from being decimated.

"But we cannot be here permanently," Lt-Gen. D.N. Khurana remarked with anguish on his face. It needs a long-term solution and the city have to find it."

The army took over as the local administration collapsed and the PAC ran amuck.

As I was talking to Gen. Khurana at the periphery of a 'basti' where he had ordered house-to-house search by his jawans, the news came of a massacre in the nearby Mallyana locality. The PAC had let loose a reign of terror on its poor, innocent people. They indiscriminately shot dead dozens of men, women and children and then set their huts on fire.

The army rushed in to prevent a holocaust, put out the fire, pulled out the dead, most of whom were charred beyond recognition "How many", I asked an officer on the spot. "They are in dozens," he threw up his arms in exasperation. In this hapless city most of the killings have been done by the PAC, a force hated and despised by members of both the communities.

The energetic reporter of *The Statesman* Neena Vyas, who was on the spot, carried the story which deserves mention:

The massacre at Mallyana began about 2.30 p.m. According to one account, a story related by a patient who had suffered gunshot wounds during the rioting that continued for several hours, the men of the Provincial Armed Constabulary instigated some local goondas to loot a country liquor shop. Crates of liquor bottles were carried away by the PAC men and residents of the locality and after some heavy drinking the carnage began.

While some people pelted stones at a particular locality in the area, PAC men took up positions and fired at them when they rushed out of their homes. Many fell dead on the spot. The PAC men also entered the hovels and shot people inside their homes. The houses were later set on fire and many people, including women and children, were trapped inside. A senior officer, who visited the spot, confirmed that many people had died inside their homes.

Entire families had been wiped out. The troops had treated more than 100 casualties on the spot by sending in medical teams.

It began as a communal riot but it soon became a shooting spree by the PAC. The army officers on the spot were shocked at the PAC's lust for killing unarmed, poor, innocent people. The opinion among senior UP congressmen is that the PAC should either be disbanded or reorganised totally. Until this is done it should not be used anywhere in controlling communal violence. The communal carnage would not have happened in Meerut had the local administration been alert. Local intelligence either had no clue to the preparations for a confrontation by the two communities, and if it had the information it just ignored it.

The riots were undoubtedly pre-planned. The amount of acid, guns and lethal weapons recovered during the house-to-house searches by the army showed the preparations were going on for a long time.

Neither the local Congress MLAs, nor the local Intelligence Bureau knew about it. The atmosphere was charged with communal tension and rumours of major communal violence were doing the rounds of the city. Some small local newspapers have been sounding warnings of communal build-up. Yet no pre-emptive steps were taken. The District Magistrate and the senior police officers were completely taken unawares by the sudden outburst.

The law enforcing authorities were paralysed as the rampaging mobs indulged in killing, looting and putting entire markets to flames. The two local dailies competed with each other in inflaming communal passions. It was journalism at its worst. The authorities took no steps in preventing the mischief despite protests by the concerned people.

Rumours did the greatest damage. The mass media were not used by the government to scotch these pernicious rumours. As I was talking to some police officers in the midst of an affected 'basti', a group of young men came rushing, shouting a dozen children had been butchered, their bodies had been skinned and they were hanging by the ropes. On checking it was found the young men were having a flight of imagination. But the police officers did nothing to scotch the rumour.

Another wild rumour was that the breasts of several women had been cut and they were dying. No such woman was admitted to any hospital, nor could the rumour-mongers produce a single such victim.

Most of the enormous damage was done by such horrifying rumours. Neither the Chief minister, who paid half a dozen visits to the city, nor the local Congress leaders did anything to deny them.

The root cause of the communal tension in the whole region is the Ram Janmabhoomi-Babri Masjid dispute. The rabble-rousers in both camps have been having a field day. Not only Meerut but the whole of Uttar Pradesh is in the grip of unparalleled communal tension. Cities and even villages are divided into two warring camps. The state is perched on the tip of a volcano: it might erupt any moment.

The dispute must be resolved without loss of time. Only the Prime minister can help find a lasting solution. He can avoid the issue at grave risk. If UP burns the whole country will fall a victim to the most heinous communal conspiracy. The damage will be irreparable and we do not have a Gandhi amongst us to revive the spirit of communal harmony.

A visit to Meerut can numb the nerves of even a hardcore believer in the country's destiny. There are two Meeruts—Hindu Meerut and Muslim Meerut. Though the members of the two communities are interdependent and will have to live together to eke out their living once again, at the moment Meerut appears a city of two 'nations' at war, a war of attrition. It's city buried in an avalanche of suspicion engulfed in hatred, a city at war against itself. The city has a death wish.

Its poor have born the brunt. Almost everybody killed, wounded or burnt alive comes from the lowest strata. I saw a man in tatters rushing out of his shack with hands thrown up searching a medicine shop. He was reeling with kidney pain. The army jawans maintaining curfew were helpless. Kuldip Nayar, who was standing next to me, could hardly control his emotions. The human misery, the human tragedy hits you in the hear.

The Ram Janamabhoomi Babri Masjid sabre-rattlers should be brought here to show what incalculable harm they done to simple human beings, Kuldip muttered in anguish.

But there is a silver lining in Meerut. When a mob invaded a newspaper printing press looking for Muslim workers, the entire Hindu workforce stood like a human wall, hid the Muslim workers behind the machines and threw the mob out. I and Kuldip went to the spot and the workers related the incident with great pride.

Meerut is not the first city to fall victim to communal violence. But it

can be the last city to have such a nightmare if the ruling party takes the required steps. In the words of that fine General who now controls the city, the government should immediately find a lasting solution to the problem. It should be dealt with on a war footing.

Current, 30.05.1987.
p. (8)

Come out of the cocoon

What do the Muslim fundamentalists in India want? A socialist, democratic, secular India, or one divided into religious, linguistic, sectarian, water-tight compartments? An India governed by an enlightened, egalitarian leadership, or one dominated by fanatics of various hues?

The Shah Bano controversy reflects the mind of a majority of Muslims of all classes—poor and rich, literate and illiterate, enlightened and obscurantist. Muslim politicians too. Whether they are in the ruling party or any other political group, except of course the Communists, they dare not cross swords with the fundamentalists, who have launched a war on the Supreme Court judgement, an enlightened piece penned by a liberal judiciary.

It is of no consequence that Shah Bano, an unlettered old lady who fought and won the case in the highest court of appeals, has gone back on her claims. She obviously retreated under pressure from this phalanx of Muslim fanatics who threaten to hit at the very concept of modern secularism. And the pity is that few Muslims, including those in the ruling party, have had the courage to challenge them publicly. Except Arif Mohammed Khan, a young minister.

The fact is that Islam, born in the early seventh century, has no concept of modern democracy or secularism—the kind of a system a vast majority of Indians have decided to live under; a system in which a man has the right to elect a government of his choice.

A majority of Muslims, whether in India or elsewhere, are not respecters of a representative system. No Muslim majority country in the world can claim to be a true democracy. They are ruled either by kings and sultans, claiming hereditary rights, or tin-pot dictators.

The irony is that Islam is against rule by a potentate, though it does not lay down norms for a democratic system either. It is this anomaly

that has kept its religious thinkers out of tune with modern ideas of governance.

Thus Shah Bano is a symptom and not the disease. The problem is not whether Muslim personal law should be amended or ended. The basic question is whether Indian Muslims are in tune with the vast majority of non-Muslim Indian intelligentsia which believes in secularism and the rule of law.

India could have chosen to be a Hindu country as Pakistan stuck to its Islamism. But India's first Prime minister was an agnostic, his daughter was not a Hindu in the classical sense of the terms and her son, who now governs the country, says he is not bound by any particular religious beliefs.

Could it have happened in any Muslim majority country? And can Saudi Arabia, the birth-place of Islam, allow a temple or a church to come up? Indian Muslim fundamentalists are serfs to a world of their own. The sooner they come out of this cocoon, the better it will be for the entire Ummat.

Current, 23.11.1985.
p. (2)

Muslims in turmoil

Muslim ministers in Rajiv Gandhi's Council of ministers are sharply divided on the burning issue of Muslim Personal Law and the Supreme Court verdict on the famous Shah Bano case. Muslim members of the Congress Parliamentary Party are also deeply involved in the convulsion in their community.

Two prominent ministers, Arif Mohammed Khan and Z.R. Ansari, have taken on the floor of the Lok Sabha diametrically opposite stands on the historic judgement granting maintenance to Shah Bano, the 78-year-old Muslim divorcee, and her shocking volte face.

Shah Bano, who fought her way to the highest court of appeal and won the case, has now come out with a statement, obviously under coercion, that the judgement should be withdrawn because it violated Muslim Personal Law.

This bizarre turn to the whole controversy has now become an issue of national debate, it is no more confined to the Muslim community alone. Parliament has been discussing it with heat and gusto. While youthful Arif leads the forces of reform, his old and seasoned colleague spearheads

the movement for the pristine purity of Quranic laws. Not a word can be changed in whatever has been ordained in the holy book.

Each of these Muslim ministers made hour-and-a-half long speeches in the last session of the Lok Sabha. Both argued their case by profusely quoting from the Quran chapter and verse and from the Hadith, the sayings of the Prophet. They went to the House loaded with holy books and buttressed their arguments in the manner of ulemas as the House listened to them in pin-drop silence.

While these debates were going on, massive processions are being organised in strong Muslim pockets of Bombay, Bangalore, Madras, Calcutta, Lucknow, Srinagar, etc.

The fundamentalists and the mullahs are having a field day. Slogans are raised against the Supreme Court verdict, walls are plastered with posters opposing any change in the Shariat and threatening to lay down lives in defence of Muslim Personal Law.

Najma Heptullah, Congress MP and vice-chairman of the Rajya Sabha, led a delegation of Muslim MPs to the Prime minister during the last session of Parliament, demanding annulment of the Supreme Court verdict and an assurance to the Muslims community that the government will not interfere in Muslim Personal Law. The isolation of enlightened Muslim men and women is as stark in the ruling party as in the community.

Rajiv Gandhi is apparently taken aback at the sudden rise of Muslim fundamentalism and has repeatedly assured Muslims that his government does not envisage any change whatsoever in the Shariat or the Personal Law of Muslims or any other religious community.

This assurance was followed by a categoric statement by minister of state for Law H.R. Bharadwaj on the floor of the House that the government will not interfere with or amend Muslims Personal law. Yet non-Congress Muslim leaders have been whipping up passions among the Muslim masses, with the Urdu press playing a prominent role.

Internal Security minister Arun Nehru's office is flooded with intelligence reports of widespread resentment among Muslims on the issue. Muslims who dare come out in defence of the Supreme Court verdict are made the targets of vituperation. They are threatened with social boycott and worse.

The Supreme Court bench headed by the Chief Justice Y.V. Chandrachud had ruled that a Muslim woman is entitled, under Section 125 of the Criminal Procedure Code, to secure maintenance from her husband who divorces her by saying *talaq* three times.

The judgment was specific and laid down that since the maintenance provision comes under the criminal law which has a universal application irrespective of caste and creed, it is not dependent on the religious faith of either the wife or the husband.

Justice Chandrachud maintained that there was no conflict between the provisions of the CrPC and Muslim Personal Law on the issue of a husband's obligation to maintain a divorced wife who is unable to support herself.

Instead of accepting the verdict with dignity, the fundamentalists launched a countrywide agitation headed by the All-India Muslim Personal Law Board. And Muslim League MP G.M. Banatwala moved in the Lok Sabha an amendment seeking exclusion of Muslims from the purview of Section 125 CrPC.

His argument is that Section 125 infringes the Quranic version of the Shariat and is violative of Article 25 of the Constitution which guarantees freedom of religion and conscience.

He has also demanded exclusion of Muslim Personal Law from the purview of the Directive Principles under Article 44 of the Constitution.

Arif Khan and Ansari spoke in the House on Banatwala's amendment. Arif's very well argued speech was hailed by all sections of the House and the national press, barring the Muslim Members of Parliament belonging to all political parties.

So far, no distinguished Muslim leader has come out in defence of Arif's justification of the Supreme Court verdict. It was in the last week of August that Arif spoke in Parliament. He did so in both his capacities—as government representative and as a young, upcoming leader of the enlightened section of the Muslim community. But so far no distinguished Muslim leader has come out in defence of his justification of the Supreme Court verdict.

Islam, Arif had said, gave equal rights to women and specifically laid down rules and conditions for ensuring equal and fair treatment to them. But the fanatics were misinterpreting these rules. He quoted several authorities on Muslim jurisprudence, including Maulana Azad in support of his argument.

Throwing a challenge to Banatwala, he said: "Islam prohibits taking interest (sood) and most monied Muslims, including those who are leading the pro-Shariat agitation, do take interest on their deposits in banks. Will Banatwala bring a bill in Parliament to disallow Muslims from taking interest on the ground that it definitely violates the letter and spirit of Islam?

Banatwala's interjection provoked laughter in the House. He suggested: "We will not take interest if the banking system is changed and no depositor is given interest. Why exclude the Muslims alone?" Banatwala and his followers would like to have the best of both the worlds.

Ansari advanced forceful argument against the Supreme Court judgement. He too quoted extensively from the Quran and the Hadith. He spoke with passion. His flowery Urdu reminded MPs of the great orator Maulana Azad.

His speech was preceded by a meeting of all Muslim Congress MPs on the previous night, which was attended by most of the Muslim ministers. The meeting decided that the Supreme Court judgement should be opposed, and requested Ansari to act as their spokesmen in Parliament.

The debate has now gone out of the portals of Parliament and the Muslim Personal Law Board, monopolised by die-hard mullahs, has been whipping up Muslim emotions to a frenzied pitch. Its effective leader, Maulana Minnat Ulla Rehmani, has given a call to his co-religionists to lay down their lives if necessary in defence of their personal law.

Speeches in Old Delhi's Jama Masjid area remind one of the 17th and 18th centuries when Muslim fundamentalism was on the rise. Almost every maulvi who speaks from the pulpit imitates Ayatollah Khomeini, and even worse.

The Muslim intelligentsia, which is largely with the mullahs and against the Supreme Court verdict, argues frantically against a common civil code. But such a code is not even a remote possibility so long as we have a one-man, one-vote system. No party can afford to antagonise the Muslims, such is their voting strength in hundreds of pockets in the country. The ruling party, which very much depends on the Muslim vote, will be the last to dare to antagonise them.

The anti-Supreme Court verdict Muslim intelligentsia would very much like to live under a secular system like ours, but they would not move an inch towards reforming their Personal Law, which was made in the 7th century in peculiar circumstances.

Before the rise of Islam in the Arabian Peninsula, the Arabs used to bury their daughters alive in the hot, burning sands because they hated the idea of their being taken away as brides. The Prophet stopped this abominable practice.

Since a lot of his young followers were getting killed in religious wars in the wake of the rapid spread of Islam he permitted people to have more than one wife and also encouraged widow remarriages.

He laid down very elaborate rules and regulations governing matrimonial life of Muslims. These and other measures gave respectability to women. In the circumstances of those days these were revolutionary steps. But they cannot be the last word for all times to come.

The fundamentalists Muslim intellectuals who insist that it is the Shariat, not the Supreme Court, that has the right to decide the fate of Muslim women are blind to the march of civilisation.

Fundamentalists like Syed Shahabuddin consider reformists as outcasts and maintain that not a word in the Shariat law can be changed: "It cannot be interpreted, it cannot be argued. For it is the word of God."

They conveniently ignore the sweeping changes introduced in Muslim countries like Algeria, Tunisia, Egypt and Indonesia with almost 99 per cent Muslim populations. The tragedy is that reformists have been far outnumbered by fundamentalists. Such is their force that Shah Bano, the eye of the storm, was coerced into changing her stand.

A Muslim can have four wives at a time, and can have dozens in the process, but the women do not have the same freedom. If a man has the right to disown his wife of several years, the mother of his children, merely by repeating *talaq* three times, why cannot a Muslim woman have the same right?

Secular India should not allow obscurantists to have their way since our Constitution is committed to equality of both sexes, irrespective of the group or community they belong to. None can be allowed to claim the protection of their outdated and obnoxious laws.

The Supreme Court judgement should have gone much beyond just upholding Shah Bano's rights. The change will have to come. Fanatics, whatever their strength and number, cannot be allowed to hold the country to ransom.

Current, 30.11.1985.
pp. (1 + 3 + 21)

Why not Shariat for men too?

Let this Bill, designed to protect Muslim women, be passed. The fundamentalists want it. Prime minister Rajiv Gandhi wants it. He strongly feels that Islamic Shariat should be the guiding factor for the Muslims in this country. They feel the Shariat must be upheld and protected in its totality. Let it be.

But why for the hapless Muslim women alone. Let the shariat be codified here and now by an Act of Parliament, otherwise Islam will be in danger of losing its pristine purity and our secularism will be in jeopardy.

The shariat, listen ye fundamentalists!, also specifically lays down the cutting of the hand of a thief, stoning to death of an adulterer and beheading of an adulterer, and whip-lashing of a boozer. Let no Muslim charge or take interest on his monetary deposits because it is a sin proscribed by the Holy Quran.

Let our Parliament legislate and codify these shariat laws before it is too late for the believers. In the absence of these laws Islam will be in perpetual danger, and Muslims, specially the fundamentalists, will continue to lead sinful lives.

The well-meaning Prime minister, who is keen to rush through the Bill, should call the leaders of the Muslim public 'opinion' and include these provisions of the shariat so Islam may be completely protected and not Muslim women alone. The Muslim Personal Law must include all these provisions: Islam has to be saved.

Our Muslim fundamentalists cannot have the cake and eat it too. Islam is a way of life. Muslims are ordained to follow it in letter and in spirit, every word of it. It is the word of God. Let the Quran be supreme. Let the hands be cut, the sinners stoned to death and let the lash be the order of the day.

There are the Fundamental Rights inscribed in the Quran and the Bill must be more comprehensive to include them. Our Parliament which is called upon to codify the shariat must not differentiate between Muslim women and men. Or scrap this obnoxious, antediluvian, retrogressive measure. It flies in the face of the Constitution. It is a capitulationist piece of legislation, an abject surrender to the obscurantist forces who want to have the best of both the worlds.

Rajiv Gandhi, a humanist and an egalitarian that he is, should have a long-range view of this country's future and not an eye on the vote banks. He should encourage the progressive, enlightened Muslims who look up to him with great hope because he himself is not given to any narrow, communal and sectarian faith. He is a non-practising, enlightened human. He should aspire to make every young Indian like him. That's what he, his mother and his grandfather have been describing as the 'scientific temper'.

This Bill speaks to promote an unscientific temper. It violates the spirit of Jawaharlal Nehru, the builder of modern, secular, socialist India. Indira Gandhi would never have dreamt of introducing a Bill of this nature, come what may. She resisted these pressures all through her term as Prime

Minister. To her the country was far greater than a bunch of fundamentalists. She wouldn't and didn't yield.

Our Constitution, our Supreme Court and our Parliament have no religion. That is what secularism is. The ruling Congress Party too has no religion. It is made up of all kinds of men and women who believe in all sorts of religions and rituals in their individual capacities. It is because of these very vital considerations that this Bill becomes irrelevant, fraudulent.

What is more revolting is that it is being rushed through under pressure from a very section of people who have not even a scant faith in secularism. Since when did the Muslim League become the spokesman of Indian Muslims or the Mullahs arrogated to themselves the role of judges and juries? It is they who kept the Muslim masses under their fanatic spell and kept them in ghettos. It pays them.

The Bill tramples on the rights of a half of the Muslim population—the women who will reject it if given the choice. The Bill also betrays thousands and thousands of enlightened Muslims who include Rajiv Gandhi's close associates. And it goes without saying that the Bill is being thrust on the Congress Parliamentary Party which has been subdued by the whip—the Islamic whip.

Rajiv Gandhi has simply been ill-advised and he is so good, so human that he thinks he is doing a great service to Muslim women by enacting the Bill.

The fact is, left to itself. Parliament will never legislate it.

Current, 08.03.1986.
p. (1)

He must be read

Had I been the Home minister I would have done the same thing as Buta Singh did. His job is to maintain law and order, keep peace, not let communal harmony be shattered. No government can afford any kind of communal or casteist commotion at this stage. The country specially the north, is perched on a communal volcano. The quick decision to ban the book has saved us from a holocaust. The election year can be the most sensitive period specially when we have Rajiv Gandhi at the helm. I am personally convinced that Rajiv Gandhi or his Home minister have not capitulated to any extraneous pressure while deciding to ban *The Satanic Verses.* Syed Shahabuddin and his ilk who have been telling

their brethren of their victory in forcing the government in banning the book have been living in a make-believe world. The difference between me and them is that while they want to 'save' Islam, I want to save India. Islam, like all other religions, has its good points. It has crores of followers in India. Syed Shahabuddin is not the only follower nor is he the only upholder of the faith. But he is the one Muslim who has a stake in being a Muslim. He thinks the mantle of protecting Islam and Indian Muslims has fallen on him. He has cast himself in the role of a medieval defender of the faith. The Babri Masjid is his baby. *The Satanic Verses* would have been another.

I am against banning books. I have not read this one by Rushdie. I think he is overrated. But Rushdie has every right to express himself against or in favour of anyone including Islam and its Prophet. To me no religion is sacred. I am an atheist. I do not believe in supernatural hoaxes. But I do believe in the right of a man to live in peace, with honour and dignity and had *The Satanic Verses* not been banned a lot of violence would have taken place. When Rajiv Gandhi asked Buta Singh to ban the book he meant to save the Muslims from unnecessary turmoil. Like any enlightened modern Indian he too is not a fanatic and his faith in the integrity of the country is beyond question. He has done a good thing in banning Rushdie's book.

Islam, the non-Muslim in this country had better, know, is a religion with a book, so is Judaism and Christianity. But few Jews or Christians, at the end of the 20th century, will risk physical violence if their Prophets are badly talked about. A Muslim would. Muslims believe in the oneness of God and Prophet Mohammed as his messenger, the last human being who spoke for Him. He was *Khatmul Mursaleen,* the very last Prophet. His word was the word of God and Quran is god's last message to humanity. Not an iota of change can be made in it. Not a comma can be taken out of it and not a full stop added. Muslims, even the liberal and enlightened ones, believe in it and no power on earth can make a dent in his rock-like faith. They die in dozens in defending this faith. Death for upholding the honour of the Prophet is a rare distinction for a Muslim. He is Shaheed, a martyr. He is directly admitted in Heaven.

Islam has its own lexicon to classify human beings. One who does believe in its god, is *mulhid,* one who denies the Prophethood of Mohammed is *munkir,* the *kafirs* are those who do not submit to Islam and its teachings.

Salman Rushdie very well knew all this. Yet he wrote *The Satanic*

Verses. His right to express his views cannot be questioned and he is free to write even much 'worse' stuff, fortunately he is living in Britain where there are no Imam Bukharis to put the Thames on fire. He will need heavy security were he to visit India and his going to any Islamic country is out of question.

It is difficult to be a Muslim. Islam does not allow dissent. Muslims have no concept of modern democracy. They do not tolerate liberalism. No Muslim country in the world has true democracy where people are free to vote and elect a government of their choice. Had Rushdie understood these hard facts of life of a nation he would not have written that open letter to Rajiv Gandhi and insisted on lifting the ban. The book must be read by all those who wish to do. The pirated copies will soon be available at street corners. It is the right of every Indian to read what he likes and it is also the right of the government to ban what it feels is dangerous to harmony and peace in the country. Syed Shahabuddin, too, should not give the impression that a mere novel based on fantasy can tarnish the image of the Prophet or Islam. I would like to read and Syed Shahabuddin too, should read it.

Current, 22.10.1988.
p. (2).

Muslim votes not for sale

They used to be Indian Muslims for centuries. Syed Shahabuddin now calls them Muslim Indians. He has put them upside down. It is his sterling contribution to widen the gulf between the majority and the minority communities. He has a monthly journal *Muslim India* which compiles facts, figures and articles written about Muslims in other journals. This ex-Foreign Service official who keeps reminding the country of the deep wounds inflicted by the partition is threatening to call a national convention of Muslim Indians at New Delhi.

He would place a charter of demands at the convention which will include political and electoral possibilities on the eve of the elections: participation or non-participation of Muslims in the political process; protection of personal law and safeguards against the imposition of a uniform civil code; proportional representation in elected bodies; statutory status for the Minorities Commission: reorganisation of the police and intelligence bodies; formation of anti-riots force with 50 per cent

representation to the minorities; liberalisation of arms licences to minorities in riot-prone areas; a ban on the senas and on military training and public drills by private organisations.

Even Mohammed Ali Jinnah had not asked for such wide-ranging concessions or made such demands. In fact, Syed Shahabuddin has demanded everything short of yet another Pakistan. He is expecting hundreds of Muslim Indians political workers, intellectuals, professionals, heads of various Muslim social and cultural organisations to flock to the capital and demonstrate their solidarity to the rest of the country whose "democratic, secular system is under siege".

Syed Shahabuddin's is a political battle in which he plans to build a solid Muslim vote bank and then bargain with the ruling party for the loaves and fishes of power. He is not the first Muslim leader to indulge in this dangerous electoral gimmicks. Many of his predecessors, including the ones in the Muslim League, have done it.

Rumours are that Syed Shahabuddin enjoys the tacit support of Home minister Buta Singh who has been entrusted with the specific task of looking after the Muslim vote bank. For the Congress it is a question of survival in the Hindi heartland and here if Muslims and Harijans do not vote for it as in the past, except 1977 the chances of a Congress victory are bleak. The Congress is known to have indulged in all kinds of electoral gimmicks in the past without giving much thought to the long-range consequences of such moves.

Had there not been a Shahabuddin, one would have been invented. Such is the tragedy of Muslims in this country. Its leaders had always been for sale. Most of them had a price tag. Muslim masses too are entirely different from their co-religionists in other countries. They tend to flock to the one who can play with their religiosity, their emotions and their ego.

They discarded Maulana Azad who pleaded with them not to have the country partitioned on the basis of faith, and opted for Jinnah, who gave them the dream of a separate homeland. "Muslims", he thundered in Bombay's Bhendi Bazar, "are not a minority, they are a nation. A nation needs a homeland", and the game was over.

Syed Shahabuddin cannot be compared to Jinnah but he has been behaving much worse than the creator of Pakistan. A democratic, secular, tolerant India has permitted him to misuse the rights enshrined in the Constitution and despite all his shenanigans, he would continue to enjoy the liberties to which an Indian is entitled. In any Muslim country he would have been in jail. He has single-handedly contributed

most of the unprecedented communal polarisation in the country though Bal Thackerays and Balasaheb Deoras have done equally enormous damage to liberal and secular traditions founded by Gandhi and Nehru. The Congress party, too, cannot escape blame. Its Home minister has been regularly parleying with people like Syed Shahabuddin, giving the impression to Muslims that he is their sole spokesman.

This unbriddled criticism of Syed Shahabuddin and his antics does not mean that Muslim are not faced with grave problems. Their sense of insecurity, the very low representation in government services, the public sector, the police and the armed forces, their deteriorating economic condition, poverty, squalor hunger, superstition, illiteracy are major constraints in the way of a progressive, healthy development among them. But these problems cannot be solved in isolation. They have to be taken as the problems of a nation. If India has to remain secular it has to be for both Hindus and Muslims. A convention of Muslim Indians cannot solve them. What Syed Shahabuddin is doing is holding an open auction of Muslim votes. It is time the Muslims refused to be auctioned.

Current, 08.07.1989
p. (2)

Muslim vote: he holds the key

Once again the Shahi Imam of Jama Masjid is the centre of attraction. He is in great demand. For the past week, the political roads have been leading to his modest fortress-looking house in a dark, congested, unkempt gali—a stone's throw from the imposing Jama Masjid.

The huge Shahi Imam with dark glasses and a maroon skull cap, is believed to be holding the key to the success of either the Congress or Janata Dal at least in U.P. and Bihar.

Come election time, and his value in the political stock exchange soars to dizzying heights. In normal periods he is undoubtedly the most maligned and despised character by these very politicians. He has been let down repeatedly. Indira Gandhi negotiated with him in 1980 and conceded almost all his demands. Once she was Prime minister she ignored him and even refused to meet him. The Imam hates her so much that he has put a huge board inside the Jama Masjid with the choices invectives written

in large and bold Urdu against her. Two black flags at the main gate of the mosque with a declaration that they are the symbol of the great betrayal of Muslims by her.

In the last one week V.P. Singh has met him three times, Devi Lal and Ajit Singh too have been frequenting his place. Rajiv Gandhi's emissary Har Krishan Lal Bhagat has held several meetings with him R.K. Dhawan's request to meet him has not yet been cleared.

Bhagat and Dhawan want him to meet Rajiv Gandhi. "Why should I meet him? If he wants to meet me, he is free to come here. I will give him a cup of tea". The Imam says it loudly to let dozens of his admirers hear him and nod. But today I interviewed him in his modestly furnished living room, soon after the Friday prayers (Oct. 27). He had almost made up his mind to strike an agreement with V.P. Singh but refused to disclose the details. The efforts from the Congress side were not to let this agreement be finalised.

The situation on the Muslim front is that the Imam's views will carry considerable weight among Muslim masses though educated Muslims take his claim of mass following with a pinch of salt.

How do you view the situation on the eve of the most crucial election in the country. Specially the alarming spread of communal violence.

Being an eminent journalist, you know this situation much better than I do. Whatever is happening in North India has disturbed my peace of mind. I am going through deep anguish and I am at a loss to find a solution. I think the government has the solution. It should wake up, and let the people know what it is going to do to solve this problem. Hundreds of Muslims are being pulled out from trains and being hacked into pieces. Their blood is flowing like water. The government is watching it, the whole country is watching and nobody, none has raised his voice of protest. Nobody has rushed to the troubled spots tc prevent the massacre, to put an effective end to this blood bath. It is not only one or two towns in Bihar, the whole state is aflame. This is their country.

I am convinced that this government of Rajiv Gandhi is very weak and inefficient. It is not capable of taking effective and strong steps. A 'holi' is being played with our blood and we really do not know what to do, where to go, how to save our lives, limbs and property. I feel so strongly about the massacre in Bihar that if I had wings I would have flown there to stand by my brothers, but ironically, this government is negotiating with me for Muslim votes while preventing me from going to

Muslims in trouble.

They think you are a dangerous communalist and may pour oil on fire.
It is wrong. It is absolutely false, I have a total commitment against communalism. To me people are neither Hindus nor Muslims. There are only two kinds of people in India. The oppressed and oppressor. Hindus are also oppressed. Millions of them have been denied the daily bread, they are starving. Muslims too are oppressed, they are more oppressed, there is delay in action in the settlement of Muslims from Ladakh in our midst. Their stories of *Zulm* are heart-breaking.

Kashmir has a Muslim Chief minister. Why can't Farooq Abdullah prevent these atrocities.
Farooq Abdullah is a despicable character. He is neither a Hindu nor a Muslim. He is an opportunist of the worst order. The opportunists have no religion. He has not inherited any quality of his father.

Why communal riots are taking place only in Congress ruled states? So far we have not witnessed any communal violence in the opposition ruled states—not even in Assam. No communal riots have taken place since the victory of AGP and since Prafulla Mahanta became chief minister.
It is a pleasant surprise, but Muslims are happy in Assam. Mahanta is so open minded on the issue that when I complained to V.P. Singh about some ill-treatment of Muslims in Assam, he immediately invited me to visit his state as his guest, meet those Muslims, bring their difficulties to his notice and promised to redress them immediately.

My question was why this communal violence in Congress ruled states.
You also know it, you very well know the reason. It is our great misfortune that this Congress government has failed to put an end to the carnage. They have no will to stop it. Though many Congress leaders visit me every day, including Rajiv Gandhi's emissaries, to assure me that their party is against communal violence. But look what has happened in U.P. and Bihar.

You seem to have believed these congressmen more than once and even had entered into agreements with them, including Indira Gandhi, and had bulk Muslim votes delivered to them.
It was a mistake. I do not trust these politicians any more. Now I will believe only when they implement their promises first and then come to me. If they don't do it means they are cheats and their only intention is to deceive us.

It is believed that the Ram Janambhoomi-Babri Masjid dispute has

escalated the communal tension.

It is a very deep rooted conspiracy against the communal harmony of the country. The conspirators have succeeded in putting Hindus against Muslims and vice-versa. It was a Vir Bahadur Singh and Arun Nehru conspiracy. It has now been proved beyond any doubt. It was done at the behest of Rajiv Gandhi, because even after punishing Vir Bahadur for the dangerous game, he promoted him in the Cabinet. Rajiv Gandhi cannot escape the responsibility.

What is the solution. Have you found some way out.

The only solution is that the mosque be handed over to the Muslims.

And the Mandir should be given to Hindus . . .

Where is the Mandir. It is a Mosque.

Do you agree with the suggestion of waiting for the Allahabad High Court decision.

My original suggestion was that let the high court judges from the south give a judgement or form a bench of judges who are neither Hindus nor Muslims. They can be Christians, Parsis and even Sikhs. Let them decide, we will accept their verdict.

Some of the Muslim leaders question your bona-fides. They say you have arrogated to yourself the right to speak for the Muslims.

This insinuation can come only from a congressman. I only listen to the voice of my conscience. I speak out loudly and boldly only when my heart asks. I have no desire to be a leader. The thought never crosses my mind.

What are your differences with Syed Shahabuddin.

None. I hardly know him, I met him only a couple of times and that too rather casually.

Isn't it interesting that your political value goes up only on the election eve. All kinds of politicians rushed to you and you also start negotiating terms and conditions with them despite your bitter experiences in the past.

Ask those worthies who have told you that I have no right to speak on behalf of Muslims. I consider myself as a very small, very humble servant of my people. Whatever I do, I do it with utter humility. I am simple faqir, a durvish.

Recently V.P. Singh visited you. I understand he had been coming to you very often.

All kinds of people are coming to me, V.P. Singh has been frequently

coming. He came yesterday also. He is a nice man, a very honest man, a sincere man. It's always a pleasure meeting him.

What does he want? Have you reached some understanding. Do you think he would fulfill the promises once he comes to power.

He is a gentleman *(Admi Sharif hai).* The question is what kind of government he would form, and what kind of people would be around him. How he would behave as Prime minister. I do not know.

Do you think he would stand by his promises.

If god wishes, he can even enact legislation to attain the mission.

Has he made any specific promise.

Yes, he has made a lot of promises. An agreement is being drafted. My representatives and his men are constantly in touch. Choudhary Devi Lal and Ajit Singh have also been visiting me. They are nice people. I have no reason not to trust them.

What are those specific issues?

I will not disclose them now. Let the time come and they will be known.

There seem to be a kind of secret negotiations. But the people would like to know V.P. Singh, himself is a firm believer in the people's right to know.

I agree with it, but there is a time for every thing. The situation may change by tomorrow. A lot of people are coming to see me. After a few hours H.K.L. Bhagat will be coming to see me. R.K. Dhawan also wants to see me. In fact both wanted to come and see me together this morning. But I have given him time later in the day.

I understand Bhagat wants you to see the Prime minister.

If you know me well and if you have known my past you must also know that I do not hang around Prime ministers. The Prime Minsiters come and go. I am a simple faqir. I stay put in this humble dwelling of mine.

Do you want the Prime minister to come here.

I have told you I don't get enamoured by these people in power. In this house everybody and anybody is welcome. Even bricks and stones can walk in and they are welcome.

Has Bhagat discussed with you any conditions.

Who is he to discuss conditions with me. It is Rajiv Gandhi who wields the final authority. There is no time to discuss conditions. The question is what they can give us now, on the spot, at this moment.

Has V.P. Singh promised to meet your demands.
Let him first come in power. An agreement is getting ready for that day.

In your view who will be a better Prime minister Rajiv Gandhi or V.P. Singh.
V.P. Singh has not yet become the Prime minister. How can I tell you about him?

And Rajiv Gandhi.
(Laughs derisively). The less said about him the better. You know that in this whole interview he is very much there, what else do you want me to say more about him. He is behind the Bhoomi-Masjid dispute and who else can be held responsible for these communal flare ups except him.

But he has made Urdu the second language in UP. Has it helped or harmed getting nearer to solutions.
Please don't provoke me. You know the reaction of this step in UP. You have seen the outcome in Badaun and other places. We do not want the country drenched in blood, we do not want anything. I repeat anything, which leads to the communal flare up, the butchery of innocent Muslims.

What is your message to the Hindus of this country.
Hindus are a wonderful people. They are a great 'Qaum' (nation). And the majority of Hindus are not communalists. They are a god fearing people. It is communal parties like RSS, the VHP, the Bajrang Dal and the Shiv Sena, which have been provoking Hindus against Muslims. They want to turn these great people into communal bigots. I am absolutely convinced that an overwhelming majority of Hindus love peace and want to lead a decent life.

As I was coming to see you a friend suggested that you and Bala Saheb Deoras should meet face to face to sort out all the differences once for all. Would you like to meet Bala Saheb Deoras.
No. Why should I meet him.

If he wants to meet you, then?
Well. He is welcome, Anybody can meet me.

Current, 04.11.1989.
pp. (1 + 2 + 3)

Secularism: a two-way street

Muslims in this country have once again landed themselves in a vulnerable position, this time on the issue of a mosque. In the late 1930s they believed in Mohammed Ali Jinnah's slogan of 'Islam in danger', identified themselves as a separate nation and destroyed the centuries old fabric of communal and religious harmony. Jinnah succeeded in creating a false sense of insecurity, isolating them from the national mainstream. The liberal, nationalist and secular Muslims watched the rise of Muslim separation in agony and, finally, yielded to the British backed conspiracy of partition.

The two-nation theory won the day. It inflicted deep wounds on the Hindu psyche. Muslims left behind in the country did not do much to heal these wounds except hide behind the smokescreen of secularism which in fact is not an Islamic concept. No Muslim country in the world, except Turkey, has adopted modern secularism as a tenet, a constitutional provision or a way of life. Islam and secularism are diametrically opposed to each other. Secularism in the Indian context means that the state has no religion but permits all religions and faiths to grow and prosper equally. The reason why secularism is under pressure here is because Muslims feel it is exclusively meant for them. The day they realise secularism is not a one way street, most of their problems can be understood by the majority in the proper national context.

The sudden rise of what is now being called saffron nationalism is a reaction to Muslim exclusivity, specially in the north. The RSS and its political wings have been there for half a century but the overwhelming majority of Hindus never permitted them to play a central role in the country's politics. They always preferred the centrist, socialist and left parties to articulate their nationalist feelings. The assassination of Mahatma Gandhi by an RSS activist had created a sense of revulsion against it among an overwhelming majority of Hindus. In their minds it is still suspect. The BJP leaders knew that the 86 seats they got in the Lok Sabha were despite RSS influence over the Hindu electorate. It was the anti-Rajiv wave unleashed by V.P. Singh that yielded them a rich harvest, and Muslims with their block vote against the Congress played a major role in giving a new turn to the political fortunes of the anti-Congress parties, including the BJP. And Muslims became anti-Rajiv only because he messed up the Mandir-Masjid dispute. They opted for VPS because of his promise that the mosque would not be demolished and that the temple would not come up on the disputed site. As if it was not enough to win Muslims, Mandal came with a powerful message that it would benefit them too. This further consolidated the Muslim block vote for the VPS-

Left alliance.

Had the BJP not taken resort to Ram, its future would have been in jeopardy. Ram therefore was Advani's master card. He knew that only in the name of Ram and *'mandir wahin banayenge'* could he shatter the established voting pattern. He has succeeded in his mission. In the process he has destroyed the centrist Congress and galvanised the upper caste Hindu voters. The backwards and the weaker sections among the Hindu electorate would have also swung to him had Mandal not been there. But he is sure that even this fortress will collapse under the pressure of Ram. The mosque may not be demolished but the construction cannot be prevented even if the Supreme Court decrees that the disputed structure is a mosque. The courts, Advani says, cannot sit in judgement on a matter of faith.

The problem is that an overwhelming majority of Hindus feel the mandir has not come up because of resistance from Muslims, which is a fact. In a rare display of stupidity and fool hardiness, Muslims have hitched their future to an old, dilapidated mosque which almost every Hindu believes is the birthplace of Ram. Muslims must realise the vital fact that we cannot conceive of an India without Ram. And if Hindus have decided to build a temple there, the least the Muslims can and must do is to rise to the expectation. Ayodhya is a sacred place for the Hindus, being the birthplace of Ram. It was the capital of his kingdom. Let them be magnanimous and offer the land and the mosque to their Hindu brethren. Once that is done, I am sure the Hindus will not demolish it. This gesture will also narrow the gulf of hatred and save the country from a holocaust. Let the river of secularism and *sadbhavana* flow from Ayodhya and let maryada purushottam Ram be a uniting factor and protector and promoter of secularism. Muslims cannot have their cake and eat it too. Secularism has to be a two-way street.

Current, 05.01.1991.
p. (2)

The real issue

The cover picture encapsules the theme of our Republic Day issue. The burqa-clad woman casting her vote while her husband watches her intently has been 'The Muslim Factor' in this country since 1952, the year our first Parliament came into being. The issue has always been a

part of our political and social fabric but assumes disproportionate intensity especially on the eve of every election. Political parties and their leaders look upon a Muslim not as a human being but a vote, a potential weapon in their hands to gain and control power. And the Muslims, conscious of the extraordinary power of the ballot, have been exercising their franchise with a rare zeal, a kind of *jihad.* To drive home the point, they vote collectively, as a bloc, especially in north India. This gives a substantial electoral clout to the so-called secular parties which benefit from the trust the Muslims repose in them while it upsets the calculations of the so-called communal parties which do not get it. So much so, it has become the root cause of the great divide between the contenders for power.

It will be wrong to assume that Muslims cast their vote against the current. Not at all. In 1972, soon after the Bangladesh war, they voted for Indira Gandhi almost en bloc because the whole country stood by her. This happened despite the fact that she was responsible for the dismemberment of Pakistan and the humiliation of its leaders. At that time Atal Behari Vajpayee had likened her to Durga. The BJP's earlier avatar, the Jana Sangh, was routed not because of the Muslims but because the overwhelming majority of Hindus had accepted her as their unchallenged leader. But in 1977 the Muslims contributed to her defeat because the whole country, especially the north, had turned against her. In 1980 she rode back to power with almost every Muslim voting for her. It reflected the mood of the nation. She would have definitely lost had she lived till the next election. Rajiv's stunning victory in 1985 was made possible because the Muslims voted for him en masse and two years back he lost power because the Muslims, like everybody else wanted a change. As a result, V.P. Singh became prime minister. Paradoxically, in 1989 the Muslims even voted for the BJP in order to prevent a return of the Congress at the helm of affairs.

In all these elections one thing has stood out: both Hindus and Muslims choose to go with the national ethos. In 1972 and the subsequent elections, a fairly large number of Muslims were elected from predominantly Hindu constituencies and vice versa. We have witnessed caste and communal barriers crumble under the weight of the national upsurge. Had the BJP not made seat adjustments with the Janata Dal, it would not have got more than two dozen seats. In the Hindi heartland of UP and Bihar its performance was pathetic despite its intense campaign on the Ram Janambhoomi issue.

What, then, went wrong with the whole process in 1990? Why the

strident slogans of pseudo-secularism and 'minorityism' and an upsurge in communal tension and violence? Why the obnoxious Hindu-Muslim divide and mutual hatred which has led to the awesome polarisation between the two communities? Why the rise in Muslim fundamentalism and Hindutva? Why has the Bhoomi-Masjid question become the main concern of the nation? Why this major threat to our secular, democratic fabric? These questions have to be answered if the country is to be saved from the impending holocaust. The BJP threatens to go to the polls on the crucial issue of the Muslim Factor. Its intention is to emerge as the only representative of the Hindu masses and capture power at the centre only on the strength of this slogan. It can attain this goal only by widening the gulf between Hindus and Muslims. Throwing the established electoral process and norms over board, it wants the country to decide between Ram and Rahim.

The Muslim factor is largely confined to the Hindi heartland, specifically UP and Bihar. The Bhoomi-Masjid dispute has been put succinctly by Ram Jethmalani in his article elsewhere in this issue: "If Ram and Rahim are one, to construct a temple dedicated to the latter must be a senseless venture . . . a hideous spectacle." But the overwhelming majority of Hindus do not take such an objective view of this emotional issue as Jethmalani does. The Hindus believe Ram was born in Ayodhya and at the place where the mosque stands. It is a matter of faith. Who are Muslims to challenge this faith and why should the so-called secular forces succumb to it? But the RSS-BJP-VHP-Bajrang Dal have gone one step further and decided to use it as a *Sudarshanchakra* in their bid to capture power. Had the ordinary Muslims realised this crucial aspect to the political game, they would not have allowed themselves to become a tool in the hands of the Save-Babri-Masjid crusaders.

The selfish Muslim leaders who control the various Babri Masjid action committees have done the greatest harm to Muslims by isolating them from the national mainstream. The dispute, after all, could have been resolved amicably. There are hundreds of mosques in Ayodhya and hundreds of thousands in the whole country. The Babri Masjid, an old structure, does not enjoy special status like, say the Jama Masjid of Delhi, If the Hindus wish to demolish it and construct a temple in the memory of Ram, the Muslims should allow it as a gesture of magnanimity. It would not only go a long way in bringing the two communities socially closer but save hundreds of Muslim lives. But as Jethmalani has put it, no Hindu, if he is a real *Rambhakta,* would ever imagine of demolishing a place of

worship. Had some mad people decided to pull down the mosque, I am sure thousands of Hindus would have rushed to Ayodhya to protect it. Had not Kamlapati Tripathi said that the temple could be built only over his dead body?

The Babri issue was raked up and made into a weapon for attaining personal ambitions by the myopic Muslim leaders, with some of them acting at the behest of the so-called secular politicians who wanted to consolidate their Muslim vote bank. These Muslim leaders, headed by Syed Shahabuddin and Imam Bukhari thought Islam and Muslims would suffer grievous, irreparable damage if the masjid was turned into a mandir. Hinduism did not disappear from the country when Muslim invaders demolished hundreds of temples, broke thousands of idols and when Aurangzeb treated them as zimmi, i.e. second-class citizens in their own country. History cannot be used as a weapon to avenge the injustice of yore but then it is not history if it does not remind people of their past. I am sure to be branded a capitulationist by the Babri bigots but I am convinced that if the Muslims have to lead a dignified existence in this country, they will have to respect Ram, his birthplace and the sentiments of millions who worship him. Religion is based not on science but on faiths. One cannot prove the existence of God. God is faith, not a reality. The Babri is not a faith, it is a structure. The Muslims have, therefore not gained anything but lost a unique opportunity by challenging the Hindu faith. Even now it is not too late. Let them think once again. They have to decide what is more important Babri Masjid or the lives and limbs of millions of innocent Muslims. It is never too late.

Coming to the *rath yatra,* every conscious Hindu is convinced that Advani's yatra was nothing but a political gimmick. He himself has admitted that it has served a political purpose and brought him closer to his goal. It was meant to isolate the Muslims and coalesce the Hindus in favour of his party, take away the high caste vote from the Congress and sabotage the Mandal process. He had planned a *padyatra* on a low key but the RSS assessment of the situation changed his plans. Advani was convinced of the climax. It was to be Mandir versus Mandal and a total isolation of the Muslims from the national mainstream. If the BJP could not capture power in the next election, such an opportunity might not come in the future. It was now or never. Advani has succeeded to a great extent in cornering the Congress. Now he is face to face with V.P. Singh in the two Hindi-speaking states and is poised to garner a huge chunk of the Hindu vote. The more the Muslims lean towards VPS, the greater are

the chances of the Hindus opting for the Mandir. Advani's accent on pseudo-secularism and minorityism has also gone down well with the educated middle class which think that Muslims have been pampered to such a great extent by the secularist parties that it's time the whole issue is decided through the ballot.

How long will the Mandir wave last and how rich are the dividends it will yield for the BJP is to be seen. But one thing is certain: that Muslims once again will vote solidly for V.P. Singh. The voting pattern of last 40 years shows that the Muslims do not vote for any Muslim political party. They invariably choose a secular party which assures their security and promises them social and political equality.

Current, 26.01.1991
p. (3).

Time to change

The mosque should not be built at Ayodhya. The centre's decision to rebuild it at the *Janmasthan* is fraught with dangerous consequences. It was taken either in panic and with an eye on the Muslim vote bank or as a design to agitate the forces of Hindutva into an unprecedented frenzy and hand over the country to the fascist goons. Narasimha Rao is not a child. He has fifty years of realpolitic behind him. Such a wizard cannot take decisions in a huff and that too without consulting his seniormost cabinet colleagues. He is too weak a prime minister to build a mosque in defiance of a hostile national mood. His game is to fan the Muslim sentiments and further widen the Hindu-Muslim divide. Had it not been so, he and his home minister would not have watched the destruction of the mosque on TV and not taken any decision for twenty-four hours. Rao's moral authority has collapsed and whatever the political authority he is left with is totally inconsequential in the emerging pattern. His bonafides are suspect especially when he mobilises the party to silence people like Arjun Singh who has been at the forefront of the fight against the BJP. Though Rao's secular credentials are beyond question, his suspicion that Arjun Singh is out to grab his *gaddi* is not only baseless but a psychosomatic case bordering on paranoia. Even now it is not too late. Rao should step down and hand over the leadership to those who have the will and the guts to stand up to the situation. The decision to build a mosque at the Janmasthan must be scrapped forthwith. Rao cannot

build it even if he puts the entire might of government behind it. He should not pour oil on the Hindutva sentiments and he must stop playing with the hurt Muslim psyche.

The Muslim fanatics who are pushing him to build the mosque at the same place are the greatest enemies of their community. Why blame Advani alone. It is they who are equally responsible for the tragedy of Ayodhya and for sowing the seeds of the Hindu-Muslim chasm. Did Rao bother to find out if men like Shahabuddin, Owaisi, Bukhari, Geelani and Javed Habib really reflect the views of a majority of Muslims or whether they are just the self-styled *thekedars* of the community. The truth of the matter is that they are the people who trade in Muslim vote in order to butter their bread at the time of elections.

With the razing of the Babri a long, painful chapter in Muslim politics is closed. It should not be allowed to be reopened again. It is time all thinking Muslims in the country exorcised these so-called Muslim leaders and opened a new chapter of understanding and reconciliation with the real, authentic leaders of Hindu opinion. The demolition of the Babri must make the Muslims realise that the Congress had used them as a mere tools to promote its own political fortunes over the past 45 years. And tools they must refuse to remain. They must explore the possibilities of an entirely new phase. Let them open a dialogue with the forces hostile to them. As Lord Krishna has said in the Gita: No defeat is permanent and no victory everlasting. No hostility can, therefore, be permanent.

Current, 02.01.1993.
p. (2).

Divided we stand

We are witnessing a vicious power struggle. December 6, the day the Babri was demolished, was the turning point in our destablished democratic ethos. On that day, not only was a mosque razed to the ground, the Constitution, Parliament and Supreme Court were shaken to their roots also. Promises made in the House, in the sanctum of the highest court and to the people from the ramparts of Red Fort were blown to pieces as a horrified nation watched in anguish.

On December 6, India hurtled into a new phase with its future enveloped in the dark clouds of uncertainty. A major question was posed : which was supreme—the will of the people or faith, the Constitution or the

manifesto, the law of the land or the machinations of a parivar, the House or the mob. Answers to these questions will have to come from the people, the final judge of the destiny of the country. We will have to wait for the national mandate whenever the ruling cliques decide to seek it afresh.

This transitional crucial phase is packed with the kind of volatility the country has never seen. The polarisation of forces has become inevitable. It is the BJP versus the rest. It will be the last ditch battle for both; no one can hazard a guess who will run away with the cake. But though the BJP has acquired a tremendous thrust, the Congress cannot be written of so easily. The ruling party is down but not out. It is still the largest party with deep roots throughout the country. It has a very large number of powerful, dedicated and determined people with a will to fight back. Its leader P.V. Narasimha Rao has indeed suffered one setback after another but his greatest advantage is that of being a good Hindu. His Hindutva has not been challenged even by his arch enemies. He cannot be accused of being pseudo-secular because he did not prevent thousands of Kar sevaks from converging on Ayodhya and pulling down the mosque with not even a teargas shell being lobbed at them. I am sure had there been a BJP prime minister, he would not have allowed the 'structure' to be destroyed.

Narasimha Rao too has staked his future on the Hindu card but in his own way. As the BJP does not expect any electoral support from Muslims, he too has written off the Muslims' votes. A mere 10-12 per cent cannot be a decisive factor in the democratic process; it is the 88 per cent who decide who should rule them. It is this realpolitic which egged Rao to compete with his rivals in a game of one-upmanship. The Muslim vote in the present situation has become irrelevant to both Advani and Rao. The competition is to entice the Hindu vote. The 88 per cent will have to choose between Rao and Advani and the odds are against the old man. It does not mean that the BJP will walk away with the cake. There are many a slip between the cup and lip.

The Congress, being the ruling party, holds the key. First, Rao is under no constitutional obligation to seek a fresh mandate for another three years. His argument is that if the BJP is keen to test the newly released strength of Hindutva, let its MPs resign and go back to the people. Rao can sit pretty for another two to three years, provided his party is not in a hurry to discard him, and go to the polls in a routine manner. Furthermore, if Narasimha Rao's trust builds a magnificent temple at the place where Babri stood, an average Hindu will rejoice and may ignore the VHP's claim. The mosque too may come up, but not at the original site. In the

process, he is discarding the claims of both Ashok Singhal and Shahabuddin.

It is undoubtedly a war of attrition between the BJP and the Congress. One will gain at the cost of the other. The BJP may sweep Gujarat but it might be humbled in Madhya Pradesh. The BJP has placed most of its eggs in the Uttar Pradesh basket but if Mulayam, V.P. Singh and Kanshi Ram put up a united front, the BJP will run for its life. In the North East, Assam, Bengal, Orissa, Bihar, Kerala, Tamil Nadu, Andhra, Maharashtra, Madhya Pradesh, Haryana and even Himachal and Delhi as also other parts of India, I can see there will be a village-to-village and door-to-door fight. The BJP is on a weak wicket in these states. It will be remembered that at the peak of the Rath yatra Advani had claimed his party would win at least 300 seats. Not only this, he declared "not I but Atalji will be our next Prime minister." The electorate cut him to size. The BJP could get only 119 seats and Advani himself won by a whisker. In the next poll too he dare not venture to contest from his home constituency.

The political reality is that with the mosque gone, the BJP's main target of hatred has been obliterated. Kashi and Mathura, as Advani has begun to repeat, are no more on the BJP's agenda. So the party is trying to highlight its other demands to keep the embers of communal hatred burning. The party is now trying to make other demands like a common civil code, repeal of Article 370, 'appeasement' of minorities, etc., the focus of its campaign. To confuse the electorate, the BJP is now saying that the Muslim Personal Law should be done away with. The point is the Muslim Personal Law is an Act of Parliament initiated by the ruling party. The Parliament which gave this law represented 88 per cent Hindus and the House comprised 90 per cent Hindus. The Muslims did demand their own personal law but the Ganges would not have been set on fire if the ruling party and Parliament had not enacted the legislation. After all, a 12 per cent minority cannot dictate to an 88 per cent majority. Parliament, if it so wishes, can do away with the MPL by legislation. Let the BJP draft a common civil code and make that document an election issue. Let the Muslims protest and howl but the will of the people should prevail. It is as simple as that.

Similarly, Article 370 is a part of the Constitution and if it has posed a threat of gigantic proportions to the nation, let it be deleted by yet another Act of Parliament. The Article does not concern Muslims; it was incorporated to save Kashmir and Kashmiris. It should be thrown in the dustbin by Parliament.

The BJP says the Muslims are not part of the 'mainstream'. Well, if

the sari weavers of Varanasi, the carpet-makers of Bhadoi, the wood-carvers of Saharanpur, the bangle-makers of Firozabad, the bakers of Bombay, the millions of Muslim peasants of Bengal, Assam, UP, Bihar, Rajasthan and elsewhere, the thousand of scientists, academicians, army officers and jawans who are guarding our borders against Pakistan are not the part of the mainstream, who is? In Bombay, where Bal Thackeray rules the roost. B.R. Chopra's tele-epic Mahabharat was created by a *malich* like Rahi Masom Raza. The captivating song *'Man tarpat Hari darshan ko'* was sung by Mohammed Rafi and composed by a fellow *malich* Naushad Ali Khan. Is not Salman Khan the heart throb of millions of mainstream boys and girls? And don't forget the dozens of outstanding classical singers, dancers and composers. In fact, this humble journalist, Ayub Syed, has been the President of the Maharashtra Ram Lila Mandal for the last 15 years. I launch the Ram Lila every year with a *havan.* So who is in the mainstream an invisible river?

The BJP raises the spectre of Muslims having four wives and breeding like rabbits. I have yet to meet a Muslim with four, three or even two wives. Keeping more than one wife can be an act of economic bravery, not Islamic exploits. Even one uneducated, unemployed wife becomes difficult to maintain for poor Muslims. As far as breeding like rabbits is concerned, successive census reports demonstrate that most urban, educated Muslims like their Hindu neighbours do not have more than three children and most uneducated Hindus and Muslims breed like rabbits. The only way to prevent excessive breeding is to make *'Hum do Hamare Do'* compulsory by an Act of Parliament, both for Hindus and Muslims. It will put an end to wild imagination.

Lastly, there is the question of the 'unyielding' Muslim leadership. But the point is that there are no recognised Muslim leaders as such. Not one has been produced since independence. The leader of Indian Muslims after independence was none other than Jawaharlal Nehru. The Muslims adored him and voted for him without demur. His daughter Indira Gandhi inherited his legacy and the vote bank until the Emergency. She did try to float some Muslims like Fakhruddin Ali Ahmed but he was always considered a dummy by Indian Muslims. Now two Hindus—V.P. Singh and Mulayam Singh—claim a Muslim following, at least in north India. No Muslim leader worth his name can claim an all India Muslim leadership.

The recent crop of so-called Muslim leaders such as Shahabuddin Shahi Imam, Salahuddin Owaisi, etc., are the creation of various political groups. Shahabuddin was created and sustained by the Janata Party and

Chandra Shekhar: now he enjoys the patronage of the Janata Dal and V.P. Singh. He is an elected Lok Sabha member on the Janata Dal ticket. The phantom of the Shahi Imam was first floated by H.N. Bahuguna and patronised by Indira Gandhi soon after the Emergency. She went to see him along with her son Sanjay and gave the impression that the establishment recognised him as a Muslim spokesman. Owaisi is the product of various Andhra Congress leaders. The two Muslim organisations floated to defend the Babri were pampered by the Congress with Shahabuddin and the Imam having easy access to the ruling elite in Delhi.

These phony leaders have done the maximum damage to Muslim masses with the national press front-paging them day in and day out. They are the main enemies of millions of poor, illiterate Muslims who are shot and killed in dozens whenever riots take place anywhere in the country. The sooner the Muslims discard them the better for them and the future of their children.

I do not subscribe to the view that Muslims must have Muslim leaders or Hindus must be led by Hindu leaders. If we want to decommunalise the society, the process has to be reversed. This can be done only when the fear of Muslim vote bank is removed. If we see the electoral pattern since the first election in 1952, we will find Muslims rejecting Muslim candidates and opting for Hindu candidates. It happened all over the country in the last two elections. In the 1989 election the Congress was their target and they voted against the Congress Muslim candidates with venageance. In the last election in Bombay they voted for Murli Dcora and Sunil Dutt ignoring V.P. Singh's call to vote for the JD candidates, one of whom was an outstanding Muslim lady. What agitates the minds of Advanis and Thackerays is that Muslims do not cast their precious vote for the BJP and Shiv Sena.

Now the situation has changed with Rao and Advani competing to corner the Hindu vote. Neither of them is interested in the Muslim vote. For whom, then, should the Muslim vote in case of an early election? Suddenly they face a political vacuum. At the moment they are in a state of shock with a massive threat to their social and economic existence.

Current, 06.02.1993
pp. (4 + 5)

Index

P

Q

R

S

T